CW00549423

Cavendish Dock, Barrow-in-Furness

THE GREEN GUIDE TO URBAN WILDLIFE

Bob Smyth

A & C Black
London

First edition 1990

Published by A & C Black (Publishers) Limited
35 Bedford Row, London, WC1R 4JH

© A & C Black (Publishers) Limited 1990

ISBN 0–7136–3137–6

A CIP catalogue record for this book
is available from the British Library

Bob Smyth has been among the country's leading urban nature conservationists. A founder member of the London Wildlife Trust in 1981, he was the Trust's chairman for four years and a council member for the Royal Society for Nature Conservation. A founder of the Fairbrother Group as the national Association of Urban Wildlife Groups, he also launched the magazine *Urban Wildlife* and was author of *City Wildspace*, the first history of the urban wildlife movement. A freelance journalist specialising in environmental and leisure topics, he now commutes between his house in North France and London and the other cities that are the subject of this book.

Printed and bound in Great Britain by
William Clowes Limited, Beccles and London

CONTENTS

London

South

West Midlands

East Midlands

Greater Manchester

Merseyside

South Yorkshire

West Yorkshire

Northwest

Northeast

Foreword

by Tim Hornsby, Director General of the Nature Conservancy Council

There has been a growing interest in the wildlife of Britain's towns and cities in recent years. The Nature Conservancy Council helped make an early contribution to an understanding that nature conservation relates not only to the countryside, but also has a very real concern with natural history in urban areas.

In the 1950s, the first round of identifying sites of special scientific interest (SSSIs) led to the designation of dozens of SSSIs in London and other major cities. The NCC published the first comprehensive survey of the wildlife resources of an entire metropolitan region, the West Midlands, in the 1970s. Localised surveys are being supported by the NCC and one of these led, in 1988, to the publication of the Nature Conservation Strategy for the metropolitan region of Tyne and Wear.

Obviously, detailed scientific assessment is necessary to act as a base for local authority planning, development control, and land management activities. But in addition, the NCC has always been conscious of the importance of public knowledge and interest in the wildlife on its doorstep. Urban county wildlife trusts and urban wildlife groups have sprung up in over 60 towns and cities during the 1980s, and many of these have benefitted either directly or indirectly from NCC assistance.

Livable cities need the very real contribution which urban ecology can make. This is increasingly being done as a genuine response to people's needs, as there in increasing interest in nature conservation, even in the most unlikely spots. It is therefore a very real pleasure to welcome this book which provides a guide for the general reader to the great variety of wildlife existing in the cities. It is particularly pleasing that this *Green Guide* is an offshoot of the familiar *Blue Guide* series. For many decades *Blue Guides* have been a *vade mecum* for travellers wishing to appreciate historic buildings and formal parks. With this book, visitors from abroad as well as those within Britain have the chance to discover the varied, and in many cases unexpected, natural heritage within England's towns and cities. It gives all of us an opportunity to explore possibilities we may not earlier have recognised, and all the delights of discovering unusual and important oases often in the very heart of what has been a harsher urban environment.

Nature in the City

by Dr David Goode

Why is it that advertisers use images of nature and the countryside to sell their products when most people live in towns and cities? Advertisers are not fools. Images of a desirable environment pay. Images of run down inner-cities don't. But what prospect is there for the dream of these advertisements becoming a reality?

Over the past ten years a concern for nature in towns and cities has developed spontaneously in many parts of Europe and North America. Recent studies of city wildlife have demonstrated that a host of plants and animals are able to thrive in the city environment, and it is becoming well established that many people value seeing wildlife where they live.

Take London for example. Since the early 19C the capital has expanded rapidly from a relatively small and closely confined city to the sprawling metropolis of today. As the city's tentacles spread they engulfed numerous outlying villages and towns together with the intervening countryside. Fortunately not everything was covered in bricks and mortar. Many fragments of the countryside survived and are now encapsulated within the urban sprawl. Vestiges of woods, river valleys, heaths and commons, even farmland with hedges, ponds and ditches can still be found among the 20C suburbs. Hampstead Heath, Dulwich Woods, Wimbledon Common and Walthamstow Marsh are examples of ancient habitats which still retain a rich variety of wildlife.

But it is the unintentionally wild places which now provide habitats for most of London's wildlife. Derelict railway depots, disused waterworks, Victorian cemeteries, railway embankments and even the roofs of buildings provide new urban habitats. Kestrels nest on city centre office blocks, herons fish in the Royal Parks, and foxes regularly raise cubs on wasteland within a stone's throw of the Old Vic Theatre. Wildlife is there but not by design.

London is not unusual. One of the wildlife spectacles of Washington D.C. is the gathering of turkey-vultures which fish for eels at the reservoirs in Georgetown. Nearby suburban woodland in the Glover-Archbold Park supports a rich variety of birds including the magnificent pileated woodpecker. New York has its attractions too. Over 200 species of birds are regularly recorded during migration periods in Central Park, and graffiti -covered subway trains pass between vast flocks of waterfowl while crossing Jamaica Bay to J. F. Kennedy Airport. In Toronto the highlight is a man-made spit, created by dumping 'landfill' in Lake Ontario, which now forms the finest wildlife habitat for miles around. The spit has breeding colonies of gulls and terns and provides hunting territory in winter for snowy owls right on the Toronto waterfront. Go anywhere in the world and you will find nature making the most of places we create.

Increasingly it is being argued that such places should be preserved, not only for their wildlife *per se*, but to provide places where people can experience nature at first hand. So Toronto has its 'Friends of the Spit' and Walthamstow Marshes in London were saved from gravel winning by a vigorous campaign led by local people. A 100 years ago others fought to save Hampstead Heath as an open space for Londoners to enjoy. We are now witnessing a period of enthusiasm and vigour comparable with the 'open spaces' movement of the Victorian era; but it no longer stems simply from a desire to protect open spaces for human enjoyment. Appreciation of wildlife is now firmly on the agenda.

Urban nature conservation differs from other more traditional approaches to conservation in that it does not place priority on rare or endangered species or habitats, but gives considerable weight to the values and benefits of urban wildlife to local people. Arguments for conservation of totally artificial habitats, such as disused railway land or neglected cemeteries have established new precendents in the case-law of planning. Moseley Bog in Birmingham, disused filterbeds in Hackney and a small piece of woodland between the railways in Chiswick—the Gunnersbury Triangle—have each provided new criteria for urban nature conservation.

A fundamental feature of urban nature conservation in Britain is that it is a grassroots movement. It is not imposed from above by statutory authorities but has grown as a response to people's needs. People who feel themselves dispossessed of nature are taking action to save even the most unlikely spots and they are winning. The proliferation of urban wildlife groups is a clear sign of the strength of the movement. During the past seven years over 60 urban wildlife groups have been set up in towns and cities throughout Britain, and more are to come. New attitudes are becoming established and a new ethos towards wildlife in the city which recognises these values is now reflected in many local plans.

But this new movement is not only concerned with nature reserves. It includes all aspects of greening from city farms and community gardens to roof gardens and window boxes. As well as the urban wildlife groups there is a proliferation of organisations devoted to greening including the national Think Green campaign and Landlife in Liverpool. Equivalents in North America include the Urban Wilderness Gardeners of Toronto, and the Green Guerillas of New York. Both are devoted to creating community gardens on vacant sites. Recent years have seen a spate of handbooks and practical guides for greening projects, one of the best of which is the Community Landscapes Pack produced by Think Green and Manchester City Council. A recent review of 'Community Involvement in the Greening' by Christine Bradley for the Groundwork Foundation identifies problems and recommends strategies for success in this rapidly developing field.

In parallel with voluntary organisations some local authorities have taken a lead in developing policies for protecting urban wildlife. London, Manchester and the West Midlands all developed strategies for conservation as part of strategic planning prior to abolition of the metropolitan county councils. In Greater London this involved a comprehensive survey and evaluation of 2,000 sites of potential value for wildlife, representing one fifth of the land area of the capital. Sites were graded according to their value in London as a whole, within individual boroughs and even at the local level. This evaluation took account of people's needs for nature as well as the intrinsic wildlife quality of individual sites. Policies advocated by the London Ecology Unit have been adopted by many of the London boroughs in their local plans, and nine public inquiries have resulted in decisions in favour of nature conservation in recent years.

Perhaps the most impressive applications of an ecological approach to planning is that of West Berlin. A complete inventory has been made of ecological factors throughout the city. All vegetation was mapped and many ecological variables measured. This data provides the basis for a rigorous process of ecological planning. Similar examples of planning for urban wildlife in the USA are contained in a recent publication by the National Institute for Urban Wildlife entitled 'Integrating Man and Nature in the Metropolitan Environment'. It seems that many ideas generated by the joint UK/USA conference on Greening Cities held in Liverpool in 1984 are now coming to fruition.

Much effort in urban nature conservation is devoted to protecting existing habitats which are increasingly under pressure for development. Especially in the densely built-up areas of inner cities local groups regularly campaign to save particular plots simply because they are the only places in the neighbourhood where anything resembling the natural world can still be seen. Such places may be poor examples of natural habitats—those concerned with urban wildlife conservation are often forced to make the best of a bad job—but such places certainly have rarity value. They have survived until now by chance, not by design. If we were to design cities to include nature the picture would be very different.

The very habitats which have developed so successfully on derelict or vacant land demonstate what is possible. They provide a particularly good guide since most of the species involved are already closely adapted to the artificial conditions of towns and cities. These are the very species which are best suited and many of them are very attractive.

Landscape designers, ecologists and horticulturalists have the skills to create new habitats. We cannot recreate ancient woodlands, or other traditionally managed habitats such as hay meadows, but many other kinds of naturalistic vegetation can be created very effectively. Technical information on habitat creation is becoming more readily available. Practical handbooks now exist for a variety of habitats and a compendium published by the Ecological Parks Trust in 1986 contains a wealth of practical information for promoting nature in cities and towns.

So far most habitat creation schemes in urban areas of Britain have been at the modest scale of ecology parks. The William Curtis Ecological Park, which existed near Tower Bridge from 1978 to 1985, was a fine example of what is possible on an inner-city site. It was remarkably successful, not only in the range of habitats and species which is supported, but also in catering for local schoolchildren who would otherwise have had little or no contact with nature. Sadly, it was only available on a temporary lease and the site is now part of the London Bridge City development, but it was an important pioneer venture. Recently a number of permanent ecology parks have been created in London including Camley Street Natural Park at King's Cross, Tump 53 Nature Park in Thamesmead, and Lavender Pond and Stave Hill Ecological Park in the former Surrey Docks. They all have dual roles, providing for education, and enjoyment by local residents. Those developed within housing schemes at Rotherhithe and Thamesmead demonstate that by careful design a variety of wildlife can be accommodated despite the close proximity of people.

It is of course possible for an ecological approach to be developed on a much larger scale. Woodlands were planted in the suburbs of Amsterdam in the 1930s and since then the Amsterdam Bos has provided a stimulus for many landscape designers. In recent years Dutch experience formed the basis of several examples of naturalistic planting in Britain. One of the best is in Warrington New Town where an ecological approach was used in the design of landscapes for housing on the former site of the Royal Ordnance factory. The result is an attractive wooded landscape within which the new town has been developed. The belts of trees with their links to the surrounding countryside can be seen as continuous threads of nature through the residential environment. A similar effect has been achieved with Russia Dock Wood, a newly created park within the docklands of Rotherhithe in SE London. Naturalistic planting, together with a series of pools and weirs, has created a remarkably natural landscape in close proximity to the housing. Reed buntings and sedge warblers have already become established, and the colony of wild ducks is much appreciated by local children. Though only recently developed this is already a most attractive park.

New approaches are becoming accepted for the use of open space in cities. Even formal Victorian parks are being converted to more natural landscapes, as in the case of Spinney Hill Park in Leicester where colourful meadows have replaced the close mown lawns. But again, this is a case of making the most of the open spaces which already exist. What is needed is a more radical approach to the landscape of cities. The vast areas of derelict land associated with declining industries in many of our conurbations offer unique opportunities to rethink the urban landscape. Some are already underway. There are proposals for extensive tracts of town woodland in the West Midlands. If woodlands, why not wetlands? Derelict docks and sewage farms offer possibilities for wetland wildlife that could be very popular in urban areas. Future plans for the vast acreage of Beddington Sewage Farm near Croydon include an extensive nature reserve with lakes, reedbeds and lagoons for marshland birds. It will be a most attractive landscape for people as well as waterfowl.

Attractive landscapes attract investors too. Although the benefits of environmental improvements are rarely quantified in conventional economics, it is clear that more natural landscapes are more desirable. 'Unspoilt' says it all. By bringing nature back into urban landscapes there is a chance that people may re-establish links with the natural world to an extent that has not been possible for many town or city dwellers since before the industrial revolution.

David Goode is Head of the London Ecology Unit

Preface

The *Green Guide* is the most comprehensive gazetteer of England's urban wildlife sites yet published. A 'Domesday Book' of city nature reserves and other areas of natural history interest, it covers over 90 towns and metropolitan boroughs in 10 regions, listing over 400 places to be visited. Within each region, towns are generally listed alphabetically as are sites within each town.

The sites include not only formal nature reserves but other areas of wildlife interest. Most have open access, though a few are private property where visiting is possible by public footpaths. A few are visitable only with a permit obtained from the county wildlife trust looking after the reserve. Addresses of such organisations are given at the end of each town's entry.

As described in David Goode's introduction to 'Nature in the City', urban nature areas come in a variety of shapes, sizes and types from 'pocket handkerchief' nature gardens to encapsulated countryside which has survived undeveloped. Some are sites of special scientific interest (designated 'SSSIs') or formally recognised as local nature reserves ('LNRs'). Some are looked after by local councils, county wildlife trusts or urban wildlife groups. Others are, however, places where wildlife has established itself on land left derelict following the demolition of obsolete factories or power plants. Most are within a built up area, though industrial sites between towns are also featured.

The *Guide* is intended for the general reader, so English names for plants and animals are used throughout (except for a few instances where there is no common name). It is, secondly, for all those involved in education from teachers to students and parents who are interested in the many educational possibilities arising in natural or semi-natural sites. It is also a significant record and hence the Nature Conservancy Council's welcome support for the project of the wildlife resources of the country's most populous areas.

Cities by their nature face continuing change. In future years, some sites here listed may be built on. Others may be added to the inventory. Readers who feel places they know of have been unjustifiably omitted are invited to draw these to the attention of the editor, c/o the publishers, for possible inclusion in future editions. Conversely, readers who are not already members of a local wildlife conservation organisation are urged to join one in the interests of assisting in the protection of the natural environment within their towns (addresses of national organisations also being given on p15).

It is safe to say that this *Green Guide*, whatever its omissions, is unlikely to be superceded in the near future. Town and city entries have been provided by on-the-spot experts, whether professionals or volunteers, and without their assistance no authoritative gazetteer would be possible. While their contributions are acknowledged at the end of each entry, special thanks are due to those providing material on whole regions.

In Greater London, Lucy Neville completed the formidable task of describing all the capital's 32 boroughs. In Greater Manchester, Carol Davenport chronicled the country's 10 varied districts. In the West Midlands, Tom Slater arranged coverage of Birmingham and its Black Country neighbours. At Leicester, the City Wildlife Project provided, with their usual efficiency, the earliest entry during what has turned out to be a three-year project.

Bob Smyth, Le Manoir, Hucqueliers, Pas de Calais

Acknowledgements

For permission to use their photographs the publishers would like to thank: Borough of Barrow-in-Furness; Benwell Nature Park; Cambridgeshire Wildlife Trust; City of Carlisle; Graeme Clayton; Cleveland County Council; The Croal-Irwell Valley Joint Committee; Gateshead Metropolitan Borough Council; P. Jepson; Kirklees Metropolitan Council; City Wildlife Project, Leicester; London Wildlife Trust; Northamptonshire Wildlife Trust Ltd; North Tyneside Council; City of Oxford; David Race; C. Rose; Southampton Common Centre; Metropolitan Borough of Stockport; David Whiteley; Metropolitan Borough of Wirral; The Woodland Trust; Friends of Wyken Slough.

Abbreviations

Entries list site owners, usually local councils: DCs being district councils, MBCs indicating metropolitan borough councils, and CCs referring to city councils or county councils. Other landowners include utilities such as the CEGB (Central Electricity Generating Board - about to be rejigged, at the time of writing, as National Power and Power Generation), BWB (British Waterways Board) or MoD (Ministry of Defence).

Organisations leasing or managing sites are listed under 'Management', these most often being county wildlife trusts (which have a bewildering variety of title such as TNCs - trust for nature conservation) or urban wildlife groups (UWGs). Other national conservation bodies include the wildlife trusts' umbrella society, the RSNC (see below); BTCV (see below); and RSPB (Royal Society for the Protection of Birds). The governmental agencies answerable to the DoE (Department of the Environment) are the Countryside Commission and the NCC (see below).

Site designations providing a measure of statutory protection include SSSIs (sites of special scientific interest) and LNRs (local nature reserves).

Contacts

Nature Conservancy Council
Northminster House
Peterborough
PE1 1AU
(0733 40345)

Countryside Commission
John Dower House
Crescent Place
Cheltenham
Glos GL50 3RA
(0242 521381)

Royal Society for Nature Conservation
The Green
Nettleham
Lincoln
LN2 2NR
(0522 732326)

BTCV
36 St Mary's Street
Wallingford
Oxford
OX10 0EU
(0491 39766)

Fairbrother Group
Association of Urban Wildlife Groups
c/o *RSNC* above

Further reading

The Wild Side of Town by Chris Baines (BBC 1986)

Wild in London by David Goode (Michael Joseph 1986)

The Greening of the Cities by David Nicholson-Lord (Routledge and Kegan Paul 1987)

City Wildspace by Bob Smyth (Hilary Shipman 1987)

LONDON

BARKING

Most of the interesting wildlife habitat of this borough occurs close to the Thames foreshore or along the river courses of the Roding at Barking Creek and the River Beam. This is a low-lying area which was undeveloped until the late 19C when the ancient grazing marshes were chosen as ideal sites for new industrial plants. These giant factories dominate the landscape not simply visually but also because of the massive amount of waterside reclamation they required. In spite of this the overall impression is still of imperfectly drained wetland, an increasingly rare habitat.

1   The Chase

Dagenham Road, Eastbrookend, Romford (TQ 513860).
LB Barking, LB Havering. 47ha.
Approach   A125, Rainham Road.
Summary   The Chase is an attractive landscape of horse-grazed grassland with a variety of small ponds and large lakes caused by the flooding of gravel pits.
History   These ancient grazing marshes were drained by a network of dykes which left rich pasture. However, they covered an area of gravel which was extracted during this century. It was leased to the London Wildlife Trust (LWT) in 1988.

The Chase

Nature interest   The grassland varies from the recently developed and relatively species poor area in the NW to the herb-rich area in the SW where several rare plants such as spiny restharrow and marshy cudweed grow in the sward. The shallow pools, some of which only exist seasonally, and the deeper lagoons provide a range of conditions suitable for amphibians such as newts and waterfowl. Reed nesting birds require the denser vegetation of the more permanent water bodies while the largely undisturbed grassland (indicated by ragged robin, devil's bit scabious and cuckoo flower) attracts ground nesting birds such as lapwing.

Management   The Chase is a wardened LWT reserve, their plans being to encourage public access by footpaths while protecting the more sensitive areas which could be damaged by too much disturbance. Some excavation work to increase the size and number of ponds will attract greater numbers of nesting birds.

Interpretation   In preparation.

Access   Restricted.

Contact   LWT warden (01 593 8096).

2   Ford Dagenham Works

Thames Avenue, Dagenham (TQ 506818).
Ford Motor Company.

Approach   Off New Road, A13.

Summary   An area of ancient Thames grazing marsh with old dyke system and breach lake still obvious.

History   The Ford Motor Company acquired the land to build their Dagenham Industrial Estate. Because of a combination of restricted access and sympathetic management this site remains an important wildlife sanctuary.

Nature interest   A reed-fringed lake caused by a breach in the river wall in 1707 (and fished by Pitt) provides breeding sites for many waterfowl including swans, tufted duck and the great crested grebe. Red-legged partridge, reed bunting and stonechat have also been recorded. A large expanse of poor soil covered by typical opportunistic plants attracts many butterflies. However, this disturbed area seems to suit the more unusual narrow-leaved meadow grass. Regionally rare wetland plants such as true bulrush, slender flowered thistle and musk thistle grow along sections of the canalised river Beam that have, as yet, escaped landscaping schemes. Black redstarts are known to use this area as a feeding ground while the dykes are particularly good for migratory birds which require the cover provided by the lush sweet grass. The nearby saltmarsh and mudflats, like those across the Thames, are of great importance to waders.

Management   The site is owned and managed by the Ford Motor Company. LWT manages an area of old dykes and fringe vegetation as a wildlife sanctuary.

Interpretation   Nil.

Access   By permit only.

Contact   Ford Motor Company (01 526 2078).

3   Thameside Community Farm Park and Ripple Levels

River Road, Barking (TQ 47820).
CEGB; LB Barking. Approx 108ha.
Approach   Renwick Road, with a public footpath from the leading to the Thames through the Levels.
Summary   The city farm incorporates a small nature reserve and is adjacent to an area of relic grazing marsh considerably affected by landfill.
History   During the early 1980s the CEGB agreed to release land to a local community group which has since created a city farm and reserve. The heavily grazed Ripple Levels are still unprotected and may be in some danger of development.
Nature interest   This is a favoured area for migratory birds which find shelter in the self-sown sallow and birch copses. Skylarks, pipits and snipe in winter occupy both the Levels and reserve which particularly attracts shelduck. Within the reserve woodland is a notable colony of common spotted and S marsh hybrid orchids which grow on the nutrient-poor soil. Along the Thames Foreshore at low tide many birds forage on the mudflats which are surrounded by a lush fringe of saltmarsh plants including sea aster and sea arrow grass.
Management   The Thameside Park Association manages the farm and reserve. Management aims are to increase the value of the pond and conserve the species-rich dykes.
Interpretation   The reserve is wardened and is available for school visits by arrangement. Two hides allow regular observation of bird populations.
Access   Open at all times.
Contact   The Thameside Park Association (01 594 8449/7352).

Further information

LB Barking and Dagenham, Parks Section, Town Hall, Barking (01 549 3880).
London Ecology Centre, 45 Shelton Street, Covent Garden WC2H 9HJ (01 379 4324).
London Ecology Unit (LEU), Berkshire House, 168–174 High Holborn, London WC1V 7AG (01 379 4352). The Unit has published a series of ecology handbooks covering habitats and individual London boroughs, including: *A Nature Conservation Strategy for London : Woodland, Wasteland, the Tidal Thames*, and two London boroughs *Lewisham* and *Barnet*; *Brent*; *Nature Conservation in Hillingdon*; *London's Meadows and Pastures*; and   *Nature Conservation in Croydon*.
London Residuary Body (LRB), County Hall, SE1 (01 633 5000).
London Wildlife Trust, 80 York Way, London N1 9AG (01 278 6612/3).
Thames Water Authority (TWA), Nugent House, Western Road, Reading, Berks RG1 8DB.
Acknowledgement   The text of this and the other Greater London entries is written by Lucy Neville.

BARNET

The borough sits between the hills of Hampstead in the E and Elstree in the W with four valleys through which run tributaries of the River Brent—the Silk Stream and Dollis Brook, and those draining into the River Lee (or Lea)—Pymmes Brook and Mimshall Brook. Away from Barnet's S core are many of London's most important unimproved grasslands. As these are managed in a more or less traditional manner they are of exceptional nature conservation value.

1 Arrandene Recreation Ground and Featherstone Hill

Wise Lane, Mill Hill, NW7 (TQ 226920).
LB Barnet. 23ha.
Approach   Footpaths from Wise Lane which divides the recreation ground from Hill Park, alternatively a footpath runs underneath Watford Way from Flower Lane.
Summary   Lying to the S of Highwood Hill and rising to include Featherstone Hill in the W, this group of fields provides a first taste of rural landscape as Green Belt merges into Hertfordshire countryside.
History   Farmed for hay in the 19C the area was acquired by the district council in 1929. LB Barnet now wishes to develop an arboretum.
Nature interest   These 12 contiguous fields although slightly affected by patchy 'digging for victory' during the last war have retained their pastoral characteristics. The dividing hedges contain field maples, oak, midland hawthorn and wild service. The fields are dominated by various grasses associated with old pasture such as cock's foot and Timothy, or oat grass and tall fescue. In the W of the recreation ground tufted hair grass is particularly abundant. Flowering plants include the common and colourful like the ox-eye daisy and rarities such as sneezewort or pepper saxifrage.
Management   The fields are cut for hay by a local farmer.
Interpretation   Nil on site.
Access   Open to the public.
Contact   LB Barnet.

2 Coppetts Wood, Glebelands and Scrublands

North Circular Road, N12 (TQ 276916, TQ 268911).
LB Barnet. 18.5ha and 5.5ha.
Approach   North Circular, Colney Hatch Lane, SW of Friern Barnet shopping centre.
Summary   These sites follow the gentle slopes of Bounds Green Brook Valley and contain a mixture of ancient woodland, scrub and open grassland with fine wetlands at Glebelands.
History   Records of pollarding in Coppetts Wood during the 18C suggest this area was once wood pasture, the usual form of tree management for trees on commonland. Combined with Glebelands and adjacent open land this was part of Finchley Common. In 1885 the area was bought by Finchley council partly for the building of sewage works. Still noticeable are the tank traps constructed during

the Second World War when woodland management declined. This was exacerbated by the sludge disaster along the E edge of the wood which, being capped with clay, is now turning to scrub.

Nature interest   The wood is dominated mostly by pedunculate oak with an understorey of coppiced hazel, hornbeam and sweet chestnut. Sycamore has become invasive, as in many ancient woods. The shade cast by this canopy suits the ivy and bramble which occupy the field layer. The Scrublands has many opportunistic species such as buddleia and nettles. Alongside these grow unusual plants like imperforate St John's wort. In the NW corner of the wood is a small pond which, being overshaded, is not as valuable to amphibians as the wetlands in the nearby Glebelands. These ponds and runnels are rich in flowering plants such as lady's smock, meadow buttercup and flag iris. Both the marsh speedwell and square-stemmed St John's wort which grow here are rarities in London. The grassy areas are also colourful with knapweed, comfrey, red campion and yarrow growing among the bent and cock's foot grass. The scrub is mostly hawthorn with silver birch and goat willow. The crack willow and horsetail reflect the underlying damp environment.

Management   Glebelands is owned and managed by LB Barnet Recreation Department, although there is no apparent conservation work. LWT has prepared a management plan for Coppetts Wood.

Interpretation   Nil on site.

Access   Glebelands is open to the public.

Contact   LB Barnet Recreation Department.

3   Mill Hill Old Railway Line

Deans Lane to Bunns Lane (TQ 203917, 235914).
LB Barnet. 5ha.

Approach   A5109, Deans Lane.

Summary   A linear reserve occupies a stretch of disused railway line which is now developing into mixed woodland with a meadow-like character towards the E of the site. Although other sections of this line have similar interest this area is likely to be formally open to the public in time.

History   When the Mill Hill to Edgware Tube line was abandoned the borough acquired this section to provide a walkway close to Lyndhurst Park.

Nature interest   As one walks along the reserve the mixed woodland of oak, hawthorn and ash alters to scrub and eventually open grassland. Beneath the woodland red campion and bluebells grow, while the grassy clearings contain rosebay willowherb, knapweed, greater stitchwort and golden rod. The mixture of cover and open areas attracts birds and butterflies such as the orange tip, comma and peacock. Slow worms have also been recorded.

Management   The site is managed as an LWT reserve. The regime emphasises the need to maintain the mix of habitats so that the scrub is controlled and grassland mowed and raked to keep it herb rich.

Interpretation   Nil on site.

Access   Restricted.

Contact   LWT (see Barking).

4   Oak Hill Woods Nature Reserve

Mansfield Avenue, Barnet (TQ 280952).
LB Barnet. 5ha.

Approach   Part of Oak Hill Park.

Summary   All but a small portion of this reserve is broadleaved woodland. It fills a NE corner of Oak Hill Park which sits in the valley of Pymmes Brook. A small tributary stream flows through the reserve, occasionally flooding downstream.

History   A map of 1817 shows part of the area to have been woodland but this seems to have been expanded sometime before a later map of 1970. The wood belonged during the Middle Ages to the Manor of Chipping and East Barnet. The landscaped 18C park was acquired by the district council during the 1930s which continued to buy adjoining land. It was finally designated as open space for sports and recreation.

Nature interest   The mature woodland is mostly composed of oak, hornbeam and ash with wild service, field maple and beech. There is some obvious invasion of sycamore and sweet chestnut as well as areas of planting with larch, cedar and Scots pine. The understorey is suffering in some areas from dense shading so that there are some areas of bare ground. However, the ground flora that survives is indicative of ancient woodland including wood melick, goldilocks, yellow archangel and bluebell. An ancient wood bank and ditch occurs along the N edge and is dominated by ash trees.

Interpretation   Nil on site.

Management   The reserve is managed by LWT which aims to improve the shrub layer of the wood and control the spread of sycamore.

Access   Open at all times.

Contact   LWT.

5 Rowley Green Common Nature Reserve

Rowley Lane, Arkley (TQ 216962).
LB Barnet. 5ha.

Approach   NW of Arkley.

Summary   An SSSI because of bog and acidic grassland features, the common is developing into scrub as birch and sallow supplement the mature oak woods in the S of the reserve.

History   Once acid heath and grassland belonging to the manor of Shenleybury, part of the common was purchased for open space by the borough council in 1934. Regular cattle grazing ceased during the Second World War and managment declined. The common was opened as a nature reserve in 1987.

Nature interest   Now mostly covered in woodland, towards the centre of the reserve is remnant acid grassland dominated by common bent grass and Yorkshire fog. Other species include heath bedstraw, tufted hair grass, common tormentil and soft rush. Also in this section is one of London's few sphagnum bogs which supports a number of wetland plants including flotegrass and lesser spearwort. Many small mammals have been recorded including pygmy shrews and voles. Bats are also known to be present.

Management   The site is jointly managed by the Hertfordshire and Middlesex Wildlife Trust (HMWT) and LWT which aims to conserve and enhance the bog communities by preventing further encroachment of the woodland. The recently desilted pond, together with a regular mowing regime, will restore and diversify the habitat.

Interpretation   Leaflet available from LWT.

Access   Open at all times.

Contact   HMWT; LWT.

6   Scratchwood (including Thistle Wood and Boyes Hill Wood)

Barnet Way (TQ 198949).
LB Barnet. 45ha.
Approach   Beside Moat Mount Countryside Park.
Summary   A large area of broadleaved woodland often linked by name to the adjacent and more obviously recreational open space. Although considerably modified in parts this is best described as predominantly ancient woodland.
History   Records dating back to the 13C show the early owners to have been the Knight Hospitallers. The woodland which formed part of the manor of Boyesland and Hendon was coppiced. The estate of Moat Mount to which it was attached was put on the market in 1923 for building development. Fortunately, Hendon council stepped in and bought this wood and a large area of farmland for public recreation.
Nature interest   Signs of past woodland management include coppiced hornbeam and hazel stools but the only area not to have been altered by later planting is to the W of the park. The canopy trees include oak (sessile and pedunculate), wild service, occasional brown birch, gean and aspen. The ground flora is typically sparse for this type of woodland with large areas dominated by bramble. However, close to the woodland streams both pendulous and remote sedge can be found. The S portion of the wood is mostly sycamore and silver birch which may indicate some colonising of open ground.

The two ponds in this section are, like many located in woods, threatened by shade and leaf fall. The more open of the pair supports water starwort and marsh cudweed. Although in places densely shaded, there are several areas of scrub, especially in Boyes Hill Wood which retains flora strongly associated with ancient woodland such as betony, bugle, dyer's greenweed and dog's mercury. The motorway embankment is covered by a conifer windbreak. Close by is a damp 'flush' which supports a number of wetland plants such as wild angelica, brooklime and goat's rue. This extensive area of openland and woods supports muntjac deer, foxes and many small mammals, as well as a wide range of woodland birds.
Management   The site is managed by Barnet parks department which carries out routine tasks such as pruning and removal of dead branches.
Interpretation   A nature trail is accompanied by a written guide.
Access   The countryside park is open during daytime.
Contact   Barnet Parks Department.

7   Totteridge Fields and Highwood Hill

Burtonhole Lane, NW7 (TQ 221935).
LB Barnet; private. 95ha.
Approach   Between Totteridge Common and the Ridgeway.
Summary   An outstanding example of traditional countryside contains small fields, streams with natural banks and an almost intact hedgerow system. Several ponds together with Dollis Brook flowing through the E corner of the fields add to the wide range of wildlife habitats.
Nature interest   These unimproved pastures and hay meadows are rare. Divided by hedgerows, which contain examples of field maple

and wild service, each field is dominated by a particular grass species including cock's foot, bent grasses, fescues or Yorkshire fog. The sward is herb rich with the colourful cuckoo flower and ox-eye daisy, and the delicate ragged robin, many vetches and trefoils. Highwood Hill has the greatest concentration of herbs including great burnet sneezewort, devil's bit scabious and pepper saxifrage. The area supports large numbers of butterflies, damselflies and dragonflies. The insect rich environment in turn supports a wide range of birds. Jackdaws and quail are two of the more uncommon species for London recorded here.

Management   The fields are still farmed although there is no formal agreement in leases from the council to protect the traditionally managed sward.

Interpretation   Nil on site.

Access   By public footpath.

Contact   LB Barnet.

Further information

LB Barnet, Borough Engineer and Surveyor, Gateway House, 322 Regent's Park Road, N3 (01 349 9121).

Hertfordshire and Middlesex Wildlife Trust, Grebe House, St Michael's Street, St Alban's, Herts AL3 42N (0727 58901).

London Wildlife Trust (see Barking).

BEXLEY

Substantial suburban development did not begin in this borough until the 1950s building boom which spread housing SW to border the rolling Kent hills and across the drained marshes towards the Thames. The NE boundary takes in the valley of the River Cray with a slice of the Dartford Marshes. The apparently inviolable Green Belt towards the Thames has been cut and squeezed by industrial, residential and leisure developments in an area of rare estuarine habitat of outstanding landscape and wildlife value.

1 Anchor Bay Saltings, Crayford Ness, Crayford Marshes

Wallhouse Road, Frith (TQ 828780).
Approx 100ha.
Approach Via the footpath along the flood embankment.
Summary More than most areas of grazing marsh, this has retained its rural atmosphere and is a poignant reminder of the once extensive river edge farmland. Although creeping development occurs in an arc around the edge of the marshes and grazing land, the overall impression is one of a landscape that has kept its integrity. The wide open aspect of the fields with the river Thames and Darenth flowing nearby is best appreciated by walking along the flood barrier.
History Less than half the ancient grazing marshes in NW Kent recorded early this century now exist. The draining and management of the saltmarsh began many centuries ago, allowing lush pasture for cattle and perhaps reeds for thatching. The tenanted Lower Farm and Howbury Farm continued to manage the land in the traditional manner throughout the 19C. Although there has been some landfilling and gravel extraction the most determined pressure which threatens to destroy the marshes began in the early 1980s. Large building schemes were rejected following public inquiries in 1983 and 1988. The Saltings is also under threat from the small marina located there which may be extended and destroy the saltmarsh.
Nature interest The saltmarsh is the upper limit on the Thames of English scurvy grass. In the reed banks sea plantain, sea arrow grass, mud-rush, sea poa and sea club rush also grow. The mudflats and marsh are important to visiting birds such as lapwing, shelduck, snipe and redshank. These and others like plover and dunlin gather on the grazing marshes. Plant species that have survived the recent completion of the flood barrier (which were recorded some 10 years earlier) include grassy vetchling and the largest area of hairy buttercup in London. Butterflies such as the gatekeeper and common blue favour the shelter of the embankment which also supports the uncommon Roesel's bush cricket.

Behind the embankment, dykes of varying water depths divide the grazing marsh. The further S these are the less they reflect the saltmarsh. The sea club-rush and glaucous bulrush change to greater pond sedge with at least one nationally rare species—the brackish water crowfoot. This network of waterfilled channels contains a minimum of 53 types of beetle and several dragonfly. They also act as corridors for a large population of reed warblers and reed buntings. Heron and kingfisher hunt among them while moorhen and mallard can easily find shelter. Breeding birds are not restricted to the secrecy of the dykes but also exploit the quiet, relatively undisturbed pasture which is dominated by such grass species as Timothy, black bent, smooth meadow or smooth brown. The richest area is grazed by cattle or horses near Howbury Farm where brooklime, gipsywort, celery-leaved crowfoot and water speedwell thrive. Regular sightings of skylarks, meadow pipits, yellow hammers and partridge are supplemented in summer by cuckoos, swifts, swallows and housemartins; and in winter by wheatears, shorteared owls and hen harriers. The rough grassland supports many butterflies and small mammals live in this rich environment.

Management   Nil for conservation.
Interpretation   Nil.
Access   Open at all times.

2   Crossness, Belverdere Marshes, Halfway Reach Bay

Norman Road, Belvedere (TQ 495808).
PLA, TWA, Thamesmead Town Ltd and private. 65ha.
Approach   Eastern Way.
Summary   A slender length of sensitive tidal mudflats, saltmarsh and grazing land stretches down the Thames, the S foreshore complementing that across the river at Barking.
History   These ancient grazing meadows were a vital part of the local economy along the low-lying farmlands providing pasture and reeds, in some cases, until well into this century. The area has been greatly altered by landfilling which has allowed the siting of similar industries, at least in scale, to those on the N bank of the Thames. Sewage works and a power station dominate the landscape and such large schemes continue to threaten this delicate habitat along with unsympathetic amenity or transport works at the river edge.
Nature interest   The marshes and mudflats are the most westerly on the Thames to have retained much of their character due to horse grazing and restricted access. This expanse of grazing marsh is broken by reedy dykes and remnants of old sea walls. These contain largely aquatic flora such as spiked milfoil, hornwort with reedmace and marsh ragwort. This is a valuable site for amphibians which benefit from substantial populations of both dragonflies and damselflies. However, it is for the wealth of birds that the area is best known.

Halfway Reach attracts some of the largest accumulations of dunlin in London. Ruffs and the occasional oystercatcher have also been recorded. The Bay itself contains a reedbed which attracts reed warblers, reed buntings and a considerable number of swans. Waterfowl particularly can be observed on the mudflats grazing on the microscopic plants and animals. Fringing these grow salt tolerant species such as sea aster, sea beet, sea arrow grass, hemlock water dropwort and scurvy grass. Many birds have taken advantage of the secluded shelter of the swampy ponds and fields at the Crossness Sewage Works for roosts and breeding. Several uncommon species needing minimal disturbance which have been recorded are shelduck, tufted duck, snipe and black redstart. Migratory birds such as stint, green and common sandpipers use the settling ponds as feeding grounds. The willow scrub developing on the drier SE corner of the works attracts little ringed plovers.

Management   Nil.
Interpretation   Nil.
Access   Via footpaths.
Contact   LWT.

3   Foots Cray Meadows

Rectory Lane, Sidcup Hill (TQ 482718).
LB Bexley. 63ha.
Approach   Close to the North Cray Woods, via footpaths from Sidcup, Old Bexley and Foots Cray.
Summary   This landscaped park includes a stretch of the River Cray running from SW to NE. The emphasis is on recreational use but the small lake and grassland could be managed to enhance their wildlife value.
Nature interest   Apart from a bewildering number of fungi and mosses which need the moist conditions, many other species associated with meadows and water edge have been recorded such as marsh marigold and purple loosestrife as well as the bright yellow flag iris.
Management   LB Bexley manages the grassland with gang mowers but a recent six-point plan by the Urban Ecology Study Unit suggests that a more sympathetic regime of seasonal cutting will encourage the spread of wetland and meadow species. If implemented, the erosion along the banks of the Cray could be controlled so that the vegetation has an opportunity to recolonise.
Interpretation   Nil.
Access   Open at all times, wheelchair access possible.
Contact   LB Bexley Recreation Department.

4   Joyden's Wood, Gattons Plantation, Chalk Wood

Parsonage Lane, North Cray (TQ 497712).
Woodland Trust; LB Bexley. 70ha, 26ha, 34ha.
Approach   Off North Cray Road.
Summary   These contiguous woods cover an area of gently undulating gravelly soil. Although some characteristics of an ancient woodland remain, the woods have been greatly modified. Indiscriminate horse riding has caused some damage especially in the damper areas.
History   The oldest sign of use is an ancient defensive ditch that crosses Joyden's Wood N to S. More recent management would have been a coppice system, although this was compromised by the use of woods for game cover in the 19C. Joyden's Wood was purchased by the Forestry Commission in 1956. Both the wood and the plantation were purchased by the Woodland Trust in 1987. Chalk Wood changed its boundary during the 19C as well as its biology when sweet chestnut was planted as the main coppice crop.
Nature interest   Chalk Wood is mainly oak and birch with obvious signs of former coppice management. The open grassy or bracken-dominated areas indicate some colonising of acid heathland. Wood anemone and bluebell carpet the wood in spring. Ancient woodland indicator species such as green hellebore also occur. Wintering birds

like woodcock, redpoll and the occasional sparrowhawk are joined by migratory species. The wood is a refuge for long-eared bats, and also provides cover for foxes, rabbits and badgers (although these are under some threat from baiters). Joyden's Wood is dominated by an extensive Corsican pine plantation, and has only two areas of broadleaved native trees with a fringe of oak and hazel along its S boundary.

Management   Joyden's Wood and Gattons Plantation are managed by the Woodland Trust which intends to replace the conifers with broadleaved native species. The Urban Ecology Study Unit of Thames Polytechnic has prepared a plan for Chalk Wood which includes the control of sycamore and the reinstatement of coppicing.

Interpretation   A nature trail leaflet is in production for Chalk Wood. Two nature trails are marked with white and green posts in Joyden's Wood.

Access   Open at all times.

Contact   LB Bexley Recreation Department; Woodland Trust.

5   Lesnes Abbey Wood

Abbey Road, Belvedere (TQ 480785).
LB Bexley. 86ha.

Approach   Off A296.

Summary   Part of an extensive area of deciduous ancient woodland surrounding a ruined abbey which occupies a steep small valley next to the borough of Greenwich and overlooking Thamesmead new town.

History   Belonging from the 12C to Lesnes Abbey and then to the charity of Christ's Hospital, the wood was coppiced to provide fuel and timber for repairs. The highest areas of the wood which contain heather suggest there has been some colonising of heathland. It was purchased by the London county council in 1930 and within a year was opened as a park. Ownership and managment passed to Bexley following the abolition of the GLC.

Nature interest   The wood was identified by the habitat survey as being of metropolitan importance with the NW section designated as a geological site of special scientific interest. One of the most striking features is the startling appearance of primarily natural wild daffodils in the spring. The more general impression is of former coppice allowed to mature with fine examples of hornbeam, gean and field maple as well as oak. The N edge of the valley is mostly on chalk and reveals ancient earthworks.

Management   LB Bexley manages the wood as a park with some areas fenced off for safety or conservation purposes.

Interpretation   Maps and leaflets from the park office.

Access   Open at all times, wheelchair access.

Contact   LB Bexley Recreation Department.

6   North Cray Woods

St Andrews Road, Sidcup (TQ 499722).
LB Bexley. 8.6ha.

Approach   Beside Foots Cray Meadows.

Summary   The wood lies close to the river Cray which flows into the Darenth.

History   A former coppice that once belonged to the Prior of St Mary Overy at Southwark, the wood was reduced to half its pre-1940 size by the building of a housing estate.

Nature interest   This is a mixed deciduous woodland dominated by pedunculate oak with an understorey of sweet chestnut and hazel. A wide ride crosses the wood so that although the wood is being invaded by sycamore, lighter clearings allow a number of species strongly associated with ancient woodland to occur such as wood anemone, wood sorrel, pignut, dog's mercury and bluebell.

Management   LWT and the North West Kent Urban Fringe Project (NWKUFB) aim to restore the woodland.

Interpretation   Nil.

Access   Open at all times.

Contact   LWT; NWKUFP.

Further information

LB Bexley, Parks and Recreation, Central Administration Offices, Sidcup Place, Sidcup (01 303 7777).

London Wildlife Trust (see Barking).

North West Kent Urban Fringe Project, Dartford Civil Centre, Home Gardens, Dartford, (0322 343556).

Woodland Trust, Westgate, Grantham, Lincs NG31 6LL (0476 74297).

BRENT

This heavily built-up borough, named after the river that flows from Barnet creating the Brent Reservoir and is feeder for the Grand Union Canal, is triangular in shape pointing towards Paddington in the SE . Near Wembley Park, in the centre of the borough, the Wealdstone-brook joins the River Brent. These wildlife arteries were once excellent habitats but only occasional stretches of river bank now exist such as at Quainton Street Open Space and Neasdon Sidings West, S of the Reservoir. Railway embankments which slice through the borough from its W edge to both the S and E are important for their length and inaccessibility. But the most valuable wildlife habitat is concentrated in the N and W at Brent Reservoir and Fryent Country Park. Both are good examples of sympathetically managed public open space with considerable community involvement in planning and activities.

1   Brent Reservoir, also known as Welsh Harp

Birchen Grove, NW9 (TQ 215871).
BWB; LB Brent. 96ha.
Approach   Off North Circular Road.
Summary   Fed by the Silk Stream and River Brent as they cross the borough boundary, the Harp is best known for its breeding wetland birds. The potentially damaging recreational activities, especially sailing, on the reservoir are increasing but educational visits and guided tours are easily accommodated.
History   The reservoir was created in 1835 to provide water for the Grand Union Canal by damming the valley of the River Brent. From the start it attracted ornithologists and day trippers so the site is particularly well documented. Protection came in 1950 with the designation of 61 hectares as an SSSI. Moves are currently afoot to declare the E and N marshes as LNRs.
Nature interest   The SSSI designation recognises the valuable range of wetland habitat from open water to reedy fens caused by this artificial lake. Swampy areas are dominated by bulrushes and common reed, while the lushly vegetated margins contain among the lesser pond sedge or soft rush, water plantain, flowering rush, arrowhead and water dock. Birds exploit all the niches they can find, from the man-made breeding rafts favoured by the common tern to the willow carr used by warblers, reed buntings and redpoll.

The more secluded areas, some of which are the result of recent habitat creation, suit waterfowl such as coot, mute swan, shoveler or pochard. The reservoir attracts the largest breeding population of great crested grebe in Greater London and a significant number of tufted duck. In summer, gadwall regularly breed, while in winter the resident birds are joined by visitors such as snipe and smew, the scarcest of the regularly wintering duck species in Britain. The woodland in the NW corner around the field study centre supports foxes, tawny owls and all three species of woodpecker. Bats are to be encouraged by a hibernaculum built in 1986 by the Brent group of the London Wildlife Trust.
Management   The management of the site is advised by the Welsh Harp Joint Consultative Committee which represents a wide cross section of both public and professional bodies such as the NCC. One of the committee's concerns is to keep the balance between the needs

of wildlife and the desires of recreational groups. This has lead to the construction of shallow lagoons to act as sanctuaries away from the disturbance of sailing. A major problem for the reservoir is the control of pollution from the River Brent, and to a lesser extent the Silk Stream, which results in the deposit of solid waste and surface oil. Booms and a trap have been installed to counteract this.

Interpretation   Educational work and guided tours are regularly undertaken with the help of a full-time ranger. Conservation tasks for volunteers occur most weekends.

Access   Open at all times; restricted in wildfowl sanctuaries.

Contact   Brent Leisure Services.

2 Fryent Country Park

Fryent Way, NW9 (TQ 195876).

LB Brent. 103ha.

Approach   The park is bisected by Fryent Way.

Summary   The country park, often referred to simply as Barn Hill after the higher of two hills that rise on either side of the road, is a popular recreational ground. It covers an area of landscaped park and traditional Middlesex countryside with fine views of Harrow and, on a clear day, even Crystal Palace, S of the Thames.

History   This is a combination of a fragment of the 18C Wembley Park and surrounding farmland. The field pattern, with ancient hedgerows on the E side of the park has altered little since it was recorded in an estate plan of 1597. Barn Hill shows many signs of landscaping by the renowned Humphrey Repton including the unfinished Page's folly, a prospect tower named after the commissioning landowner, Richard Page. Part of this area was taken for a golf course at the end of the 19C, which fell into disuse during the First World War. From 1927, when the district council acquired 20 hectares, the park grew piecemeal with the fields leased to a local farmer until 1957. For the last 30 years the park has been designated as public open space.

Nature interest   The most striking feature of the park is the retention of extensive hay meadows. Many were ploughed during the Second World War but have recovered due to judicious management, so that over 100 wildflower species are still to be found. Apart from an abundance of buttercups and vetches in the sward of meadow foxtail and other grasses, there are such notable species as sneezewort, devil's bit scabious and adder's tongue. The ancient hedgerows, one of which was a parish boundary hedge between Kingsbury and Harrow, contain midland and hybrid hawthorn as well as elder, blackthorn and the rare wild service tree. The nationally rare narrow-leaved bitter-cress has colonised the bases of at least six hedges. The woodland on Barn Hill was planted around 1793 with oak, field maple, hornbeam and beech, which is not naturally found in this area. The pond at the summit of the hill is also part of this landscape scheme. Young oak woodland in the W of the park is colonising the old golf course. Such a mixture of habitats is particularly good for woodland birds. Ten old farm ponds have been supplemented by four that have recently been dug to encourage invertebrates and wetland plants.

Management   The site is managed by LB Brent Leisure Services Department for both recreation and conservation. The voluntary Barn Hill Conservation Group is involved with keeping species records and undertakes regular practical work. Proposals for the setting up of a joint consultative committee are being considered for interested groups to become more involved in the management and other issues affecting the park.

Interpretation   A leaflet, *Countryside in Brent,* is available from local libraries and council offices. A 12-point nature trail and guide begins at the car park off Fryent Way. As well as supporting year-round activities, a countryside ranger gives lectures and guided walks.

Access   Free public access.

Contact   Brent Leisure Services.

Further information

LB Brent, Leisure Services, Brent House, High Road, Wembley, Middlesex HA9 6SX (01 903 1400).
London Wildlife Trust (see Barking).

BROMLEY

Bromley could comfortably fit within its bounds the three inner London boroughs on its N border. Its suburban character is largely due to pressure for development following the First World War, which also sparked off demands for Green Belt legislation. As a result, the S and E edges of the borough retain a Kentish farmland appearance. Bromley also encompasses a number of ancient commons and is well known for its network of woodlands which cover the ridges of numerous small hills that rise to meet the North Downs. Their proximity allows them to behave as almost one biological unit linked by hedges and streams across Bromley's significant inheritance of chalk grasslands.

1   Chislehurst Common, St Paul's Cray Common and Petts Wood

St Paul's, Cray Road (TQ 441702, TQ 450687).
Chislehurst Common Conservators, National Trust. 36ha, 28ha, 54ha.
Approach   W of Scadbury Park.
Summary   A cluster of relic heaths and ancient woodland with heavy visitor pressure mainly concentrated in the N at Chislehurst Common. Although fringed by housing in the S and E, from the SW border with Tong Farm to Scadbury Park in the NE, this is a considerable stretch of rural landscape.
History   The two commons were once heaths controlled by grazing. They were protected under the Metropolitan Commons Supplemental Act of 1888 which established a board of elected conservators to oversee management. A famous fire that raged out of control for two weeks in 1870 across St Paul's Cray Common may well have encouraged the succession of woodland that the decline in grazing had begun. Petts Wood, named after a family of Tudor shipwrights, was saved in 1958 following 30 years of opposition to various housing schemes affecting the former Hawkwood estate.
Nature interest   The ground of both commons is fairly well drained and results in a typically poor acid soil. Former gravel extraction and pockets of clay have caused a number of ponds to form, most of which are in need of sympathetic management to maintain their wildlife interest. Those on Chislehurst Common are suffering from trampling although examples of bur-marigold, marsh penny wort and purple loosestrife still decorate the banks. In contrast, the three central ponds in St Paul's Cray are choked with purple moorgrass. The secondary woodland is mostly oak and birch with an understorey of holly, hawthorn and bracken. Patches of acid grassland survive near the Cockpit at Chislehurst and in two clearings near St Paul's Cray Road. The W clearing has the best example of relic heathland dominated by heather. The E clearing has suffered from insensitive management in the past.

The woodland becomes damper towards the boundary ditch with Petts Wood with sedges and buckthorn replacing the meadow grasses of the higher ground. Eventually this develops into an unusual area of alder wood which covers the banks of four feeder streams of the Kyd Brook which flows S of Petts Wood. Under this canopy notables such as lady and male fern as well as broad-buckler fern grow. The W stream is especially rich with these and other species such as meadowsweet, bugle and ramsons. Elsewhere is mainly oak and birch ancient woodland with former sweet chestnut coppice and stands of hazel in the W and S.

Management Petts Wood is owned and managed by the National Trust. The commons are managed by the Chislehurst Common Conservators. There is some attempt to extend the area of acid grassland and heath by controlling the encroaching woodland.

Interpretation Nil on site.

Access Open at all times.

Contact The Chislehurst Common Conservators; National Trust.

2 Crofton Heath

Orpington (TQ 436665).

LB Bromley. 68ha.

Approach S of Petts Wood.

Summary The heath occupies flattish ground which slopes towards the NE. The site contains former coppice and farmland so that a variety of habitats accommodate an especially wide range of insects.

Nature interest The site is dominated by pedunculate oak with former hazel coppice. Together with brown birch, aspen, crab apple this results in a well-developed shrub layer which in spring allows bluebell, wood anemone and wood sorrel to flower. This contrasts with the secondary woodland which has grown across the centre of the heath and contains hawthorn, blackthorn and sallow. In the frequent grassy clearings the brightly coloured tormentil, meadow buttercup and knapweed grow, with the common spotted orchid making an appearance near the E edge of the central woody area. A stream flowing to the Kyd Brook crosses the NE sector, encouraging the growth of many wetland species including flote grass, wild angelica and remote sedge. As the stream passes through the centre of the heath, rosebay willowherb, meadowsweet combine with substantial areas of reed canary grass.

Management LB Bromley.

Interpretation Nil.

Access Open at all times.

Contact Bromley Parks Department.

3 Hayes Common

Baston Road, Bromley (TQ 411161).

LB Bromley. 92ha.

Approach A232 crosses the common E to W.

Summary The once open appearance of the common is only hinted at in an area of closely mown recreational grassland as natural succession combined with some planting has converted this heath to scrub woodland.

History As in many ancient commons that survived the main bout of 19C enclosure, conservators took over management. By the 1920s grazing declined and finally ceased during the following decade. In 1954 the common was acquired by LB Bromley.

Nature interest The W edge contains the opposing influences of modern ornamental planting and ancient earthworks. The area is now dominated by oak with some silver birch. The varied understorey of bracken, bramble and gorse allows wavy hair grass to grow, while mosses and lichens take advantage of damper areas. A recent excavation for a gas pipe line which cuts across the common is now colonised by gorse. The most intricate and valuable mix of habitats occurs towards the E edge. Especially interesting is the large patch of heather which contains such notables as the rare dwarf gorse, cross-leaved heath and bell heather; this area has been identified as a proposed SSSI. The open environment extends to grassland in the N which supports lizards, grass snakes and adders.

Management   LB Bromley.
Interpretation   Two nature trails begin at the E entrance.
Access   Open at all times.
Contact   Bromley Parks Department.

4   Highbroom Woods

Monks Orchard Road, Beckenham (TQ 376666).
LB Bromley. 8.2ha.
Approach   Eden Park BR Station.
Summary   A long slim wood flanks the meandering river Beck which neatly divides it in two.
History   Formerly ancient coppice on which wartime tipping took place, creating the higher ground in the middle of the site.
Nature interest   An alder wood is supplemented by small pockets of wetland supporting kingcup, wavy bitter-cress, mosses and liverworts.
Management   Nil for conservation. Heavy visitor pressure and some tipping is cause for concern.
Interpretation   Nil.
Access   Open at all times.
Contact   Bromley Parks Department.

5   High Elms

High Elms Road, Bromley (TQ 438610).
LB Bromley. 86ha.
Approach   Near Downe House.
Summary   An area of mature woodland lies on the W slopes of a dry valley which runs N on the Downs.
History   High Elms was the landscaped estate of the Lubbock family who bought the land in the early 19C. In 1938 it was sold to Kent county council which in turn passed it to the borough council as part of green belt open space.
Nature interest   Evidence of former use can be seen at this site as the wood was used for game cover by the Lubbocks and was planted with conifers by the Forestry-Commission which, as in many other schemes, were never harvested. The top of the W escarpment is chiefly of oak and beech. Lower down this changes to hazel coppice with a rich ground flora, including examples of tooth wort and spurge laurel with green hellebore and the occasional bird's nest orchid.
Management   High Elms is managed by LB Bromley and has a study centre.
Interpretation   Nature trail with leaflet.
Access   Open at all times; to use centre, contact LB Bromley.
Contact   LB Bromley Recreation Department.

6   Keston Common

Westerham Road (TQ 418641).
LB Bromley. 176ha.
Approach   Fishponds Road.
Summary   One of the best examples of true relic heathland left in
London contains a rare valley bog to add to its attraction. Heavily used
for recreation which, together with some encroachment by scrub and
non-native species, is causing some damage.
History   The series of reservoirs near the N edge of the common
were dug for John Ward during the last century to supply his house
with fresh water. The two large ponds were created by damming a
stream which once fed the river Ravensbourne running close to the
NE edge of the common.
Nature interest   The heathland vegetation of the common is dominated by heather and wavy hair grass on the acid soil. The gorse and
birch scrub occur around former conifer planting. Oak and beech
woodland occur towards the S. The SSSI designation that protects the
common is largely aimed at conserving the sphagnum bog which
supports the rare bog asphodel and sundew.
Management   The common is managed by LB Bromley which
provides fishing facilities and picnic areas.
Interpretation   Nil.
Access   Open at all times.
Contact   Bromley Recreation Department.

7   Ravensbourne Meadows

Lakes Road, Keston (TQ 417645).
LB Bromley. 6ha.
Summary   Close to Keston and Hayes Common these damp meadows slope towards the N and E into the valley of the Ravensbourne.
History   The meadows belonged to the Tate & Lyle Ravensbourne
Estate but were acquired by the borough council in the 1970s.
Nature interest   The clay soil is very damp towards the NE of the
meadows allowing the growth of lush wetland vegetation. Kingcups
and purple loosestrife are plentiful in this area but as conditions are
drier in the S and W, meadow grasses tend to dominate. The ponds
support amphibians and snakes are also recorded.
Management   The meadows retain much of their character due to
the recent loss of grazing; however, LB Bromley now mows only parts
for hay in early spring and summer.
Interpretation   The Ravensbourne Nature Trail is available from
LB Bromley.
Access   Open to the public who are asked to not walk in the
sensitive wetland habitat.
Contact   LB Bromley Recreation Department.

8   Scadbury Park Nature Reserve

Perry Street, Chislehurst (TQ 454700).
LB Bromley. 117ha.
Approach   Sidcup by-pass.
Summary   An area of formerly traditionally managed farmland
retains many hedgerows, meadows, ponds and streams. The SW half
of the park is dominated by woodland of various ages.

History   The reserve was formerly an enclosed hunting park owned by the De-Scathebury family and later the influential Walsinghams. By the 20C ownership had passed to the Townshends. The park was acquired by the borough council for housing in 1983 but opened in 1985 as a new public open space.

Nature interest   The woodland has a core of former wood pasture with massive oaks estimated to be around 400 years old. The NE section has been planted with sycamore but as this was formerly coppiced, extensive areas of bluebells survive. The S portion of the wood below the main ride seems to be colonised farmland with field boundary hedge species in abundance such as gean and field maple. Typically, the ground flora of the former wood pasture is dominated by bracken, while the ancient woodland contains wood anemone and wood sorrel. The diversity of woodland structure supports many woodland birds including nuthatches, tawny owls and all three British woodpeckers. Shallow streams, several large drainage ditches and nine ponds provide important habitats for various amphibians such as the great crested newt. Damp conditions in the NE section suit the broad-buckler as well as other kinds of fern along with opposite-leaved golden saxifrage and many mosses and lichens.

Management   The reserve is managed by Bromley Parks Department.

Interpretation   A two-mile circular walk begins at the St Paul's Cray Road and Perry Street entrances.

Access   Open except across farmland, where footpaths must be followed, and around the excavation of the former moated manor house.

Contact   LB Bromley Recreation Department.

9   The Warren

Crockenhill Road, St Mary Cray (TQ 482678).
Private. 12ha.

Approach   Via footpaths from Crockenhill Road or Sheepcote Lane.

Summary   Sitting in rolling farmland the reserve is on a small plateau and contains a mix of glades and shady woodland with two interconnected large ponds. The Warren suffers from the enthusiasm of motorcyclists who have damaged a patch of open grassland which offers magnificent views of the railway cutting and wooded landscape.

History   Late 19C maps show the area as completely wooded so the reserve may have been part of the Kevington Woods. The ponds once formed a single boating lake which together with the large stands of rhododendron shows clearly the desire to ornament ancient woodland which affects many of Bromley's woods.

Nature interest   The reserve is mostly covered with broadleaved native trees. Towards the W edge the woodland of oak and hornbeam changes to colonising silver birch. In this dry and open area bracken tends to dominate. The S section is damper than elsewhere and contains two restored ponds and another less stable dank hollow hidden at the very edge of the reserve. Work begun in 1985 has left a large expanse of open water with banks covered in rushes and yellow flag irises. The marshy area between the ponds is a reminder of natural succession which would have let willow and flote grass choke the water. The wetland supports amphibians including the rare great crested newt. An area of former coppiced sweet chestnut and hazel fills a NE spur which also includes examples of field maple, spindle and blackthorn. Rabbits graze the grassland at the W edge and the site supports many small mammals including moles, shrews, woodmice and yellow necked mice, as well as grass snakes.

Management   The reserve is managed by LWT which aims to control the spread of sycamore and rhododendron, as well as reinstating a coppice regime to improve the woodland structure.

Interpretation   LWT leaflet.

Access   Open at all times.

Contact   LWT.

10   West Kent Golf Course

Luxted Road, Bromley (TQ 423603).

West Kent Golf Course Club. 85ha.

Approach   Near Biggin Hill airport.

Summary   A gentle hill and fairways retain much of their original chalk downland character.

Nature interest   The woods that embrace the W edge of the course and thicken out along the S boundary vary from fine mature beech and hazel in the N to oak and birch on the higher S slope. Other canopy trees include rowan, elder, gean and sweet chestnut. Among the typical ground flora are such surprises as white helleborine and twayblade in the E section of the wood. The chalk downland which is divided by three arms of this wood is rich in aromatic herbs such as wild marjoram and thyme, or wild parsnip smelling of coconut. Other species include many orchids, yellow rattle and the delicate quaking grass. The grassland is favoured by such butterflies as the small blue and marbled white.

Management   LWT has a management agreement covering the more important areas of chalk grassland.

Interpretation   Nil.

Access   Restricted, via public footpath only.

Contact   West Kent Golf Club.

Further information

LB Bromley, Recreation Department, Administrative Offices, Civic Centre, Bromley, Kent (01 464 3333).

London Wildlife Trust (see Barking).

CAMDEN

Camden extends from the steep ridge of hills at Hampstead down to the river terraces of the West End and City. Three main valleys dividing the Haverstock, Highgate and Parliament hills once channelled streams into the lost rivers of the Fleet and Tyburn. Open spaces of value to wildlife are concentrated in the N so it is not surprising that railway embankments and the Regent's Canal have become important, if sometimes impermanent, reserves in this highly built up borough.

1   Camley Street Natural Park

12 Camley Street, NW1 0NX (TQ 298835).
LRB. 1ha.

Approach   At the back of St Pancras and King's Cross stations on the Regent's Canal.

Summary   A highly successful habitat creation scheme focuses on wetland and a pond alongside the Regent's Canal. A wooded embankment protects the park on the street side, while a broadwalk allows visitors to wander without causing damage to vulnerable wetland plants.

History   Coal brought up to London along the Regent's Canal was off loaded at this site throughout the last century. The coal depot, which changed into a rubbish dump, was acquired by the former GLC for a lorry park in 1981. After lobbying from LWT and the GLC's own ecologists an ecological park was agreed instead and opened in 1985. By 1986 such was the success of the park that it became the first habitat creation scheme to be designated a Local Nature Reserve, and

Camley Street Nature Park

only the third LNR in the Greater London area. The park is currently under threat from proposals to build the Channel Tunnel terminus at King's Cross.

Nature interest   The most obvious feature of the park is the pond with substantial reed beds which encourage the blue tailed damsel-flies and dragonflies and hide toads and frogs. The pond contains hornwort, water milfoil and arrowhead, and along the banks can be seen yellow flag irises, water mint, marsh marigold and bogbean. The two areas of woodland are mainly of sallow and alder. The cover provided by this and the location of the park attracts around 50 species of bird from the common blackbird and sparrow, to chiff-chaffs, heron and black redstart.

Management   The park is managed by LWT which aims to keep the waterside habitat open while keeping the woodland dense by coppicing. A warden and on-site teacher organise workdays, events for the local community and surveys.

Interpretation   A field study centre is packed with information on what can be seen and studied at the park. A series of leaflets are available.

Access   Open 10am–5pm every day, this access is extended during summer months. School parties must pre-arrange visits.

Contact   LWT Camley Street warden (01 833 2311).

2   Hampstead Cemetery

Fortune Green, NW6 (TQ 249851).
LB Camden. 15ha.
Approach   Off Finchley Road.
Summary   The cemetery is still used for burials but in addition to the area of well-tended graves are two pockets of woodland and a fine old hedgerow.
Nature interest   The W half of the cemetery is occasionally mown so that scrub while encroaching has not taken over areas of herb rich grassland which includes clumps of bird's foot trefoil. The ornamental trees grow alongside copses of ash and yew. However, the most notable feature is a boundary hedgerow mostly of hawthorn, which could well indicate 19C enclosure.
Management   The   site   is   managed   by   Camden   Parks Department.
Interpretation   Nil
Access   Open daylight hours.
Contact   Camden Parks Department.

3   Highgate Cemetery

Swains Lane, N6 (TQ 285872).
Friends of Highgate Cemetery, to be reformed as Highgate Cemetery Charity. 15ha.
Approach   Off Highgate High Street.
Summary   The splendour of this landscaped Victorian cemetery is now dominated by secondary woodland, with trees poking from grave edges and occupying the once open ground. Glades and meadow-like areas can be found in the S portion of the W half although the E cemetery is generally more open.

History   The cemetery was opened in 1839 to provide for burials that could no longer be accommodated in the small churchyards and metropolitan cemeteries. Geary and Bunstone Bunning landscaped the W cemetery allowing the planting of specimen trees in a park-like setting. In 1854 an extension to the cemetery had been added across the lane. But as the burial plots were bought and used so the revenue of the company inevitably declined, and sometime during or after the Second World War maintenance ceased. In response to the closure of the by then overgrown cemetery in 1975, the Friends of Highgate Cemetery (FOHC) was formed. They campaigned and have managed it for over a decade.

Nature interest   The cemetery is mainly secondary woodland consisting of stands of sycamore or ash. A number of large mature trees hint at both the original layout and of the neglect the site fell into. Over 100 different species of wild flowers have been recorded, although some of these are due to deliberate introduction. The woodland cover attracts many birds and protects the resident foxes.

Management   The management by FOHC consists of balancing the needs of wildlife and protection of the architecture of the cemetery. Sycamore and ash, which tend to take over after the former has been removed, are both controlled. Grassland mixes have been sown experimentally in a S glade. Volunteers work on site and staff the information centre.

Interpretation   Information booklets and a film are available from the FOHC, who also undertake tours and lectures.

Access   Restricted. Tours take place April–Sept 10am to 4pm and Oct–March 10am to 3pm. Parties may book a visit.

Contact   FOHC, 5 View Road, Highgate, N6 4DJ (01 348 0808). The General Manager, Highgate Cemetery, Swains Lane, N6 (01-346 1834).

4 Hampstead Heath

East Heath Road, NW3 (TQ 270865).
Corporation of the City of London, 319ha.
Approach   Highgate Road, West Heath Road.
Summary   The heath is a remarkable expanse of open land only four miles from the City. S views across this mixture of park, ancient woodland, scrub and acid grassland take in the harsh outline of the financial centre and, on a clear day, the hazy curves of the Crystal Palace ridge on the far side of the Thames.
History   Some two centuries before the famous 40-year fight to stop the Victorian lord of the manor, Sir Thomas Maryon Wilson, from building across the commonland, the creation of numerous small reservoirs and the uncontrolled digging of gravel and sand had altered the smooth rolling aspect of the heath. Another factor in the alteration of the grazing lands was 'beautification'. The landscaper, Humphrey Repton, planted exotic trees to create pleasant views. The pressure to tidy up continued to threaten the heath throughout the 19C and indeed still does. Public pressure to protect the heath culminated in the initial purchase by the Metropolitan Board of Works of 220 acres. This area has steadily increased, so that Kenwood, Golders Hill Park, West Heath and the Heath Extension all contribute to the semi-rural atmosphere. In 1897 the Hampstead Heath Protection Society, now the Heath and Old Hampstead Society, was formed

and their independent role as a watchdog has been fundamental in the protection of the heath.

Nature interest   Only one plant of the heather *Calluna vulgaris* is left, its location kept secret, to remind visitors who may stumble across it that this was once a heath of gorse and heather. It also shows that recreation rather than conservation for many years ruled the management programme. The central N area is an SSSI and the Westfield Bog near Kenwood is similarly protected. Birch encroachment is being controlled around this rare sphagnum bog but adds to the tree cover across the heath. Many of the flowering plants are common such as cow parsley, yarrow and daisy, but patches of cranesbill occur across a central belt, while bugle, wood anemone, bluebells and the uncommon nettle-leaved bell flower can be found in the woodland areas. One or two patches of cowslips, primroses and false oxlip appear on the E edge but it is the general environment of the heath which is attractive to visitors and wildlife alike. Many of the ponds are used by waterfowl including the great crested grebe, tufted duck and reed warblers. The woodland attracts chiffchaffs, woodpeckers and stock doves, with kestrels hunting over the grassland.

Management   Conservation is seen increasingly as a major aspect of management to prevent erosion and to enhance habitat. Planting to attract butterflies, the retention of dead standing trees for nesting sites and new mowing regimes are just some of the signs of a more sensitive approach to the natural history of the heath.

Interpretation   Many historical pamphlets and guides are available, some from the Manager's office. An excellent handbook is available from the London Ecology Unit (see Barking).

Access   Open at all times.

Contact   Heath and Old Hampstead Society.

Further information

LB Camden, Works Department, Old Town Hall, Haverstock Hill, London NW3 (01 435 7171).
London Wildlife Trust (see Barking).

THE CITY

The heart of London is the city square mile where the original settlement was built on two low hills on either side of the now lost River Walbrook. As the capital expanded, Moorgate, an extensive marsh to the N, was drained and all available land built on. The City Corporation always had interests in land outside its jurisdiction, but it was only at the end of 19C that the City became involved in the saving of large areas of open land. Their offer to take over land once on the outskirts of London usually followed large public outcries against enclosure of commons, where lawsuits and even imprisonment had heightened resentment. Its Open Spaces Committee now owns and manages Hampstead Heath (Camden, etc), Highgate Wood (Haringey), Epping Forest/Wanstead Flats (mainly in Essex), Farthing Down, Riddlesdown, Coulsdon Common, Kenley Common (Croydon) and Threehalfpenny Wood/Spring Park (border of Bromley and Croydon). They have recently become the managing body for Hampstead Heath.

Further information

Corporation of the City of London, Open Spaces Committee, Guildhall, EC2 (01 606 3030).

CROYDON

The ancient market town of Croydon sat in the valley between the S chalk hills of the North Downs and the clay capped ridge of Norwood once covered by what is popularly known as the Great North Wood. The borough is of special interest to geologists as it covers almost the entire range of rock types found in the London basin.

The difficulties of farming on the highly permeable chalk explains why the bulk of valuable wildlife habitat occurs on the S dry valleys, which were grazed by sheep well into this century. Yet Croydon has the largest population of any London borough and the lack of open space of any kind, let alone of wildlife interest, in the N of the borough is an indication of the pressure on habitat. The dry valleys and chalk ridges are subject to the conflicting demands of recreation or housing and what is often seen as half-hearted management of this sensitive landscape. Two causes for concern are the erosion of Croham Hurst and the Addington Hills and the encroachment of scrub across considerable areas of chalk grassland. There are, however, new threats from major road and rail building proposals which could fragment and destroy many of the borough's important wildlife sites.

1 Biggin Wood

N Covington Way, SW16 (TQ 317702).
LB Croydon. 5.2ha.
Approach   Off Beulah Hill.
Summary   This ancient woodland covers a SW facing slope of the clay-capped Beulah Hill. Since a botanical survey by Edward Lousley in 1959 the wood has declined, as he predicted, because of a combination of unsympathetic management and heavy recreational pressure.
History   Part of the chain of sessile oak woods associated with Norwood, this was a coppice belonging to Biggin Farm whose fields are now covered in housing or allotments. It was opened to the public in the 1950s having been acquired by LB Croydon some years earlier.
Nature interest   The wood has clearly differentiated sections with changes in type of vegetation and structure. A bank of elm suckers surrounds the E entrance. N of the central concrete path is an area of former oak coppice extending to an ancient boundary ditch with several oak pollards. This section has poor ground flora and considerable patches of bare ground. Towards the NE many garden species such as snowberry and laurel grow, but on the central slope in an area which appears to have been cut some time in the last decade the light has allowed ground flora to flourish. Many flowering plants indicative of ancient woodland such as greater stitchwort, celandine and lords and ladies edge the paths among the bramble. The S portion of the wood is either an oak plantation or a series of selected standards completely lacking an understorey, with a small brook running along the E edge. The dark shade and bad erosion is threatening the few patches of ground cover that survive.
Management   Croydon Parks Department appears to confine its activities to removing fallen leaves and maintaining the concrete path.
Interpretation   Nil on site.

Access   Open at all times.
Contact   Croydon Parks Department.

2   Bramley Bank Nature Reserve

Riesco Drive, Addington (TQ 354633).
LB Croydon. 10ha.
Approach   S of the Addington Hills.
Summary   This is an L-shaped area of mostly broadleaved secondary woodland but some large oaks and beeches indicate a previous use as wood-pasture. It covers a plateau and W facing slope.
History   Bramley Bank was part of the Heathfield estate owned by the Riesco family who left the wood to the people of Croydon by bequest to the council in 1945. In 1984 the site was licensed to LWT which began management by restoring the larger of two ponds on the reserve.
Nature interest   The N section of the reserve contains a number of mature oaks and beeches which are now surrounded by silver birch and ubiquitous sycamore. The shade cast by such a dense canopy results in a poor ground flora although wood sedge, an unusual plant for London, can be found among the other shade-tolerant species. Two plantations of Austrian pine occupy the W edge but the bulk of the woodland surrounding these and the remainder of the S wedge of the reserve is secondary and has large patches of bluebell and bracken. In a central area of this wedge, abutting an unofficial bridlepath, is an important remnant of acid grassland mainly composed of bent and fescue grasses, with heath bedstraw, mouse-ear hawkweed and a small amount of heather. Common woodland birds like thrushes and various tits are resident with bullfinch, chaffinch and tawny owl taking advantage of the diversity of habitat on the reserve.
Management   An LWT reserve. Management aims are to improve the ponds, extend the acid grassland and encourage a more varied woodland.
Interpretation   Nil on site.
Access   Open at all times.
Contact   LWT.

3   Coulsdon Common

(TQ 322570).
Corporation of the City of London. 55ha.
Approach   B2030.
Summary   A piece of the jigsaw of open landscape at the S edge of Croydon linking with Farthing Down and Happy Valley, the common is mostly wooded and crossed by mown rides. There is a tiny area of acid grassland but on the whole the vegetation reflects the underlying chalk soil. There has been some planting of exotic trees along the mown rides.
History   Similarly to other commons in this area it was purchased by the City of London in 1883.
Nature interest   The most interesting aspect of the common is in comparing the acid areas in the S with the chalk areas in the N.

Pedunculate oak with silver birch cover the S section but because the larger trees are widely spaced this may indicate the colonising of open grazed land. The rest of the common is covered by wood composed of oak, wild cherry, ash and lime with an understorey of hazel coppice. The ground flora includes patches of bluebells, wood anemone, woodsorrel and male ferns and pale violets.

Management   The City of London management includes the regular mowing of the acid grassland and tends to reflect park practises rather than conservation of habitat.

Interpretation   Nil.

Access   Open at all times.

Contact   City of London Corporation, Kent and Surrey Commons Department.

4   Coulsdon Coppice Nature Reserve

Rutherick Rise, Coulsdon (TQ 307590).
LB Croydon. 3.5ha.

Approach   The W edge of the reserve has a number of access points through St Davids or Rutherick Rise.

Summary   A varied area of woodland is surrounded by housing.

History   Once a coppice that belonged to the Byron Estate, the wood was threatened by the break up of this in the 1920s. Building took place around its borders but when the last estate was built in the 1980s permission for development required that an area which includes the coppice should be left open.

Nature interest   The reserve includes Bleakfield Shaw, an area of mature woodland with the S being ancient. The former coppice is of oak and ash with an understorey of holly, hazel and blackthorn. The ground flora is typical of ancient woodland, while Deadman's Haugh which adjoins this section is more shrubby. Larkins Copse to the E is also a coppice of overgrown hazel stools, whereas Larkins Dean alongside is grassland with scattered trees and scrub encroaching. The grassland consists of flote grass and giant fescue, with agrimony and perforate St John's wort adding colour. The variety of structure and habitat attracts many birds from rooks and sparrowhawk to thrushes, tits and bullfinches. Butterflies use the chalk grassland which has wild basil, meadow cranesbill, moschatel and hairy St John's wort as some of its herbs. The reserve is also known for its Roman snail colony.

Management   LWT manages this reserve and has begun by esta-blishing paths around it. It intends to improve and maintain the diverse woodland structure.

Interpretation   LWT leaflet.

Access   Open to the public.

Contact   LWT.

5   Croham Hurst

Upper Selsdon Road, S Croydon (TQ 342629).
LB Croydon. 34ha.

Approach   Selsdon Road (B275).

Summary   The site is a mix of ancient woodland and heath which slopes downwards to include chalk grassland on the S side of the hills.

The habitats of this site reflect strongly the underlying soil, offering the opportunity to see species associated with both acidic and chalky conditions.

History   A wooded ridge, the E side of which was laid out as the Croham Hurst Golf Course.

Nature interest   The site, which is an SSSI, rises to form a plateau with a substantial covering of heather and grass broken by exposed pebble beds. Oak woodland grows on this slightly acid soil but the abrupt change from bracken understorey to hazel along the SE side of the site marks the boundary of soil types. The woodland is yet another marker at the base of the hill with obvious indications of ancient woodland such as dog's mercury and bluebell as well as the rarer Solomon's seal and lily of the valley. Unfortunately, the S area of chalk grassland adjoining these woods is developing into scrub.

Management   The Hurst is managed by Croydon Parks Department which is attempting to control the scrub and protect the soil from increasing erosion.

Interpretation   Nil on site.

Access   Open at all times.

Contact   Croydon Parks Department.

6   Farthing Down and Happy Valley Park

Ditches Lane, S Croydon (TQ 309568).
Corporation of the City of London, LB Croydon. 157ha.

Approach   Coulsdon Road, Fox Lane.

Summary   An arc of anciently worked chalk downland and woods bestrides a steep ridge and winding valley which meets Coulsdon Common on its E edge.

History   The Farthing Down appears in a list of lands belonging to Chertsey Abbey but the survival, now obscured by scrub, of extensive Celtic fields and barrows indicates some form of cultivation from the Neolithic period. The grasslands were traditionally managed by sheep grazing but this declined at the beginning of this century. The City of London bought Farthing Down, along with three other commons in the area in 1883 after an enclosure dispute. The adjoining Happy Valley and Devilsden Wood was acquired in stages by the council between 1937 and 1938 to be leased for farming. With the decline in rabbits after the introduction of myxomatosis in the 1950s, the grazing gap once filled by sheep widened and hawthorn scrub began to take over the grasslands. LB Croydon instigated the clearance of two areas at the edge of Happy Valley at the end of the 1960s. The area is threatened by proposals to cut a new road through the adjacent Devilsden Woods.

Nature interest   Much of the area has been designated as an SSSI. The chalk worked many centuries ago is not the easiest land to cultivate and the coarse sward reflects the harsh conditions plants have to be able to withstand. On the shallow dry soil low tufted bristle leaved fescues, upright brome and false oat are among the many species of grass which can survive. Especially in the areas cleared of scrub, and on the W slope of the down, this sward is dotted with the deep-rooted salad burnet, knapweed and wild carrot. The greater part of the entire British population of greater yellow rattle is located in this area.

The boundary hedges of Farthing Down include eight tree species such as maple, oak, ash and dogwood. The E hedge merges with an ancient yew grove along the ridge of the down which falls steeply S into Happy Valley. The escarpment has been invaded by mainly hawthorn, but other trees such as the wayfarer tree can also be seen. The NW edge has been cleared of this scrub and the glades are filled with rich chalk grasslands. At least seven species of orchid thrive in this and similar areas, from the bee orchid to the man orchid and twayblade. The wide valley floor extends the area covered by grass and supports, in addition, carnation sedge, the stiff rest harrow and hairy St John's wort. Running alongside is Devilsden Wood and nearby Piles Wood which straddles the border with Surrey. Both are dominated by pedunculate oak with ash and wild cherry. Below the well-developed understorey, ground flora associated with ancient woodland grows, including species such as wood anemone, bluebells and lords and ladies. The 24 species of butterfly recorded in this area include many dependent on chalk grassland herbs, such as the small blue and chalkhill blue, and rarities like the green hairstreak, the dark green fritillary and dingy skipper. Foxes and badgers are resident in the valley, while birds such as nuthatch and treecreepers keep to the woods. Kestrels and skylarks need the stretches of open grassland.

Interpretation   A 28-point nature trail beginning at the Welcome Tea Rooms at the SE corner of Farthing Down is accompanied by a series of booklets pointing out seasonal changes.

Management   Both the City of London and Croydon Parks Department manage their sections to control the scrub and promote the grassland. The paths are in some places hard to follow and, unfortunately, these spots tend to coincide with features pointed out in the booklets.

Access   Open at all times.

Contact   Croydon Parks Department.

7   Hutchinsons Bank and Chapel Bank Nature Reserve

Featherbed Lane, Addington (TQ 383615, TQ 386606).
LB Croydon. 36ha.

Approach   S of Addington Court golf courses.

Summary   The reserve occupies a SW facing slope at Hutchinson's Bank, and a W facing slope and valley at Chapel Bank. Under heavy recreational pressure and encroachment from hawthorn scrub the downland character has changed. Chapel Bank especially has suffered from motorcycles and landrovers plunging down the hillside to the valley bottom.

History   The area was grazed by sheep that kept scrub at bay and encouraged a short sward.

Nature interest   Scrub invasion has swamped much of the chalk grassland on both sites followed the decline of grazing. However, an intricate pattern of small clearings and glades has survived. On both areas this is of high quality and contains the scented and brightly coloured herbs associated with this habitat including burnet saxifrage, lady's bed-straw, hairy St John's wort, marjoram, and field scabious. The rare small blue butterfly thrives on the large numbers of kidney vetch found towards the bottom of Hutchinson's Bank. A variety of orchids also grow on this well-drained and sunny slope such as pyramidal orchid, man orchid and twayblade.

Chapel Bank has been maintained by rabbit grazing. A central area of grassland contains carline thistles, wild thyme, sheep fescue, milkwort and man and twayblade orchids. The scrub of hawthorn and dogwood has a rich field layer of sanicle, primrose, moschatel, woodruff, violets and yellow archangel. At least 21 butterfly species have been recorded including the fairly common brimstones, small tortoiseshells and meadow browns, and the more unusual dark green fritillary, white letter hairstreak and dingy skipper. Apart from rabbits at Chapel Bank, foxes and badgers have also been recorded with slow worms, adders and common lizards clearly indicating the importance of this kind of habitat to wildlife.

Management   LWT manages the site to conserve and extend the areas of chalk grassland, and also to maintain areas of scrub and woodland to provide a variety of habitat. Measures have been undertaken to formalise paths and prevent access to motorcycles and cars which have caused erosion on Chapel Bank. It is seen as a fine area for educational use, being close to housing and local schools.

Interpretation   Nil on site.

Access   Open at all times.

Contact   LWT.

8   Kings Wood

Kings Wood Way, Sanderstead (TQ 351603).

LB Croydon. 57ha.

Approach   Hazelwood Grove footpath.

Summary   A large block of ancient woodland S of Selsdon Park Golf Course.

History   Linear earthworks run across the site in the N and there may well have been an ancient farmstead nearby. The coppiced wood was altered to accommodate game shoots by the addition of a grid of wide rides and conifer tree markers in the 19C. The local council acquired the wood under the Green Belt scheme.

Nature interest   This oak dominated wood has a well- structured understorey mostly of holly and hazel, although there is evidence of planting like the presence of sweet chestnut. The ground flora is indicative of ancient woodland with bluebells flowering in spring, followed by yellow archangel, pignut, wood sorrel, male and broad-buckler fern. The field layer is of bracken and bramble which taken as a whole shows the underlying conditions of the wood to be acid soil. However, like many sites in Croydon the change in geology at the N of the wood where chalk is present allows the growth of field maples and hazel. Around 50 bird species have been recorded.

Management   Croydon Parks Department.

Interpretation   Leaflets available from LB Croydon.

Access   Open to the public.

Contact   Parks Department.

9   Riddlesdown

Riddlesdown Road, Purley (TQ 531600).

City of London Corporation. 66ha.

Approach   Near Caterham.

Summary   Here an ancient trackway that once joined London to the S coast crosses the ridge of chalk which is the E boundary of the

Caterham Valley. A railway line cuts diagonally to the S of the Down using a viaduct over the Rose and Crown chalkpit. The slopes are covered with a mix of chalk grassland and scrub.

History The name may have derived from Middle English meaning an area cleared of wood, and this area was certainly sheep or rabbit grazed well into this century. In the 1820s chalk extraction began on the SW edge of the Down, and only halted in the 1950s. The grassy common was saved by the City of London in 1883 along with other commons in the Croydon area in order to resolve a legal dispute about common rights with the lord of the manor. In 1937, the council added 37 acres, though most of this is still a tenanted farm.

Nature interest The decline of sheep grazing and the decimation of the rabbit population have left Riddlesdown with the same problem of natural succession that applies to other chalk downs. The wooded side of the Down rises to a terrace of herb- rich grassland mostly of upright brome or sweet vernal grass, with the elegant quaking grass and carnation sedge. Wild thyme, the lemon coloured kidney vetch, marjoram, wild parsnip and low growing restharrow are among the many herbs to be found as well as the nationally rare round-headed campion. Towards the S and E the sward is less rich being close to an area of improved grassland. Encroaching chalk scrub which includes spindle, dogwood, buckthorn and wayfaring tree merges into oak woodland. The understorey of this contains ash, whitebeam and hazel and, on the NW slope, hawthorn. This section joins an area of dark ancient yews which grow on either side of the trackway.

The Rose and Crown chalk pit which has a SW aspect is jagged with terraces and slopes. Opportunists such as rosebay willowherb and ragwort have a foothold on these platforms which also support species typical of old chalk grassland such as those on the upper slopes of the Down, including bee and pyramidal orchid and a large colony of common spotted orchid. The nationally rare white mullein together with its yellow relation grow on the pit floor. The pond, surrounded by scrub, supports a breeding population of toads, while the generally sheltered and sunny environment attracts common lizards and slow worms. A colony of the small blue butterfly relies on its food plant, the kidney vetch, which is found on the spoil heaps. The colony is one of the two largest in Greater London, the other being at Hutchinson's Bank, also in this borough. Another 12 species have been recorded with two rarities, the dingy skipper and chalkhill blue.

Management The City of London is managing it to control scrub and is cutting the hay to maintain the sward.

Interpretation Nil on site.

Access The Rose and Crown chalk pit has no public access.

Contact The City of London Corporation, Kent and Surrey Commons Department.

10   Selsdon Wood Nature Reserve

Old Farleigh Road, S Croydon (TQ 364617).
National Trust. 81ha.

Approach Near Selsdon Vale.

Summary This is modified ancient woodland with conifer and beech plantations. There are considerable areas of open grassland and a network of paths have protected them, so that a well-developed understorey of interesting plants is easily seen without trampling.

History   The reserve was a holding of Selsdon farm in the old Croydon Crook portion of the borough which throughout the 19C was owned by the Smith family. The ancient technique of coppicing continued until the Second World War. The wide rides and plantings indicate the wood was partially managed to provide game cover as well. During the first two decades of this century the wood changed hands until it too, like the surrounding land, was in danger of being lost for building. The appeal for funds to purchase the 16 acres described as a bird sanctuary in 1923 by the Croydon Natural History and Scientific Society and the Surrey Garden Village Trust, blossomed over the following 10 years. By 1936 a reserve of around 200 acres was handed over to the National Trust.

Nature interest   The wood is a collection of plantations and oak coppice with large clearings mostly in the W corner. Several areas are fenced off to protect the understorey. The N edge, Court Wood, is dominated by pedunculate and sessile oak with hazel as the shrub layer. In the spring, this area is carpeted by wood anemone and bluebells. An unusual area of ash-maple woodland has a good understorey again of hazel with common and midland hawthorn, crab apple and spindle. The rich ground flora includes examples of wood spurge, dog's mercury, primrose, goldilocks and the purple and twayblade orchids. Considerable planting schemes of thousands of larches, spruces and beech have taken place since 1969 on the advice of LB Croydon. A central area called Steven's Larch was planted sometime before the Great War and harvested during the six years of the Second World War. The range of woodland habitat adjacent to open land attracts at least 62 species of birds such as nuthatches, woodpeckers, treecreepers and tawny owls. Small mammals such as shrews, voles and mice have been recorded as well as weasels, badgers and the diminutive Chinese muntjac deer.

Management   Although owned by the National Trust the reserve is managed by LB Croydon. Some coppicing takes place on the SE boundary, and fencing is used to protect the wood from trampling.

Interpretation   Booklets on the history of the reserve are available from Croydon Parks Department.

Access   Open during daylight hours.

Contact   Croydon Parks Department.

11   South Norwood Country Park

Long Lane, Elmers End (TQ 354683).
LB Croydon. 48ha.

Approach   On the border between LB Croydon and LB Bromley.

Summary   An important site not only because areas of wildlife interest are rare in the N of the borough but more importantly because Croydon has little standing or running water. The park contains a mosaic of grassland, scrub and woodland with wet meadow fed by a spring-fed stream.

History   Originally farmland, the site was acquired by the local council piecemeal from the mid-19C until 1951, for use as a sewage farm. Two methods were tried, drying out and containing, neither of which was successful. Since 1966 the site has become a haven for wildlife. Threats to the old sewage farm which straddles the border with Bexley emerged recently. Local pressure against development certainly encouraged LB Croydon to develop this park with the main emphasis on nature conservation, in the area they own. The fate of the Bexley area is not yet clear. During 1987 and 1988 the area was landscaped as a country park which opened in May 1989.

Nature interest   Most of the park has retained its former habitat which is wetland. There is some habitat creation and landscaping—most obviously the view point mound near thesports arena to the S of the park. To the W of the site office is a meadow area which was seeded where rubbish was tipped. The more characteristic habitat is, however, to the N of the park. Beside an extensive area of grassland runs a feeder stream leading in a N arc to a large lake, which has been developed to retain water at different levels to encourage drangon-flies and damselflies. Bird species formerly recorded in the area which was dominated by reed canary grass and reed sweet grass included warblers and reed bunting. Elsewhere, benefitting from the mix of 'wasteland' and wetland were grey herons, snipe, water rail, golden plover or stonechats and even partridges. To the credit of the park's designers this mosaic of habitat has been retained so it is to be hoped that many of these species will continue to be found here. Tree cover is provided by· four species of willow—white, grey, great and crack. These grow naturally in the park. New planting for cover has been undertaken in the meadow area while the wasteland area and grassland have been allowed to keep their more open character.

Management   The park is managed to conserve wildlife with recreational activities catered for in the S part of the site. A wide network of footpaths will protect the area of habitat as well as allow wheelchair and pushchair access.

Interpretation   Another of Croydon's trim trails takes visitors around the park but there is a leaflet available which shows habitats and main footpaths for the more leisurely visit. The park office is to the S of the park.

Access   Open access from morning to dusk.

Contact   Croydon Parks and Recreational Department, Taberner House, Park Lane, Croydon CR9 3JS. (01 760 5584).

12   Spring Park and Threehalfpenny Wood

Addington Road, Addington (TQ 377648).
City of London. 31ha.

Approach   A2022 border of LB Bromley and LB Croydon.

Summary   Running parallel to the main road, the wood covers a narrow ridge of sand and clay. Many informal paths cut through stands of trees and across the boundary ditch on the SE slope leaving many areas bare of vegetation. A wedge of woodland extends N, and along its edge is the beginning of the river Beck, which disappears below ground to re-emerge in High Broom Wood.

Nature interest   This SSSI is significant for being the only site in Greater London to contain stands of the graceful small-leaved lime which are locally abundant close to the boundary ditch. The overall impression is of overgrown sweet chestnut with canopy trees of oak and birch. The shade of the wood may well have contributed to the decline of the light-sensitive hazel stands. In some parts of the W half the understorey is poor but towards the centre of the site bramble dominates with plants such as sanicle, wood sorrel and wood melick.

A spring in the W half encourages the growth of alder and sphagnum moss as well as the notable hard fern.

Management   The wood is owned and managed by the City of London.

Interpretation   Nil on site.

Access   Open at all times.

Contact   Corporation of the City of London.

Further information

LB Croydon, Parks Department, Taberner House, Park Lane, Croydon (01 686 4433, 01 760 5584).

Corporation of the City of London, Kent and Surrey Commons Department (see City).

EALING

The Grand Union Canal continues its journey to Paddington from Ealing's W border while its main branch stretches towards Uxbridge and the Midlands. The River Brent similarly winds along a curving valley from the border with Brent to enter the Thames near Syon House. Away from the largely industrial and residential S and E, where open space tends to be small manicured parks, the borough rises to Hanger, Castlebar and Horsenden Hills. Between and across these lie the bulk of wildlife habitat with the canal and river pulling thin threads of water-edge flora through otherwise formal parks and golf courses. Despite this, a strategic overview taken during the early 1980s identified the borough as being deficient in wetland habitat. The concept of the extended Brent River Park to counter this blossomed from a previous nature conservation policy which describes management plans for open spaces and the considerable area of farmland around Horsenden Hill.

1 Foxwood

Hillcrest Road, W5 (TQ 182822).
LB Ealing. 2ha.
Approach   Next to Hanger Hill Park.
Summary   A small reserve survives at the edge of the park on a hillside overlooking the Brent Valley. Around a mainly secondary woodland surrounded by housing on its N and W borders, some effort has been made to help the reserve blend into the surrounding recreational grassland by retaining a buffer meadow zone.
History   The woodland occupies part of the site of a former reservoir. Following its construction in 1888 it developed faults and was finally drained in 1943, although this was primarily to prevent it being used as a navigational aid for enemy bombers. In 1949, the council purchased the land partly for housing. For the following 20 years plants began to colonise the reservoir, but sadly between 1969 and 1972 the basin was filled by rubbish. A young local resident, David Stubbs, compiled records over the next few years which indicated the value of the site to wildlife. In 1982, the meadow-like areas were turned into playing fields leaving wooded banks. The increasing public interest in nature conservation led to the creation of this reserve during the ensuing years, where local LWT group members have undertaken surveys and practical tasks.
Nature interest   The reserve acts as a bird sanctuary for at least 60 species. The vigorous young woodland is balanced with areas and individual trees of a greater age. Oak and sycamore tend to dominate with an understorey of hawthorn, holly and bramble. Ground flora on the crest of the hill is indicative of ancient woodland and hedges, including bluebells, wood anemone and lesser celandine. Apart from the impressive bird list which records chiffchaff, blackcap, tawny owl and other woodland species, butterflies such as the Essex skipper, speckled brown and the holly blue also enjoy the site.
Management   An LWT reserve. Management aims include diversifying the woodland structure with some control of sycamore and other invasive species. A useful site for school visits.
Interpretation   A five-point nature trail has been constructed on site with an accompanying explanatory leaflet available from LWT.
Access   Open at all times.
Contact   LWT Regional Officer (01 747 3881).

2   Hanwell Springs

Church Road W7 (TQ 147808).
Private. 1ha.
Approach   Near Brent Lodge Park.
Summary   The reserve, otherwise known as The Hermitage, consists of broadleaved woodland. A lake is fed from a pure spring emerging from the wood. It lies close to an ox-bow of the river and is within the Brent River Park.
History   The reserve was originally protected by the Selborne Society but management has now been undertaken by LWT.
Nature interest   The wood slopes N down to a lake so that a diversity of habitats is contained within this small reserve. Oak, hornbeam and cherry with some horse chestnut form the canopy. The ground flora is rich in some areas with wild garlic, archangel, primrose and goldilocks. The spring-fed stream has moss and fern covered banks. At its mouth is the rare moss *eurynchium riparicides*. Meadowsweet and purple loosestrife edge the lake, which LWT has desilted, and now supports a good range of dragonflies and other aquatic insects.
Management   Restoring the lake has been a major aim of management and LWT intends to continue to upgrade this habitat and conserve the woodland cover for birds.
Interpretation   Nil on site.
Access   No public access. Visits can be arranged through LWT.
Contact   LWT Regional Officer (01 747 3881).

3   Horsenden Hill

Horsenden Lane North, Greenford (TQ 160844).
LB Ealing. 100ha.
Summary   The highest point in the borough with views across London and four other counties, Horsenden Hill is valued as ancient rural landscape with ponds and hedges patterning the often unimproved meadows and pastures.
History   The area was pasture and arable in the 18C but was increasingly used for hay to feed London's working horses. This would have been transported by barge along the canal, and the importance of this supply is apparent with the conversion of the entire area by the end of the following century. During the 1930s the grasslands were bought piecemeal by the neighbouring councils of Wembley, Ealing and the county of Middlesex. Following the Second World War the last arable farm closed. As public space developed across former fields, with the emphasis on sports facilities, a lack of expertise in managing the area to conserve habitat became clear. In 1984 a countryside ranger was employed to formulate and implement a combined policy for recreation and nature conservation. The initial reintroduction of haymaking has been successful, and restoration of Horsenden Wood is also now in hand.
Nature interest   The most interesting habitat of Horsenden Hill is its varied grassland. Near the Canal, on either side of the lane, the damper slopes encourage meadow buttercups, agrimony and ragged robin to grow in the sward of red fescue, cocksfoot, meadow foxtail and Timothy grass. As the slope rises rye grass is dotted with field scabious and black medick. The damper patches contain marsh foxtail, or sweet vernal grass. Sports pitches intersperse the less interesting upper grassland but there are occasional patches of cut-leaved cranesbill even in that unpromising environment. The

steeper grass slopes in the SE, although suffering from the encroachment of scrub, are now cut by hand to retain the locally rare dyer's greenweed, pepper saxifrage, rest harrow and zig-zag clover. The tall hedgerows contain many typical woodland plants probably indicating their origin as woodland strips left after surrounding land was cleared. Around Horsenden Wood this process took place during the 19C leaving hedges containing hornbeam and wild service, also found in the wood itself. This was a coppiced oak woodland, but over-zealous park-type management and visitor pressure has destroyed the former hazel understorey and much of its ground flora. The nearby Perivale Wood suggests what this wood must have once looked like.

Management   The whole area is managed by LB Ealing, which consults nearby landowners and users. Survey work has been undertaken by the LWT and volunteers are encouraged to take part in practical tasks.

Interpretation   A countryside walk of just under three miles has been devised with an accompanying booklet and interpretation boards. Guided tours and illustrated talks are regularly undertaken.

Access   Open at all times.

Contact   Countryside Ranger, Ealing Parks and Amenities.

4   Perivale Wood

Sunley Gardens, Greenford (TQ 159836).
Selborne Society. 11ha.

Approach   S bank of the Grand Union Canal.

Summary   An important example of broadleaved ancient woodland, Perivale Wood sits between the railway line and the Grand Union Canal.

History   Since 1904 the wood has been owned and managed by the Selborne Society, who took their inspiration from Gilbert White. Although coppicing declined in the 1920s it played no small part in gaining the wood's designation as a Local Nature Reserve. The regime is being reintroduced, so continuing a tradition of management which provides material for fencing nearby fields.

Nature interest   One of Britain's oldest LNRs, the wood's importance is obvious from the well-developed hazel understorey (an increasingly rare sight) beneath the canopy of pedunculate oak and ash. Ground flora flourishes with a spring carpet of bluebells and betony, goldilocks and common violet. The wood is noted for its unusually large examples of field maple, crab apple and wild service. Many features indicate the wood's link with surrounding farmland such as the old parish boundary hedge along its E border, and the regenerating elm, associated with hedgerows, in the SW. On its S and E borders are old species-rich pastures which, combined with those on nearby Horsenden Hill, make this area important for its open aspect as well as the sheltered environment of woodland.

Management   The Selborne Society manages the wood and is reintroducing coppicing which will help keep the structure of the wood.

Interpretation   Booklets are available from the Selborne Society.

Access   There is no public access, but visits may be arranged.

Contact   The Selborne Society, c/o 12 Hanwell Drive, London W7.

Further information

LB Ealing, Technical Services, 24 Uxbridge Road, London W5 2BP (01 579 2424).
London Wildlife Trust (see Barking).

ENFIELD

Enfield is the northernmost borough of Greater London. The ancient E boundary is drawn by the river Lee that once divided Middlesex from Essex. The ground near the river, once prone to flooding, was used formerly as meadow and market gardens but, where the land rises to the western clay hills, woodland and heath predominated. Most of this landscape was enclosed as Enfield Chase in 1136 and even in the 19C was considered to be wild and distant from the capital, as names like Botany Bay suggest. Building development was hastened by the arrival of the railway in 1872. The wharves and industry located along the Lee were supplemented by terraced houses covering the grounds of former country mansions. Habitat of value to wildlife tends to occur in the Green Belt area where the mix is of farm and parkland, but even in open space such as Grovelands Park former coppices belonging to the Chase can still be seen.

1   Covert Way Field

Near Hadley Wood (TQ 265974).
LB Enfield. 6.5ha.
Approach   Covert Way, Camlet Way.
Summary   North of Hadley Common this small triangular reserve occupies former pasture which has been colonised by scrub.
History   The reserve was established in 1975 by LB Enfield with the support of the Hadley Wood Association.
Nature interest   This is an area of scrub and tall grassland close to a railway line. The dominant tree species is ash, but oak and hawthorn also occur. Field edge tree species such as crab apple and maple are also present with elm occupying an E shelter belt supplemented by conifers. The grassland has also been invaded by other common hedge species such as bramble and dog rose. A regular mowing regime has been established to encourage a herb-rich sward.
Management   The reserve is managed by LB Enfield parks department with the co-operation of an advisory committee of various natural history groups led by HMWT. Some coppicing and mowing have been undertaken to prevent the entire reserve developing into woodland.
Interpretation   HMWT leaflet.
Access   Unrestricted.
Contact   HMWT.

2   Trent Park

North Enfield (TQ 2997).
LRB. 167ha.
Approach   Cockfosters Road.
Summary   A landscaped park with areas of woodland towards the Hadley Road edge adjacent to Merryhill Farm.
History   Formerly part of the Chase, the park includes the moat of the lost mansion of the 14th Earl of Hereford. The two large lakes are the result of 18C landscaping by the busy Humphrey Repton (see Barnet). The process that he began for Dr Jebb, physician to George III, was continued by subsequent owners especially Sir Philip Sassoon, who planted specimen trees and collected exotic waterfowl.

During the Second World War the mansion became an interrogation centre. In 1952 Middlesex County Council had acquired the house and grounds, and the park was opened to the public in 1973. The mansion is part of Middlesex Polytechnic.

Nature interest   The woodland of this landscaped park still contains oak and hornbeam with gean and hawthorn echoing the woodland characteristics of this borough. The ground flora has been greatly modified by the extensive planting of cultivated daffodils.

Management   The park is managed by LB Enfield and some coppicing has been undertaken. Dead wood is left to encourage fungi and invertebrates.

Interpretation   Trails include the woodland trail for the blind, created by a former blind resident, Ron Stevenson, and George Matthews, the former park manager. Beginning at Cockfosters Gate this allows visitors to complete a three mile walk guided by raised logs and braille information posts.

Access   Unrestricted.

Contact   Trent Park Manager (01 449 8706).

3   Whitewebbs Wood

North Enfield (TQ 325996).
LB Enfield. 50ha.

Approach   Along Clay Hill.

Summary   This modified ancient woodland occurs at the NE corner of Whitewebbs Park and golf course. Along the S boundary of the wood runs Cuffley Brook, a tributary of the Lee, which favours the growth of water plants, extending the wetland habitat of the private lake which lies S of the wood.

History   In 1570 Elizabeth rewarded her physician, Dr Huicks, with a grant of Whitewebbs House on land which, although part of the Chase, was once commonland. James I incorporated more land to the N of this to form the enclosed Theobalds Park. By 1790 the house was demolished and the estate was bought by the noted agricultural innovator, Dr Abraham Wilkinson. Some 30 years later, with the division of ancient commonland between the neighbouring parishes, the wood went to the doctor, increasing the size of his already large estate. In 1955 the local district council acquired the estate to form Whitewebbs Park with the house becoming an old peoples' home in 1973.

Nature interest   The wood lies on clay acidic soil on a S-facing slope. Dominant tree species are oak and hornbeam which were formerly coppiced, as elsewhere in this borough. Additional species such as alder, mature beech and ash occur, with wild service tree growing particularly in the W section. Where the understorey of bramble and bracken allows there is a typically poor ground flora associated with hornbeam woods. Even so this includes examples of lady's smock, lesser celandine, wild strawberry and wood anemone. The streams running through the wood encourage the growth of remote sedge and wood sorrel, but as they drain into Cuffley Brook more species take advantage of several damp hollows. This richer habitat includes examples of comfrey, water mint and other common wetland plants as well as crack willow. A large number of butterflies have been recorded and a good range of mammals such as voles and shrews, grey squirrels, rabbits and the occasional muntjac deer have been recorded.

Management   LB Enfield Parks Department.
Interpretation   A nature trail of just over a mile in length has been laid out by the local group of the RSPB and can be started from either of the two car parks. Guides and local maps are available from the Forty Hall Museum nearby.
Access   Unrestricted.
Contact   LB Enfield Parks Department.

Further information

LB Enfield, Parks Department, Civic Centre, Silver Street, Enfield (01 366 6565).
Hertfordshire and Middlesex Wildlife Trust (see Barnet).
London Wildlife Trust (see Barking).

GREENWICH

The borough is renowned for its sweeping wooded hillsides, plunging down to meet the Thames in the N. Greenwich Park was
enclosed in 1619, but the wastes and commons of the Kentish
borough were either eroded by 18C landlords who built large houses
in secluded grounds such as Castle Wood or by the military who
needed barracks and arsenals. Much of the 3,000 acres of open space
of this borough is either former commonland or landscaped park
created from the heaths and grasslands. Only a faint echo of the
rough and windy gorse covered Blackheath remains, although some
attempt to encourage habitat is likely on a section which slips into
Lewisham. With the loss of low-lying wetland to Thamesmead Town
during the 1970s, the most important expanse of habitat is the
ancient woodlands, though voluntary groups are concerned to retain
ponds and what is left of the once marshy land of the Kidbrook area.
The Green Chain Walk links many sites, but in itself does not offer
any protection to wildlife habitats which are threatened mainly by
road schemes.

1   Bostall Woods and Heath

Bostall Hill, SE2 (TQ 46778, 47782).
LB Greenwich.
Approach   Numerous footpaths lead from Plumstead Cemetery or
from Bostall Hill Road which divides the heath from the woods.
Summary   The penultimate N section of woods and grasslands that
slice across the borough forming a chain from the Abbey Woods S to
Avery Hill.
History   Originally part of the commons of the manor of Plumstead, Bostall was the focus for dramatic protests following attempts
by the landlord, Queen's College Oxford, to sell the land as private
property in 1866. In 1877 the heath was acquired by the Metropolitan
Board of Works. The LCC later doubled the area of open space by
purchasing the woods in 1893 from Sir John Goldsmid who had
campaigned vigorously against Queen's College and agreed to sell
the land cheaply.
Nature interest   The woods are mainly secondary broadleaf, modified by the planting of Scotch fir and larch. However, there is some
evidence of coppice and pollarding, once the most widely used
method of cutting wood on commons in this area. Originally, oak, ash
and birch were the main species but there has been some planting
with sweet chestnut. The acid grassland is threatened by scrub
encroachment and erosion by cyclists.
Management   LB Greenwich Parks Department.
Interpretation   Nil on site; Green Chain Walk leaflet 1.
Access   Free public access.
Contact   LB Greenwich Leisure Services.

2   Charlton Sand Pit

Pound Park Road, SE7 (TQ 419786).
LB Greenwich. 4ha.
Summary   Notified as an SSSI in 1959, the 50 foot high cliffs reveal
a sequence of geological strata considered to be a 'text book classic'
in relation to sedimentation of the Woolwich Beds.

History   The sand pits, otherwise known as Gilbert's Pits, were dug for glass works and for moulding purposes at the Royal Arsenal at Woolwich.

Nature interest   From the pebble beds at the base of the pits to the sucession of silts and shell beds rising to chalk, this site reveals a geological history of the area. This is the nearest site to central London where such strata can be studied.

Access   By permission only.

Contact   Greenwich Parks Department.

3 Dot Hill

Dothill Road, SE9 (TQ 446773).

LB Greenwich, LWT. 1ha.

Approach   Take the unmade footpath along the top edge of allotments from Dothill Road. Entry is through large wooden gates.

Summary   A wooded embankment on the N slopes of Shooters Hill, bordered by a housing estate on E edge and allotments on the W, offers views across the Thames to the Royal Docks.

History   Once used as allotments, in 1987 it was licensed to LWT as a nature reserve.

Nature interest   The grassy upper part of the slope is dotted with brambles which spill down towards the damper, lower area where cover is dense. A natural spring feeds a stream which becomes a pond surrounded by soft rush, hairy willowherb, sweet grass and common reed. Tree species include oak, ash, birch and even the rare wild service tree. A hawthorn hedge has been planted along the western edge. A good population of frogs and birds such as blackcaps, willow warblers and tits benefit from the seclusion of this site which is the northernmost section of the arc of open space that leads to Oxleas Woods.

Management   The site is managed by LWT which aims to enhance the wetland habitat and maintain the grassland while encouraging public access.

Interpretation   Nil on site.

Access   Open access.

Contact   LWT.

4 Kidbrooke Green

Rochester Close, Rochester Way, SE3 (TQ 412760).

Approach   No access at present. Nearby is Birdbrook Road Pond close to the Kidbrooke Estate.

Summary   A mix of lightly grazed grassland and marshland interspersed with small ponds.

History   A last glimpse of the once extensive marshlands along the length of the Kidbrooke, it is now used for rough pasture. Some drainage channels and hedges can still be seen which are found in old maps of the area. A campaign by local conservation groups aimed to protect the wetland gained momentum when construction of football pitches disturbed ponds.

Nature interest   Wildlife takes full advantage of the damp environment so that lizards, toads, frogs and newts are to be found in the shallow pools and ditches. Small mammals and a good range of birds, including snipe, redwing and fieldfare have been recorded.

Management   LB Greenwich, LWT.
Interpretation   Nil on site.
Access   No public access.
Contact   LB Greenwich Leisure Services, and LWT.

5   LESSA Pond

Butterfly Lane, SE9 (TQ 432739).
London Electricity Sports and Social Association (LESSA).
Approach   Access is along an ally between 87 and 91 Footscray Road. Close to Royal Blackheath Golf Club and numerous playing fields adjoining Avery Hill Park and College.
Summary   A pond tucked in the corner of a playing field beside a car park is adjacent to Pippenhall Meadows (qv).
History   Part of former farmland, the pond has been licenced to LWT since 1985.
Nature interest   This large pond retains its place in a network of old hedgerows that criss-cross land now devoted to sports. Although vandalism is a problem, as with most city ponds, there is a good selection of aquatic and marginal vegetation including water milfoil, celery-leaved buttercup, various rushes and sedges. Cover for birds is provided by oak, ash and willow. It is best known for amphibians—frogs, toads and newts. Bats are present as are foxes.
Management   The site is leased and managed by LWT which aims to maintain the pond for amphibians and birdlife.
Interpretation   Nil on site.
Access   From ILEA footpath access is freely available.
Contact   LWT (see Barking).

6   Oxleas Wood, Shepherdleas Wood and Jack Wood

Shooters Hill, SE18 (TQ 440759).
LB Greenwich. 77ha.
Approach   On the E slope of Shooters Hill.
Summary   Edged by the Roman road between London and Dover and cut by various modern alternatives, this cluster of ancient woods covers the S slopes of the highest hill in inner London.
History   From the 12C to the 14C the woods were managed as coppice for the royal manor of Eltham, where one of the Tudors' favourite palaces was built. Crown ownership ended in 1679 when the woods were granted to Sir John Shaw. For the next 200 years they were managed under leaseholds. The War Office took them over in 1871 and the LCC in 1930, which opened the woods to the public in 1934 and reintroduced coppicing in 1983. The woods are under threat from proposals to build the East London River Crossing. The curving course of the road scheme cuts through Shepherdleas and Oxleas Woods, and is likely to destroy almost two thirds of the plant species associated with this particular group of ancient woods. Local and regional opposition led to a lengthy but unsuccessful campaign to protect this important habitat, including evidence presented at a public inquiry in 1985.
Nature interest   The woods are some of London's most important and are nominally protected by being designated as an SSSI. The range of species, stand types and varied structure of each wood

contribute to the value of the whole of this extensive area of woodland. Each wood has its own character, reflecting the underlying geology and slightly different management. An interesting comparison could be made between the pedunculate oak dominated Oxleas and Shepherdleas Woods and the sessile oak of Jack Wood. Although coppice management is general, the best example is Shepherdleas Wood where, though the plant species are fewer, there are particularly fine examples of the rare wild service tree. This tree occurs throughout these woods with examples of both mature and young contributing to the understorey. In Oxleas Wood, where the understorey is dominated by hazel and sweet chestnut, grows the widest range of ground flora from the spring flowering bluebells and wood anemone, to wood poa, wood millet and wood sage among the bramble and bracken.

The damp environment which feeds ditches and streams—one of which crosses Oxleas Wood, supports rushes, sedges and tall brome. The most interesting of the streams runs in Jack Wood. In or beside it grows remote sedge, tufted hairgrass and yellow pimpernel. Another rarity to be found in Jack Wood is butcher's broom, a member of the lily family. A wide range of plants associated with a wet flush in the N edge of Oxleas and numerous fungi and lichens contribute yet more species to a list which provides interest throughout the year. The structure of the woods supports a wide range of birds which benefit from a similarly healthy insect population. Along with the rare, for London, wood warbler, occur nuthatches, tree creepers, woodcock and woodpeckers. Woodmice, bank voles and short-tailed vole as well as foxes have been recorded.

Management   LB Greenwich.
Interpretation   Trail by Green Chain Walk, the accompanying leaflets obtainable from LB Greenwich.
Access   Open at all times.
Contact   LB Greenwich Leisure Services.

7   Pippenhall Meadows

Butterfly Lane, SE9 (TQ 438744).
LB Greenwich; various tenants. 5.8ha.
Approach   The Green Chain Walk, or from Bexley Road via the stables.
Summary   A mix of unimproved and semi-improved grassland with a damp central area is caused by a natural spring. Five pastures are divided by hedges with a pond and a brook which eventually feed the River Shuttle.
History   Watercress beds in the NE were fed by the spring but are now used for grazing.
Nature interest   The N area is regularly mown but still supports plenty of field woodrush while the hedges in this vicinity are noted for their spring foxgloves. The strongest feature of the meadows is the damp environment which supports many wetland plants such as ragged robin, cuckoo flower, greater bird's foot trefoil and fleabane. The central pastures which provide most of the examples of these seem to have remained unimproved while the S area which is drier is less rich, although bluebells are particularly plentiful. The old hedges provide cover for warblers, greenfinch, dunnocks and thrushes; the flush and pond for snipe and mallard.

Management   Managed as grazing land with some mowing, both need to be carefully monitored to protect wildlife habitat.
Interpretation   Nil on site.
Access   Open at all times.
Contact   LB Greenwich Leisure Services.

8   Tump 53

Bentham Road, SE28 (TQ 467804).
Thamesmead Town Trust. 1.4ha.
Approach   Off Windrush Close.
Summary   A moated island surrounded by reedbeds.
History   The man-made tumps were used as ammunition stores in the late 19C, the area being sold to the LCC in 1960. Its successor, the GLC, carried out landscaping works before 1985 when LWT took over management. A similar scheme awaits Tump 39 in Crossway Lake further N beside the Thames.
Nature interest   Woodland of elder, hawthorn and silver birch fills the tump itself while dense reed beds and much aquatic vegetation occupy the moat.
Management   Managed by LWT primarily as an educational reserve.
Interpretation   Leaflet available from LWT. A nature study centre is planned for the early 1990s.
Access   Open to the public.
Contact   LWT Warden (01 310 5100);   Thamesmead Town Ltd, Company Office, Harrow Manor Way, Thamesmead, SE2 9XH.

Further information

LB Greenwich, Leisure Services, 147 Powis Street, SE18 (01 854 0055).
London Wildlife Trust (see Barking).

Tump 53

HACKNEY

Before Domesday this inner London borough was 'Hacca's well watered land'. Although fundamentally altered by 19C building developments the remaining wildlife habitat is rooted in this wet past from the three miles of the River Lee along Hackney's E border, to the reservoirs in the N and the Regent's Canal, which travels nearly two miles linking Shoreditch to Victoria Park. 15% of the borough is public open space but this is mostly formal parkland although these too have sometimes retained characteristics of their history as meadow or pasture. The borough council has expressed some interest in habitat creation in the green desert of the Hackney Marshes. An excellent report records the value of the canal to wildlife, and proposals to protect the small Wenlock Basin are being considered. However, the bulk of valuable habitat depends on the River Lee and the New River, the latter's future being uncertain.

1   Abney Park Cemetery

Stoke Newington High Street, N16 (TQ 333868).
LB Hackney. 13ha.
Approach   Through a magnificent gateway from the high street.
Summary   An atmospheric secondary woodland with grass walks between graves. Once inside, it is difficult to keep a sense of direction.
History   Part of the estate of Sir Thomas Abney which was used as an arboretum, the cemetery eventually declined during this century. Local groups interested in the wildlife as well as the historical value of the cemetery now participate in a management committee, although volunteers are not encouraged to do practical work on site.
Nature interest   The woodland is valuable for birdlife as it is the only large tree-covered area in the borough. The dense undergrowth is good for small mammals and insects which in turn attract owls and bats.
Management   LB Hackney Parks Department undertakes management tasks, local community and conservation groups which mounted a campaign to save the cemetery being represented on a committee.
Interpretation   Nil on site. Booklet available from the Save Abney Park Cemetery Committee.
Contact   LB Hackney Parks Department; Save Abney Park Cemetery Committee, c/o 204 Lea View House, Springfield E5 9EA.

2   River Lee, Hackney Cut and the Middlesex Filter Beds

The Lee forms most of the E border of the borough (TQ 358864).
Lee Valley River Park Authority, TWA (Filter Beds).
Approach   Easily seen from the towpath which may be followed for most of the river's three miles. This continues along the Hackney Cut which links the Lee to the filter beds.
Summary   An important stretch of running fresh water which enters the Thames at Limehouse, the Lee is canalised along much of its London section. Further S glimpses of a naturally steep banked river can be seen, as can the river plants and birds that take

advantage of this corridor through the borough and the few wild footholds that still exist especially at the filter beds and various small islands.

History   Alongside what was once a navigable river a new channel was dug in 1768 and is known as the Lee Navigation or Hackney Cut. The Filter Beds were dug between 1852–54 by the East London Water Works. By 1969 the beds had fallen into disuse and the sand and gravel removed, leaving the way open for wildlife. The LVRPA, set up in 1967, hopes to save the filter beds by negotiating a lease with TWA.

Nature interest   On the E edge of the N section of the river are the Walthamstow Marshes which clearly show what might have been the appearance of those at Hackney before they were drained to become acres of featureless football pitches. Along the river, stands of bulrushes, with exotics such as Himlayan balsam, Russian comfrey and hogweed, provide cover for waterfowl such as mute swan, pochard and tufted duck. This river-edge habitat continues S of Lee Bridge Road, and as the river curves into the cut below Leyton and Walthamstow Marshes are the filter beds. Various stages of succession from open water to dry grassland are demonstrated in sections which radiate out like cheese wedges. Reed beds with poplar and crack willow, lesser reedmace, great pond sedge and nodding bur-marigold hide waterfowl. Continuing down the Cut are some areas of substantial vegetation with arrowhead and bulrush on a shallow ledge while hornwort, curled pondweed and various kinds of duckweed remain submerged.

Down the Lee, E of the Cut is Bully Point, opposite the Eastway Cycle Track. This former marsh was drained and then tipped on. As its height increased so its flora changed and now reflects a truly urban setting. This nature reserve is noted for 14 species of butterfly, many birds and small mammals.

Management   The LVRPA manages a number of conservation areas along the length of the river.

Interpretation   LVRPA, LWT.

Contact   LVRPA, PO Box 88, Enfield (71711).

3   New River, Stoke Newington Reservoirs and Filter Beds

On the border with Haringey, close to Finsbury Park (TQ 235573—the reservoirs).

TWA. 12ha (East Reservoir), 15ha (West Reservoir).

Approach   Although followed by a path in Haringey the New River is less accessible in Hackney, but as it emerges near Islington it can again be followed. Green Lanes runs between the filter beds and the reservoirs, while Lordship Road splits the two apart.

Summary   Shaped like a pair of spectacle lenses with the river as the top frame, the reservoirs are well known for waterfowl, while the river—although an aqueduct—has an extensive range of wetland plants.

History   The New River was built by Hugh Middleton between 1609–13 to take spring water from Amwell in Hertfordshire the 38 miles to the Angel, Islington. In Hackney most of the river lies underground while the reservoirs it feeds occupy old gravel workings that were expanded in the 1830s to quench the thirst of the growing metropolis. Trading the TWA are creating a new ring main around London which will not require either the river or the reservoirs and filter beds (built in the 1930s and 1940s). A campaign to save them has been growing since 1985, and the New River Action Group was formed in 1987 to spearhead over 35 organisations which have joined the protest. Plans include a retail park on the filter beds, with the entire East Reservoir and most of the West developed, while the river level will drop.

Nature interest   Over 225 plant species have been identified down the course of the river ranging from rarities in London such as water dropwort to cover provided on the banks of the reservoirs by common spike rush and great willowherb. The general depth of these is around 5–6 metres with emergent vegetation concentrated on the West Reservoir because of its gently sloping edges. Grassland with an area of woodland in the SE of the East Reservoir composed of old hawthorn and pedunculate oak are among the attractions of this site for birds. Around 23 species breed here, with around 77 species regularly visiting. Great crested grebe, mute swan, pochard, tufted duck, smew, common terns and kingfishers use this habitat. In winter the reservoirs assume even more importance as the water tends to remain ice free, giving vital respite to birds. The nine shallow rectangles of open water on the far side of Green Lanes are the filter beds which attract geese and tufted duck which also benefit from the surrounding four hectares of relatively undisturbed grassland.

Management   TWA currently manages the river and its append-ages, but its future depends on the result of a public inquiry into plans for redevelopment of the land. The reservoirs are presently stocked with fish for angling, and grassland is mown in the late summer.

Interpretation   Nil on site. A nature trail is available for the Canonbury Road section in the neighbouring borough of Islington. LWT, the New River Action Group and TWA hold various reports, surveys and plans.

Access   Restricted.

Contact   New River Action Group, 74 Bramley Road, Southgate, London N14 4H5 (01 449 6112); LWT; and the TWA (see Barking).

4   Springfield Park

W of the River Lee (TQ 346875).
LB Hackney. 15.9ha.

Approach   Numerous footpaths cross the park with the lodge entrance facing Spring Hill.

Summary   An interesting park for grasslands varying from neutral to wet and acid.

History   Ancient pasture brought by the local council in 1905 for public open space.

Nature interest   The Park is surprisingly rich in species associated with meadows and pastures. In the NW corner the neutral grassland retains examples of common catsear, common sorrel and red clover. The grassland is composed of creeping soft grass, sweet vernal and crested dogstail among the more usual ryegrass. Sloping down towards the River Lee in the E, the area is damper and supports marsh foxtail, red fescue, fine bent and Timothy grass. Some species of tree illustrate yet more about the park's history with, apart from elm and hawthorn, the wayfaring tree.

Management   At the moment the park is managed in the usual way for public open space by the parks department. A change in the mowing regime is considered to be one of the simplest ways of encouraging the habitat.

Interpretation   See LWT report on Hackney sites.

Access   Open access.

Contact   LB Hackney Parks Department.

Further information

LB Hackney, Parks Department, Stoke Newington High Street, N16 (01 241 8928).
London Wildlife Trust (see Barking).

HAMMERSMITH AND FULHAM

Bordering on Ealing and Kensington and Chelsea, the bulk of Hammersmith is covered by housing with rather formal parks providing some relief. Sadly, the largest area of real value is fated to become a depot for Channel Tunnel rolling stock, so even railway embankments do not provide sanctuary to wildlife in this borough. However, a small nature reserve is being established on the edge of the large redevelopment site formerly famous for greyhound racing at White City.

Wormwood Scrubs, Scrubs Wood and Little Scrubs Wood

Scrubs Lane, NW10 (TQ 745817).
LB Hammersmith, British Rail. 80ha, 8ha, 5ha.
Approach   Wormwood Scrubs is unenclosed by fencing and may be entered along Braybrook Street, a turning off DuCane Road.
Summary   By far the largest public open space in the borough, together with Kensal Green Cemetery just the other side of Scrubs Wood and the Grand Union Canal, it forms an important wedge of variable habitat between major roads and railway lines.
History   The park was commonland and is protected under the Wormwood Scrubs Act of 1890 which protects the right of access for military training established early in the 19C. This is still observed, but in 1980 the former GLC suggested that activity should be confined to the W section which has been maintained as rough grassland as a result. The woods lap the top of the park but are destined to become the 'North Pole' development. Local opposition, vigorously lead by the young Lester Holloway, gained national publicity for the woods during the Save Scrubs Wood campaign, which led to an appearance before the parliamentary committee considering the Channel Tunnel Bill in 1987.
Nature interest   Away from the S sports pitches, the rather bleak park in its W reaches attracts many birds with kestrels hunting above the open grassland. The woods have grown up in disused sidings. The E Little Scrubs Wood, which acts as a link into Kensington and Chelsea, has grown up in the last 10 years on an area used for cleaning trains. The finest area of scrub which sheltered many birds was recently destroyed by bulldozers which have a practice area here. The main section known as Scrubs Wood has been developing for 50 years so that a good mix of habitats from birch and hawthorn scrub, rabbit-cropped grassland and damp runnels have provided a stable home to a wide range of wildlife. Birds better known as country dwellers such as white-throat and fieldfares are recorded among other inhabitants. The sunny embankments support a breeding population of lizards and slow worms. With voles and foxes completing the food chain Scrub Wood is a successful urban habitat whose disappearance will seriously affect the borough's ability to retain wildlife.
Management   The woods are unmanaged. The Park has potential for encouraging wildlife.
Access   Wormwood Scrubs is open at all times. No access to either woods.
Interpretation   Nil on site. Surveys available from LWT.
Contact   Hammersmith and Fulham Amenity Trust.

Further information

LB Hammersmith & Fulham, Leisure and Recreation Department, 181–187 King Street, London W6 9JU (01 748 3020 / 736 7181). Hammersmith and Fulham Amenity Trust, c/o above address. London Wildlife Trust (see Barking).

HARINGEY

The borough rises in the W with lower ground towards the Lee Valley. Open space is well distributed, but proportionally lower than that of Camden to the S. However, various conservation iniatives have put this borough ahead of others in the effort to encourage wildlife. When Alexandra Palace was acquired in 1980 a nature reserve was established in the surrounding park. This grassy open space is linked by a walk to the southernmost of Haringey's woodlands. The other occur to the NW of the borough abutting the large St Pancras and Islington Cemetery.

1 Alexandra Park

Alexandra Park Road, Hornsey, N10 (TQ 300900).
LB Haringey. 65ha.
Approach   Footpaths cross the park from either Alexandra Park Road or Grove Avenue. Most descend from the Palace at the ridge of the hill.
Summary   In the borough's largest public open space the reserve lies to the E next to the Wood Green reservoir and filter beds.
History   Once probably grassy heath surrounded by woodland, the palace built on the hill was named in honour of Princess Alexandra, wife of the future Edward VII. While never quite reaching the popularity of its rival, the Crystal Palace, even with the addition of a circus and a race course, it gained fame with the first live television transmission by the BBC in 1936. The GLC took over the park from its predecessor which acquired it 1956. In 1980, with much of the palace damaged by fire, ownership passed to the borough.
Nature interest   Heath grass on the NW slope of the central hill suggests the ancient character of the park. A range of habitats have grown up during the last 20 years, with wood, scrub and grassland providing cover for the 46 bird species that have been known to breed. Butterflies, too, are a common sight. A wide range of small mammals occur, from woodmice to short-tailed vole and weasels. Foxes, grey squirrels and hedgehogs are regularly seen. A pond was built in the nature reserve in the early 1980s, which has already added new species to the list such as common sandpiper, water rail and kingfisher.
Management   Managed by LB Haringey Leisure and Recreation Department.
Interpretation   Borough surveys by LWT and North London Polytechnic.
Access   Open to the public.
Contact   LB Haringey Leisure and Recreation Department.

2 Coldfall Wood

Creighton Avenue, N10 (TQ 277903).
LB Haringey. 13.8ha.
Approach   NW of Muswell Hill.
Summary   An oak/hornbeam wood has, like Highgate Wood, darkened—in this case due to lack of management which does nothing to counter considerable recreational pressure.
History   Once a woodland on the edge of Finchley Common, this coppice was bought by Hornsey Council in 1930 from which time it appears to have been left unmanaged.

Nature interest   The future for this wood seems bleak. The shade cast by the canopy of uniformly aged trees allows few of the species associated with ancient woodland to survive, although near the SE entrance a wet area supports distant flowering sedge.

Management   Some removal of brambles but no clear strategy seems to have been developed. Sycamore and beech seedlings are colonising the wood which needs a radical plan to improve its chances of survival as a viable wildlife habitat.

Interpretation   LWT borough survey.

Access   Open to the public.

Contact   LB Haringey Leisure and Recreation Department.

3 Highgate Wood and Queen's Wood

Archway Road, N6 (TQ 283887, TQ 288886).
Corporation of the City of London, LB Haringey. 28ha, 22ha.

Approach   Muswell Hill Road separates the two woods from each other. The entrances to both woods may be found off this road, but Highgate has an extra one on Archway Road and Queen's Wood may be entered from Queen's Wood Road which cuts off a chunk of woodland from the main area.

Summary   There are many indications that these were ancient coppices but Highgate Wood, the larger of the two, has become dark and gloomy while Queen's Wood, which covers a steep hillside, seems to have benefited from the inaccessibility this causes and the light it allows in.

History   Both woodlands were once hornbeam/oak coppices. Highgate Wood may have been used in the manufacturing of beer as its 17C name was Brewer's Fall. This was retained (Fall replaced by Wood) until the NW corner was dug in 1813 and was called Gravel Pit Wood. By 1842 the Earl of Mansfield had leased the wood which he left unmanaged. The woods were saved, when the lease expired, by a vigorous campaign which lead the Ecclesiastical Commissioners, which took it over, to give the wood to the City of London, which continues to manage it to the present day. Queen's Wood was called Old Fall Wood during the 17C but by the time it was bought by Hornsey in 1889 it had become Church-yard Bottom Wood. Once bought, it was renamed in honour of Queen Victoria.

Nature interest   Highgate Wood has a poor shrub layer compared to its neighbour. The oak canopy is dense although formerly coppiced hornbeam can still be found. This, together with examples of hazel, wild cherry and ground flora plants such as pendulous sedge, lesser stitchwort and wood violet, indicates that this is ancient woodland. In the SW section wild service trees grow. During the last 15 years many conifers have been planted so that Douglas fir, western hemlock and Corsican pine near the entrance add to the general gloom of the wood. Three large enclosures have been planted with beech which seems to have been a misguided effort to improve the understorey. The same range of trees appear in Queen's Wood, but an indication of how much lighter this wood is might be the wide distribution of hazel. Wild service grows in the E and midland hawthorn in the N. The shrub layer includes holly, guelder rose, elder and hawthorn. Streams cross the N section and encourage the growth of yellow flag iris, cuckoo pint and remote sedge. As in its neighbour, ornamental trees have been planted along the perimeter of the wood and the grassy area tends to be mown short. A disused adventure playground in the E is giving way to a community of ruderal plants. Both woods are good for birds with at least 63 species recorded.

Management   The Open Space Committee of the Corporation of the City of London pays for the maintenance of Highgate Wood. It aims to broaden the narrow age range of the trees and to plant mainly traditional species. Small areas are cleared to enable this to take place without causing too much public anxiety, and the enclosing of other areas allows undergrowth to remain free from trampling. It has been suggested that coppicing could be re-introduced to improve the structure of the wood. Queen's Wood is managed by LB Haringey.

Interpretation   Booklet on Highgate Wood from Open Spaces Committee of the City Corporation.

Contact   Highgate Wood can be contacted on 01 444 6129.

4   Parkland Walk

Stapleton Hall Road, Finsbury Park, N4 (TQ 293898, TQ 314875). LB Haringey. 13ha, approx 5½ miles).

Approach   Links Alexandra Park to Cranley Gardens at the edge of Highgate Wood, running from there to Archway and Finsbury Park.

Summary   It seems that the rather formal entrances combined with a buffer zone of gardens for much of its length has helped to protect this green corridor from unintentional disturbance. The walk is known for a wide range of birds and butterflies.

History   This was the Great North Railway Line taking visitors to Alexandra Palace. The service opened in 1873 and was finally closed in 1970. Since then records have been kept of this length of land which was bought by the borough for housing in 1976. Local people formed an association to save it and succeeded in their aim in 1978 following a public inquiry. The borough accepted the evidence and provided a warden for the site in 1980, opening the walk two years later.

Nature interest   The site has a wide range of habitats which support at least 19 species of butterfly. Well over 233 plants species (of which 20% are now native) provide nectar and food for large and small skippers, the green-veined white, the clouded yellow and the usually rural silver-washed fritillary. Among the 52 bird species recorded are red-legged partridge and yellow hammer. With 24 species breeding, the level of access has not, as yet, apparently threatened a healthy bird population. There has been some invasion by sycamore and bracken but hare's foot clover and nettle-leaved bellflower can still be found. With so many flowers to be seen this walk is worth a visit most of the year.

Management   Managed by LB Haringey which aims to control the spread of sycamore, Japanese knotweed and horsetail.

Interpretation   The information centre in the Station House, Stapleton Hall Road provides leaflets and information.

Access   Open to the public.

Contact   The Warden, The Station House Information Centre, Stapleton Hall Road, N4.

Further information

LB Haringey, Leisure and Recreation Department, The Lodge, Church Lane, N17 (01 808 7604).
London Wildlife Trust (see Barking).

HARROW

Famous for its public school built in the S of the borough, surburban Harrow covers the high ground on the border of London with Hertfordshire. The rural N hills are protected by various conservation policies but pressure to build in this area, once known for metro-land style development, continues. The Harrow Weald is drained by numerous streams, some feeding the River Colne, others the Dean Brook at Edgware. Wildlife habitat, as elsewhere on the outskirts of London, is often protected alongside archaeological features. Field systems, woods, ponds and lakes are frequently associated with ancient dykes, Roman roads or Saxon remains. However, even the more urban S at Harrow on the Hill, the school grounds and nearby blocks of farmland remain important habitats along the line of hills which cross the borough boundary with Ealing.

1   Bentley Priory

Common Road or Uxbridge Road, Stanmore (TQ 155928).
LB Harrow. 65ha.
Approach   Entrance from Old Lodge Way off Uxbridge Road.
Summary   An important grassland with open water and woodland to the E of Harrow Weald Common with, as the ground rises, magnificent views across the Thames Valley.
History   A 12C Augustinian Priory survived until the Reformation. The building was demolished in the 18C and the estate belonged to James Duberly and subsequently the Marquess of Abecorn. The estate declined in the 19C and was finally broken up in 1926. 40 acres went to the Air Ministry with the rest going to Middlesex county council. The open land was leased out and eventually in 1964 went to the borough council. The nine acre nature reserve around the artificial Summerhouse Lake was established in 1975.
Nature interest   An SSSI with habitats ranging from neutral grassland to various waterbodies and woodland which covers a Y-shaped area pointing to the Priory in the N and the Priory House in the E. Surrounding the fenced off lake, the woodland varies from an oak/hazel mix with alders in the wetter areas, to oak/hornbeam in the S. The wet flushes support wood bitter cress and remote sedge. The oldest single oak in Middlesex is found here, being dated at around 400 years old. As a pollard it could indicate the character of much of the area as pre-18C pasture. The open grassland in the N is unimproved.

The drier pastures contain common bent, red fescue and meadow foxtail. The devil's bit scabious, harebells and eyebright are among around 200 species of flowering plant.

The streams support brooklime, rushes and great hairy willowherb. Rarities such as water horsetail and marsh St John's wort have been found in these marshy areas while around the famously shaped Boot Pond in the S tip of the park, stands of burreed and reedmace are the main edging, with yellow flag iris, water plantain and celery leaved water crowfoot. Around the large Summerhouse Lake in the centre of the park grow reed sweet-grass and pendulous sedge. Across the open water are yellow and white water lilies. The lake attracts herons and kingfishers among over 95 species recorded in the park. Tawny owls and sparrowhawks visit with migrants such as ouzels, great grey shrike and pochard swelling their numbers.

Management   Managed by LB Harrow Parks Department, with the reserve being managed by HMWT. Rabbits and mowing maintain the sward rich.
Interpretation   HMWT.
Access   The park is open to the public but the reserve is only open to HMWT members.
Contact   LB Harrow and HMWT.

2   Harrow Weald Common and High Weald Wood

Oxhey Lane, Common Road (TQ 143298 and TQ 139122).
LB Harrow.
Approach   Footpaths from Old Redding, off Oxhey Lane.
History   The ancient Grim's Dyke and Old Redding alongside the common must have cut across an area of heath and woods bordering on Hertfordshire. Later, Bentley Priory, established in the 12C, probably acquired land from this extensive tract. Attempts to sell off the common in 1886 were prevented by public opposition which secured its protection under the 1889 Metropolitan Commons Act, a board of governors being set up to manage the common.
Summary   Lying on an E–W axis this area is adjoining open ground to the N much of it golf courses. There is a mix of heathland, wet flushes and woodland.
Nature interest   In an SSSI, the tussocks of purple moor grass (a rare plant for London) together with ling suggest the type of heath this was before birch began to colonise. By the Kestrel Grove offices in the N a few rare heath rush plants can be found. The S is occupied by oak and hazel dominated- wood with aspen, hornbeam and birch creating a good understorey. Many ancient woodland indicators can be found such as wood avens, wood sage, ferns and the rare wood horsetail. The flushes that occur on the NW border of the wood contain soft rush, the greater stitchwort, tufted hair grass and sphagnum moss. The High Weald Wood, S of Old Redding, is an ancient hornbeam coppice which, like the common, was formerly dug for gravel leaving waterlogged hollows supporting more wetland plants. The woodland close to open ground supports many birds from those that require the seclusion of tree cover like goldcrests and tits to the redpolls, bull finches and goldfinches that take advantage of the range of local habitat. In winter fieldfares and blackcaps can be seen. At least 18 butterfly species have also been recorded including brimstone, common blue and orange tip.
Management   Owned and managed by LB Harrow Parks Department.
Interpretation   The Harrow Natural History Society provide a nature trail leaflet.
Access   Open to the public.
Contact   Harrow NHS.

3   The Rattler

Vernon Drive, Belmont (TQ 166906).
LB Harrow. 2km.
Summary   A parkland walk mostly of shrubbery and herb-rich grassland.

History   This was once the Harrow–Stanmore Railway line which closed in 1964 only to be reopened 20 years later as a small reserve.

Nature interest   Sycamore, silver birch and hawthorn have colonised with open areas filled with grasses such as creeping bent, Timothy and red fescue. This sward is dotted with flowering plants such as ox-eye daisy, white and red clovers, doves-foot cranesbill and wild carrot which attract butterflies.

Management   The site is licensed and managed by LWT which aims to keep the range of habitat.

Interpretation   Nil on site.

Access   Open to the public.

Contact   LWT Regional Officer (01 747 3881).

4   Stanmore Common and Little Common

Warren Lane, Stanmore (TQ 156939).

LB Harrow. 52ha.

Approach   Off Dennis Lane, Wood Lane or Warren Lane.

Summary   A large area of woodland N of Bentley Priory with several ponds at its SE corner.

History   Once open heath the curious pillow mound may have been a warren to encourage rabbit breeding when rabbits were first introduced to Britain in the Middle Ages. The common is the remains of the commonland of Great Stanmore enclosed in 1813.

Nature interest   An SSSI, the common is interesting for its damp environment created by streams, contributing to its renowned numbers of fungi. The canopy of the woodland is oak and beech with birch, with an understorey of bramble and bracken.

Management   Owned and managed by LB Harrow Parks Department.

Interpretation   Nil on site.

Access   Open to the public.

Contact   LB Harrow.

5   Stanmore Country Park and Pear Wood

Dennis Lane, London Road, Stanmore (TQ 172933).

LB Harrow. 74ha.

Summary   An area of farmland adjacent to Watling Street with two areas of woodland, Pear Wood and Cloisters Wood. The area is part of an important belt of landscape from Harrow Weald Common northwards.

History   The country park was once part of the Warren House estate which passed to the GLC from Middlesex county council which had acquired it as part of its green belt policy. In 1976 the GLC designated the former farmland a country park, but little as yet seems to have been done to facilitate this.

Nature interest   The country park lies to the S of Pear Wood. Many features indicate its former use as pasture; anthills in the acid soil and various plant species such as heath bedstraw, sheep's sorrel and pepper saxifrage are associated with unimproved grasslands. Tussocks of tufted hair grass, with bugle and large bird's foot trefoil add to this character. However, there is a mix of habitat as a spring line emerges from the wood supporting sedges and rushes, while the woodland shows signs of its ancient origin and more recent usage. The canopy of beech with birch is dotted with planted Scots pine,

sweet chestnut and rhododendron. These plantings by the Duke of
Chandos in the 19C do not hide the ancient woodland of hornbeam,
ash and wild cherry with the ground flora of wood sorrel, dog's
mercury and various woodland grasses. Wildlife includes one of only
two colonies of wood ants in Hertfordshire and Middlesex, with small
mammals ranging from woodmice, weasels, to the larger foxes and
perhaps badgers. The wide range of birdlife includes, apart from
regular woodland occupants, cuckoos, woodcock, tawny owl and
sparrowhawk. A pond in the E of the park supports carp, tench, rudd
and perch which in turn attract herons and kingfishers.

Management   LB Harrow.

Interpretation   A marked nature trail runs through the park.

Access   Open to the public although visitors need a permit for Pear
Wood.

Contact   LB Harrow.

Further information

LB Harrow, Parks Department, Station Road, Harrow (01 863 1551).
Hertfordshire & Middlesex Wildlife Trust (see Barnet).
London Wildlife Trust (see Barking).

HAVERING

Over 300 ponds have been found in Havering, a borough whose valuable wildlife habitat focuses on small woodlands and wetlands. At the extreme E of Greater London, Havering has developed as a generally rather bleak suburb with fairly large tracts of farmland still keeping a foothold in the increasingly threatened low-lying Essex landscape. Many woods dot the higher N and E of the borough like Jermains Wood (TQ 571909) or the Osiers (TQ 554935), but most are inaccessible. Large parks like Dagnams or Havering country park (including a sliver of Hainault Forest) have natural history interest, but the S of Havering has nationally important river edge and estuarine sites such as the Ingrebourne Valley and the Rainham Marshes.

1 Cranham Marsh Reserve

Argyle Gardens (TQ 572855).
LB Havering. 13ha.
Approach   Footpaths from Argyle Gardens.
Summary   Three distinct sections make up this reserve dominated by wet woodland.
History   Pasture acquired by LB Havering in 1976.
Nature interest   The woodland is a mix of ancient and secondary with several springs contributing to areas of marsh. S of the woods is pasture often covered with surface water. Lack of grazing has allowed lesser pond sedge to dominate which discourages marsh marigold, fen and marsh bedstraw or sneezewort which also grow on the reserve. Middle Wood, the central area of the reserve is ancient woodland surrounding and protecting Eastern Marsh which supports meadowsweet and marsh horsetail. Bonus Wood is, as it sounds, an extension to the reserve but separated by a sliver of farmland and not open to the public.
Management   The site is managed by the Essex Naturalists' Trust which intends to reintroduce grazing in autumn and early spring to prevent natural succession drying the marsh out. It hopes to resume coppicing and to redig some drainage ditches to recover the rare meadow rue whose seeds may still be viable but covered in peat.
Interpretation   Nil on site.
Access   Main area is open to the public.
Contact   Essex Naturalists' Trust warden (0462 23384).

2 Duck Wood

Sheffield Drive, Harold Hill (TQ 555923).
LB Havering. 9.5ha.
Approach   Through gate off Sheffield Drive.
Summary   A reserve of former hornbeam coppice surrounded by housing and edged by a bank and ditch in the N and E. A cluster of 10 ponds occur in the centre of the wood.
History   This was a coppice belonging to the Dagnam Estate which was broken up and divided into a golf course and Dagnam Park. In 1985 negotiations began which led to the wood becoming an LWT reserve.
Nature interest   The now large hornbeams which were once coppiced have shaded areas of woodland and prevented a good

understorey from growing in some areas. However, hazel, crab apple, blackthorn and hawthorn are all present so that where the 1987 storm felled mature trees young growth is bound to be encouraged. Bluebells and wood anemones occur in spring, which, with lesser celandine, bugle and lords and ladies, indicate ancient woodland. The ponds are in various stages of succession and attract frogs and toads. They support many wetland plants such as water starwort, celery-leaved buttercup and pendulous sedge.

Management   Leased to LWT which plans to re-instate coppicing. The ponds have been restored but with the intention of keeping them at different successional stages for habitat variation.

Interpretation   Leaflet from LWT.

Access   Open to the public.

Contact   LWT (01 593 8096).

3   Rainham Marshes

Ferry Lane, Rainham (TQ 5280).

LB Havering; MoD. 400ha.

Approach   Ferry Lane edges Rainham Marshes, with access on W edge.

Summary   A wedge of marshland of international importance to birdlife because of its size, position and mosaic of wetland habitat.

History   Sea walls were unreliable until the late 17C when the various lords of the manors of this area combined to build a more effective barrier across the Wennington Creek, the Achilles heel for previous attempts. However, some 300 years later, in 1953, this was breached again with major flooding affecting the land which had become cattle pasture. This had ben maintained along traditional lines until 1906 when the War Office bought 400 acres for rifle ranges. The Danger Zone still covers these at Purfleet in the E but during the 1960s the PLA constructed silt lagoons in which to dump dredgings from the Thames. By 1977 the use of the ranges of the W were recognised as of little value to the MoD and reports began circulating about the release of excess land. The MoD sold the W end to the local authority for commercial development. They proposed various schemes such as steel stockholding yards or industrial development regardless of the area's SSSI designation. The unsympathetic attitude of both the MoD, which may now sell the rest of the marshes, and the local authority means that schemes for development, such as hotels, a massive theme park and housing are currently under consideration. In 1986 the DoT added their plans to the cocktail of threats. The re-routing of the A13 straight across the marshes together with these other schemes have focussed opposition, lead by LWT and the Essex Naturalists' Trust.

Although an obvious candidate for an international nature reserve, the marshes are not even protected by Green Belt legislation due to ownership.

Nature interest   170 species of birds have been recorded including varieties like the hen harrier and sandpipers. Three areas make up the Marshes—the Rainham Marshes, the central Wennington Marshes (silt lagoons) and the Purfleet Marshes (rifle ranges). Criss-crossed by dykes and ditches as far as the lagoons, the character of these ancient grazing marshes is gradually changing. However, the tussocky appearance in the W is due to the consistent pattern of cattle use whose trampling and eating down the decades has unwittingly added to the complex habitat which has attracted thousands of birds. Some require the marshes for breeding, others for food—especially true of the treacherous silt lagoons on which waders, but not human visitors, can wander. Flocks as large as 4,000 teal have been recorded, but many other species also accumulate in great numbers, sometimes on migration and sometimes for over wintering. Pintails, gadwalls, shovelers, lapwings, redshanks, stonechats, winchats and yellow hammers are just a few of the species that can be seen.

Shelduck, little ringed plover and skylark shelter in the grasslands, while reedwarblers and red bunting hide in the taller vegetation. But the marshes are not only important for birds. Insects such as the scarce emerald damselfly and ruddy darter, amphibians and reptiles also benefit from the range of wetland habitat. Plant species range from salt marsh to rough grassland. False oat, cocksfoot and meadow grass give way to marsh foxtail, sea club-rush and hard rush in the wetter areas. In water-filled hollows and dykes greater pondsedge or sweet reed grass grow with marginal vegetation made up of rushes, fool's watercress, comfrey and the stiff saltmarsh grass. The grassland habitat is subtle and delicate. The wide open quality of this landscape where the view, unlike at Crayford with its rising hillsides nearby, seems uncluttered by buildings. This is a rare habitat and provides an unrivalled opportunity for birdspotting only possible on marshes where these species can gather in great numbers.

Management   Nil for conservation.
Interpretation   Nil on site.
Access   Only de facto from Ferry Lane. No access to the silt lagoons which have their own dangers, as do the Purfleet rifle ranges which are also restricted.
Contact   London Wildlife Trust.

Further information

LB Havering, Recreation and Amenities, Mercury House, Mercury Gardens, Romford (70 66999).
Essex Naturalists' Trust, Fingringhoe Wick Nature Reserve, South Green Road, Fingringhoe, Colchester, Essex CO5 7DN (0206 28678).
London Wildlife Trust (see Barking).

HILLINGDON

Bounded by the River Colne in the W and the River Crane in the E, Hillingdon is criss-crossed by streams, brooks and rivers arising from the Chilterns. This is the third largest London borough with its built-up zone mainly in the S and E while the NW remains rich in valuable wildlife habitat. Much is retained through sympathetic agriculture and the maintenance of wetland, 20% of the entire capital's standing water being found in Hillingdon. As many of the sites are privately owned they are not accessible, though some may be viewed from footpaths.

1   Fray's Farm Meadows and Fray's Island

Western Avenue and Money Lane, Denham (TQ 055973, 057859). LB Hillingdon; private. 46ha.
Approach   To the island from Money Lane, while the meadows can be viewed from a track below the Shire Ditch.
Summary   The island is a thin strip of wooded land along the River Colne. The meadows lie between the River Colne and Fray's River to the E of Denham Lock.
History   Currently threatened by yet more gravel extraction with the idea of opening another lake after the operation finishes. Opposition has been consistent but may be undermined by plans to remove gravel from the railway track which will affect the hydrology.
Nature interest   The enclosed and sheltered aspect of this pastoral landscape is due to the mix of low-lying damp grasslands and flowing water. This SSSI has plant communities which have existed for centuries on these ancient wetlands, such as colourful purple loosestrife, ragged robin and meadowsweet with a background of sedges. The grasslands are rich in flowers as is the railway cutting which retains characteristics of its meadow past. The uncommon marsh marigold and the, only in name, common skullcap can be found attracting a wide variety of dragonflies and butterflies. The ditches attract amphibians and the extensive habitat supports wildfowl and waders like snipe, jack snipe, lapwing, teal and shoveler. Wet alluvial grassland is rare and threatened in the London region so making Fray's Farm especially important.
Management   The meadows are still grazed and cut.
Interpretation   Hillingdon Natural History Society(HNHS); LWT.
Access   No public access, but views from the towpath along the Grand Union Canal.
Contact   HNHS; LWT.

2   The Grove

Royal Lane, West Drayton (TQ 068824).
LB Hillingdon. 2ha.
Approach   End of drive at Royal Lane.
Summary   A triangular-shaped reserve with a collection of ponds and mixed woodland.
History   Formerly part of the grounds of a large house at the edge of Hillingdon Village which was demolished in the 1970s.
Nature interest   A mix of native and exotic tree species make up the scrub and woodland of this small reserve. Sycamore, false acacia and

horse chestnut occur alongside oaks, ash and silver birch. Reminders of the old grounds include the remnants of yew and holly hedges with rhododendron and cherry laurel as not entirely welcome additions to the understorey. Brambles and ivy attract insects and birds with foxgloves and bluebells appearing in spring. In the W and central area the grasses include meadow foxtail and false oat together with flowers like lady's bedstraw, St John's wort and taller species such as meadowsweet. The ponds are surrounded by yellow flag irises, rushes and sedges. The N marsh area has reed sweetgrass and hairy willowherb.

Management   LWT reserve where management includes preventing scrub encroachment and restoration of the ponds.
Interpretation   Nature trail leaflet available from LWT.
Access   Open to the public.
Contact   LWT Regional Officer (01 747 3881).

3   Harefield Place Nature Reserve

Harvill Road, Harefield. (TQ 058867).
LB Hillingdon. 30ha.
Approach   Through Uxbridge Golf course.
Summary   Broadleaved woodland with pond and grasslands.
History   Once part of the Harefield Estate.
Nature interest   The woodland of oak, hornbeam, beech and lime was once dominated by wych elm and English elm destroyed through Dutch elm disease. The ground flora includes bluebells, wood avens, remote sedge and dog's mercury. Alder grows near the pond which is edged with reeds and meadowsweet. Nightingales occupy the wood and the uncommon Leisler's bat has also been seen.
Management   Managed by HNHS for the last 25 years.
Interpretation   HNHS.
Access   Permit from HNHS.
Contact   HNHS.

4   The Mid-Colne Valley

Ickenham and Harefield.
LB Hillingdon, private.
Approach   As this is an area rather than one individual site, the towpath along the Grand Union Canal is one way to see some of the habitats mentioned.
Summary   This river valley contains not only the River Colne but Fray's River and the Grand Union Canal. The valley covers a range of habitats from lakes and adjoining grasslands to flowing water and woodlands.
History   Most of the standing water is the result of extensive gravel digging in the area during the 19C.
Nature interest   The former gravel pits attract large numbers of birds. Over 70 species have been recorded. The winter wildfowl includes pochards, shovelers and the great crested grebe. The largest pit, known locally as Broadwater, together with Tile House South and Moorhall are attractive to Canada geese, little ringed plover and cormorant. The whole area from Denham Green to South Harefield Road is an SSSI. The canal passes alongside the Colne to Uxbridge and close beside the Fray until turning E at Yiewsley. In the N

Alderglade (S of Western Road) is a small nature reserve along a disused railway line which includes alder and willow woodland emphasising the link with the river. The renowned and private Fray's Farm lies further S which is separated from the wet Denham Lock Wood which varies from alder and crack willow to marshy areas of reed with meadowsweet and sedges lining the dykes. It is a mark of the area's importance that nightingales still can be heard in St John's Covert which lies close to Denham Lock Wood.

Management   Denham Lock Wood SSSI is managed jointly by LWT and Hillingdon Natural History Society; HMWT manages Alderglade.

Interpretation   Nil on site.

Access   Restricted.

Contact   LWT, HNHS, HMWT, Colne Valley Park Volunteers.

5   Old Park Wood

Hill End Road, Harefield (TQ 045913).
LB Hillingdon. 24ha.

Approach   A public footpath runs through the wood from Summerhouse Lane to Hill End Road.

Summary   A large proportion of this wood is considered to be ancient woodland covering a varying geology of chalk or sand and gravel.

History   Formerly belonging to the estates of Harefield Park.

Nature interest   On the ridge, oak and birch woodland dominates with a bracken field layer. Oak and ash occupy the lower slopes, shading into alder woodland along the springline valleys. Rare plants such as opposite-leaved golden saxifrage are still found here, although herb Paris—once plentiful in the wood—seems to have disappeared. Early purple orchid and coral root are just a couple of species that contribute to the unusual environment.

Management   Owned and managed by LB Hillingdon with a reserve (7ha) managed by HMWT.

Interpretation   Nil on site.

Access   Mostly open access.

Contact   LB Hillingdon, HMWT.

6   Ruislip Woods, Poor's Fields, Tarleton's Lake Nature Reserve

Ducks Hill Road, Ruislip (TQ 077895).
LB Hillingdon. 331ha.

Approach   Numerous footpaths from the main road enter Mad Bess and Copse Woods. Park Woods can be entered from Ruislip Common. Bayhurst Wood Country Park can be entered along footpaths from near Breakspear House. The country park has a car park.

Summary   One of London's finest clusters of ancient woodland is crossed by several tributaries of the River Pinn. Copse Wood and Mad Bess Wood are divided by a main road, with Park Wood separated from them by Ruislip Common and Bayhurst Wood Country Park by a thin belt of farmland. Tarleton's Lake lies immediately adjacent to the park while a nature reserve adjoins Poor's Fields.

History   The woods were managed as hornbeam/oak coppice with Park Wood perhaps enclosed for game as the name suggests. The name Mad Bess is 18C but no one is sure why. Poor's Fields refer to what was common grazing land. Threatened by building development at the beginning of this century, plans foundered during the First World War so that with consistent local residents' pressure the woods were saved and opened to the public in the 1930s.

Nature interest   An SSSI, these woods are predominantly hornbeam and oak, both sessile and pedunculate, mostly of ancient origin but with areas of secondary woodland as in Copse Wood and around Tarleton's Lake. The largest area of woodland is Park Wood which has the added attraction of an earthwork emerging from the SW corner. The habitat varies from former hornbeam coppice to young woodland in a strip where former pylons once stood. The S section has a notable stand of aspen and wild cherries seem numerous. The ground flora is typical of hornbeam woods with wood melick, Forster's wood rush and wood poa being amongst the species that cope with the environment. Hazel contributes to the shrub layer near the stream that flows through the wood. Sedges, ragged robin and other waterside plants benefit from the opening of the canopy along its length.

Lying to the N of Park Wood is Poor's Fields which varies from neutral grassland in the S to grassy heath in the N. Plants such as heather, heath bedstraw and sheep's sorrel are typical of more acidic conditions. The open environment is interrupted by a sprinkling of birch which may well threaten the grassland. Reptiles such as grass snakes, slow worms and adders favour this vicinity. Adjoining the field is the nature reserve managed by the Ruislip and District NHS, consisting mainly of marsh with a number of reedfringed ponds. Abutting this open habitat is Copse Wood where the number of species and structure has been considerably altered since it was managed as pure coppice. In the SE 19C clearance has led to the establishing of younger woodland. The rides and young woodland allow light to penetrate, helping the growth of woodland plants such as woodsage, or soft rush and remote sedge that enjoy the damp. The stream which enters the wood in the N supports pendulous sedge.

Across the road in Mad Bess Wood, in the W, two more streams support similar plants, and the woodland is benefitting from the reinstatement of coppicing. Bayhurst Wood is noted for its unusual mix of mature hornbeam and beech standards. There are many breaks in the canopy where scrub grows, or bramble and bracken. Among this field layer can be found woodland grasses, wood rush and tufted hairgrass. On the NW edge is Tarleton's Lake Nature Reserve which, being dominated by a lake and marsh, supports wetland species from reedmace to the delicate water forget-me-not.

Management   The woods are owned and managed by LB Hillingdon which has long-term management plans for Mad Bess, Copse and Park Woods, with a separate plan for Bayhurst Wood country park. The reserves are managed by HMWT.

Interpretation   Records are held by the local societies and LWT. A nature trail and information on Bayhurst Wood can be obtained from the centre at the country park.

Access   Open to the public.

Contact   LB Hillingdon Leisure Services, LWT, HMWT, Ruislip and District NHS.

7   Uxbridge Moor

St John's Road, Uxbridge (TQ 047838).
LB Hillingdon. 5ha.
Approach   De facto access through the industrial estate, or along towpath.
Summary   Part of a chain of habitats along the River Colne close to urban Uxbridge. The river is clean at this point and, where the banks have not been trampled, aquatic plants grow on the island where the Colne divides.
Nature interest   The S of the island is mostly unmanaged willow wood with an understorey of elder and hawthorn, while scrub occupies the W part of the island. Impenetrable brambles provide cover for birds while the N of the island is open grazed fields with typical wetland pasture species such as ragged robin and tufted hair grass. Unusually for a London river, the Colne here supports a good range of aquatic vegetation with the banks covered by hairy willow-herb, sedges and rushes. Typical river birds are supplemented by kingfishers and herons.
Management   LWT manages the woodland, thinning some of the dense willow to encourage wetland species to grow.
Interpretation   LWT.
Access   Open through footpaths.
Contact   LWT Regional Officer (01 747 3881).

8   Yeading Brook Fields, Hare's Hollows, Gutteridge Wood and Ten Acre Wood

Charleville Lane, Hayes (TQ 098834).
LB Hillingdon, LB Ealing, private. 160ha.
Approach   Footpaths and bridleways cross the area. LB Hillingdon is proposing a trail to connect the woods with the Yeading Valley.
Summary   The Yeading Valley contains valuable wetlands and woods bordered by recreational grounds on the E and W, and S of Northolt aerodrome.
Nature interest   Gutteridge Wood and Ten Acre Wood are in the N of this area surrounded by pasture and hedgerows. Gutteridge Wood is ancient with oak and hazel coppice, and ground flora such as wood poa and broad helleborine will benefit from the reinstatement of this woodland system. The nearby unimproved pastures and meadows contain meadow vetchling, lady's bedstraw, marsh thistle and the now not so common skullcap. Nearby is the small Cutthroat Wood with the adjacent Ten Acre Wood.

Triangular in shape and bordered by the Yeading Brook, this oak plantation has a meadow in the NW attracting butterflies which benefit from the continued grazing of horses and cattle. Brimstones, meadow browns, clouded yellows (recorded in great numbers in 1983) and speckled wood occur as do dragonflies and the rare Rossel's cricket. This serves an introduction to the Yeading Brook Fields (or Meadows) which lie to the S below Covert Wood. The grasslands, especially of the S tip, contain a concentration of plants associated with fen-like conditions making this area exceptionally interesting to botanists. Hare's Hollows in the S, together with the hay meadow on the W edge of the brook, are rich in notable flower species such as orchids, grass vetchling and the nationally rare narrow-leaved water dropwort. The hollows have retained these species associated with undisturbed grassland mainly because plans for digging a couple of lakes during the 1950s were abandoned. N of Kingsmill Avenue the fields are dominated by tufted hair-grass, bent grass and Timothy grass. Great burnet, sneezewort, ragged robin and the rare red bartsia all reflect the underlying damp environment. Willows and hawthorn are dotted through the area. These species are not restricted to the valley but can be found in the outlying recreational fields. Sparrow-hawks, kestrels and house martins are among the birds and mammals attracted to this contiguous area of habitat.

Management   The fields are managed by grazing and hay cutting.
Interpretation   LWT leaflets and LB Hillingdon.
Access   The trail runs through Cutthroat Wood, S of Gutteridge Wood, SE to Kingshill Avenue to the Yeading Valley Open Space.
Contact   LB Hillingdon; LWT.

Further information

LB Hillingdon, Leisure Services, Civic Centre, Uxbridge, Middlesex (0895 50111).
Colne Valley Park Volunteers', c/o Denham Court Mansion, Village Road, Denham, Bucks.
HMWT (see Barnet).
Hillingdon NHS, c/o 42 Middleton Drive, Pinner, Middlesex HA5 2PG (01 868 0207).
London Wildlife Trust (see Barking).
Ruislip & District NHS, 18 Rynchester Close, Ickenham, Middlesex.

HOUNSLOW

During the last 100 years the borough of Hounslow has changed from an area dominated by its river-based life to one of many of London's residential and industrial suburbs. Hounslow covers a terrace of the Thames, along which a chain of man-made islands or 'aits' were built to support the transport of goods to and from the capital. Most of the boat repair yards have gone but the aits now act as refuges for birds, especially waterfowl. These and the Duke of Northumberland's River, a cut joining the River Colne to Crane, are a reminder that massive altering of the landscape is not just a feature of this century. Wildlife habitat is confined in this borough to water features and railway embankments, most famously at the Gunnersbury Triangle and at the disused Feltham Marshalling Yards beside the River Crane. The ancient Hounslow Heath that so disturbed William Cobbett's peace of mind as he began his rural rides, has shrunk and lost much of its character. But here, as at Syon Park, attempts are being made to save and encourage what is left.

1   Gunnersbury Triangle Local Nature Reserve

Bollo Lane, Chiswick (TQ 201787).
LB Hounslow. 2.5ha.
Approach   Entrance opposite Chiswick Park underground station.
Summary   An area of damp secondary woodland surrounded on all sides by railway lines.
History   During the 19C this land seems to have in part been used as an orchard, although in places gravel or sand was excavated. In 1869 the railways arrived and effectively isolated this triangle. Since the 1940s the area was undisturbed and woodland began to colonise. Development proposals emerged in 1982 which included warehouse and factory units on what had become a quietly popular site. A vigorous campaign was mounted by the Chiswick Wildlife Group which eventually succeeded in defeating BR's plans at a public inquiry. The borough bought the land with GLC assistance and since 1984 it has been an LWT reserve.
Nature interest   The woodland is mainly birch with a central, wetter area supporting mostly willow. A new pond with a number of seasonal ponds attract a good range of birds, such as redpoll, tawny owl and the sedge warbler. Where a test boring was dug by BR in 1982 a wet ride has developed with aquatic vegetation including bulrush, water plantain, rushes and celery-leaved buttercup. The reserve supports small mammals and a family of foxes in an area dominated by housing and major roads.
Management   LWT management includes maintaining the grass sward and woodland structure.
Interpretation   There is a small on-site field study centre, nature trail and leaflet.
Access   Open six days a week. There is access for the disabled.
Contact   LWT Warden (01 747 3881).

2   Hounslow Heath

Staines Road, Feltham (TQ 123743).
LB Hounslow. 80ha.
Approach   Paths from Frampton Road off Staines Road.
Summary   An area of flattish grassland with scrub and a number of
ponds beside a recently landscaped golf course.
History   Across what was once over 4,000 acres of heath, the
Romans constructed a road to Silchester in the W known as Stane
Street (now the A30). Later the heath became part of the Forest of
Staines and so it remained until attempts to enclose it began in 1495.
In the 16C the Duke of Northumberland constructed his river across
the heath but it was the army that gradually fragmented the heath
from the 17C. The 19C saw the heath divided by enclosure which
resulted in the War Office gaining 300 acres. More land went to an
airstrip in 1919, this time for civil use. Followingthe Second World
War, Heathrow Airport prevented the heath frombecoming housing
because of the unacceptable noise of overhead planes. In 1977 the
borough council laid out a rather uninspiring golf course, with the
GLC buying the rest of the heath for a park.
Nature interest   In the E gravel pits are now ponds attracting
amphibians but most of the site is grassland dominated by cock's foot
and Yorkshire fog. Towards the SE is an area of young woodland.
Scrub dots the grasslands, hinting at former times as it includes
gorse and broom often found on heaths. Grassy heathland can still
be found in the E and beside the River Crane. Dwarf gorse, heather
and petty whin near the railway line are all that is left of the once
common species, but there is enough habitat to attract over 70
species of bird including partridge, dunnock, reed bunting and
goldcrests. The short-eared owl, stonechat and white-throat are
unusual for London and, like the skylark, are attracted to the heath
by the coarse grassland. This also supports butterflies, and small
mammals such as watervoles benefit from the rare, for London,
stretch of natural riverbank along the Crane. Weasels, three families
of foxes, grey squirrels and rabbits are also found, helping to earn
Hounslow Heath its designation as an SSSI.
Management   Increasingly managed with nature conservation in
mind by the borough parks department.
Interpretation   A nature trail with 13 stops has been laid out
around the heath with an accompanying leaflet.
Access   Open to the public.
Contact   LB Hounslow Parks Department.

3   Kempton Park Wood and Reservoirs

Sunbury Way, Hanworth (TQ 113705).
TWA. 38ha.
Approach   From E end of site.
Summary   A mixed deciduous woodland surrounds old waterworks
N of the Kempton Park Race Course.
History   A consortium called Themeworld proposed to build a
leisure complex across this site hoping that the retaining or creation of
new lake would defeat local opposition. In 1987 a public inquiry was
held and the land was later designated as Green Belt.
Nature interest   Close to the largest heronry in Surrey, these
partially drained reservoirs and woodlands attract waterfowl which

need the mud and reedbeds. Around 60 species of bird visit the site including winter migrants and rarities like the little ringed plover. The flocks of gadwall and shovelers enjoy the relatively undisturbed habitat as do tufted duck and pochard.

Management   Nil for conservation.
Interpretation   Nil on site.
Access   By permit only.
Contact   TWA, New River Head, Roseberry Avenue, EC1R 4TP.

Further information

LB Hounslow, Parks Department, Civic Centre, Lampton Avenue, Twickenham YW3 4DN (01 570 7728).
London Wildlife Trust (see Barking).

ISLINGTON

This inner London borough was once famous for its clear wells and streams like those at Sadlers Wells and the Fleet River descending from the Hampstead hills. The filthy Fleet was arched over in the 18C and is now a sewer pipe reaching the Thames through a hole in the embankment. The pastures have long gone, rampant speculative building having covered the borough in the 19C, so that Islington now has very few public open spaces. Various small greens, Highbury Fields and Caledonian Park are all that is left, with wildlife habitat restricted to railway cuttings and small community projects such as the Gillespie Park nature area, Culpepper Community Garden or a small reserve off St Paul's Road along the New River Walk (see Hackney).

Gillespie Park

Gillespie Road, Highbury, N5 (TQ 313862).
BR; LB Islington. 1ha.
Approach   The nature garden adjoins the park.
Summary   A habitat creation scheme on railway sidings.
History   A project on sidings which were once used for coal, it is only a few years old but is currently under a closure threat, although the council would like it to be added to the park.
Nature interest   A small site offers a mix of culinary herbs, grassland and a pond, the site attracting birds and insects. A hybrid grass was discovered recently which may well only exist on this site.
Interpretation   A leaflet is available.
Management   The site is managed by an LB Islington warden.
Access   Open to the public.
Contact   The warden (01 266 6393).

Further information

LB Islington, Parks and Reccreation Department, 345 Holloway Road, N7 (01 607 7331).
London Wildlife Trust (see Barking).

KENSINGTON AND CHELSEA

This long, thin royal borough has the least open space in London. The area was popular in the late 17C and 18C for the acquiring of landed estates by those wealthy enough to escape the overcrowded City and the results of the Great Fire of 1666. Residents now look to Westminster for Hyde Park and Kensington Gardens, or to Ealing and Wormwood Scrubs. The latter is close to Kensal Green Cemetery, which with the more damaged Brompton Cemetery attracts some wildlife. The remnant of one of the 18C estates, Holland Park, provides the most accessible habitat, although this needs some enhancing as does the canal which runs through the borough.

1   Holland Park

Kensington High Street, SW8 (TQ 248798).
Royal B of Kensington and Chelsea. 20ha.
Approach   Either through the formal gates fronting the High Street or through Abbotsbury Road in the W.
Summary   A popular recreation ground with many formal elements, the park occupies the S slope of Campden Hill.
History   A series of open pastures belonging to a Jacobean mansion, this area was not far from the old Uxbridge Road. The first Lord Holland (Henry Fox) bought beeches from Goodwood in 1749 to decorate his new style park. This ornamental planting continued throughout the 19C but much of the structure of the schemes were damaged during Second World War bomb raids. Over 2,000 elms and sycamores were lost to disease after the war so that there has been an extensive replanting programme.
Nature interest   This centres on the secondary woodland and scrub which provides shelter for a wide range of birds. The native trees like oak and ash are supplemented by many exotics such as Turkey oak and horse chestnut. The understorey is mainly of holly underneath the beech but elsewhere it is mainly bramble, and ivy with cow parsley. The pond in the S is a potentially valuable addition although it will need to be restored.
Management   A plan prepared by LWT in 1986 suggests a woodland management regime and restoration of the pond, as well as a sympathetic mowing regime.
Interpretation   LWT report.
Access   Open to the public.
Contact   RB of Kensington and Chelsea.

2   Kensal Green Cemetery

Harrow Road, W10 (TQ 230825).
General Cemetery Company. 22ha.
Approach   Alma Place entrance.
Summary   Part of a complex of habitat which, together with the Grand Union Canal which forms the S boundary and Wormwood Scrubs, provides a belt of wild space in a built-up area.
History   Opened in 1832 to provide space for the ever-expanding metropolis, the cemetery is still run privately for burials and cremations.
Nature interest   Woodland fringes the N and S and fills a central

circle of this landscaped cemetery. Wood anemone and bluebells may suggest that at an earlier period there were hedges around damp meadow. The open areas are mainly neutral grassland with herbs like great burnet, sneezewort, yellow bedstraw and field woodrush. Orange tip, green-veined white and peacock are a few of the butterflies recorded as using the cemetery, as do 85 bird species, foxes, weasels and bats.

Management   Some management for conservation by volunteers balanced with visitors' needs.

Interpretation   Nil on site.

Access   Daily.

Contact   LWT.

Further information

RB Kensington and Chelsea, Parks and Open Spaces Department, Town Hall, Hornton Street, W8 7NY (01 937 5464).
London Wildlife Trust (see Barking).

KINGSTON UPON THAMES

Another royal borough with little public open space, surburban Kingston benefits from the Surrey countryside across the border in the S, Wimbledon Common in next door Merton and Richmond Park to the N. Much open space is inaccessible to the public, such as the large Coombe Hill Golf Course in the N, or the interesting habitat at Seething Wells and Bonesgate Pastures. Initiatives such as the Hogsmill River and Tributaries Open Space have not yet safeguarded the rivers from abuse. The Hogsmill, running through the centre of Kingston, and Beverley Brook, which forms its E boundary, are badly polluted from sewage treatment works. A policy of pocket handkerchief sites scattered across the borough may well encourage management regimes sympathetic to wildlife.

1   Coombe Wood

Henley Drive, Malden (TQ 217753).
RB Kingston Upon Thames. 2.4ha.
Approach   From Henley Drive.
Summary   In an area dominated by the golf course, the reserve lies along the edge of the Kingston By-Pass.
Nature interest   Former hazel coppice with oak standards, the woodland's ground flora includes lords and ladies. The two clearings are dominated by bracken or ruderal plants, but near the two ponds at either end of the wood there is soft rush and great willowherb.
Management   LWT.
Interpretation   Nil on site.
Access   Restricted.
Contact   LWT.

2   Hogsmill Wood Nature Reserve

Kingston By-Pass, New Malden (TQ 205670).
RB Kingston Upon Thames; LWT. 0.69ha.   '
Approach   Beside sports grounds off Windsor Avenue.
Summary   This small woodland beside the Hogsmill Open Space provides a sliver of habitat bordered by extensive sports grounds.
Nature interest   On the whole this is oak/sycamore secondary woodland with regenerating elm suckers. The ground flora is not yet interesting but there is still enough to attract watervole, fox and squirrels. Near the river in the W, crack willow grows and both kingfishers and heron have been recorded.
Management   LWT intends to improve the woodland structure.
Interpretation   Nil on site.
Access   Restricted.
Contact   LWT.

3   Richard Jefferies Bird Sanctuary

Oak Hill Grove, Surbiton (TQ 182672).
LB Kingston. 0.5ha.
Approach   Part of the park called The Wood.
Summary   A woodland reserve at the E of the park.

History   This long-established bird sanctuary was licenced to LWT in 1987.

Nature interest   Noted for covering a steep escarpment, the wood is dominated by oak with an understorey of holly. A seasonally wet area adds to the variety of habitat.

Management   LWT manages the site and will increase sensitive use by the public.

Interpretation   Nil on site.

Contact   LWT.

Further information

RB Kingston Upon Thames Directorate of Education and Recreation, Guildhall, Kingston Upon Thames, Surrey (01 546 2121).

London Wildlife Trust (see Barking).

LAMBETH

A 1982 ecological survey of this inner London borough identified two important wildlife sites—Eardley Road Sidings and Shakespeare Road Sidings. Both are now to be lost to development. Although both Brockwell Park and Ruskin Park, named after John Ruskin who lived in nearby Denmark Hill, have nature trails, management has not been altered to promote interesting habitats. The large gang-mowed Clapham Common and Streatham Common, once rough grassland, have become flat green deserts within this century. Small community initiatives include the Tulse Hill Nature Garden and Knights Hill Wood, but residents must look to Sydenham Hill in Southwark for the nearest substantial area of wildlife habitat.

Further information

LB Lambeth, Amenity Services, Park Division, 164 Clapham Park Road, SW4 7DQ (01 622 6655).
London Wildlife Trust (see Barking).

LEWISHAM

Lying in the Ravensbourne Valley, Lewisham during its history has been dominated by this river and its tributaries the Quaggy and Pool. Floods were common—with its tidal mills and meadows, at least, benefiting from the varying water levels. Now canalised and deepened, the Ravensbourne retains very little water edge habitat although the River Pool has a natural appearance at Bell Green. The borough was farmed well into the 19C and its largely rural atmosphere was only finally lost this century. Its land rises to the Sydenham Hill ridge in the W where a number of public parks huddle along its length. Several sites of interest for wildlife are located on railway lines.

1 Beckenham Place Park

Beckenham Hill Road, SE6 (TQ 383707).
LB Lewisham; LB Bromley. 96ha.
Approach Entrances from either Beckenham Hill Road in the E, or Beckenham Place Park in the S.
Summary A recreational park with formal decorative plantings and a large golf course, with wildlife benefiting from a central block of ancient woodland.
History Formerly the grounds of Beckenham Place, built by the timber merchant John Cator who became lord of the manor in 1773, the park belonged to his descendents throughout the 19C. It was opened to the public two years after the LCC acquired it from the family in 1927.
Nature interest An 18-hole golf course includes acid grassland and one of the park's two ponds. Elsewhere, the grounds are dominated by recreational grasses like rye but the presence of bent grass and sheep sorrel help to indicate underlying acid conditions. The pond is securely fenced off but this has more to do with the treacherous mud than for protecting the habitat. Around the edges hawthorn and willow grow, while to the W, scrub of various species has developed. The main block of woodland is to the N of the pavillion and S of the Ash Plantation. The oak-dominated ancient woodland has been modified by some planting of exotics such as sweet chestnut and cherry laurel. Hornbeam and ash add to the canopy and the understorey consists of natives like wild service, blackthorn, hazel, holly and hawthorn. The ground flora includes bluebells and dog's mercury. Towards the E alder can be found which, with remote sedge, show a damp environment. The development of this habitat is not continuous as the park slopes towards the Ravensbourne in the E. The river has been canalised to prevent flooding but in some places looks natural where the bank is covered with water edge plants like reed-canary grass or bistort. Such a range of habitats attracts many birds. Some 45 species have been recorded although this marks a decline on numbers taken 25 years ago when 65 species were noted.
Management Lewisham Parks Department.
Interpretation A nature centre has been housed in the former mansion but was closed at the time of writing. Nature trails leaflets are available.
Access Open to the public.
Contact Nature Conservation Officer (01 695 6000 ext 5058).

2 Devonshire Road Nature Reserve

Devonshire Road, Forest Hill, SE23 (TQ 361744).
BR; LB Lewisham. 2.8ha.
Approach   Entrance opposite Tyson Road.
Summary   One of a chain of reserves following the railway line to
London Bridge.
History   The site was saved following a campaign led by the Forest
Hill Forum which opposed the cutting down of vegetation by British
Rail which began in 1979. A licence was granted to the borough
council which promotes the site as primarily an educational reserve
with considerable community involvement in its management.
Nature interest   The mix of wood, grassland and scrub attracts a
good range of birds and butterflies. The secondary woodland is
mainly oak and birch with blackthorn, hawthorn and ash. There is
some invading Japanese knotweed and giant hogweed, and the
grassland contains opportunists like ragwort and golden rod. Yarrow
and yellow toadflax are only two of the species attracting moths and
butterflies.
Management   LB Lewisham, with regular work undertaken by
volunteers such as the LWT Lewisham Conservers.
Interpretation   Nature trail with accompanying leaflet.
Access   Restricted to educational use, but open to the public
2pm–4pm on Saturdays.
Contact   Nature Conservation Officer (see Beckenham Place Park).

3 Downham Fields

Side Road, Downham (TQ 396715).
LB Lewisham. 10ha.
Approach   Downham Way entrance.
Summary   A public open space on a gentle hill slope to the S of the
Downham Estate.
History   The nearby Downham Estate was built on open land
belonging to the old Shroffold's Farm whose name derives from an
ancient manor in the area.
Nature interest   Habitat of interest focuses on the relatively herb-
rich grassland which is dominated by species such as common bent,
Yorkshire fog and red fescue.
Management   The grassland is regularly mown by LB Lewisham
throughout spring and summer.
Interpretation   Nil on site, but the estate is mentioned in Green
Chain leaflets available from the parks department.
Access   Open to the public.
Contact   Lewisham Parks Department.

4 Hither Green Nature Reserve and Hither
   Green Cemetery

Baring Road, SE12 (TQ 396736, 397728).
LB Lewisham. 2.4ha; 14ha.
Approach   From public footpath off Baring Road to the reserve,
while the entrance to the cemetery is from Verdant Lane.

Summary   To the W of the railway line lies the cemetery which together with the reserve, at the S tip of the railway sidings on the E, forms a block of open grassy habitat.

History   Following a public inquiry in 1987, a covenant has allowed the retention of this small area which had been recognised locally as being important for wildlife for some years.

Nature interest   Best known for its lizards and slow worms, the nature reserve is sloping and mainly well drained although there are some damp areas which attract amphibians which will benefit from the new pond. Where the grass cover is broken, lichens and mosses grow. The mix of the scrub and grassland of this reserve attracts birds and butterflies which also benefit from the seclusion of the nearby cemetery. The interesting grassland surrounding the graves is rich in flowering species such as agrimony and self heal, so is particularly colourful throughout the spring.

Management   LB Lewisham carries out regular mowing in the cemetery, while volunteers carry out conservation tasks at the reserve.

Interpretation   Leaflet available from LWT.

Access   The reserve is open to the public; the cemetery has restricted access.

Contact   Lewisham Parks Department for the cemetery, Nature Conservation Officer for the reserve (see Beckenham Place Park).

5   New Cross Gate Cutting Nature Reserve

Vesta Road, New Cross, SE4 (TQ364764).
BR. 7ha.

Approach   Best seen from Vesta Road which overlooks the site which lies to the N.

Summary   An unusually wide and steep cutting close to New Cross Gate station varies from woodland to grassy embankment in an area of little public open space and less wildlife habitat.

History   The 19C railway lines were cut across the country below the hilly lands belonging to farms at Brockley. The embankments have been left largely undisturbed for many years, attracting not only wildlife but the attention of LWT which in 1988 gained an agreement to manage the site.

Nature interest   Split in half by the railway which runs N to S, the reserve can be divided into three types of habitat. The widest section in the NW is well wooded with birch, regenerating elm, sycamore and hazel. The clearings in this section are covered by acid to neutral grassland with false oat and cock's foot grasses giving way to sward containing birds-foot trefoil, vetches, sheep's sorrel and toadflax. The large anthills give some indication of how little the reserve has been disturbed. More grassland occurs in the S of the W section which is otherwise dense hawthorn scrub made almost impenetrable by brambles. Birds are protected by this, and among those already recorded are dunnocks, warblers, blackcaps with other species usually associated with a more rural environment like the white-throat and lesser white-throat.

Management   LWT.

Interpretation   Leaflet available from LWT.

Access   Access by prior arrangement.

Contact   LWT.

6 Dacres Wood Nature Reserve

Silverdale, SE26 (TQ 355721).
LB Lewisham. 2.4ha.
Approach   From Silverdale.
Summary   A small reserve along a railway embankment in Lower Sydenham.
History   The railway siding reserve includes a section of the cut of the old Croydon Canal.
Nature interest   Mature woodland with a few exotics such as Turkey oak growing along the embankment extend the range of habitat which otherwise is mainly grass. With appropriate management and the addition of the pond this will become more interesting.
Management   LB Lewisham plans include the construction of a large pond.
Interpretation   Nil on site.
Access   No access at present.
Contact   Nature Conservation Officer (see Beckenham Place Park).

Further information

LB Lewisham, Directorate of Environmental Services, Borough Engineer's Branch, Parks and Open Spaces, Deptford Town Hall, New Cross Road, SE14 (01 692 1288).
London Wildlife Trust (see Barking).

MERTON

The fate of the two large commons at either side of this former garden suburb reflect an underlying ambivalent attitute to nature conservation in this borough . Only Wimbledon Common with its neighbour Putney Heath have had the benefit of fairly benign management. Other natural features like the once sparkling river Wandle which cuts through Merton from the former Beddington marshes to Wandsworth, or Mitcham Common, have until very recent years been neglected or even purposely damaged.

Open space is scattered in an arc from the SE corner of the borough around Morden and NW to Wimbledon with dense inter-war building development elsewhere. The emphasis tends to be on formal parks or golf courses which do not necessarily promote the retention or restoration of habitat.

1 Cannon Hill Common

Cannon Hill Lane, SW20 (TQ 239683).
LB Merton. 17ha.
Approach   Entrance either from Parkway or Cannon Hill Lane.
Summary   A recreational ground with small nature reserve S of playing fields and tennis courts, with small area of woodland.
History   Part of the estate belonging to the 12C Augustinian Canons of Merton Priory, this continued to be agricultural land until the hill was enclosed and landscaped. 'Gentleman's Park' was offered for sale after the First World War for building development. However, public opposition succeeded in saving 60 acres which the local council purchased in 1926 with the help of local benefactors.
Nature interest   The LWT reserve lies towards the middle of the park, close to the pavilion. The most interesting grassland belongs to the S slope of the hill. A good range of birds have been recorded, many breeding in the bird sanctuary. Butterflies are a common sight, with the mixed woodland and hawthorn scrub adding to a range of habitat which suit those preferring dappled light like speckled wood and others needing open grassland like the meadow brown.
Management   The reserve is managed by LWT.
Interpretation   Nil on site.
Access   Open to the public. Restricted to the reserve.
Contact   LB Merton Parks Department; LWT.

2 Mitcham Common

Croydon Road, Mitcham (TQ 287680).
Mitcham Common Board of Conservators. 184ha.
Approach   Footpaths cut across the common from Cedars Road to Windmill Road.
Summary   This greatly modified relic of heathland is basically triangular and sliced by numerous roads including Croydon Road which divides the large golf course from the smaller recreational area.
History   A chequered past of unsympathetic management seems to be on the wane. Once a large common, extending from Waddon Marsh in the S, four neighbouring parishes used it for pasture and disfiguring gravel digging. George Parker Bidder QC is the most well-known of several vigorous campaigners against the resulting

despoilation of the common whose efforts lead to the setting up of a Board of Conservators which bought out the lords of the manors. However, within less than 50 years they had allowed the dumping of vast amounts of rubbish and in turn found themselves pressured by the formation of the Mitcham Common Preservation Society. Old battle lines were redrawn in 1984 when new proposals for dumping were agreed by the agents of the Board, LB Merton Parks Department. However, this threat was averted (as have been various landscaping schemes around Seven Island Pond) and a more recent plan shows a welcome attempt at some conservation management.

Nature interest Relic heathland can be found on the N edge of the golf course where heather and dwarf gorse grow. Other flowering species that have kept a foothold include tormentil, restharrow, petty whin and orchids. The common once extended to Waddon Marsh in the SE and some areas still reflect this damp past, albeit only seasonally. Three ponds now exist but these are due to former gravel extraction. The largest, Seven Island Pond, lies to the N of Croydon Road and included in its emergent vegetation is bogbean. Other man-made features include a puzzling earth mound created in the 1950s. The encroaching woodland is composed of willow and birch, and ash provides cover for birds, some unusual like stonechats and barn owls. It is for butterflies that Mitcham Common is, however, best known, with 21 species recorded ranging from the familiar tortoiseshells to rarities like the four-spotted, silverhook and wormwood shark.

Management A management plan dating from 1986 still emphasises a park-style regime but the needs of wildlife habitat have been acknowledged.

Interpretation Nil on site.

Access Open to the public.

Contact LB Merton Recreation and Arts Department.

3   Pyl Brook Nature Reserve

Rutland Drive, Morden (TQ 251670).
LB Merton. 0.4ha.

Summary A wooded strip of land alongside the Pyl Brook surrounded by housing.

History An area altered by 'digging for victory' during the Second World War has succeeded to secondary woodland.

Nature interest This band of woodland which includes examples of wild cherry, elderberry and crack willow is bordered by the Pyl Brook on its N edge.

Management The site is managed by LWT.

Interpretation Nil on site.

Access Restricted.

Contact LWT.

4   Wimbledon Common, Putney Heath, Farm Bog and Fishponds Wood

TQ 227720, 225715, 217708.
LB Merton; LB Wandsworth. Over 400ha.

Approach The heath and common are unfenced so can be entered along Roehampton Vale or Parkside.

Summary   Criss-crossed by bridlepaths, fringed by playing fields in the W and dominated by a golf course, this is still one of London's most important acidic heathlands.

History   Anciently settled, as can be seen by the circular earth-works at Caesar's Camp, the common and heath were saved following one of the legendary protests against 19C enclosure. The Spencer family as lords of the manor had allowed extensive gravel digging and brickmaking over and above usual common rights. Lord Spencer's aim was to enclose the common for a park and building development by virtue of a private Act of Parliament. This was presented in 1864 and was swiftly opposed by residents led by the MP Henry Peek. By 1871 Peek and his supporters had seen the successful passing of another Act which protected the entire area instead.

Nature interest   The common and heath occupy a poorly drained plateau which slopes towards the W. The SSSI designation for most of the area is due to rare wet heath and unimproved acidic grassland. Small variations in habitat indicate the slightly different underlying conditions. Semi-natural broadleaved woodland covers the W slope and central area dominated by pedunculate oak and birch with holly forming most of the understorey. However, both hazel and alder buckthorn (rare in London) add to this. The field layer generally consists of bracken and bramble while clearings support acid grassland or heath vegetation. The former is dominated by common bent and sheep's fescue but where conditions are wetter wavy hairgrass, purple moorgrass and soft rush are found. A similar pattern repeats itself with dry heath species varying from dwarf gorse to heath rush and brown sedge—another unusual plant for London. Wetland habitat is fed by several streams particularly to the S of Robin Hood Road at Farm Bog which, although slightly the worse for lack of management, still supports a number of different types of sphagnum moss. To the W of this reserve are the reserve's ponds which give their name to Fishponds Woods close to Warren Farm. More park-like open water can be found at the N edge of the common and in Putney Heath at Kingsmere and Queensmere, while those close to Windmill Road are the result of 19C gravel extraction. Such an expanse of habitat attracts many birds, while mammals, too, benefit from the varied terrain and vegetation, so that records reveal foxes, rabbits and badgers.

Management   There has been some planting of horse chestnut and encroaching scrub could offer a threat to heathland habitat. The maintenance is undertaken on behalf of the Board of Conservators by LB Merton Parks Department. The board levy a sliding scale of local rates so that those nearer the common pay more than those at a greater distance. LWT manage Farm Bog and Fishponds Wood.

Interpretation   The Conservators of Wimbledon Common and Putney Heath; LWT.

Access   Access is unrestricted to the LWT reserves as well as the heath and common.

Contact   The Conservators of Wimbledon Common and Putney Heath, The Rangers House, Wimbledon Common (01 788 7655).

Further information

LB Merton, Recreation and Arts Department, Morden Park House, London Road, Morden (01 543 2222).
London Wildlife Trust (see Barking).

NEWHAM

Newham lies between the last few curvaceous miles of the River Lee and River Roding, as they pass largely ignored to the Thames at Bow Creek in the W and Barking Creek in the E.

Much of the borough was once low-lying marshes that gradually rose to the edge of the once extensive Royal Forest of Waltham. All that is left in acknowledgements of this past, in a borough dominated by long chains of Victorian terraces, are names like Forest Gate. The web of channels and streams where the Lee splits around and through Temple or Mill Meads were identified along with Bow Limmo in 1984 for their historical and ecological interest. Sadly, it seems that residents only have a few formal parks to visit. Rare opportunities to see and protect the local wildlife habitat, which has strong links with Newham's waterside industrial heritage, have drifted by so that even such strong natural features as the peninsula of Bow Limmo will be forgotten as the London Docklands Development Corporation route a railway across the river meander to the City.

1   Barking Creek

Jenkins Lane, East Ham (TQ 450826).
TWA. 10.5ha.
Approach   Via the sewage treatment works.
Summary   On the W bank of the River Roding is an area of landfill which still retains some wetland habitat close to the large sewage treatment plant.
Nature interest   Subject to tidal influences, there are still reed beds along the creek with some saltmarsh species such as scurvy grass and wild cherry or those of freshwater like yellow flag iris. Several ponds and channels vary the habitat which is mainly hummocky infill which support great reedmace and celery-leaved crowfoot. A good range of birds have been seen here including dunnock, grey wagtails, lapwings and reed buntings.
Management   Nil except by rabbits.
Interpretation   Nil.
Access   Restricted, permission is needed from TWA.
Contact   Beckton Sewage Works, Jenkins Lane, Barking, Essex IG11 0AD (01 591 3911).

2   Bow Creek, the Limmo Peninsula and Thames Wharf

Silvertown or Dock Road, Canningtown (TQ 395810).
BR, LDDC, TWA. 17ha.
Approach   From steps in the N from pavement of Dock Road.
Summary   After unremitting industrialised river edge, suddenly S of the junction of several major roads is a dramatic meander of the Lee (Bow Creek) only a few hundred yards from its entry to the Thames, with a slice of habitat on the E bank and a fringe of habitat around the peninsular itself.
History   The Lee mouth has been greatly affected by its past uses as wharves, railway sidings and industry.

Nature interest The main disturbance has been from tipping, which vegetation has covered. Species reflect the nutrient-poor under-lying soil. However, in a culvert at Thames Wharf several uncommon plants like the fennel leaved pondweed and hemlock water dropwort have been recorded. In the N of the site is a large grassy area with a ribbon of saltmarsh beside the creek which contains plants such as sea aster and sea clubrush. A band of intertidal mud attracts wading birds, while around the bend in the river is the pear-shaped Limmo peninsular on which vegetation reflects both former tipping and the river edge environment.

Management Nil.

Interpretation Nil on site.

Access De facto access.

Contact LWT; LDDC, West India House, Millwall Dock, London E14 (01 515 3000)

3 Bully Fen

Temple Mills Lane, E15 (TQ 376854).
LVRPA.

Summary Part of the area under the control of the LVRPA, the small reserve lies close to the Eastway Cycle Track.

History In the distant past this was marsh belonging to the Knights Templar but in more recent times they were set aside for flood alleviation. These plans were dropped and the marshes were infilled in 1952.

Nature interest Lying to the S of the uniform Hackney Marshes this site has wet woodland and colourful ephemeral plant communi-ties particularly good for invertebrates.

Management The reserve is managed by LVRPA.

Interpretation LWT.

Contact LVRPA (see Hackney).

4 St Michael's Churchyard

High Street South, East Ham E6 (TQ 429824).
2ha.

Approach Private cemetery from Norman Road.

Summary Straight down the road from Woodgrange Park Cemetery this is a sympathetically managed burial ground.

Nature interest Mainly secondary woodland.

Management Management allows both for the tending of graves and for wildlife.

Interpretation Information centre beside the church.

Access Open at all times.

Contact Information centre (01 470 4525).

5 Woodgrange Park Cemetery

Romford Road, Manor Park E7 (TQ 418852).
Private. 10ha.

Approach Entry at end of Tenbury Close.

Summary A private burial ground close to railway line which passes through Woodgrange Park Station.

History   The area was once known as Little Ilford but the cemetery was yet another Victorian scheme which is still used for burials.

Nature interest   Part of a chain of small sites which eventually lead to the Wanstead Flats, this site has a good canopy of lime and oak with an understorey of hawthorn and holly. Wild roses and rosebay willowherb add colour and variety which increases as the habitat becomes more open towards the railway line. Here rarities such as barren fescue and even some wavy hairgrass have been recorded.

Interpretation   Nil on site.

Access   Strictly by prior arrangement.

Contact   (01 472 3433).

Further information

LB Newham, Directorate of Engineering and Surveying, High Street South, E6 (01 472 1430).
London Wildlife Trust (see Barking).

REDBRIDGE

Bordering on Essex countryside, Redbridge is edged by the parallel valleys of the rivers Roding and Ching in the W rising to a series of hills continuing across the Greater London boundary at Hainault. The borough suffers the rippling effect of post war housing development which is still suburbanising even much-appreciated captive farmland, now threatened by proposals for modern village complexes. Wildlife habitat is dominated by the influence of the former royal forests of Hainault in the E corner and by Waltham (Epping) which slips into the S at Wanstead Park and Flats.

1   Claybury Woods

Manor Road, Woodford Bridge (TQ 435912).
Regional Health Authority. 15ha.
Approach   Via footpath off Tomswood Hill passing the disused farm buildings.
Summary   The ancient woodland lies on the S slopes of Tomswood Hill beside a large Victorian hospital.
History   Probably an enclosed woodland on the edge of Hainault Forest, it and surrounding farmland became the grounds of an asylum which opened in 1893. As with most large mental hospitals there are plans to sell off Claybury after its closure in 1992.
Nature interest   The former hornbeam coppice is open enough to have retained quite an interesting ground flora. Although there are a few Turkey oaks or conifers, most of the woodland trees are native so that the canopy of hornbeam and pedunculate oak is supplemented by such species as wild service. There is a particular concentration of these just N of the Forest House. The understorey is better developed in the E of the wood and makes an interesting comparison with the more sparse shrub layer in the W. In the lighter, younger woodland the ground flora is rich with bluebells and wild garlic in the spring, and herbs such as dog's mercury or wood anemone. Forster's woodrush can be found towards the centre of the woods, as can another unusual species butcher's broom, which contribute to Claybury being considered as an SSSI.
Management   LWT volunteers have restored the pond and hope to re-introduce a coppice system with the agreement of the RHA.
Interpretation   Leaflet available from LWT.
Access   Open to the public.
Contact   LWT; RHA, Claybury Hall, Woodford Bridge (01 505 6241).

2   Fairlop Plain

Forest Road, Fairlop (TQ 456902).
Norstead Leisure Ltd; LB Redbridge. 120ha.
Approach   Either from entrances off Forest Road, or from riding stables at the end of Aldborough Road North.
Summary   A small proportion of this wide flattish former farmland is to be developed in a habitat recreation scheme concentrating on wetland.
History   Farmland which still retains hedges was used in both World Wars as an airstrip but was bought in the 1950s by Ilford council

for gravel or sand extraction and for the disposal of rubbish. Of over 1,000 acres just over half may continue to be farmed but the rest of the site is to become a country park and golf course.

Nature interest   5.5 hectares, which include former gravel workings, is to be a lagoon nature reserve at the suggestion of LWT. Birdlife has long been attracted to the open water and many rare species have been recorded such as whimbrel, smew and the bar-tailed godwit.

Management   Norstead Ltd are to landscape the lagoon
Interpretation   Nil on site.
Access   Yet to be decided.
Contact   LB Redbridge; LWT.

3   Hainault Forest Country Park

Fox Burrow Road, Romford Road, Chigwell (TQ 475333).
LB Redbridge; LB Havering; Essex County Council. 400ha; 33ha in Redbridge.

Approach   From the recreational grounds off the New North Road.
Summary   This large country park includes sports grounds, a fishing lake, woodland and farmland with a quarter of the area managed as a golf course.

History   The Forest of Hainault once belonged to the Abbey of Barking and was continually encroached upon from the 17C onwards. Nothing caused such a public outcry as the callous destruction of 92% of this magnificent wood-pasture which followed the passing of a disafforestation act on behalf of the Crown in 1851. The shock of losing so much to agriculture in a mere six weeks began a long campaign to save what was left for the public, led by a verderer of the neighbouring Epping Forest, North Burton. With the support of newly established pressure groups such as the Commons and Footpaths Preservation Society and the National Trust a nucleus of 803 acres was acquired by the LCC in 1903. This was gradually extended so that now the bulk lies in Essex, with recreational grounds concentrated at Redbridge and farmland at Havering.

Nature interest   The structure of the former wood-pasture, demonstrated by numerous contorted ancient hornbeam pollards, is the chief interest of the forest. A variety of other habitats contribute to this being an important wildlife site. On the S and E of Cabin Hill younger woodland curves around a rising grassy slope. Composed of birch, with oak and hawthorn scrub with the occasional mature oak there are still other scattered ancient woodland tree species such as wild service and crab apple. Across the Greater London boundary are many pollards with a typically poor accompanying ground flora, although nonetheless interesting for this. Various streams like Sheeps Water in the W or those trickling around Lambourne Well contribute wetland flora such as pendulous, remote and wood sedge. Damp conditions can also be found in clearings in the W where well-structured woodland has resulted from management and greater light. In this area trees give way to bracken and acid grassland. The sheltered and considerable variety of habitat of the forest encourages numerous birds and mammals. Foxes and squirrels are regularly seen, while stoats and badgers are harder to spot.

Management   The management regime includes re-introducing pollarding while grassy clearings are kept open by flailing.

Interpretation   A nature trail leaflet is available from the park centre.
Access   Open to the public.
Contact   LB Redbridge.

4   Wanstead Flats and Park

Wanstead Park Road or Warren Road, E11 (TQ 416877, 410862).
City of London Corporation. 56ha; 85ha.
Approach   Entrances from Warren Road or Northumberland Avenue lead to the park while the flats are unfenced and can be entered anywhere along their borders.
Summary   Redbridge border rides over the City of London Cemetery and misses the large pond on the Flats but takes in the rest of the area which includes two golf courses and the park.
History   The grounds of Wanstead House were enclosed from lands once part of the Forest of Waltham in 1545. From the 17C the park began to be landscaped. One scheme was the creation of the fishponds. However, the fortune of the Child family collapsed in the early 19C which eventually led to the demolishing of the mansion. The land and flats were acquired by the City of London in 1878 under the Epping Forest Act which continues to manage what is left.
Nature interest   The flats and park contain grasslands and ponds of value to wildlife although it is surprisingly the flats that need to be managed more sympathetically so that the sports pitches do not eclipse the pasture that cattle still graze. Scrub and woodland provide the park with native species like oak and silver birch mixing with familiar park favourites like standard beeches. The dense understorey encourages birds of which at least 50 species out of over 100 recorded are believed to breed on site.
Management   The Corporation of the City of London manages the entire area.
Interpretation   Booklets are available from the Open Spaces Committee of the City Corporation.
Access   Open to the public.
Contact   Open Spaces Committee (see City of London).

Further information

LB Redbridge, Recreation and Amenities Division, Town Hall, Ilford (01 478 3020).
London Wildlife Trust (see Barking).

RICHMOND UPON THAMES

The Thames was once the naural divide between Middlesex and Surrey. The meadows and hilly pastures attracted the attention of the Crown, which not only enclosed many acres for hunting but also ornamented the former working landscape as at Bushy Park and what became Kew Gardens. Over a third of the borough is public open space, but the greatest proportion of this belongs to the parks and gardens where the emphasis has not always been primarily concerned with the managing of habitat. However, like other London boroughs wildlife has gained a number of footholds in former public utility sites, such as the disused reservoirs at Barnes, although these places seldom have the formal protection of their pampered cousins, the ornamental parks.

1 Barn Elms Reservoirs and Barnes Common

Rocks Lane, Methyr Terrace, SW13 (TQ 22971; 223758).
TWA; Church Commissioners. 34ha and 50ha.

Approach   A small lane on the bend of Rocks Lane as it becomes Castelnau is one entry; an alternative is in the N near Hammersmith Bridge via the filter beds. The common can be entered from any of the roads that cut across it.

Summary   The distorted square formed by the four reservoirs are separated from the Thames by only a slip of land. To the S lies Barn Elms Park through which the last few yards of the Beverley Brook flows S of the park below intersecting roads in the grassy Barnes Common.

History   Barnes Common has had a peaceful past. The Dean and Chapter of St Paul's, as lords of the manor since the 11C, assured its safekeeping by not insisting on the purchase of their manorial rights. As a result the borough is able, on behalf of the subsequent owners, the Church Commissioners, to maintain the common. The reservoirs, the oldest and shallowest in London, have recently become the focus of a possible bird sanctuary to be managed by the Wildfowl Trust.

Nature interest   These sites demonstrate the severe limitations of SSSI designation in the protection of habitat, and more significantly in the potentially disastrous consequences arising from the removal of such a designation. The SSSI status of the common is due to the acid grassland of 20 hectares close to Mill Hill which has survived draining and the planting of rows of standard trees. The tree cover, bramble and bracken have provided a mixed habitat away from the sports pitches which have nibbled away the edge of the common. This is the only known site in Greater London for the burnet rose.

By far the most well known and favoured site for birds lies to the N at the reservoirs. Sadly, recent counts have revealed a decline in their numbers so that the NCC has removed the SSSI designation. Unable, due to the specific character of scientific evaluation, to answer the claim that the volunteer recorders who congregate on Sundays may disturb the flocks, or that the NCC's action is often misread as some sort of announcement of the site's fall from grace, its status lurches from the dizzy heights of scientific recognition straight to vacant land. Yet the reservoirs offer haven to large gatherings of seagull, gadwall, shoveler and pochard as well as the rare smew and tufted duck. These are only a few of the wide range of birds which include those associated with marshland like the sedge warbler or passerines such as sandpipers and wagtails.

Management   Nil for conservation. The common is managed by LB Richmond parks department.
Interpretation   Nil on site.
Access   While the common and park are open to the public there is de facto access to the reservoirs.
Contact   TWA (see Hackney); Barn Elms Protection Association, Barnes Community Association, 70 Barnes High Street, SW13; RB Richmond Parks and Recreation Department.

2   Crane Park Island Nature Reserve

Ellerman Avenue, Hounslow Road, Twickenham (TQ 128728).
LB Richmond. 1.8ha.
Approach   The island reserve opposite the Shot Tower lies to the W of Crane Park which protects a wedge of land on either side of the river Crane for over a mile.
Summary   A former mill pond is surrounded by mixed broadleaved woodland.
History   This man-made island was created to provide a head of water for a gunpowder mill in 1776. Manufacturing finally ceased in 1926, leaving the island to develop into secondary woodland. All that is left to hint at the former use is the nearby Shot Tower. In 1981 Richmond and Twickenham Friends of the Earth identified the site as a possible nature reserve, and LB Richmond's agreement began what became known as the Crane Park Project, with subsequent provision of a warden and on-site teacher.
Nature interest   At the centre of the wooded island is the millpond which, since being drained in the 1960s, is now seasonally wet. The rich alluvial soil supports willow, balsam and nettles of well-known importance to butterfly caterpillars. The varied speed of water flows on either side of the island promotes the growth of water crowfoot which withstands the fast flowing backwater, while arrowhead enjoys the deep and slow flowing mainstream.
Management   An important educational reserve which is now staffed by LWT, practical management tasks are undertaken each month by volunteers.
Interpretation   The Shot Tower is being converted into a study centre and leaflets are available from LWT.
Access   Open to the public.
Contact   LWT Warden (01 808 9582/01 755 2339).

3   Ham Lands, Petersham Meadows and Terrace Field

Riverside Drive, Ham (TQ 164729).
LB Richmond. 80ha.
Approach   From the riverside towpath from Petersham Road to Teddington Lock.
Summary   A stretch of low-lying fields in the N extend into grasslands and scrub, sometimes of considerable width following the curve of the Thames on the S bank.
History   Recently saved from threats of development by the council, part of these lands once belonged to Secrett Farm, part were half yearly Lammas lands. Much of Ham belonged to the notorious Dysart family (see Ham Common) who were keen on maintaining

their privacy but this did not save these lands being dug for gravel in the late 19C.

Nature interest   Freshwater marsh plants provide some of the flora for this strip of diverse habitat with Teddington Lock similarly indicating the tidal limit of the Thames estuary. In the N, at the meadows which lie below the steeply sloping Terrace Fields, brook-lime and pink waterspeedwell can be found, while opposite the man-made Eel Pie Island three types of orchid grow. This is partly due to the chalky character of the infill used at the former gravel workings. Other unusual species found in these former water meadows include the bloody cranesbill and salad burnet which also reflect this underlying substrate. The common plants like rosebay willowherb or yarrow are balanced with dittander and moth mullein. This length of well-vegetated riverside attracts a wide range of insects, 19 species of butterfly having been recorded. The hawthorn and willow scrub is cover for numerous birds from woodpeckers and white-throats to willow warblers and reed buntings. Amphibians are also recorded and much threatened like the reptiles and grass snake. To the S of the Thames Young Mariners base, close to the edge of the Greater London, is a rare opportunity to see a surviving area of flood meadow.

Management   LB Richmond manages with the advice of numerous conservation groups including LWT.

Interpretation   Nil on site; report by LWT Richmond Group.

Access   Open to the public, restricted at the Thames Young Mariners base.

Contact   LB Richmond; LWT.

4   Lonsdale Road Reservoirs

Lonsdale Road, SW13 (TQ 218773).
LB Richmond, management committee. 9ha.

Approach   From the Thames towpath.

Summary   The 'Leg of Mutton', like its larger neighbour the Barn Elms Reservoirs, has only a thin strip of land dividing it from the Thames.

History   The loss of this early 19C reservoir was only narrowly averted by dogged opposition of local people, spearheaded by the Barnes Wildlife and Animal Welfare Group which kept up its guard for over a decade following the reservoir's decommissioning in 1960. First the group campaigned against water board plans to build houses in 1968, which successfully resulted in LB Richmond refusing planning permission—which then found itself forced to purchase the site for £1 million. To offset this the borough then proposed its own building scheme, which was also rejected following a public inquiry in 1972. Undeterred, three years later the council altered the plan to include a formal park—which met once more with widespread public disapproval. This was dropped when the funds available to the council declined in the late 1970s, the site gaining its belated nature reserve status in 1980.

Nature interest   With the dropping water level since its use as a reservoir, various stages of natural succession around the margins of the reservoir are a major feature of its wildlife interests. The gently sloping sides help diving species such as pochard and tufted duck to feed easily. To encourage waterfowl a number of floating rafts have been made which together with surrounding young woodland will, it is hoped, lead to settled breeding.

Management   Voluntary conservation groups have planted over 1,000 native trees to create hedges and a woodland belt. This is part of the management committee's aim to protect the birdlife and encourage educational use. A jetty will allow pond dipping without too much water edge disturbance, while observation hides will leave the birds to continue with everyday activities unaware of the binoculars trained on them.

Interpretation   Barnes Wildlife and Animal Welfare Group.

Access   Permit only.

Contact   BW&AW Group.

5   Richmond Park, East Sheen Common, Ham Common and Palewell Common

Queen's Road, Petersham (TQ 200735).

DOE, National Trust; LB Richmond. Over 955ha.

Approach   Numerous roads, footpaths and bridleways cross the enclosed park, with Sawyers Hill cutting it in half.

Summary   A magnificent area of rolling captive countryside. The occasional ornamental planting, such as the Isabella Plantation and Sidmouth Wood, tend to act as a honey pot to visitors, taking pressure off sites of importance to wildlife. Around its circumference are three radiating wooded commons—Ham in the W, East Sheen in the N and Palewell in the NE.

History   The park was wrung from the unwilling lords of the manor by the high-handed action of the autocratic Charles I, who annexed and enclosed the entire area in 1637. The wall he constructed around its perimeter, allowing access to commoners only from strategically placed ladders, became the focus of protest for the next two centuries. If anything could better the arrogance of Charles I it was the action of Princess Amelia when she became the park 'ranger' in 1751. Her need for exclusivity led her to remove these ladders so that the commoners could no longer collect wood for fuel. In the ensuing furore parts of the wall were knocked down, but is was an action brought against the gate keeper by a local brewer, John Lewis (who later died in abject poverty partly due to the costs this entailed), which finally had the ladders replaced, although Amelia made sure they could only be climbed by the young and fit.

Ham Common, too, had a colourful history with the Dysart family, who owned much of the land in this area, constantly warring against their neighbours. Ignoring local people and the vestry, they claimed the common as strictly private property. Their posture was seriously challenged in 1891 after public notices they had erected threatening prosecution of trespassers were sawn down. Undaunted, Lord Dysart presented a private bill to parliament in 1896 hoping the council would not notice that thereby they would be forced to exchange an area of their land for public ownership of the common. The Commons and Footpaths Preservation Society vigorously protested and helped the bill's rejection. Instead, in 1902, another Act was passed which finally protected the Common. Meanwhile, the National Trust had rescued East Sheen Common from the gravel digging enthusiasm of the Spencer family.

Nature interest   The SSSI designation is once again focused on a very specific target to protect the rich beetle fauna found on mature trees and deadwood throughout the park. The main impression of the park is, though, one of extensive grassland which varies from dry and acidic to marshy with fescues and sedges indicating the underlying conditions. Around the man-made Pen Ponds in the centre of the park and near Roehampton Gate, sedges are particularly abundant. The herds of fallow and red deer tend to congregate in the woodland N of the park near Bog Lodge, which also supports a wide range of smaller mammals such as foxes and weasels. Unfortunately, in an attempt to promote luxuriant pasture for the deer by the dumping of tons of de-activated sludge, Thamesgro, some habitat was directly damaged while far more was threatened. The superintendant was not, it seemed, primarily concerned with the SSSI designation. Indeed, in the 1950s, the former superintendant objected to the NCC's decision, pointing out that the land had been drained in places and planted in others, which seemed to him to undermine their conclusions. There could be an underlying contradiction in the deer management, with culling being undertaken to keep numbers down while habitat is altered for their benefit alone.

This attractive landscape slips into the E edge of Ham Common, which away from the sports pitches is wooded, as is East Sheen Common and Palewell Common in the N. Over 100 species of bird have been counted including heathland residents such as stonechats or those of open countryside like skylarks. Other species prefer the cover of the wooded Ham Common or the mature trees surrounded by acid grassland.

Management   The park is managed by the DoE, while Ham Common is managed by LB Richmond.

Interpretation   There is a nature trail in the Isabella Plantation but otherwise no interpretation on site.

Access   Open to the public in daylight hours.

Contact   Friends of Richmond Park, 22 Woodland Avenue, New Malden, Surrey (01 942 6125); Bailiff of the Royal Parks, DoE, 2 Marsham Street, SW1; LB Richmond Parks and Recreation Deparment.

Further information

LB Richmond upon Thames, Parks and Recreation Department, Langholme Lodge, Petersham Road, Richmond, Surrey (01 940 8351). London Wildlife Trust (see Barking).

SOUTHWARK

The borough combines the once wide flood plain of the Thames, which allowed the river to lap the land far into Walworth, and the ridge of wooded hills that begin in the E at Nunhead and reach their highest point along the Sydenham Hill ridge (the ancient border between Lewisham in Kent and Camberwell in Surrey).

Relief from the overwhelmingly urban character of terraced houses and large estates in the centre and N of Southwark is provided by two formal parks, but the bulk of open land is found across the hillsides of the sharp S triangle. On either side, descending from the Sydenham ridge, a glimpse of Southwark's mostly subterranean river tributaries can be seen: the Peck at Peckham Rye Park and the Effra at Belair Park.

While protection of small, created habitats such as Lavender Pond and a series of community-based pocket handkerchief nature gardens such as Benhill Road or Goldsmith Road has been supported by the council, its attitude has not been consistent. As a result, little or no protection has been given to naturally occuring wildlife sites such as the once magnificent grasslands of the disused Bricklayer's Arms Depot.

1   Camberwell Old Cemetery

Forest Hill Road, SE22 (TQ 348741).
LB Southwark. 6ha.
Approach   Formal entrance gates from Forest Hill Road.
Summary   One of three cemeteries between the neighbouring hills of Nunhead and Honor Oak.
Nature interest   Secondary woodland and scrub have developed across the cemetery although some has been recently cleared. A wide range of tree species including oak, hornbeam, ash and hawthorn grows alongside park favourites like horse chestnut and poplar, but the dominating species is the ubiquitous sycamore. Brambles and ivy roll over graves and ground so that ground flora is best seen along the path edges where vetches or ox-eye daisies supplement nettles and cow parsley.
Management   Nil for conservation.
Interpretation   Nil on site.
Access   Open to the public.
Contact   Southwark Leisure and Recreation Department.

2   Dulwich Upper Wood

Farquhar Road, SE19 (TQ 337712).
LB Southwark. 2.4ha.
Approach   The wood fringes the road and the entrance is from its S tip.
Summary   A strip of secondary broadleaved woodland covering an embankment.
History   Woodland has colonised the grounds of Victorian houses although some mature oaks suggest the ancient woodland that once covered the site. The site has been managed by the Trust for Urban Ecology (TRUE) since 1984.
Nature interest   Over a period of 40 years or so secondary woodland has been dominated by sessile and pedunculate oak.

However, cherry laurel, rhododendron, false acacia as well as sycamore have been retained, darkening the woodland floor which is therefore dominated by ivy and bramble. Hedge species and wildflowers have been planted to increase the range of species.

Management   The site is managed by TRUE which has created a small area of coppice and a nature trail.

Interpretation   The trail leads around the wood and information is available from the warden whose base is the portakabin classroom.

Access   Open to the public.

Contact   The warden (01 761 6230).

3   Lavender Pond

Lavender Road, Rotherhithe Street, SE16 (TQ 364803).
LB Southwark. 0.7ha.

Approach   A fairly short walk from the Rotherhithe tube station.

Summary   A popular pond with half the circumference given to a flood meadow and curving embankment.

History   Once belonging to the 19C Surrey Docks system, Lavender Dock was finally closed in the 1970s but a corner was retained for this innovative scheme which opened to the public in 1982 under the management of TRUE.

Nature interest   Despite problems caused by anglers, this is an attractive site. Emergent species like branched bur-reed, yellow flag, greater reedmace and watermint have been planted while the wet meadow in the E includes examples of purple loosestrife, kingcup and the aromatic meadowsweet. Young tree cover is provided by alders. Amphibians are plentiful in this area while waterfowl like mallard, moorhen and the occasional swan appreciate the cover surrounding the open water.

Management   A management committee advises the warden whose task has included control of the dense algal bloom which grows in response to the need for the constant topping up of the water level. In spite of this, Lavender Pond is a much-used educational resource.

Interpretation   Leaflets are available from the warden and a teacher is based at the site office.

Access   Open to the public. Access to the flood meadow across the swing bridge is restricted.

Contact   The warden (01 232 0489).

4   Nunhead Cemetery

Linden Grove, SE15 (TQ 354753).
LB Southwark. 24ha.

Approach   Large formal entrance gates lead into the N edge away from the S area still used for burials.

Summary   One of London's large Victorian cemeteries, like others it is dominated by secondary broadleaved woodland. One third is open land available for new burial plots.

History   Once hill top pasture, this former garden cemetery with its winding paths and ornamental plantings, designed by James Bunstone Bunning, opened in 1840. Like most private cemetery companies, by the Second World War its management had declined. Vandalism and apathy lead to its acquisition for £1 by LB Southwark in 1969. Nearly half the area was to be retained for burials with the rest set aside as a park and nature reserve.

Nature interest   The nature reserve in the NE is dark secondary woodland composed of ash and sycamore beneath which a field layer of bramble and several types of ivy grows. At the opposite side of the cemetery in the NW a more open environment reveals red and white clover, with bird's foot trefoil and chamomile—which may be the result of a seed mixture spread by LB Southwark. To the S of this area on the crown of the hill is a damp grassland where wood rush can be found. Specimen trees are scattered throughout the cemetery so that Turkey oaks and even a gingko interrupt the young woodland. The sheltered environment supports a wide range of birds including thrushes and tits, woodpeckers and tawny owls.

Management   Work by volunteers organised by the Friends of Nunhead Cemetery (FONC) has been undertaken to control sycamore and restore the monuments, while other works are undertaken by LB Southwark public works department.

Interpretation   Nil on site. Guided walks and printed information are provided by FONC.

Access   De facto access daily.

Contact   FONC, c/o 144 Erlanger Road, SE14 5TJ.

5   One Tree Hill and Camberwell New Cemetery

Honor Oak Park, Brenchley Gardens, SE23 (TQ 355743, 357745). LB Southwark. 7ha; 11ha.

Approach   Steps alongside St Augustine's Church lead to the top of the hill and the park, while the formal entrance to the cemetery is half way along Brenchley Gardens or from Brockley Way.

Summary   Also known as Honor Oak Hill, the wooded slopes form a wedge of open space on the border with Lewisham.

History   The status of the hill was in some doubt in the late 19C but was believed by local people to be 'waste' or common land, so that the enclosing of the area for a large private golf course in 1896 resulted in widespread public protest. In the autumn of that year many thousands of people gathered and began to pull down the newly erected fences. When these were re-erected, even larger crowds were inspired to pay a visit. It took another six years before the neighbouring councils were able to finally save the hill by organising its acquisition under the LCC's General Powers Act of 1904.

Nature interest   Timothy, cocksfoot and meadow grasses occur in the more intensively managed cemetery which is otherwise dotted with specimen trees. Towards the park, oak and sycamore grow with an understorey of elder and hawthorn. The ancient character of the area is hinted at in the greatly disturbed acid grassland of the park which is now wooded. Heath grass, smooth hawksbeard and sheep's sorrel can still be found in the otherwise dull rye-grass sward. Crab apple, hawthorn and oak are plentiful in the S with the Honor Oak itself, nearly a century old, reminding visitors of the strength of feeling that saved the hill.

Management   Southwark's parks department manages the hill but with little active conservation of habitat.

Interpretation   Nil on site.

Access   Open to the public.

Contact   Southwark Leisure and Recreation.

6 Stave Hill Nature Park and Russia Dock Wood

Salter Road and Redriff Road, SE16 (TQ 361799, 362796).
LB Southwark; London Docklands Development Corporation (LDDC). 2ha; approx 14ha.

Approach   The park may be approached from the wood along the winding footpath.

Summary   Two created habitat schemes, with the nearby Lavender Pond (see above), complete a trio of imaginative attempts to design new public open space. The Stave Hill tumulus, created in 1984, gives stunning views across the Thames, new housing and light industrial buildings.

History   In an area once dominated by the 19C Surrey Commercial Docks, many of which were seriously damaged during the last war, few features remain of this trading past apart from the Lavender Dock Pump House and the dockside embodied in the woodland scheme commissioned by the council and opened in 1980.

Nature interest   The tree species used in both schemes is similar, consisting of rowan, maple, ash, hazel, dogwood and hawthorn among the wide range chosen. The well-kept Russia Dock Wood is fairly dense and already attracts a good range of waterfowl including mallard, moorhen and even reed bunting. The ponds of both sites are less successful than Lavender Pond as the varying water levels do not retain aquatic vegetation except where shallow shelving allows.

Management   The eco park is managed by TRUE which hopes to develop it as an educational centre similar to Lavender Pond. LB Southwark manages the wood where seasonal mowing of grass along the paths encourages wildflowers.

Interpretation   Nil on site.

Access   Open to the public.

Contact   TRUE warden, Timber Dock Road, SE16 1AG (01 237 9175); Southwark Leisure and Recreation.

7 Sydenham Hill Wood Nature Reserve and Dulwich Wood

Sydenham Hill, SE21 (TQ 370724).
LB Southwark; Dulwich College Estates Governors. 11ha; 20ha.

Approach   The nature reserve can be entered either from Cox's Walk, a steep footpath from Dulwich Common, or from steps at Crescent Wood Road. Dulwich Wood may be seen and entered from Low Cross Wood Lane opposite Sydenham Hill station.

Summary   An extensive area of ancient woodland is bordered on the N by a large private golf course.

History   These adjoining woods once belonged to the Abbey of Bermondsey and formed part of a chain of woods which linked New Cross with Norwood Common and were popularly called the Great North Wood. In the 17C they were acquired by Edward Alleyn, founder of Alleyn's College of God's Gift—or Dulwich College. By the end of the 19C the newly formed board of governors had begun building development along the ridge, while a railway line was cut through to Crystal Palace. In the 1960s while the Victorian houses declined, another large section was lost to an estate. In 1979 LB Southwark bought the lease for Sydenham Hill Wood and its environs with a view to partial development for council housing. For a number of years since then, a campaign to protect the woods has been spearheaded by LWT, which has managed the Sydenham Hill Wood nature reserve since 1981.

Nature interest The reserve occupies a steep N facing clay hillside and is a mosaic of woodland habitat. Dominated by sessile oak and hornbeam of various ages, the canopy is broken by a number of glades. The understorey is mostly composed of holly and some hazel. Non-natives such as cherry laurel and rhododendron have taken root, although where they have been removed native seedlings are growing. Ancient woodland indicators can be seen especially in a central belt where bluebells, wood sorrel, lesser celandine and wild garlic grow close to the former railway trail.

Along the ride, at the bottom of the slope the young woodland consists of willow, ash and birch with a group of wild cherries near the railway footbridge. A number of poplars and beeches outline the ride, although the latter contribute increasingly more to the fungi of the wood than to the canopy. Foxgloves and red campion occur in considerable numbers close to the small woodland pond which, although of a low level in the summer, is known to flood in winter. Up the slope close to a large cedar of Lebanon, a relic of the plants in the grounds of the Victorian houses, is a damp hollow of uncertain origin. Numerous woodland birds have been recorded within the wood from the tiny goldcrest to all three British woodpeckers and nesting kestrels. Nuthatches and treecreepers can be seen walking up and down the trunks of mature trees, while fox families occupy the more secluded part of the ridge and grey squirrels climb across the spreading branches.

The adjacent Dulwich Wood has similar characteristics sharing the 50 or so bird species and 14 types of butterfly. The formerly managed structure of the wood is clear, with standard oaks still obvious even with the loss of the coppice. A further section of the wood lies to the W of Low Cross Wood Lane, where the understorey is poor but a large patch of wild garlic grows.

Management The LWT reserve is managed to encourage the recovery of the woodland structure, especially where erosion has caused bare earth. Steps and a nature trail have been constructed.

Interpretation The 8-point nature trail for the wood is marked by white posts and accompanied by a leaflet obtainable from the on-site display centre or from the LWT office. Leaflets on management of the wood and a book on the history of the woods are also available.

Access The reserve is open to the public; there is de facto access to Dulwich Wood.

Contact LWT Warden (01 699 5698); Estates Governors of Dulwich College, The Old College, SE21 7AE.

Further information

LB Southwark, Leisure and Recreation Department, Chatelaine House, Walworth Road, SE17 1JJ (01 703 3499).
LB Southwark, Planning Department, Angel Court, 199 Borough High Street, SE1 1JA (01 403 3322).
London Wildlife Trust (see Barking).
Trust for Urban Ecology (TRUE), PO Box 514, SE16 1AS (01 237 9175).

SUTTON

In 1986, a working party convened by the borough council identified around 20 sites with wildlife potential with few of current value. The Sutton Conservation Group was set up, suggesting a changing attitude to the natural environment in a borough with surprisingly few patches of public open space and a depressingly familiar pattern of management. The list included a wedge of land on the border with Merton which contains one of Sutton's most famous habitats. This is the Beddington Sewage Treatment Works, once the extensive fresh-water marshes that linked Waddon to Mitcham Common. Ironically, the sludge lagoons attracted large numbers of birds to its 40 acres (most of which are now likely to be lost to gravel extraction), though its discharged effluent contributed to the injuries inflicted on the E arm of the River Wandle. The management of this once sparkling chalk-fed river still seems problematic after centuries of abuse. Anxiety about its health has concentrated the efforts of individuals and conservation groups since the 19C which at its beginning saw 90 mills along its banks, dependent on its flow for power and waste disposal. The decline of industry rather than environmental concern has probably caused a relative drop in the chronic pollution. But the Wandle has a long way to go before it can emulate the cleaner reaches of the Hackbridge branch, which drains from the chalk downs of Banstead just across the Greater London border.

1 Ruffet and Big Wood

Richland Avenue, Woodmansterne (TQ 28603).
Private owner. 7.5ha.
Summary   Mature sycamore woodland with interesting ground flora, surrounded by playing fields in the W and S, and horse pasture in the E and N. Heavy recreational use with BMX cyclists causing damage.
History   Appears to be sycamore coppice.
Nature interest   Sycamore is not the only tree providing cover in this wood, oak occurs in the N while in the W a number of fine beeches grow. Wild cherry, ash, field maple, whitebeam and rowan perhaps reflect the underlying chalk which influences the character of the landscape S of the borough. Dog's mercury, bluebells, goldilocks buttercup and lesser celandine demonstrate the openness of the canopy which is due to former coppicing and the gaps created by fallen dead timber. Woodland birds include mistlethrush, wren, blackcap and goldcrest.
Management   Nil for conservation.
Interpretation   Nil on site.
Access   De facto access.
Contact   LB Sutton.

2 St Philomena's Lake

Shorts Road, Carshalton (TQ 277645).
Private. 1ha.
Approach   The lake is located in the grounds of the St Philomena's convent and school.
Summary   A recently restored spring-fed lake.
History   Carshalton House was built for Queen Anne's physi-

cian in the 18C, eventually becoming a school and convent of the English Province of the Daughter's of the Cross. The lake pre-dates this, having been traced at least to the 15C.

Nature interest   Rare plants like water sedge complement the planting of small reed grass, water mint and watercress (beds of which can still be found along the Wandle at Shepherds Road). The lake supports newts, toads and frogs as well as a good range of dragonflies and a rare aquatic snail, *limnea palustris*.

Management   LWT have restored the lake and built a weir to maintain the water level.

Interpretation   Information from LWT.

Access   Restricted.

Contact   LWT.

3   Seear's Park and Waterworks

St Dunstan's Hill, Cheam (TQ 246642).
LB Sutton. 5.4ha.

Approach   Love Lane footpath runs along the edge of the park.

Summary   A new and intensively managed park lies to the S of an area of scrub and grassland.

Nature interest   The heavily used wood which merges into hawthorn and elder scrub also contains some regenerating elm. Lesser celandine, wood anemone and wood avens contribute to the ground flora. The habitat changes in the N to an area of grasses and ruderal plants.

Management   A new pond has been created which might encourage sympathetic management of the park.

Interpretation   Nil on site.

Access   Open to the public.

Contact   Sutton Technical Services.

4   Wilderness Island

River Gardens, Carshalton (TQ 282655).
LB Sutton. 2ha.

Approach   A footbridge from Mill Lane crosses the river branch.

Summary   Reedbeds and wetland occupy an area between the confluence of two branches of the Wandle. Nearby are Nightingale Road Spinney in the N and Carshalton Ponds in the S.

History   Part was formerly an orchard while the bulk is simply isolated backland which has been licenced to LWT since the mid 1980s.

Nature interest   The secondary woodland with a herb-rich meadow in the S of the island alters to reed and sedge beds in the N. A good range of aquatic plants including water plantain, yellow flag, reedmace, pendulous sedge and greater pond sedge are found, testimony to the fairly clean water supply. These together with crack willow pollards suggest the type of management that could improve river habitat along the rest of the Wandle.

Management   LWT intend to keep a mix of habitats with areas of open water. Volunteer tasks take place each month.

Interpretation   An 8-point nature trail is obtainable from LWT.

Access   Open to the public.

Contact   LWT.

Further information.

LB Sutton, Park Section, Technical Services Department, 24 Denmark Road, Carshalton, Surrey, SM5 2JG (01 661 5000).

Sutton Conservation Group, The Old Rectory, Honeywood Walk, Carshalton, Surrey SM5 3NX (01 669 5025).

London Wildlife Trust (see Barking).

TOWER HAMLETS

The small villages—hence 'hamlets'—outside the City's square mile overtook the meadows, pastures and even woods that once belonged to the Bishop of London. The E edge of the modern borough is the River Lee, to the W of which were the rich pastures of Stepney Marsh including the Isle of Dogs. Here were built the docks that are now being redeveloped. Most of the borough's open space was thereafter found alongside the Lee or the Regent's Canal. The poor conditions of the East End attracted social reformers and political campaigners, but local people too demanded change. The first result of their petitioning was Victoria Park on the N border with Hackney, opened in 1845, linked to it by the Regent's Canal. Similar pressures led to the development of a new park at Mile End during the 1980s. City farms have been a popular development in the borough, most taking their inspiration from the Mudchute on the Isle of Dogs started in the 1970s. An undertow of support for nature conservation has resulted in a number of sites being saved, such as St Jude's Nature Garden.

1   Old Ford Island

Fish Island, Dace Road, E3 (TR 374840).
TWA.
Approach   From footbridge over the Lee Navigation.
Summary   A wedge of scrub and meadow lies beside the Northern Outfall Sewer.
Nature interest   The meadow and neutral grassland is rich in herbs such as salad burnet and St John's wort, much appreciated by the 16 species of butterfly so far recorded on the reserve which include the notable small copper.
Management   LWT aims to maintain the grasslands.
Interpretation   Nil on site.
Access   Restricted.
Contact   LWT.

2   Regent's Canal, Hertford Union Canal, Meith Gardens

Regent's Canal towpath (TQ 358833).
TWA; BWB. 6km.
Approach   The Hertford Union and Regent's Canal can be seen from Victoria Park.
Summary   The relatively clean water of the canals has contributed to wateredge and aquatic vegetation.
History   The Regent's Canal was opened in 1820 with the Hertford Union Branch opening some 10 years later.
Nature interest   The footpath is wooded in places, especially beside Victoria Park, so that the colonising sycamore, elm and ash meet exotic oaks and the usual rye grass of recreational grounds. Squeezing from walls and the canal banks species like wild angelica mix with rarities like hemlock water-dropwort or the vigorous colonisers found in many of London's now increasingly threatened 'wasteland sites'. Notable species like hornwort, arrowhead and water starwort can be found as the Hertford Union meets the Lee in the N, close to the Old Ford Island reserve. Meith Gardens on the W edge of Regent's Canal is a mix of small scale marshes and meadows.

Management Meith Gardens and canal project work are managed by LWT.
Interpretation Nil on site.
Access The canal towpath is open to the public.
Contact LWT.

3 St Jude's Nature Park

Middleton Street, E2 (TQ 359830).
LB Tower Hamlets. 0.5ha .
Approach From St Jude's Road behind the Raine's Foundation School.
Summary A popular small reserve particularly useful for school visits.
History One of the earliest of London's nature gardens, it was laid out in 1980.
Nature interest These small sites are often begun when an area of colonised wasteland or gardens are saved. However, new management can sometimes overwhelm the original habitat usually by tree or seed planting. The main feature of this site is the pond which attracts both human pond dippers and aquatic life.
Management The park is managed by the Tower Hamlets Environment Trust (THEI) which has a warden on site.
Interpretation THEI.
Access Open to the public.
Contact THEI, Spitalfields Centre, Hanbury Street, EI (01 377 0481).

4 Tower Hamlets Cemetery

Southern Grove, E3 (TQ 370823).
LB Tower Hamlets. 11ha.
Approach Ropery Street entrance.
Summary The largest area of woodland in the borough lies S of the London Hospital.
History This private Victorian cemetery which opened in 1841 was taken over by the GLC in 1966 which began some landscaping work before passing ownership to the borough when the GLC was abolished. Rumours have, for years, led many to hope that this will become a nature reserve but recent careless work in the course of removing gravestones with a bulldozer, chosen as a cheap management technique, is not felt to augur well.
Nature interest Areas of landscaping and planting were undertaken by the GLC partly as a result of the need to make the unsure ground safe. Long meadows and secondary woodland of mostly sycamore and ash attract birds which have their own fenced sanctuary in the SW.
Interpretation Nil on site.
Access Open to the public.
Contact Cemetery office (01 980 4414) or Poplar Neighbourhood One Stop Shop, Bromley Public Hall, Bow Road, E3 (01 981 2522).

Further information

LB Tower Hamlets, Neighbourhood Offices, c/o Town Hall, Patriot Square, E2 (01 980 4831).
London Wildlife Trust (see Barking).

WALTHAM FOREST

Both the E and W borders of the borough contain some of London's much-altered Essex landscape. Though dominated by the presence, and taking its name from, the ancient Forest of Waltham, a large portion of which is Epping Forest, little woodland habitat has been retained within the Greater London boundary. The river Ching, which drains from High Beach in the forest proper, provides a long length of Waltham Forest's E border. Separate sections of Epping Forest survive as far S as Higham's Park. The W border is the river Lee, the ancient course of which is still shown on maps meandering through the Walthamstow Reservoirs. Most open space is concentrated on these borders.

1 Ainslie Wood

Ainslie Wood Road, E4 (TQ 377920).
LB Waltham Forest. 1.75ha.
Approach   Three entrances exist—Royston Road, Woodside Gardens and Underwood Road.
Summary   Associated with Larks Wood to the NE, the reserve is ancient woodland bordered on the N by sports pitches.
History   Larks Wood itself was part of Epping Forest although this cluster of small woods have been separated from the main area of woodland for 300 years, 20C housing replacing farmland.
Nature interest   Mixed oak and hornbeam woodland with a boundary ditch along its N edge even with considerable disturbance provides cover for tawny owl, blackcap and even spotted flycatcher.
Management   LWT hopes to control the adverse effects of heavy recreational pressure and embark on woodland management.
Interpretation   Leaflet from LWT.
Access   Open to the public.
Contact   LWT.

2 Epping Forest to Higham's Park and Walthamstow Forest

Bury Road, E4 for Epping; Oak Hill, Woodford Green for Walthamstow Forest.
Corporation of the City of London. 2,430ha; 52ha.
Approach   A walk out of Greater London into Essex along the Centenary Walk forms a journey of 15 miles from Manor Park in the S to Epping Underground station.
Summary   As the land rises to the gravel-topped hills of Essex, Epping Forest, with its woods and grassy clearings, begins to dominate. Only a small area pierces the Greater London boundary at Pole Hill, a vantage point for viewing the valley of the river Lee as it descends to the Thames. Nearby is the grassland surrounding the Queen's Hunting Lodge, which in fact was an open observation gallery. Higham's Park and Walthamstow Forest were once continuous with Epping and show many of the features of this shared past.
History   Once known as the Forest of Waltham, Epping (the name is first found recorded in 1662) was one of six Essex hunting forests declared in the 12C. Commoners retained various rights to wood and grazing in the woodland and pasture which were most seriously

threatened in the middle of the 19C. By then many acres had succumbed to piecemeal enclosure, but it was the attempt of the local squire (also the rector) to take 1,000 acres to sell as small building plots, that spurred the elderly labourer Thomas Willingale to protest. In 1865 he was determined to renew the annual common rights, much to the annoyance of the squire who had arranged a drinking party instead.

Eventually Thomas and his two sons gained the support of the Commons Preservation Society and the City of London and succeeded in taking the squire to court. In the subsequent Epping Forest Act of 1878 the area was saved. Even sections that had formerly been enclosed were returned, including Walthamstow Forest. The act was one of the first to declare that the land should be managed to protect its 'natural' aspect.

Nature interest   The Forest is a mix of grassland and woodland with 150 ponds, assorted streams, heath and marsh. The SSSI is famous for the strange forms of 400 year pollarded hornbeams and the towering beeches. The gravelly hill tops support the beech and birch, while lower slopes contain oak and hornbeam, as in Walthamstow Forest. Over 300 flowering species have been found, a reflection of the size and variation of habitat in this large tract of countryside. Ferns and fungi have their niches in the damp environment provided by wet flushes and streams flowing through the woods. In clearings and especially at the S tip of the forest proper at Chingford Plain, part of which is managed as a golf course, acid grassland can be found.

At Pole Hill dyer's greenweed grows, while along the banks of the Ching stitchwort and foxgloves flourish. A wide range of wildlife occupies Epping, including over a 100 species of bird and many invertebrates. Amphibians may settle now that ponds are beginning to be managed after years of dumping and neglect. The area is perhaps best known for fallow deer.

No such large mammals occur in Walthamstow Forest in the S but many plant species and features are held in common with Epping. Damp flushes allow wavy-hair grass and rushes to grow with oak contributing to the canopy. Field maple and the rare wild service tree are found in the NW of the wood. Both Epping and Walthamstow contain young woodland. In the case of the former this is often in the form of birch colonising former grass or heathland. The rare heather, cross-leaved heath and the more obvious gorse and broom could well succeeed to woodland if management of the land does not include some scrub clearance.

Management   Epping Forest is managed by a team of 12 workers under the guidance of the corporation and verderers.

Interpretation   The Queen's Hunting Lodge is a museum with many displays about the history and management of Epping Forest, while the Epping Forest Conservation Centre at High Beach, opened in 1970, is run by the Field Studies Council.

Access   Open to the public.

Contact   Epping Forest Conservation Centre, High Beach (01 508 7714); Friends of Epping Forest, 39 Smeaton Road, Woodford Bridge, London IG8 8BD.

3   Walthamstow Marshes

Spring Hill, Clapton, E5 (TQ 350887, 372960).
Lee Valley Regional Park Authority. 32.5ha.

Approach   Via the towpath which runs along the W edge of the marshes and continues N to the reservoirs.

Summary   A wedge of alluvial meadows separated from the reservoirs by the Coppermill Stream is ideally seen from the towpath which provides views of the open flat landscape, brimming with water-loving plants.

History   This is the last area of the river Lee's once wide freshwater marshes long since destroyed by drainage or gravel extraction. When plans were announced for gravel digging in the late 1970s, the Save the Marshes Campaign argued against the destruction of the last marshes of the lower Lee Valley. Following a public inquiry in 1981, when the GLC supported the Campaign against LVRPA and both the neighbouring borough councils, the site was saved and designated an SSSI.

Nature interest   An outstanding count of 340 plant species has been recorded at the marshes including those of grassland, meadow and fen. Reeds, horsetails, many types of sedges, great water grass, comfrey, silverweed and meadowsweet are only a few of the wetland flora noted. The rare Roesel's bush cricket and the emperor dragonfly have been found here as have over 40 bird species such as avocet, lapwing, greenshank and wheatear.

Management   The marshes are now managed by the LVRPA which cuts the vegetation in summer and allows grazing until the spring.

Interpretation   Guided tours are undertaken by the LVRPA and a leaflet is available from the authority.

Access   Open to the public, although a number of sanctuary areas protect the habitat from too much disturbance.

Contact   LVRPA.

4   Walthamstow Reservoirs

Ferry Lane, Tottenham, N17 (TQ 352900).
TWA. 133ha.

Approach   Forest Road cuts across W–E the cluster of reservoirs and footpaths from Coppermill in the S lead between them.

Summary   An extensive area of open water divided between Hackney on the W and Waltham Forest in the E. With the Walthamstow Marshes to the S this is one of London's most important stretches of open water.

History   The dozen or so reservoirs which lie on the Essex border were constructed from the 1850s until the First World War.

Nature interest   The shallow, shelved reservoirs have the unusual feature of a number of small islands which are famous for the heronry they support. Other breeding birds including great crested grebe, pochard and shoveler, which find much of London's river edges unsuitable, can be found nesting here. However, it is for the large flocks of migrating birds that the reservoirs are most well known, which have resulted in the area being designated an SSSI.

Interpretation   Nil on site; leaflets available from the LVRPA.

Access   Open to the public.

Contact   LVRPA.

Further information

LB Waltham Forest, Town Hall, Forest Road, E17 (01 527 5544).
Lee Valley Regional Park Authority (see Hackney).
London Wildlife Trust (see Barking).

WANDSWORTH

This large London borough, which looks like a jagged tooth along the S bank of the Thames, is split down the middle by the river Wandle. Nowhere along its length is there any concession made to the river. No park is allowed to be influenced by its presence although some river-edge habitat can be found just as the Wandle escapes the land and enters the Thames at Bell Creek near the old gas works.

Woodland touches Tooting Bec Common in the S where the railway slices through it, providing a slim ribbon of wildlife habitat which then runs through Wandsworth Common and along other lines S of Battersea Park. A good inheritance of common land has been subjected to the rigours of park-style management although the potential for change can be seen at Wandsworth Common.

1 Battersea Park

Albert Bridge Road, Carriage Drive, SW11 (TQ 280773).
LB Wandsworth. 80ha.
Approach   Fenced entirely around its border, the park can be entered from formal gates on both its W and E sides and in the SE opposite the Queenstown roundabout.
Summary   The park has a number of features including ornamental flowerbeds, a large lake and a small nature reserve developed from a former leaf dump now called 'Mist's Pitch'.
History   Battersea Fields were gained from the Thames in the 16C by embanking and used for a variety of purposes which began to include rowdy gatherings. It was an attempt to prevent these that led to their acquisition in the 1840s for a public park. Infill to raise the low-lying field came from the Victoria Docks extension to the E of London and the innovative design which gave the park its formal integrity was the work of Sir James Penethorne. The park was opened in 1864.
Nature interest   The main focus of interest is the reserve named after an enthusiastic local naturalist and keen recorder of the park's wildlife, Brian Mist. Butterflies are particularly abundant in Mist's Pitch. Birds are also attracted to the recently desilted lake with its large false boulders. Shelduck, pochard and great crested grebe have been recorded among the more numerous park familiars.
Management   The reserve is managed by Brian Mist to enhance its wildlife value.
Interpretation   Nil on site.
Access   Open access when the park is open.
Contact   Park Office (01 871 6347).

2 Wandsworth Common

Spencer Park, Bolingbroke Grove, SW18 (TQ 274743).
LB Wandsworth. 70ha.
Approach   An open common, it can be entered anywhere along its perimeter.
Summary   A much divided flattish common, it is the area known as the 'Scope' which attracts wildlife, the rest being mowed grassland with the usual standard trees.
History   The common once touched both Wimbledon and Clapham but many acres were lost to encroachment and enclosure in the late

18C. Once again the Spencer family as lords of the manor allowed this and extensive gravel extraction which aroused public concern. By 1877 the Metropolitan Board of Works had begun to manage the common which included Neal's Farm, W of the railway, which continued until the last war.

Nature interest   The SW corner under a new management policy is developing into gorse and tree scrub of importance to birds and butterflies which, with a new pond intended to support amphibians, could show other parks how wildlife habitat may be accommodated.

Management   The common is managed by LB Wandsworth, volunteers assisting in the SW corner.

Interpretation   A nature study centre lies close to Dorlcote Road in the area once belonging to Neal's Farm.

Access   Open to the public.

Contact   LB Wandsworth.

Further information

LB Wandsworth, Technical Services, Town Hall, Wandsworth High Street, London SW18 2PU (01 871 6347).
London Wildlife Trust (see Barking).

WESTMINSTER

The City of Westminster was the Crown's answer to the independence of the City of London. Famous for the church on Thorney Island, now Westminster Abbey, the area was once greatly influenced by two of London's lost rivers, the Tyburn and the Westbourne which channelled their way from the hills of Hampstead to meet the Thames. The borough's open space derives from Henry VIII's efforts to reserve the land W of his court as royal forest. The surviving parks were protected from the tide of development by the Crown from Charles I onwards allowing the public to visit, keeping eventually only the grounds of Buckingham Palace for private use. Although these have a large population of waterfowl, the often foul water and sparsely vegetated banks of their lakes are a poor substitute for the former rivers.

1 Green Park, St James's Park, Hyde Park and Kensington Gardens

Kensington Gore, Piccadilly.
DoE. 312ha.
Approach   Formal entrances occur at regular points around all these parks.
Summary   These are recreational grounds, with St James's retaining the more intimate atmosphere, which are all similarly used with jogging, dog walking and feeding grey squirrels or ducks some of the most popular activities.
History   Many acres of this area belonged to the Manor of Hyde which formed part of the estates of the Abbey of Westminster gained by the Crown after the Reformation. St James's Park was used as a nursery for deer ready for their release into the new hunting grounds, and long after Charles I had first opened the reduced area these animals could still be seen. In 1851 the Great Exhibition was held in the Crystal Palace built along Kensington Gore to house not only vast numbers of manufactured goods but also the trees and birds belonging to the acres of former park.
Nature interest   Wildlife is mostly confined to birds attracted to the open water (and by public feeding) at both St James's Park and Hyde Park, nearly 100 species having been recorded. Along the Serpentine, LWT has created an artificial kingfisher bank in the hope of attracting these choosey birds back into the heart of London. A bird box scheme is also envisaged for the future.
Management   Park-style management is now influenced by the needs of wildlife, especially birds.
Interpretation   Nil on site.
Access   Open to the public.
Contact   DoE (see Richmond).

2 Regent's Park and Primrose Hill

Regent's Park Road, Prince Albert Road, NW1 (TQ 282827, 278837).
DoE. 191ha, 25ha.
Approach   Formal entrances around the orbital road give access to Regent's Park. Primrose Hill may be entered from Regent's Park Road.

Summary   An ornamental park famous for its theatre, boating lake and Queen Mary Garden devoted to roses.

History   Like the other royal parks, Regent's Park was part of the agricultural lands seized by Henry VIII. It was managed for pasture and hay until John Nash was asked by the Prince Regent to design his commercially-inspired park, the pattern for later 19C city parks.

Nature interest   This is centred on the heronry on an island in the boating lake which is thought to be in decline. Primrose Hill and its grassy banks gained notoriety when DoE staff refused to allow the London Wildlife Trust at its launch in 1981 to include the planting of a few examples of the park's namesake where not a single plant existed. Some time later and away from the public gaze, the staff did create a primrose bank.

Management   Nil for conservation.

Interpretation   Nil on site.

Access   Open to the public.

Contact   DoE (see Richmond).

Further information

City of Westminster, City Hall, Victoria Street, SW1E 6QP (01 798 1145).
London Wildlife Trust (see Barking).

SOUTH

BRIGHTON

The favourite resort of the Prince Regent, Brighton is sandwiched between the sea and the South Downs—once a small agricultural and fishing community called Brigthelmstone. Outside London, Brighton is the largest town in the SE of England with a population of a quarter of a million within the conurbation. The formation of Greater Brighton was largely the result of the energy and foresight of Sir Herbert Carden (1867–1941) a local solicitor and councillor. Carden realised the need to encircle the town with a green belt of Downland and he persuaded the council to buy over 4,900 hectares at a cost of about £800,000. This has restricted building on the Downs and left access for wildlife into the town centre.

1   Brighton Marina

Black Rock, Brighton (TQ 335033).
Brighton Marina Company Ltd. 51ha.
Approach   Buses along Marine Parade.
Summary   The largest marina in Britain with berths for 1,900 boats.
History   The harbour and berths were completed in 1978. Bought by Brighton council, it was subsequently sold to Brent Walker who began constructing the Marina Village in 1986. With the inspiration of local garage owner and yachtsman, Henry Cohen, Brighton marina is near completion with its village square and large hypermarket. The harbour is formed by a huge breakwater of 110 caissons, each one 12 metres high and weighing 600 tons. The chalk cliff above the 'undercliff walk' to Rottingdean is diverse in its geological strata, fauna and flora.
Nature interest   The water of the harbour is surprisingly rich in marine life while the breakwaters are a popular spot for bird watchers, particularly during the spring and autumn migrations. Kittiwakes, cranes, skuas, purple sandpiper, velvet scoter, smew, black tern, roseate tern, shag, gannet and hoopoe have all been seen here in recent years.
Interpretation   Nil on site.
Access   There is public access to parts of the inner harbour and the E and W breakwaters.
Contact   Brighton Marina Company Limited, Brighton Marina Village, Brighton.

2   Castle Hill

Castle Hill National Nature Reserve (TQ 367074).
Brighton BC. 45ha.
Approach   Buses to Woodingdean from Brighton.
Summary   Unimproved chalk grassland and scrub.
History   Castle Hill lies to the SW of Kingston Village and on the edge of Woodingdean. Part of this beautiful and peaceful area of the Downs is an NNR. It is also an SSSI and part of the Downs an AONB (Area of Outstanding Natural Beauty). It is easy to reach from the

B2123 Rottingdean—Falmer road by the W path from which views
to the E can be seen of the white cliffs of the Seven Sisters. Below
to the W runs the parallel Juggs Lane, an old footpath into Lewes
over the Downs, along which local women carried the catches of
fish in 'juggs' on their heads from Rottingdean to Lewes to sell in
the market. The site was declared an NNR in 1975.

Nature interest   Common spotted and fragrant orchids can be
found in abundance in some years with field fleawort, sainfoin,
lesser centuary, chalk milkwort and round-headed campion. The
reserve is also noted for its butterflies among which can be found
the small blue, the grizzled and dingy skipper. The most common
breeding birds are white-throat, linnet and yellowhammer; turtle
dove, whinchat and corn bunting can also be seen.

Management   The reserve is leased to the NCC. Scrub is cleared
at intervals and cattle graze the reserve during the winter.

Interpretation   A leaflet is available from the NCC.

Access   A permit is required off the public bridleway.

Contact   Nature Conservancy Council, The Old Candlemakers,
West Street, Lewes.

3 Devil's Dyke

Devil's Dyke Road (TQ 258111).
Brighton BC. 76.9ha.

Approach   No. 24 bus from Brighton during summer months.

Summary   This spectacular downland coomb or dry valley and
prehistoric hill fort site with unimproved chalk grassland, scrub
and woodland is an SSSI.

History   Eight kilometres NW of Brighton, the Dyke is a deep
ravine with steeply sloping sides cut into the Downs. Legend has it
that the Dyke was dug into the chalk by the Devil to allow the sea
to rush in to submerge the churches of the Weald. The ravine is
obviously water worn, yet unlike other downland watercourses is
not open to the sea but closed at either end. Popular in the
Victorian era, with a rail link from Brighton, it boasted a hotel,
cable car, funicular railway and other attractions. During the last
war most of these features were destroyed but the dyke still
affords spectacular views from the top and has a cafe and čar park.
It was bought by Brighton Corporation in 1928 for £9,000.

Nature interest   Autumn gentian, carline thistle, squinancywort,
devil's bit scabious, small scabious and common spotted and pyramidal orchids flourish in the grassland with juniper and buckthorn
appearing among the scrub and moschatel in the woodland at the
bottom of the downs. Invertebrates to be found here include the
round-mouthed snail, small copper, common blue and speckled
wood butterflies, the six-spot burnet moth and the speckled bush
cricket. Birds commonly seen are green woodpeckers, goldfinches,
long-tailed tits, swallows and house martins.

Management   Mechanical clearance and burning have been
used to reduce the areas of scrub and sheep grazing has been
reintroduced to maintain the short downland turf.

Introduction   Nil on site.

Access   Open at all times.

Contact   Brighton BC Parks and Recreation Department.

4 Lewes Road and Bear Road Cemeteries

Lewes Road and Bear Road, Brighton (TQ 321058).
Brighton BC; Brighton and Preston Cemetery. 38ha.
Approach   Buses along Lewes Road and up Bear Road.
Summary   Victorian cemeteries and crematoria in a wooded valley with some semi-natural chalk grassland, flower beds and ornamental ponds.
History   This area was first consecrated as a burial ground in 1851 by which time the parish churchyards had become full.
Nature interest   Foxes are often encountered here as well as common lizards and both common frogs and toads breed in the ponds. Kestrels nest here and green and greater spotted woodpeckers, chiffchaffs and long-tailed tits can be seen as well as winter visitors such as fieldfare and redwing. In the Lewes Road cemetery, areas of chalk grassland, where the turf has completely covered the gravestones, support small scabious, fairy flax, mouse-ear hawkweed, common rockrose and autumn ladies tresses, while in the Brighton and Preston Cemetery great mullein, primrose and small toadflax can be found.
Management   Trees felled in the 1987 storm are still being cleared. The council-owned cemeteries are mown frequently and much tidied while the privately owned Brighton and Preston cemetery is much wilder and overgrown in parts and is managed by strimming and the use of weedkillers.
Interpretation   A historical, geological and natural history trail of the Extra Mural Cemetery is available from the Booth Museum of Natural History.
Access   Open to the public between the times stated on noticeboards at the gates.
Contact   Brighton and Preston Cemetery, Hartington Road, Brighton; Woodvale, Lewes Road, Brighton; Downs Crematorium, Bear Road, Brighton.

5 Moulsecoomb Wild Park

Lewes Road, Brighton (TQ 332080).
Brighton BC. 36.4ha.
Approach   Buses along Lewes Road.
Summary   Largely unimproved downland valley with chalk grassland, scrub, woodland and recreational areas.
History   Bought by Brighton Corporation and opened to the public in 1925, the park was never set out in a formal way but was left, as its name implies, in a wild state. Described as a 'glorious stretch of wild, almost rugged downland with deep valleys and furze-clad heights', the N slopes of Hollingbury became Moulsecoomb Wild Park. It is a remarkable feature to be found existing only three kilometres from Brighton town centre. At the top of the hill, 150 metres above sea level, is Hollingbury Camp, an Iron Age hill fort.
Nature interest   The sheltered S-facing slopes make this an excellent site for butterflies such as the chalkhill blue, the brown argus and the green hairstreak. Their larvae feed on common rockrose and horseshoe vetch growing in the scrub clearings. Orchids such as the common spotted and early purple grow here and in the very short turf the frog orchid can be found. Other chalk-loving plants here are columbine, common gromwell, yellow-wort and ploughman's spike-

nard. Among the birds to be seen here are cuckoo, linnet, spotted flycatcher, goldfinch, bullfinch, willow warbler and ring-necked parakeet. Until quite recently nightingales were nesting in the ever-decreasing scrub.

Management   Regular scrub clearance is undertaken to maintain a variety of habitats.

Interpretation   A nature trail has been set out and a trail guide is available from Brighton BC.

Access   Open at all times.

Contact   Brighton BC Parks and Recreation Department.

6   Roedean to Saltdean Undercliff Walk

Roedean, Rottingdean and Saltdean (TQ 344031 to 382018).
Brighton BC. 4km.

Approach   Buses along A259 coast road. Entrance to undercliff walk at Roedean, St Dunstan's, Rottingdean and Saltdean.

Summary   Chalk cliffs, mobile shingle beach and extensive rockpools.

History   The undercliff walk and sea wall was built by unemployed men from Sussex, Wales and the N of England during the Depression. The bed of the extension of Volk's electric railway can still be seen on the rocks. A train on stilts, known as 'daddy-long-legs', ran in the sea from Black Rock to Rottingdean.

Nature interest   Plants at home on the crumbling sheer chalk cliffs here include hoary stock, lesser sea spurrey, rock samphire, sea lavender, sea heath and thrift. Fulmars nest on these cliffs and other birds to be seen here are rock pipits, oystercatchers and black redstarts. The great expanse of rock pools, exposed at low tide, harbours butterfish, shore rocklings, blue-rayed and slipper limpets, chitons, beadlet anemones, bristleworms, sand masons, porcelain and hermit crabs, periwinkles, top shells, piddocks and prawns.

Management   None.

Interpretation   Leaflet available from Booth Museum of Natural History.

Access   Access along undercliff walk sometimes restricted due to chalk falls and repair to sea wall.

Contact   Booth Museum of Natural History.

7   Stanmer Park and Stanmer Great Wood

Stanmer, Brighton (TQ 343087).
Brighton BC. 258ha.

Approach   Buses along Lewes Road. Nearest station is Falmer.

Summary   Semi-natural woodland, plantations, chalk grassland and recreational areas.

History   Approximately six and a half kilometres N of Brighton, Stanmer lies off the A27 to Lewes. There are footpaths through the park and woodland. The name is derived from the Anglo-Saxon word for 'a pool of stones', referring to the large stones which surround the pond beside the flint church. The estate and house were owned by the Pelham family of Lewes from the early 1700s. During the last war the depleted estate of some 2000 hectares was used as a battle training ground and in 1947 sold to Brighton Corporation. Sussex University now occupies 80 hectares of the estate, the rest being preserved as farmland and a public park. The village of Stanmer lies N of the chuch and contains 18C and 19C buildings and was one of the last 'working villages'. There is a small rural museum run by a local preservation society.

Nature interest   The mixed-age woodland of broadleaved trees and conifers attracts a variety of woodland birds such as blackcap, treecreeper, nuthatch, goldcrest, chiffchaff and green and greater spotted woodpeckers. Many different species of fungi can be found in the wood in autumn. Adder's tongue fern grow here as well as flowering plants such as twayblade, yellow archangel, pyramidal orchid, round-headed rampion, harebell, field scabious, dwarf thistle and autumn ladies tresses. Fine displays of bluebells can be seen in spring.

Management   The Great Wood, badly damaged in the storm of 1987, is in the process of being cleared though in some areas fallen trees will probably be left where they are. Some replanting has already begun. Some of the chalk grassland is only mown once a year to allow the flowers to bloom and set seed.

Interpretation   Trail guide from the Parks and Recreation Department.

Access   Open at all times.

Contact   Parks and Recreation Department; Stanmer Preservation Society, 3 The Deeside, Patcham, Brighton.

Further information

Brighton Borough Council, Parks and Recreation Department, Moulsecoomb Place, Lewes Road, Brighton.

Booth Museum of Natural History, 194 Dyke Road, Brighton.

Sussex Trust for Nature Conservation, Woods Mill, Shoreham Road, Henfield, W Sussex BN5 92D (0273 492630).

Brighton Urban Wildlife Group, c/o STNC.

Acknowledgement   Text written by Anna Borsey, Tony Spiers and Lavender Jones.

BRISTOL

Bristol is arguably S England's most dramatic city, lying on limestone hills through which the Avon Gorge slices towards the Bristol Channel. Its once flourishing docks are now an enormous recreational water area, surrounded by refurbished warehouses and studiously picturesque modern development. Upstream of the city centre, the Avon provides a deep valley where further new construction is replacing former industry. The largest of its tributaries, the River Frome, has created one of the area's many side valleys—Siston Brook in the Kingswood district being the location of the Avon Wildlife Trust's Willsbridge Mill field centre. Diverse habitats range from the Leigh Woods overlooking the Gorge to the fields of Dundry Slopes, also including the wet meadows of Lawrence Weston Moor on the Severnwards side of the King's Weston Hill ridge. The city and its neighbouring districts have been well served by the efforts of the Avon Wildlife Trust, founded in 1980.

1 Avon Gorge

The Portway, BS8 (ST 565731).
Bristol CC.
Approach   Buses to the Downs or Clifton Suspension Bridge.
Summary   The Avon Gorge, spanned by Brunel's Clifton Suspension Bridge, must be Bristol's most famous landmark. The steep rock face, to which rare plants cling precariously side by side with the ever-present rock climbers, contrasts with the densely wooded edge of the Leigh Woods NNR on the W side of the Gorge.
History   The deep gorge, through which the River Avon now runs, was cut in the last Ice Age. When Bristol was an important port the Gorge was a dramatic entrance to the city. In 1836 work started on the Clifton Suspension Bridge and was finished in 1864, and it remains the best viewing point for the Gorge.
Nature interest   The Gorge is internationally famous for its rare plants, but most of these are confined to inaccessible ledges. Some of these plants, however, such as the attractive spiked speedwell and spring cinquefoil, can be seen from public footpaths along with a diverse range of limestone grassland plants. Flower spikes of the parasitic ivy broomrape can be found among the scrub.
Management   The NCC and Bristol city council have cleared considerable areas of scrub which were overshadowing the rarer plants and the limestone grassland is cut annually.
Interpretation   Nil.
Access Open at all times.

2 Badocks Wood

Lakewood Road, BS10 (ST 580777).
Bristol CC.
Approach   Buses to Southmead or Westbury on Trym.
Summary   Badocks Wood lies in NW Bristol in a steeply sided valley through which flows the River Trym. The sides of the valley are clothed in trees, although in places Dutch elm disease has left gaps in the canopy and the tree growth is now more scrubby.
History   There is every reason to believe that there has always been woodland here, as the valley is unsuitable for cultivation or develop-

ment. Badocks Wood is a good example of a wood which has become encapsulated by urban development.

Nature interest   A good variety of woodland plants are found below the tree canopy, including yellow archangel, wood anemone and wood melic. Along the banks of the stream, water forget-me-not and water figwort can be found.

Management   A community initiative was set up here by BTCV to improve access around the wood and increase its value to wildlife, but much of the work is now carried out by Bristol city council. A footpath has been constructed and selective thinning and replanting has improved the variety of trees found in the wood.

Interpretation   Information and a leaflet on Badocks Wood is available from Bristol CC.

Access   Open at all times.

Contact   Parks Manager, Bristol CC.

3   Blaise Castle

Kingsweston Road, BS10 (ST 560783).
Bristol CC.

Approach   Buses along Kingsweston Road or Henbury Road.

Summary   The centrepiece of a green swathe dominating the skyline of NW Bristol, the woods and rock faces of Blaise Castle provide a dramatic landscape in a busy urban area. Large numbers of people come to walk in the woods and the spectacular gorge cut by the River Trym through the limestone hills; the grassland areas are popular picnic sites.

History   The surviving buildings at Blaise Castle date back to the 18C, but the two small Iron Age hill forts testify to the area's longer history. Records suggest that much of the site has always been wooded and there is evidence of old coppice systems. Landscaping of the estate began in the 18C and this included the planting of exotic trees and shrubs.

Nature interest   Despite suffering from the landscape modifications and present day disturbance, the woodlands are of high quality. Widespread plants include wood anemone and sanicle, as well as rarer ones such as green hellibore. The secretive hawfinch possibly breeds here and other woodland birds include nuthatch and woodpeckers. The grasslands range from damp meadows with cuckoo flower to dry downland with wild thyme and horseshoe vetch.

Management   Bristol city council, which manages the estate, is improving woodland quality by the gradual removal of non-native trees such as holm oak and by increasing the diversity of woodland structure.

Interpretation   A guide to Blaise Castle Estate is available from the council.

Access   Open at all times.

Contact   Bristol CC.

4   Brandon Hill Nature Park

Jacobs Wells Road, BS8 (ST 579728).
Bristol CC.

Approach   Buses to Queens Road or Park Street, easy walking distance from central Bristol.

Summary   Brandon Hill Nature Park is an interesting and unusual habitat creation project set in one of Bristol's finest and most historic parks. Set in the centre of Bristol, commanding fine views of the city, Brandon Hill is a very popular area of the city. The nature park, with its wildlife ponds, wildflower meadow, heathland, woodland and butterfly garden, provides a complete contrast with the formal Victorian-style landscaping of the rest of the park.

History   Brandon Hill is one of the oldest parks in Bristol, dating back to 1174 when it became part of the hermitage dedicated to St Brendan. The public were given freedom to walk over the hill in the 16C and later it played an important part in defending the city from the Roundheads in the Civil War. The nature park was first proposed by Avon Wildlife Trust in 1980 and since then five acres of the park have been used to show how wildlife habitats can be created in the centre of the city. Avon Wildlife Trust now has its headquarters in the old police station on the W of the park which includes an urban wildlife centre.

Nature interest   The wildlife of the nature park is well documented and each year new species are discovered. Many species of butterfly are found in large numbers including small tortoiseshell, meadow brown and small and large skipper. The ponds attract frogs, toads and newts as well as common species of dragonfly and damselfly. Many bird species and a family of foxes have taken up residence in the woodland and scrub.

Management   Management of the nature park is quite intensive to keep it attractive to visitors and improve the park for wildlife. The meadow is cut annually for hay, but also each year more wildflowers are planted. The butterfly garden is kept stocked with nectar-rich flowers and a new footpath system now links this with the woodland where a variety of trees and shrubs have been planted. In 1987 a small heathland was created using native and non-native heathers, gorse, broom and other typical heathland plants.

Interpretation   A trail guide is available from AWT.

Access   Open at all times.

Contact   Avon Wildlife Trust.

5   Bristol Docks

Close to The Centre, BS1.

Approach   Within easy walking distance of central Bristol.

Summary   Bristol owes much of its heritage to its history as a seaport, and although commercial traffic has greatly declined, the docks are a reminder of the past. The docks vary greatly in character, from active industrial land and derelict sites to prestigious new housing developments and recreational areas.

History   The docks were at their busiest in the early part of the last century. Since the decline in commercial traffic, they have become an important recreational site—attractions include an art gallery, a media centre and an industrial museum.

Nature interest   The plantlife of the docks reflects their history, with a wide diversity of non-native species introduced by the grain stores and seed-crushing mills. These plants range from fig trees to small annual grasses which spring up anywhere in the area. The docks attract common birds, with herring and lesser-black backed gulls nesting on nearby roofs, where in winter starling and pied wagtail roosts provide easy pickings for sparrowhawks. Hard weather in winter may bring in less usual waterbirds such as rare grebes and there is always a chance of spotting a black redstart.

Management Management for wildlife here has been restricted to providing floating platforms for birds which attract mute swans in particular.

Interpretation Nil.

Access Open at all times, regular boat-trips during the summer.

6 Clifton and Durdham Downs

Blackboy Hill, BS9 (ST 565745).
Bristol CC.

Approach Buses to the Downs.

Summary Wildlife co-exists with recreation at one of Bristol's favourite play grounds. Known to Bristolians as the Downs, this area is spacious and open with scattered trees and dense scrub. Much of the area is used for football.

History The Downs are common land and commoners' rights are preserved by bringing sheep onto the Downs every 11 years. In 1860 an act of parliament laid down the right of public access to the Downs, and the practice of sheep grazing was maintained until the 1920s when the increasing number of people and cars drove the sheep away. The Victorian years saw much 'beautification' with widespread planting of trees and shrubs.

Nature interest When sheep grazed the Downs, they were one of the classical botanical sites of Britain. Few plants have survived the management practices of recent years, although the occasional cowslip and common spotted orchid still appear. Former lead workings contain scraps of rich limestone turf. Resident birds are scarce but spring and autumn bring a variety of resting migrants.

Management Since the last war, the Downs have been closely mown throughout the year and depressions have been tipped in. Fertilizers and herbicides have not been widely used, fortunately, giving hope that some of the Downs' former botanical riches still survive.

Interpretation Nil.

Access Open at all times.

Contact Parks Manager, Bristol CC.

7 Coombe Brook Valley (The Gosey)

Between Mayfield Park South and Holly Lodge Road, BS5 (ST 625748).
Bristol CC.

Approach Buses to Whitefield Road, Lodge Causeway or Fishponds Road.

Summary The steep sides of this small valley, known locally as the Gosey, are clothed in dense scrub and have been a popular unofficial playground for generations of children. Compared with the nearby flat unimaginative playing fields, the Gosey makes a welcome contrast and is an important oasis for local wildlife.

History The Gosey is one of the only stretches of this small brook which has not been culverted and the valley filled in and landscaped. The valley was probably cleared of its natural vegetation many years ago and then left untouched, resulting in the mature scrub which is here today.

Nature interest   The mature scrub, mostly of hawthorne and elder, and trees such as ash and sycamore provide an important habitat for wild animals in this valley. Foxes, butterflies and a wide variety of common birds are found here.

Management   The Frome Valley group of Avon Wildlife Trust has been managing the Gosey since 1982. Selective thinning of some of the over-mature hawthorn and sycamore has been followed by the planting of a wide variety of trees and shrubs. Extensive rubbish clearance and the provision of a footpath and bridges have helped improve the appearance of the valley and increased its use by local people.

Interpretation   Information is available from AWT.

Access   Open at all times.

Contact   Avon Wildlife Trust.

8   Crabtree Slipwood and Horseshoe Bend

The Portway, BS9 (ST 527767).

Approach   Buses along the Portway.

Summary   Situated downstream of the better-known Avon Gorge, this small complex of sites occupies an attractive position overlooking the lower reaches of the River Avon with open countryside beyond. Although the first impression gained of the area is of lorries thundering past on the A4 and of the nearby industrial complex at Avonmouth, it can be surprisingly tranquil and even the views towards central Bristol give a very rural impression.

History   This area has been greatly modified by the construction of the Bristol to Avonmouth railway and the A4, both of which follow the river. The building of the road and railway have led to the construction of deep cuttings which have been colonised by a variety of plants.

Nature interest   The most interesting habitats here are the areas of unimproved limestone grassland which are rich in plant species, including the less common wild liquorice and the more common rock rose and yellow wort. The mixture of scrub, woodland and grassland attracts many butterflies, with large numbers of marbled white, common blue and purple hairstreak.

Management   The largest area of grassland is mown annually for hay, and some woodland management work is carried out. The other areas are unmanaged, but the shallow depth of the soil prevents scrub growth in many places.

Interpretation   None.

Access   Crabtree Slipwood, which includes both grassland and woodland, can be reached from the lay-by on the A4 and access is unrestricted. Access to other areas is less easy but the areas can be seen from the road.

Contact   Avon Wildlife Trust.

9   Crox Bottom

Between Hartcliffe Way and Hengrove Way, BS13 (ST 581688). Bristol CC.

Approach   Buses along Hartcliffe Way and Hengrove Way.

Summary   A small park which, on the whole, is traditionally managed. Pigeonhouse Stream runs through Crox Bottom and feeds two small lakes. Slopes of the park are steep and some areas of scrub are dense.
History   Crox Bottom a is typical example of an urban park landscaped over the last 30 years. Lakes have been created and a formal footpath network introduced.
Nature interest   The lakes are the focus of the park's wildlife which attract small numbers of water birds in winter and provide breeding and feeding grounds for a wide variety of dragonflies. Although much of the grassland is unimproved, it is close mown and plants are difficult to see. In 1987 a small area was turfed with wildflower-rich grassland rescued from nearby Hawkfield Meadows. This is to be managed as a traditional hay-meadow and may attract a variety of butterflies.
Management   Crox Bottom is managed by Bristol city council as a formal park. Unfortunately unmown steep banks are being threatened by scrub.
Interpretation   Nil.
Access   Open at all times.

10   Dundry Slopes

S Bristol, BS13 (ST 564664).
Approach   Within easy reach from Hartcliffe and Withywood.
Summary   Dundry Hill is a SW outlier of the Cotswolds which forms a physical barrier to the S expansion of Bristol. There are fine views of the city from the hill and Hartcliffe Community Farm is conveniently nearby. A distinctive feature of Dundry Slopes is the nature of the hedgerows, which are immensely thick and sprawling, like narrow woodlands. Many of them include small streams and a line of springs form small flushes along the hillside.
History   The Slopes now form part of Bristol's green belt.
Nature interest   The fields vary greatly in their wildlife value, some of them having been badly damaged by horse-grazing or by agricultural improvement. The better fields have common-spotted orchids, devils-bit scabious and dyers greenweed and many grassland butterflies are found. The hedges are attractive to birds and woodland plants such as primrose and moschatel can be found while the flushes have ragged robin and sedges.
Management   Horse-grazing has been a problem here and Hartcliffe Community Farm, which manages some of the fields, hopes to lessen these effects by introducing a rotation of grazing animals using cattle and sheep.
Interpretation   Nil.
Access   Open at all times.

11   Frome Valley

Start at Fishponds Road, BS5 (ST 615753).
Bristol CC.
Approach   Buses to Eastville Park or Frenchay.
Summary   The Frome Valley follows the River Frome from the fringe of the city right into Eastville Park near the centre. The valley changes in character along its course, passing through woodland and

grassland at Oldbury Court Estate through to the more traditionally managed Eastville Park with its playing fields and formal flower beds.

History   The history of the Frome Valley is long and varied. Villages developed along the banks of the River Trym which are now part of the City of Bristol. However, this area of Bristol still retains a rural feel. Oldbury Court Estate forms part of the valley and was once a hunting lodge of Kingswood Chase. The house no longer exists but the estate is now owned and managed by the city council. On the left bank of the river was a French prison, built in 1779, housing prisoners in appalling conditions.

Nature interest   The wildlife of the valley varies considerably along the river. Bird life is very rich and dippers, hawfinches and lesser spotted woodpeckers are not uncommon. The woodlands are predominately broadleaved but a number of exotic species have been planted in the past. Woodland plants such as hairy woodrush and early dog violet suggest that at least some parts are ancient.

Management   Little management is carried out apart from general maintenance and grass cutting and the valley could benefit from some management to improve wildlife.

Interpretation   A trail guide for the Frome Valley by the Bristol Naturalists Society is available from the City Museum.

Access   Open at all times.

12   Lawrence Weston Moor

Lawrence Weston Road, BS11 (ST 545790).
Bristol CC.

Approach   Buses along Long Cross.

Summary   The Somerset Levels extend up as far as Bristol and few areas are as well preserved as Lawrence Weston Moor. The Moor is flat, low-lying and wet, being on the flood plain of the Severn Estuary. The small fields are divided by lines of pollarded willows giving a sense of seclusion and the characteristic drainage ditches, known as rhynes, are rich in wild flowers.

History   NW Bristol has suffered very much in the recent past from industrial development at Avonmouth, the construction of the motorway and from large-scale rubbish tipping. The motorway isolated Lawrence Weston Moor from any remaining farmland and for many years it was forgotten.

Nature interest   The wildlife of the Moor varies with the water level. Near the motorway the fields are well drained and contain hay meadow plants such as meadow rue and knapweed. Areas of reed and sedge beds are found in the wetter fields and these provide cover for a variety of birds including snipe. The intermediate fields are dominated by reeds and sedges with many wetland flowers.

Management   AWT leases the site from Bristol city council and has recently introduced a management plan. A hay crop is taken from the drier fields and cattle graze the damper ones. The willows will soon be pollarded and the rhynes cleared on a rotational basis. Trees have been planted to provide a shield from the motorway.

Interpretation   The Trust hopes to formalise the footpath system and provide interpretative material in co-operation with nearby schools.

Access   Open at all times.

Contact   Avon Wildlife Trust.

13 Kingsweston Down

Kingsweston Road, BS9 (ST 550780).
Bristol CC.
Approach   Buses along Kingsweston Road.
Summary   Kingsweston Down is a long ridge of downland surrounded by woods, which in summer is alive with butterflies and ablaze with wildflowers. Despite its hilltop situation, the long expanse of grassland is sheltered by the trees and can be a suntrap. Footpaths criss-cross the Down but it is a surprisingly quiet and tranquil place.
History   There is no evidence of any human occupation of the Down since the Iron Age. The ramparts of an Iron Age hillfort can still be traced at the NE end of the site. The quality of the grassland indicates that it has been traditionally managed for hay or grazing for a considerable number of years.
Nature interest   The limestone grassland is characteristically rich, with plants such as rock-rose and harebell widespread. This richness, and the shelter provided by the surrounding woods, result in large numbers of butterflies. Common grassland species such as common blue and brown argus occur on the Down itself, with purple hairstreak found at the woodland edge.
Management   Kingsweston Down is managed by AWT under an agreement with Bristol city council. An annual hay-cut of alternate halves of the grassland is taken by a local farmer, while the Trust management involves creating bays in the scrub to encourage butterflies.
Interpretation   Information is available from AWT.
Access   Open at all times.
Contact   Avon Wildlife Trust.

14 Moorgrove Wood

Between Kings Weston Road and Windmill Lane, BS10 (ST 555789).
Bristol CC.
Approach   Buses along Kings Weston Road.
Summary   Moorgrove Wood straddles a hilltop among the housing estates of NW Bristol. The wood is dominated by large mature trees, criss-crossed with many footpaths. The dense canopy provides a damp atmosphere where wetland plants flourish around small pools.
History   Woodland has probably always clothed this hill before the expansion of Bristol swallowed up the surrounding area. Though it was left unmanaged for many years, a recent initiative has opened up the wood to the general public.
Nature interest   The range of woodland plants at Moorgrove Wood is wide and in spring the displays of wood anemone and yellow archangel are spectacular. A pond and wet area add further diversity and common valerian and pendulous sedge are among plants found here.
Management   A variety of management work has been carried out recently, including selective thinning of trees, footpath construction and pond clearance.
Interpretation   Nil.
Access   Open at all times.

15 Narroways Junction

Mina Road, BS2 (ST 508751).
British Rail.
Approach   Short walk from St Werberghs City Farm, buses to St Werberghs.
Summary   A small site set in the centre of the city, Narroways Junction has breath-taking views over a large part of Bristol. The mixture of grassland, woodland, wasteland and scrub provide an impressive variety of wildlife in an area where open space is scarce.
History   Once a hill, this site got its name from the three railway lines which have cut through it. One of these lines recently became disused, allowing unofficial access on to the site and making it popular with local people. In 1987 the nearby St Werberghs City Farm obtained a lease from BR to use the site as part of their farm.
Nature interest   The limestone grassland which is found on most of the site is particularly rich with species such as greater knapweed and broomrape common. Butterflies are found here in abundance, with a large population of marbled whites. Common lizards, foxes and slow worms are found in the disused allotments.
Management   St Werberghs City Farm manages the site with wildlife in mind. Grazing of the grassland is carried out using sheep and goats so as not to damage the turf. Thinning of the woodland to diversify the age structure is planned, as are a nature trail and various educational activities.
Interpretation   Contact St Werberghs City Farm for more information.
Access   Open at all times.

16 Stoke Park

Romney Avenue, BS16 (ST 612769).
Frenchay Health Authority.
Approach   Buses to Romney Avenue.
Summary   This large expanse of open space is an important landscape feature of the city, being visible from many parts of Bristol. It leaves a striking impression, with its mixture of woodland and grassland, when driving down the M32 motorway which leads into the city.
History   The large house on Stoke Park dates back to 1563 when it was built by Sir Richard Berkeley to replace the original derelict manor house. The park formed the estate and was landscaped to include the woodlands and rolling grasslands present today. The park and the house are now part of Stoke Park Hospital.
Nature interest   Much of Stoke Park consists of intensively farmed pasture but areas of wildflower rich grassland can be found on the steeper slopes. These contain species such as stemless thistle, devil's bit scabious and salad burnet. Stock are allowed into the woods which have caused some damage. However, many birds can be found, including nightingales and turtle doves.
Management   Little management work is carried out except that necessary to allow cattle to graze the grasslands.
Interpretation   Nil.
Access   Open at all times.

17 Troopers Hill

Troopers Hill Road, BS5 (ST 629731).
Bristol CC.
Approach Buses along Summerhill Road (Upper Bristol Road, A431).
Summary Troopers Hill is bare and windswept, overlooking the River Avon and the wealth of other wildlife sites along its banks. The vegetation is short and trampled except in gullies and on the steep slopes. There are many relics of Troopers Hill's industrial past, including the chimney on the summit.
History Bristol is not often associated with coal mines and foundaries, but it is Bristol's past as a centre of heavy industry which has shaped Troopers Hill. Part of the hill is a sandstone outcrop, an unusual feature in Bristol, and the rest is composed of industrial waste which is over 150 years old. This waste has become colonised with a variety of plants which have spread from the natural hill.
Nature interest The soil on the site is acidic, in contrast with the limestone derived soils which predominate in Bristol. Plants restricted to acid soils, such as heather, are found here and nowhere else in Bristol as is the locally scarce butterfly, the grayling. Most of the plants are small and insignificant, but botanists and non-botanists alike cannot fail to be impressed by the lonely atmosphere of Troopers Hill.
Management Troopers Hill is unmanaged, but the trampling feet of weekend visitors replicates the effect of grazing sheep very well.
Interpretation Nil.
Access Open at all times.
Contact Parks Manager, Bristol CC.

18 Stockwood Open Space

Between Hungerford Gardens and The Coots, BS14 (ST 625688).
Bristol CC. 24ha.
Approach Buses to Stockwood or short walk from Bath Road.
Summary Stockwood Open Space comprises 60 acres of old farmland surrounded by housing estates, a municipal tip, a golf course and a school. Despite this, its size gives the impression of being in the countryside and it takes a long time to explore the variety of meadows, hedgerows, ponds and woodland.
History Once a farm, managed in the traditional way, it was abandoned with the expansion of SE Bristol and the construction of the housing estates at Stockwood. It was bought by Bristol city council and became public open space. The usual grazing and hay-cutting virtually ceased until AWT took over management in 1981.
Nature interest The size and variety of the different habitats make Stockwood Open Space an important area for wildlife. The meadows are rich in wildflowers, with species such as dyer's greenweed and field scabious. A wide variety of butterflies and birds are also found and the ponds and marsh attract a good range of amphibians and insects such as dragonflies. The woodland known as Ilsyngrove is thought to be ancient with plants such as Bath asparagus and bluebells, and the remains of a ditch and bank boundary.
Management AWT's management of the site has included the reintroduction of an annual hay-cut on most of the fields, some scrub clearance on the most neglected fields, coppicing of the woodland,

pond clearance and the introduction of a horse-riding trail and footpath system.

Interpretation   A trail guide is available from AWT.

Access   Open at all times. Tarmac footpaths allow some access to wheelchairs.

Contact   Avon Wildlife Trust.

19   Willsbridge Valley and Willsbridge Mill

Between Willsbridge Hill and Long Beach Road, BS15 (ST 665707). Kingswood DC.

Approach   Parking in Long Beach Road, buses to Willsbridge or Bitton.

Summary   Just outside Bristol in Kingswood, Willsbridge Mill is the county's first wildlife visitor centre. The 18C corn mill and barn, and the mostly wooded valley are the scene of many activities run by AWT and make a sharp contrast with the new housing estates which surround it.

History   The valley was once part of the Kingswood Forest and later became the scene of much coal mining activity from the 17C through to the early 20C. A tramway, still visible today, was built through Willsbridge Valley linking the coal mines with the River Avon. Soon after 1716 an iron mill run by four five metre diameter water wheels was built in the valley using the fast flowing brook for power. After bankruptcy in 1820, this mill was demolished and the present mill powered by a large turbine was built soon after. This mill continued to be used up until a great flood in 1968, when the dam wall was smashed. The mill then fell derelict until 1981 when it and the valley were leased to AWT.

Nature interest   The valley, with its variety of habitats, is home to a variety of common wildlife as well as a few rarer species. A colony of bats, including the greater horseshoe, roosts in the old tramway tunnel and pine trees. Dippers and kingfishers have been regularly sighted in the stream but this suffers from sporadic pollution from factories further upstream.

Management   As well as the usual management of the woodland through selective thinning and planting, a variety of habitats have been created. Three ponds have been built, one over 21 metres long, and a wildlife garden faces the mill.

Interpretation   Written material is available on the wildlife and history of the valley. The mill houses a 'hands on' exhibition on two floors with buttons to push and wheels to turn. A variety of activities are available for schools and the general public both in the valley and the barn.

Access   The valley is open at all times. The mill is open from April to October and access is available to wheelchairs (please telephone for parking arrangements).

Contact   Willsbridge Mill (0272 326885) for details of events.

Further information

Parks Manager, Bristol City Council, Colston House, Colston Street, Bristol BS1 5AQ (0272 266031).

Avon Wildlife Trust, The Old Police Station, Jacobs Wells Road, Bristol BS8 IDR (0272 268018/265490).

Acknowledgement   Text written by Ralph Gaines and Rupert Higgins of AWT.

OXFORD

Sited at the junction of the rivers Thames and Cherwell, Oxford is an extremely green city. This greenness results partly from the profusion of local authority and university parks and gardens, but also from the survival of substantial areas of countryside some of which reach nearly to the heart of the city.

1 Aston's Eyot and the Kidneys

Jackdaw Lane, S Oxford (SP 518050).
Oxford CC (The Kidneys) and Christ Church (Aston's Eyot). 16ha.
Approach Jackdaw Lane (Aston's Eyot) or Meadow Lane (The Kidneys).
Summary An interesting wilderness area alongside the Thames. Both areas were rubbish-tipped this century. Aston's Eyot has developed into a fascinating wilderness area with woodland, scrub and 'weeds'. The Kidneys has been maintained in a more open condition.
History This area was probably snakeshead fritillary meadows until about a century ago, they were both used for domestic refuse tipping between about 1900 and 1930. Apart from an abortive attempt to convert it to a sports ground, Aston's Eyot has been allowed to develop along natural lines. Both areas are now much used for informal recreation.
Management Ranger Service to maintain and enhance the existing wildlife interest.
Nature interest Rich in bird and plant life. Butterfly interest includes an unexpected colony of brown argus.
Interpretation Boards at main entrances.
Access Open at all times.
Contact Ranger Service.

2 Chilswell Valley

S Hinksey (SP 502037).
Oxford CC. 12ha.
Approach By Chilswell Path, off A34 service road, at the rear of Johnson's Garden Centre.
Summary This attractive, steep-sided valley W of Oxford contains reedbed, woodland and calceous grassland in a peaceful setting. There are wonderful views of Oxford's historic buildings.
History A naturally steep-sided valley–too steep for agricultural use–given to Oxford city in the 1930s has largely been unmanaged since that time.
Nature interest Reed and sedge warblers are to be found in the reedbed; woodpecker, owl and woodland flowers in the wood; and cowslips, bee orchids and marshland white butterflies on the grass-bed. There are also magnificent fruit-rich hedgerows and scrub thickets.
Management A Ranger Service maintains and enhances the existing variety of wildlife.
Interpretation Boards at the entrance.
Access Open at all times.
Contact Ranger Service.

3   Grandpont Nature Park

Whitehouse Road (SP 510054).
Oxford CC. 1.6ha.
Approach   Whitehouse Road or Thames towpath.
Summary   A mixture of herb-rich meadow and native shrub thickets planted on Oxford's old gas works site alongside the River Thames.
History   A working gas works until the 1970s and a well-known landmark on the Oxford–London railway line. The buildings and holders have now gone and the site has been levelled, landscaped and planted up as a nature park.
Nature interest   Increasing.
Management   Ranger Service to promote an attractive and ecologically interesting area of countryside close to the city centre.
Interpretation   Boards at main entrances.
Access   Open at all times.
Contact   Ranger Service.

4   Iffley Fields

Iffley (SP 535035).
Oxford CC. 22ha.
Approach   On foot via Donnington Bridge Road, Iffley Lock or the Southern Bypass.
Summary   A substantial area of Thames-side unimproved grassland. Many of the meadows flood each winter and in spring and summer they are rich in natural history interest.
History   Known to have been good for snakehead fritillaries for at least a century, these meadows are thought never to have been fertilized or ploughed.
Nature interest   SSSI. Here herb-rich meadows support a several thousand-strong colony of snakeshead fritillaries. Many other interesting plants occur including ragged robin, marsh marigold and sedges. Wintering flocks of snipe.
Management   Berkshire, Buckinghamshire and Oxfordshire Naturalists Trusts (BBONT).
Interpretation   Nil on site. 'Handbook'.
Access   Open at all times.
Contact   BBONT's Oxfordshire Officer or Ranger Service.

5   Lye Valley

Girdlestone Road, Headington (SP 545060).
Oxford CC. 12ha.
Approach   By bus along The Slade.
Summary   A steep-sided valley surrounded by housing. Features of note include areas of scrub, alder carr, reed bed and herb-rich fen. The valley has an air of peace and tranquility, astonishing considering the proximity of dense housing.
History   Formerly known as 'Headington Moors' the valley been encroached on by housing from all sides and is now the only remnant of a previously much more extensive area of attractive countryside.
Nature interest   SSSI. The area of fen has plants such as grass of

Parnassus, butterwort and marsh helleborine. The carr and scrub support interesting birds such as siskin and redpoll; sedge- and reed-warbler sometimes breed in the reeds.

Management   Ranger Service to maintain and enhance the existing variety of wildlife.

Interpretation   Boards at the main entrances.

Access   Open at all times.

Contact   Ranger Service.

6   Magdalen Quarry

Old Road, Headington (SP 552071).

Oxford CC. 1ha.

Approach   William Kimber Crescent.

Summary   A small ecological SSSI surrounded by housing.

History   Quarried for building stone until about a century ago, the cliff is one of the few remaining exposures in Headington Quarry.

Nature interest   Some interest is provided by a small patch of grassland and peripheral scrub. Foxes are regularly seen.

Management   Ranger Service to maintain and enhance the existing variety to wildlife.

Interpretation   Board at main entrance.

Contact   Ranger Service.

7   Port Meadow

Walton Well Road, Jericho (SP 502078).

Ownership claimed by Oxford CC. 160ha.

Approach   By bus from Walton Street to Walton Well Road entrance Wolvercote to Godstow Road entrances.

Summary   A substantial riverside urban common in the NW of Oxford used for cattle and horse-grazing by those with common rights. This is a flat, characterful meadow.

History   Aerial views show evidence of Bronze and Iron Age settlements. Documentary evidence shows that it has been used as pasture for many centuries, although there were two hay crops taken during the Civil War period. Complicated ownership and common rights disputes have ensured continuity of management.

Nature interest   SSSI. Botanical interest centres on its marshland flora including the only known English site for creeping marshwort. Rich for migrant birds in winter including waders, duck and geese plus an ever-present flock of feral geese.

Management   The grazing animals, commoners' associations and Oxford city council are all involved in the management of the meadow and a part-time ranger is employed by the city.

Interpretation   None.

Access   Open at all times.

Contact   Ranger Service.

8   Raleigh Park

Southern Bypass, Botley (SP 494054).

Oxford CC. 5ha.

Approach   A34 or Westminster Way.

Summary   An attractive, unimproved meadow with mature trees to give a parkland feel. Splendid views of the historic buildings of the city centre.

History   An ancient area of grassland which has been neither fertilized nor ploughed for many years. The field was diminished in area by the construction of the A34 some decades ago. Recent planting of ash and oak are intended to replace the mature elms lost through disease about 10 years ago.

Nature interest   There is rich grassland flora including fleabane, knapweed and spotted orchids. There is also a substantial flushed area of giant horsetail and a small pond with rich dragonfly fauna.

Management   Ranger Service to maintain and enhance the existing variety of wildlife.

Interpretation   None.

Access   Open at all times.

Contact   Ranger Service.

9   Rock Edge

Old Road, Headington (SP 550064).
Oxford CC. 1.6ha.

Approach   By bus (junction of Old Road and Windmill Road, Headington).

Summary   A geological SSSI with an area of scrub and calceous grassland.

History   A remnant of a Headington Quarry, with a long low cliff, where digging ceased more than 100 years ago. The rectangular depression in the ground is evidence of the former municipal restaurant which was dismantled in the 1960s.

Nature interest   The scrub provides food for many species of birds. Attempts are being made to improve the diversity of the grassland, which was sown with rye grass.

Management   Ranger Service to promote the wildlife interest of the site.

Access   Open at all times.

Contact   Ranger Service.

10   Shotover Country Park

Grovelands Road, Headington (SP 565063).
Oxford CC. 124ha.

Approach   By bus along Old Road.

Summary   A substantial area of open countryside on the S side of Shotover Hill. Habitats present include acid grassland, heath, mixed woodland, coppiced woodland, marsh and neutral grassland. The intimate mixture of habitats gives many parts of the country park a feeling of wilderness.

History   A former royal forest (disafforested in 1660), it has in practice been a country park for at least 100 years, and owned by the local authority for about 50 years.

Nature interest   SSSI. Features of note include ancient woodland with magnificent spring flowers; locally rare heath and acid grassland; a full range of breeding birds; and a strong colony of black hairstreak butterfly.

Management   Ranger Service to maintain and enhance the existing variety of wildlife.

Interpretation   Free nature walk booklet (available from Rangers or Oxford Town Hall), Infopoint dispensing machine and interpretive

boards at main entrance.
Access   Open at all times.
Contact   Ranger Service.

Further information

The Countryside Ranger Service is c/o Department of Engineering and Recreation, Town Hall, Oxford OX1 1BX.
Most of the above sites feature in the round walks described, together with maps, in the booklet *Countryside Walks in Oxford* available from the above department for £2 incl. p&p.
Berkshire, Buckinghamshire and Oxfordshire Naturalists' Trust, 3 Church Cowley Road, Rose Hill, Oxford OX4 3JR (0865 775476).
Acknowledgement   Text written by David Steel, Countryside Officer, Oxford CC.

Pollarded Oak, Brasenose Wood, Oxford

PLYMOUTH

Plymouth is unusually fortunate in possessing a wide variety of habitats of high quality. The rocky shore, coastal cliffs, estuarine and woodland habitats present are of good quality and are supplemented by nationally important geological exposures and by colonies of several species of nationally rare plants. The existence of such a rich and varied landscape contributes greatly to the city's amenities and to this end the Plymouth local plan makes reference to setting up local nature reserves to conserve plant and animal life in areas within the city of particular ecological importance.

1 Ford Park Valley, Central Park

Between Gilbert Lane and Central Park Avenue, Peverell, Plymouth (SX 475560).
Plymouth CC.
Approach   Buses from city centre to Pennycomequick Roundabout.
Summary   A deeply incised valley tending NW–SE, of approximately one kilometre in length. It is bounded by a public park on three sides and a cemetery on the fourth.
Nature interest   The valley contains a variety of plant and wildlife habitats ranging from mature mixed woodland, formal tree and shrub planting to a pond and a stream.
Management   Carried out by the city council, with assistance and advice from the Plymouth Urban Wildlife Group and BTCV.
Interpretation   To be from posters mounted on stone plinths in the valley.
Access   Open at all times.
Contact   Planning department.

2 Southway Valley

N outskirts of the city immediately W of Plymouth Airport, 6km N of the city centre (SX 485605).
Summary   This narrow, steep-sided valley contains a small stream, one of a series of small tributaries draining W to Tamerton lake on the Tamar Estuary. Most of the land comprises woodland, including a coniferous plantation and scrub, though a central portion of the valley bottom has been infilled and used for recreation. Total area approximately 32 hectares.
Nature interest   Rich in wildlife, the valley bottom provides some wetland habitats in addition to areas of grassland and scrub. The site is an integral part of a network of urban biological corridors and a proposed LNR.
Management   Plymouth city council owns and manages the N half of the valley. The E half, including the coniferous plantation is privately owned with informal access.
Interpretation   None at present.
Access   The area is almost totally surrounded by residential development. At the E end well-used metalled paths cross the valley. A number of paths have been constructed through scrub and woodland. Informal paths exist along the valley bottom on both sides of the stream.
Contact   Planning department.

Whiteleigh Wood, Plymouth, Photo: The Woodland Trust

3   Whiteleigh Wood

In the NW corner of the city, running approximately NW–SE from near the head of Tamerton Lake, Plymouth (SX 475603).
Woodland Trust. 25ha.

Approach   Buses from city centre to Southway or Tamerton Foliot.

Summary   The area is principally of woodland on the SW side of a wet valley along the bottom of which runs a perennial stream. The woodlands are on a fairly steep slope bisected longitudinally by a terraced ride created as a result of the installation of a mains water pipeline.

Nature interest   The wood contains a variety of important habitats which with appropriate careful management offers considerable opportunities in the study of woodland, tall ruderal, marsh and aquatic communities. The site is an integral part of a network of urban biological corridors, and is a proposed LNR.

Management   Owned and managed by the Woodland Trust.

Interpretation   None at present.

Access   Open at all times via three good access points off Tamerton Foliot Road and the entrance to Borrowdale Close.

Contact   Woodland Trust, Westgate, Grantham, Lincs NG31 6LL (0476 74297).

4   Woodland Wood Valley

Within the N suburbs of Plymouth, 5km from the city centre, forming an elongated area following a valley from the head of Budshead Creek (SX 460602) SE towards Crownhill (SX 482592).

Plymouth CC. 2.5km.

Approach   Several bus routes from the city centre.

Summary   It comprises 43 hectares of woodland, scrub, grassland and streamside habitats largely bounded by residential development.

Nature interest   Woodland Wood Valley contains valuable habitats in Budshead and Woodland Woods and their associated areas of scrub. The site is an integral part of a network of urban biological corridors.

Management   City council.

Interpretation   None at present.

Access   Most of the area is surrounded by housing development and is extensively used by local residents. E of Woodland Wood the open space is freely accessible on all sides. Paths also run through Budshead Wood and Woodland Wood.

Contact   Planning department.

Further information

Plymouth City Council, City Planning Officer, Civic Centre, Plymouth PL1 2EW (0752 668000).

Plymouth Urban Wildlife Group, c/o Department of Natural History, City Museum, Drake Circus, Plymouth PL4 8AJ (0752 264878).

Acknowledgement   Text written by Ray Williams of the Planning Department and David Curry of the Plymouth UWG.

PORTSMOUTH

Portsmouth is now the most densely populated city area in Britain, so green space in the city is at a premium and under constant threat from development. The open space that remains is thanks mainly to military and post-war land reclamation. Apart from the sea front, with its shingle beach, which still maintains some interesting shingle flora such as yellow horned poppy and sea holly, and despite encroaching caravan parks and grass planting, there are only two main areas on Portsmouth Island itself of major wildlife importance. However, surrounding Portsea Island are some very interesting wildlife areas.

1 Farlington Marshes

Off Eastern Road, Farlington (SU 679045).
Portsmouth CC. 120ha.
Approach   Sandwiched between the A27 and Longshore Harbour, the marshes can be reached by a track from the junction of this road and Eastern Road.
Summary   An LNR, with their diverse habitats the marshes support almost 500 plant species—300 of which are grasses representing over one third of all grasses known in Great Britain. A breeding ground and winter refuge for over 230 bird species, it is a place where over 80 species can usually be seen on any day.
History   The marshes were reclaimed from the mudflats of Langstone Harbour by the Lord Mayor of Farlington between 1769 and 1773. Flint tools and pottery found all over the marshes show that prehistoric people hunted, fished and grazed their cattle here. The 18C reclamation was for grazing, which continues today and preserves a type of habitat once typical of land bordering the shores of S coast harbours—namely rough pasture, drainage dykes and scattered ponds with wet areas liable to flooding by rain or occasional high tides. Managed by the Hampshire and Isle of Wight Naturalists' Trust (H&IoWNT) since 1962, the marshes were purchased by Portsmouth council in 1970 and designated an LNR.
Nature interest   The marshes' importance as an over-wintering area and staging post for migrant bird lies in its area of sheltered water, protected to the N by Portsdown Hill, abundant food in the form of plant and animal species in the marshes and mudlands, and freedom from disturbance. The most famous visitors are the Brent geese breeding in Arctic Russia and migrating to the warmer climate of W Europe for the winter. Recent counts have exceeded 5,000 individuals, a significant proportion of the world's total. Flocks of over 1,000 wigeon and shellduck and mallard in hundreds can regularly be seen. Short eared owls, long eared owls and bearded tits (visitors from E Anglia) also winter here. During the spring and autumn migrations between the N and more exotic climes, the bushes are alive with warblers, redstarts, flycatchers, wheatears, stonechats, and whinchats, with occasional rarities such as blue throat or woodchats shrike. Birds breeding here include red shank, oyster catcher, ringed plover, lapwing and shellduck. Large numbers of field voles live in the grassland, while in the brambles and hawthorn woods bank voles and woodmice are an attraction for birds of prey such as sparrow hawk and kestrel. In winter marsh harriers and hen harriers comb the reedbeds for small birds. There is a flourishing rabbit colony, though myxomatosis is present, and hares, too, were present but have declined in recent years.

Management   H&IoWNT maintain a grazing regime by arrange-
ment with local farmers to preserve the area's traditional character.
Interpretation   Nil on site.
Access   There is public access·to the vantage point on the fringe of
the marshes.
Contact   H&IoWNT.

2   Hilsea Lines

Scott Road, Hilsea (SU 660044).
Portsmouth CC.
Approach   Part of South Coast Walk.
Summary   Semi-natural woodland has grown up around the
ramparts and moat of the old fortifications, the only woodland on the
island. The moat and tidal creek are a mixture of different habitats
with freshwater and inter-tidal mudflats within a few metres of each
other.
History   In 1740 when French invasion seemed imminent the
ramparts and moat of Hilsea Lines were built along the N shore of
Portsea Island to protect the naval base from attack from the land. The
Lines were remodelled in 1858 and became redundant soon after with
the development of long range portable guns.
Nature interest   Before Dutch elm disease the woodland was
mainly elm with sycamore, but few elms are left now. The moat is
mainly freshwater, becoming brackish towards the E and to the N in
Ports Creek. Moorhen and coot swim in the open water, and heron
can occasionally be seen fishing for eels. Where the moat connects to
Ports Creek and is flooded at high tide, a diverse brackish water
community thrives. Swarms of opposum shrimps form food for fish
such as mullet, eel and flounder as well as for dragonfly and damselfly
nymphs. In the Creek, particularly where it broadens into Langstone
Harbour, diving birds such as great crested grebe and little grebe can
be seen, especially in winter. In the evening tawny owls and the
occasional barn owl hunt for small mammals in the grassland on the N
side. Towards the mouth of Langstone Harbour an area of reclaimed
land contains three freshwater lakes, the only other freshwater
location on the Island. Milton Lakes (2) are off Moorings Way (SU
675010) but are under threat from the proposed extension of the
Eastern Road.
Management   Originally, the ramparts were grass and probably
mown regularly, as part of the Lido area to the W is today. With the
growth of trees the grass has been killed off and the slopes are so
steep that rainwater streams prevent most ground flora from becoming established. The surface of the monument is fragile and the major
erosion factor today is children playing.
Interpretation   Nil on site.
Access   Open at all times.
Contact   Cumberland House Museum and Aquarium.

3   Portsdown

Portsdown Hill Road (SU 660065).
Portsmouth CC.
Approach   On either side of the hilltop road between Fort Widley
and Fort Purbrook.
Summary   Recently declared an SSSI, the area has remnants of
chalk flora and fauna.

History   While Portsmouth and its suburbs have encroached up to the steep slope of the chalk hillside, this prevents further expansion into the Hampshire countryside. The forts were built during Palmerston's time during a mid-19C scare about possible French invasion.

Nature interest   Bee and fly orchids as well as ladies' tresses and the commoner spotted orchids are found. Dogwood, typical of chalky conditions, is common, while tall broom rape, a parasite on greater knapweed, occurs in quite large numbers. Insects abound, with at least 20 species of butterfly breeding regularly. Common blue and chalkhill blue can be seen, though the small blue is becoming rather rare. Marbled white and grayling are occasionally spotted, but the dark green fritillary is now rare. In late summer and autumn the great green bush cricket can sometimes be noted. Many small birds flock on the open slopes including corn buntings which like chalk habitats. Jackdaws nest in the forts where in the past barn owls have also nested. Badgers have setts on the N slopes, while on sunny days in summer common lizards and adders sun themsleves on the S slopes.

Management   Slight.

Interpretation   Nil on site.

Access   Open at all times.

Contact   Cumberland House Museum.

Further information

Portsmouth City Council, Cumberland House Museum and Aquarium, Eastern Parade, Southsea, Portsmouth PO9 9RF (0705 827261).

Hampshire and Isle of Wight Naturalists' Trust, 8 Market Place, Romsey, Hants S05 8NB (0794 513786).

Portsmouth Urban Wildlife Group, c/o Community Environment Project, Ferry Gardens, South Street, Gosport, Hants PO12 1EP (0705 503354).

Acknowledgement   Text written by Peter Sewell, Keeper of Natural Sciences, Cumberland House Museum. Additional assistance provided by Christine Seaward of the Community Environment Project.

READING

Reading was a small market town, a bridging point over the River Thames a short distance above its junction with the River Kennet, until the mid-19C. With the coming of the railways its position in close proximity to London was fully exploited. Since then the town has developed rapidly, with continuous and rapid expansion into the surrounding countryside, hampered only by the major gravel workings in the Thames and Kennet Valley.

1 Devil's Dip

Prospect Park, Bath Road (SU 690723).
Reading BC. 0.5ha.
Approach   Buses along Bath Road, getting off at Circuit Lane.
Summary   Reading's first urban nature area, a joint project between Reading council and Reading Urban Wildlife Group (RUWG), lies on the S side of the park.
History   The Dip is an old pit, the product from which may have been clay. Its subsequent use has been to take land drainage water so there is permanent water in the bottom.
Nature interest   The steep sides of the pit have become colonised with scrub and emerging trees for nesting birds, while a sunnier slope has been planted for butterflies. There is a traditionally managed hedgerow and a spring and summer meadow where linnets are regularly seen feeding.
Management   The area has been cleared of rubbish, fenced and gated, young hedge planted, pond and marsh dug and planted with native species. Routine management is carried out by the Wildlife Group except for mowing which is done by the council.
Interpretation   A leaflet about the Dip is available from Reading UWG.
Access   Open at all times.
Contact   Reading UWG.

2 McIllroy Park and Round Copse

Pottery Road (SU 677745).
Reading BC.
Approach   Bus or car along Norcot Road, thence to Pottery Road.
Summary   In W Reading, McIllroy Park is one of the least intensively managed parks with spectacular hilltop views over the Thames Valley from the grassy summit. The scarps are wooded with some fine beeches along an ancient track.
History   Originally known as Beecham Hill and Kentwood Grove, McIlroy was a famous family in the town, running a prestigious department store. Between the wars residential development skirted the hill to make it an urban park.
Nature interest   Two distinct types of woodland exist, one with a dense holly understorey, and the other a more open scrub oak carpeted with bluebells in the spring. Many species of bird are to be found and buzzards nested in the early 1980s. Round Copse is to be found at the S extremity of the site, with its wide diversity of woodland species including sanicle.
Management   The grass is cut infrequently and the woodland left

unmanaged so that the full woodland cycle of growth, death and decay, followed by regeneration can be observed.

Access   Open at all times.

3   River Kennet

(SU 715727).

Reading BC.

Approach   The footpath along the W side of the River Kennet may be joined off Berkeley Avenue just S of the town centre.

Summary   The River Kennet and the Kennet and Avon Canal flow through the S of Reading to their junction with the Thames to the E of Reading Gaol. Much of the river is well served with footpaths and famous for its wealth of wildlife.

Nature interest   Some of the richest water margin flora in the area is to be found here including the attractive flowering rush. The area attracts many migratory birds including breeding nightingales, and kingfishers patrol the river.

Management   The footpath is maintained by Reading council while the river is the responsibility of Thames Water.

Access   Open at all times.

4   River Thames Towpath

Caversham Bridge (SU 710746).

Approach   Bus or car to Caversham Bridge, car park off Richfield Avenue.

Summary   Westwards on the S side of the river the towpath skirts a tongue of low-lying agricultural land between river and railway where cattle graze in season.

History   The River Thames is a historically major waterway with low-lying islands and banks utilised by boat-builders, ferrymen, bargemasters and basketmakers among others. Ancient houses belonging to these artisans still stand on the N side of the river. Today the river is given over to leisure pursuits but where the banks are less intensively managed there is plentiful wildlife, using the adjacent open land for nesting and foraging.

Nature interest   This part of the river is known for the uncommon club-tailed dragonfly, while in the damp meadows of the adjacent park and farm may be seen snipe, reed bunting, yellowhammer, whinchat and skylark. The species-rich ditches of Cow Lane are worth the short diversion from the towpath.

Access   Open at all times. Adjacent farmland private.

5   Shinfield Park

Shinfield Road, Shinfield Green (SU 727690).

Berkshire CC.

Approach   Entrance to the park at various points.

Summary   The woodland covers a four hectare site on W facing slopes of the park in the grounds of which lies the county council HQ. A heavy London clay extends throughout the site and the nature of the woodland is variable according to historical landuse.

History   In the early 19C much of the area was given over to arable crops. However, by the end of the century it had reverted to woodland and was used for cover for shooting gamebirds. Consequently these woods have never been managed for timber.

Nature interest   Among the butterflies attracted to the grassy glades is the white admiral. Nuthatches and treecreepers breed in the woodland, as does the migrant cuckoo. The fire ponds on the edge of the woodland attract a wide range of dragonflies and damselflies and are well stocked with fish.

Management   Paths kept clear.

Interpretation   Enquire at reception desk of Shire Hall, adjacent, for interpretative leaflet.

Access   Open at all times.

Further information

Reading BC, Leisure Services, Civic Offices, Civic Centre, RG1 7TD (0734 575911).

Reading Urban Wildlife Group (BBONT), c/o Denton Pastures Country Park, Davis Street, Hurst, Reading RG10 0TH (0734 341721).

Acknowledgement   Text written by Linda Carter of the Reading UWG.

SOUTHAMPTON

Roman Southampton was established in the 1C AD on the Bitterne Manor peninsula on the E bank of the River Itchen. The Saxon town of Hamwic was founded in the 7C on the W bank of the River Itchen, while the medieval town developed during the 10C on the higher land overlooking the River Test. During the 18C and 19C, the town expanded to cover the whole of the peninsula between the two rivers. Important features of the modern town are the common and the city centre parks. The status of the common probably dates to the 8C or 9C, while the parks were the common fields of the Saxon town.

The development of the modern town arose from the construction of the docks in the 19C, a process which led to the gradual reclamation of the extensive mudland foreshore around the Southampton peninsula. This process continued with the construction of the Western Docks in the River Test during the 1930s and with the post-war construction of the container port at Redbridge.

Southampton's boundaries were increased to take in the E side of the River Itchen in the 1920s and have been extended on several occasions since 1945. The linear open spaces in the many stream and river valleys leading into the Test and Itchen are important in terms of recreational use and wildlife conservation.

1 Chessel Bay

Athelstan Road, Bitterne (SU 442128).

Approach   Track across railway off Athelstan Road.

Summary   An expanse of mudflats exposed by the ebbing tide, bordered by areas of crack willow, sedges and rushes, scrub/rough grassland and a predominantly oak woodland where a bank provides protection from the esturine waters. The mudflats are situated along the E (outer) edge of a large bay formed by a meander in the river below Northam Bridge. The area is important as it is one of the last stretches of natural shoreline below Riverside Park. A railway runs the entire length forming a boundary which restricts access and hence minimises disturbance.

Nature interest   The woodland suffers from trampling in places but does have areas where wood anemone, wood spurge and winter heliotrope survive. Trees include beech, rowan, holly and hazel.

The major interest is the shoreline, and bay coastal wild flowers such as sea aster and sea campion grow along the shore and the common shrimp and shore crabs abound. The organic material in the mud supports a rich shoreline food chain including several species of mollusc. Waders such as oystercatchers, redshanks, ringed plover and dunlin are present most of the year and are joined by migrants such as greenshank and green and common sandpipers. Herring gulls breed locally but blackheaded gulls are by far the commoner gull. Non-breeding guillemots have been seen from mid-summer and cormorant frequently fish the bay. Large numbers of small fish such as young flatfish and gobies can be seen along the shore and attract grey herons and kingfisher to fish the shallows. Winter visitors include grebes, diving ducks such as tufted duck and goldeneye; scarce visitors have included scoter and smew.

Management   Nil.

Interpretation   Nil.

Access   Inaccessible; best birdwatching is from a boat.

2 Frog Copse

Between Woodmill Lane and Meggason Avenue (SU 449148).
Southampton CC. 1.25ha.

Approach   Several access points along Woodmill Lane and Meggason Avenue (both bus routes) and from the corner of Northfield Road.

Summary   A small, mixed deciduous woodland situated in the NE
corner of an area of rough grassland, along a N–S running steep slope.
Water collecting at the base of the slope allows alder to flourish.
Sycamore dominates the drier areas with silver birch scrub at the S
(uphill) end. The copse has a dense understorey including hazel,
holly, bramble and a rich assortment of woodland plants including an
impressive array of ancient woodland indicator species. A thin belt of
scrub separating the copse from rough grassland adds variety.

History   The area has probably been wooded for over 200 years, the
copse being in existence for at least 160 years. In the early 1960s the N
part of the wood was destroyed as part of the development of Townhill
Park Estate. The extent of the copse prior to the mid-1800s is not clear.
Several ancient coppiced field maples possibly indicate an old
boundary line near the top of the slope.

Nature interest   This site is particularly noteworthy for its long
history under woodland and the resultant wide variety of woodland
plants. Flowering bluebells carpet the woodland floor in spring,
accompanied by patches of wood anemone, wood-sorrel, Solomon's
seal, lesser celendine, yellow pimpernel and yellow archangel and
(opposite-leaved) golden saxifrage. Butterflies include speckled
wood, orange tip and occasional green hairstreaks. Frogs are found in
the damper spots, but the lack of deeper areas of water minimises
breeding success. The upper, sandy, part of the woodland slope has
several fox earthworks and local badgers frequent the wood and have
a sett nearby. An abundance of dead/dying wood encourages green
and greater spotted woodpeckers and in some years lesser spotted
woodpeckers. Late October brings siskins to the alder cones and
several hundred can be seen during late winter in a 'siskin year'.

Management   Tipping and several trampled thoroughfares
threaten the woodland flowers and neglect in woodland management
has led to sycamore taking over some areas. Vandalism and cutting of
firewood also contributes to the disfigurement of the trees. The local
secondary school has worked in the area since 1986, their management plan includes removal of sycamore and increasing the numbers
of oak, ash, hazel and other native species, and the removal of rubbish
from possible amphibia breeding areas.

Interpretation   Nil.

Access   Open at all times.

Contact   Leisure, Tourism and Amenities Department, Southampton CC; Bitterne Park Secondary School (School Conservation Corps).

3 Lower Itchen Valley

Mansbridge Road, Swaythling (SU 448158).
N, Eastleigh BC; S, Southampton CC.

Approach   Car park off A27 N of Mansbridge or alongside White
Swan pub E of bridge.

Summary   An area of park adoining Riverside Park (see 4) with
views over alder carr, herb-rich wet land and grazed meadow land
intersected by a network of carriers and drains. A small shallow

reservoir gives variety and the Itchen Navigation towpath can be followed as far as Winchester to give a fascinating day's walk through a variety of landscapes along the Itchen Valley.

History   The Itchen Navigation canal has slowly silted up since it ceased to carry commercial barges towards the end of the 19C. A small stream survived along the lower section until the construction of the M27 caused it to be redirected into a nearby drain. Large areas of the canal are now virtually dry.

Much of the land was managed as water meadows, and then parts were grazed by horses and cows. Sheep have now been introduced, resulting in a shorter and hopefully more species-rich sward. The area N of the reservoir formerly extended to the edge of Southampton Airport and had a population of particularly fine specimens of common spotted orchid, a few of which remain.

Nature interest   The reservoir is surrounded by hawthorn and sallow scrub, popular with migrant warblers. Several species stay to breed, including blackcap and lesser white-throat, with sedge and reed warblers in the marshier areas. During autumn/winter flocks of goldfinch and siskin can be seen in the alders along the river with occasional water rail and green sandpiper along the drains. Cetti's warbler has been recorded during cold spells, probably wandering from the population further up the valley. Sparrowhawk, kestrel, tawny and little owls are resident, short eared owls quartering the area during the winter. Cuckoos and reed buntings are also noted.

At least 16 mammal species have been recorded including stoat, weasel, harvest mouse and three species of shrew. Fox and badger activities are evident. More than eight dragonfly and damselfly species are present including the spectacular banded damoiselle and the emperor dragonfly. A colony of S marsh orchid can be seen in the meadow S of the M27. An abundance of comphrey provides food for unusually large numbers of scarlet tiger moth, and other lepidoptera and insect life abound. Great green bush crickets and vanessid butterflies are common among the nettle beds. Recent construction of the M27 resulted in an abundance of wasteland species, including mush mallow, meliot and impressive numbers of large-flowered evening primrose.

S of the A27 an area of reed, sedge and bramble scrub is backed by woodland where green and greater spotted woodpecker can be seen, with the occasional lesser spotted. Spotted flycatcher and cuckoo frequent the boundaries with the wood.

Management   Management of non-park areas is in a state of flux due to recent changes in ownership.

Access   Views from park, and the towpath N under the motorway is open at all times.

Contact   Eastleigh BC.

4   Riverside Park

Manor Farm Road, Bitterne Park (SU 441157).
Southampton CC.

Approach   Buses to Bitterne Park Triangle; access at S via track on each end of Cobden Bridge, also several points along Manor Farm road. Car park off Woodmill Lane near Woodmill.

Summary   Mainly parkland with recreation use. The W edge follows the meandering riverside, small reedbeds and shrubberies creating quiet corners away from the main public pressure. Woodmill is the N extent of the tidal influence. Above this the river has been channelled, with a gravel path alongside the entire length.

History   Marsh and reed beds were formerly more extensive until a seawall was erected and the landward side infilled to create more parkland in the 1960s.

Nature interest   Access to over 2.5 kilometres of river gives good birdwatching; waders such as redshank, snipe and common sandpiper are regularly seen. Blackheaded gulls are omnipresent and often joined by up to four other species of gull and the occasional common tern. Up to 100 swans are present throughout the year and kingfishers are regularly seen.

Winter visitors include great crested grebe and dabchick with occasional smew, golden-eye and Slavonian grebe (mainly on the saltwater section near Cobden Bridge). The water just below Woodmill is brackish enough to support several freshwater fish and large numbers of mullet follow the tide in summer. The freshwater section above Woodmill is extensively fished with large shoals of young dace just below the surface on hot summer days. Moorhen and watervole breed along the far bank and sea trout and salmon can surprise visitors with their antics during late summer/autumn. Daubenton's bats can be seen skimming the river, especially just downstream from Mansbridge. Grey wagtail breed along the banks. Hedgerow butterflies such as green veined white and orange tip are common during the spring and early summer. Colour is given to the water edges by Indian and orange balsam, purple loosestrife and silted up corners can be yellow with kingcups (marsh marigold). Pendulous-flowered helleborine has recently been found on an inaccessible muddy area under willows.

Management   Managed as a park by the council.

Access   Open at all times.

Contact   Leisure, Tourism and Amenities Department, Southampton CC.

5   Southampton Common

The Avenue, Southampton (SU 415145).

Southampton CC. 146ha.

Approach   Buses along The Avenue. 15 minute walk from city centre.

Summary   An extensive recreational area of mainly parkland noteworthy for its variety of habitats and proximity to the centre of the city.

History   The first written record of the common was in 1228. The area was the main source of permanent pasture for the cattle and horses of the town and was managed accordingly. Earthbanks and hedges were erected around the boundaries to keep the stock in and groves of trees/bushes were encouraged to provide shelter and shade. The earthbanks still visible around the N and W side are probably part of the enclosure of 1577. Flooding of a disused gravel pit created the Cemetery Lake by 1881. The Ornamental Lake was originally constructed (beginning 1888) as a double, cresent-shaped lake separated by a weir, but the NE section gradually shrank and had gone by 1933. The addition of an island near the weir in 1910 gave the present lake.

Until 1945 various houses stood on the site of the old brickmaker's house. The area then became a tree nursery until 1961 when a zoo

The Ornamental Lake, The Common, Southampton

(pet's corner) was opened. This was closed in 1985 and demolished and a new Urban Study Centre is planned to open in 1989. Southampton is one of the few places to still have a Court Leet.

Nature interest   Areas where mowing is not too regular support meadow plants such as fleabane, knapweed, devilsbit scabious and tufted vetch. Some wetter areas have adder's tongue fern and common spotted, S marsh and twayblade orchids. Short mown turf is favoured by large populations of autumn ladies' tresses, especially near the covered reservoir in the N. Green winged orchids also grow here in varying numbers. Until it was enlarged in 1949, the reservoir banks supported bee orchids. A few plants of this species have appeared annually since 1984 further S.

Many woodland plants are present but scarce, mainly due to the dense woodland canopy, picking by humans and the history of grazing. Broad-leaved helleborines appear occasionally in scattered localities, mainly to the E of the Avenue. Ox-eye daisies grow in profusion in the cemetery, accompanied by harebells and star of Bethlehem has been recorded in the past. Several garden escapees also occur as a reminder of past dwellings.

The range of habitats support a large variety of insects, including over 200 moth species. Butterflies such as large and small skippers, meadow brown, gatekeeper and purple hairstreak are common. Brimstone breed on the large quantities of alder buckthorn and occasional white admirals, dark green fritillaries and clouded yellows are seen. Holly blues can be common, especially around the cemetery. Over 100 species of bird have been recorded; woodland species such as treecreeper, nuthatch, green and greater spotted woodpeckers are well represented. Lesser spotted woodpeckers are seen more rarely and a few wood warblers appear most years. Pied flycatchers are annual visitors especially during August/September and many warblers appear on passage. Blackcaps, chiffchaffs and willow warblers are among the few that stay to breed.

Heathland species are restricted to a few remnants of a once widespread habitat. A few common lizards survive, mainly in the cemetery, and grass snakes are occasionally reported from the N. A large population of great crested newt are present, with smooth and a few palmate newts. Common frog and toad can be found in the lakes and many of the ditches.

Carp, tench, perch, pike, roach and eels are present, mainly in the Ornamental Lake. Aquatic insects were well represented in this lake, but recent dredging has set back their populations. Several species of dragonfly are still present and a few water-scorpions and hydra remain. Freshwater shrimp and water boatmen are still common and clouds of daphnia are present in the Boating Lake during summer.

At least three species of bat occur (Daubenton's, pipistrelle and noctule). Foxes are very common and weasel and stoats are occasionally seen. Over 100 species of fungi have been recorded.

Management   Mainly managed as a park by the council. The mowing of some areas has been modified to encourage certain plants, especially orchids, to flourish.

Interpretation   Southampton Common Studies Centre exhibition area, information and animal room. Staff lead regular public walks; private parties catered for. Open daytime weekdays, afternoons 2–5pm.

Access   Open at all times.

Contact   Southampton Common Studies Centre, Cemetery Road, The Common, Southampton SO1 2NM (0703 36094).

Further information

Leisure, Tourism and Amenities Department, Southampton City Council, Civic Centre, Southampton SO9 4WY (0703 223855).
Schools Conservation Corps, c/o 3 Canton Street, Southampton SO1 2DJ (0703 631801).
Acknowledgement   Text written by Andy Welch of the Southampton Common Studies Centre.

WEST MIDLANDS

BIRMINGHAM

1   Bromwich Wood

Between M5 and Scotland Lane, B32 (SO 998813).
Birmingham CC. 4ha.
Approach   Bus from Birmingham, Bromsgrove or Halesowen to
Balmoral Road. Access off Scotland Road.
Summary   Although quite small, the woodland contains a wide
diversity of plants and trees. The main footpath which crosses the
wood is accessible to disabled people and there are open picnic areas
as well as more densely wooded areas. The footpath links with
another path which leads to the Woodgate Valley Country Park.
History   Old maps, along with plant species to be found here,
suggest the wood contains relics of ancient woodland. The wood was
probably coppiced from medieval times to provide fencing and
firewood, while standard trees would have been left for use in
building.
Nature interest   The wood is predominantly oak but also includes
ash, sweet chestnut, alder, hazel, hawthorn, blackthorn and elder.
During the spring there is a carpet of bluebells and also other
traditional woodland flowers such as wood anemone and yellow
archangel. The damper areas of woodland are also valuable for
wildlife and wood horsetail is among the species to be found here. The
wood is home to many birds including nuthatches, tree creepers and
jays, while nightingales have also been seen.
Management   Birmingham Recreation Services.
Interpretation   Leaflet produced by Birmingham city council.
Access   Open at all times.
Contact   Head Ranger, Woodgate Valley Visitor Centre, Clapgate
Lane, Bartley Green, Birmingham, B32.

2   Hill Hook

Between Clarence Road and Lichfield Road A5127, B74 (SK 106004).
Birmingham CC. 8ha.
Approach   Bus from Sutton Coldfield to Clarence Road. Train to
Blake Street Station. Access Clarence Road, Hill Hook Road.
Summary   This attractive reserve includes areas of marsh, wet
woodland and scrub, centred around an old mill pond. Well-laid paths
provide easy access and wooden bridges cross the very wet places.
Careful development has helped retain its very natural character.
History   There was a corn mill, mill pond and mill race on the site
from the mid-19C. The mill was in use until the 1940s and some local
residents can still remember it as a meeting place and recreation area.
The dam was rebuilt by Birmingham CC when housing development
took place. The mill pond has been extended and during redredging
the original dam location was found. The islands in the mill pond now
mark the position of this first dam. There is also a marker in the shape
of a mill wheel to show where the mill once stood.

Nature interest   The variety of habitats encourage wildlife. Alder in the wet woodland supports siskins and redpolls in winter, and in summer the air is full of bird song. A rich cover of woodland wildflowers include pink purslane, wood anemone and bluebells. Reed mace and marsh marigold grow in the marshy areas and the rare bogbean can also be found.

Management   Hill Hook is managed by Birmingham city council. It is hoped that Hill Hook, which is currently designated public open space, will soon be designated an LNR.

Interpretation.   Nil.

Access   Open at all times.

Contact   Birmingham Recreation and Community Services.

3 Queslett Quarry

Off the Queslett Road A4041 close to the M6, B43 (SP 063948). Birmingham CC. 14ha.

Approach   Bus from West Bromwich/Walsall to Queslett Road or from Birmingham to Aldridge Road.

Summary   A large pool surrounded by areas of open grassland and edged with young trees and saplings.

History   A former gravel pit, the quarry was landfilled and land-scaped once gravel extraction was completed. The Urban Wildlife Group (UWG) was involved in ensuring that one pool and an area of willow carr was retained. The pool which was kept is now a valuable attraction to wildfowl and waterbirds. In addition UWG helped with the planting of thousands of small trees and these are already providing cover for many birds and other wildlife.

Nature interest   Established areas of scrub and grassland have a variety of plants including a beautiful array of S marsh and common spotted orchids. From the shelter of the trees you can see swans, tufted duck, coot and several species of gull.

Management   Birmingham council.

Interpretation   Leaflets are available.

Access   Open at all times.

Contact   UWG or Birmingham Recreation and Community Services Department.

4 Woodgate Valley Country Park

Clapgate Lane, Woodgate, B32 (SP 000835). Birmingham CC. 80ha.

Approach   Buses from Birmingham via Harborne to Woodgate Valley.

Summary   A habitat creation site on former farmland.

History   A beautiful stretch of natural countryside and old farmland raised to country park status by Birmingham council.

Nature interest   The area still contains a considerable number of hedgerows reflecting the site's former use as farmland. Although primarily hawthorn, the hedges contain a variety of species including holly, blackthorn, oak, ash, elder, hazel and bramble. There are patches of bluebells, dog's mercury and wood anemone. Trees are scarce in the area and those present are associated with the hedger-ows and brook that run through the site. The small area of woodland consists basically of oak, with hazel coppice as well as beech, birch, hawthorn, holly, rowan and gorse.

Management   Maintained by the council's Recreation and Community Services department.

Interpretation   There is a visitor centre at the site which provides facilities for a number of educational and recreational activities.

Access   Open at all times.

Contact   Head Ranger (see Bromwich Wood).

Further information

Birmingham City Council, Recreation and Community Services, Auchlinbeck House, Five Ways, Birmingham B15 IDS (021 235 3217). Urban Wildlife Group, 131–133 Sherlock Street, Birmingham B5 6NB (021 666 7474).

Acknowledgement   Text of this and other West Midlands entries (except Coventry and Telford) written by UWG staff coordinated by Tom Slater.

COVENTRY

At the very heart of England lies Coventry, a freestanding city of some 300,000 people. The city dates back to before Anglo-Saxon times. Legend claims that Lady Godiva rode naked through the streets of Coventry in protest against the high taxes that her husband imposed on the town in the 11C. In medieval times Coventry was among the great cities of England with wealth built upon the weaving of woollen cloth. In the 19C clock and watchmaking skills provided the basis upon which the city's 20C engineering industry was based. Coventry has strong links with the motor industry and car manufacture is still one of the cornerstones of the city's economy. However, the city is now diversifying again, with new high technology industries becoming increasingly important.

Coventry is surrounded by the Warwickshire countryside, large areas of parkland and open space remain in the heart of the city itself.

1 Canley Woodlands

S of Charter Avenue, CV4 (SK 287772).
Coventry CC. 29ha.
Summary   Canley Woodlands comprise two woods, Park Wood and Ten Shilling Wood, both found on the S side of Charter Avenue in the SW of Coventry.
History   Both are ancient woodlands appearing much the same today as they did on maps 200 years ago. The woods formerly belonged to the Stoneleigh Abbey Estate, and were bought by Coventry CC in the 1920s. A section of Park Wood planted with conifers was felled during the Second World War to provide pit props for local mines.
Nature interest   Of particular interest in Park Wood are remnants of a sweet chestnut coppice, and a fine avenue of birch along the centre of the wood.
Management   Coventry CC.
Interpretation   Guide leaflet available.
Access   Open at all times.
Contact   Coventry Leisure Service Department.

2 Kenilworth Road Woodlands

Either side of Kenilworth Road, CV3 and 4 (SK 320770).
Coventry CC. 53ha.
Summary   The Kenilworth Road into Coventry is surely one of the most beautiful approaches to a city anywhere. The straight road is lined with mature woodlands along its entire length, with two larger historic woodland areas attached at Stivichall Common and Wainbody Wood.
History   The ancient Coventry to Kenilworth Road was turnpiked in 1775, at which time three rows of oaks were planted along the road on both sides. Gibbet Hill at the S end of Kenilworth Road takes its name from the gibbets which were located there until 1810. Three highwaymen were executed at that spot in 1765.
Nature interest   The woodlands provide a superb wildlife corridor running into the heart of the city. Squirrel, fox and rabbit are common, and muntjac deer are regular visitors.

Management   Kenilworth Road was designated a conservation area in 1968. The woodlands are managed by Coventry CC.
Interpretation   Guide leaflet available.
Access   Open at all times.
Contact   Coventry Leisure Services Department.

3   Stoke Floods

Off Binley Road, CV2 (SK 374787).
Coventry CC. 8ha.
Summary   The reserve is centred around a lake lying in the Sowe Valley on the E side of the city. The lake is surrounded by extensive reedbeds. There are areas of tall herb and scrub to the N of the lake.
History   The lake was created this century by mining subsidence.
Nature interest   Bird life on the lake is of particular interest with swans, Canada geese, mallard, great crested grebe, plus occasional more exotic winter visitors.
Access   Open at all times.
Contact   Warwickshire NCT.

5   Tile Hill Woodlands

Tile Hill Lane area, CV4 (SK 280786).
Coventry CC. 55ha.
Summary   Four woods in close proximity in the Tile Hill area in the W of Coventry.
History   All the woods were part of the Stoneleigh Abbey Estate until they were bought by Coventry in 1926. As with the majority of woodland in the Coventry area, the woods were once almost certainly part of the great Forest of Arden which covered a large part of the Midlands.
Nature interest   Tile Hill Wood is an SSSI some 30 hectares in extent. A mixed deciduous and coniferous woodland, it is noted for its rich flora and fauna which have been carefully recorded over the last 50 years by the Coventry and District NHS.

   To the S of Tile Hill Wood is the much smaller six hectares mixed woodland, Pig Wood. The name probably relates to the use of the wood for the grazing of swine on fallen acorns and beech mast in years gone by. To the S is Plants Hill Wood, another mixed woodland, containing sessile oak among numerous other species.

   The final wood of the Tile Hill group is Limbrick Wood, over half a kilometre to the E of the others. This 10hectares woodland is now surrounded by residential development. The wood is of high re-creation and amenity value and its many paths much used by the public.
Interpretation   Interpretative leaflet available.
Access   Open at all times.
Contact   Coventry Leisure Services Department.

6   Tocil Wood

North of Gibbet Hill Road, CV4 (SK303755).
Coventry CC. 4ha.
Summary   Despite considerable public use, Tocil Wood is a fine example of Warwickshire woodland.

History   Old woodland area in the SW of the city adjacent to the University of Warwick is probably relict woodland dating back to the ancient Forest of Arden. There is evidence of pottery kilns and associated habitation in the wood dating from Roman times.

Nature interest   Woodland includes a damp area with attractive flora, particularly marsh marigolds.

Management   The wood is managed by Warwickshire NCT. In the N part of the wood a traditional coppice with standards management regime has been re-established. The S part of the wood is managed as high forest.

Access   Open at all times.

Contact   Warwickshire NCT and Coventry CC.

7   Willenhall Wood

Between Middle Ride and Yarningale Road, Willenhall, CV3 (SK 371783).

Coventry CC. 9ha.

Summary   Willenhall Wood is situated in the SE of Coventry S of St James Lane between Middle Ride, Yarningale Road and the city boundary at Willenhall.

History   A wood with a well-documented history dating back to the 13C.

Nature interest   The wood is a mixed deciduous semi-natural woodland containing a diverse canopy of oak, ash, birch, wild cherry and rowan, while the shrub layer contains hazel, elder and hawthorn. In spring the wild flora of the wood, dominated by bluebells, presents a fine display, particularly at the E end of the wood.

Management   Coventry CC. Historically the wood has been managed as coppice with oak and ash standards.

Interpretation   Interpretative leaflet available.

Contact   Coventry Leisure Services Department.

8   Wyken Slough

Site bounded by Aldermans Green Road, Eburne Road and the M6 motorway, CV2 (SK 362834).

Coventry CC, Warwickshire NCT and Friends of Wyken Slough. 40ha.

Summary   Another reserve site centred around a lake in the Sowe Valley on the E side of the city.

History   The lake was created by mining subsidence in the 19C, and was surrounded by agricultural land until the 1960s when the M6 motorway cut through the area, at which time much of the farmland fell into disuse. This lack of use enabled the area to develop into a valuable area for wildlife and recreation. With positive management in recent years, the area is developing into an informal country park on the edge of the city.

Nature interest   The pool is a regular haunt of large numbers of swans in the winter, with mallard, coot, moorhen and little grebe residing here. There is a small marsh area at the N of the pool frequented by snipe, reed bunting, sedge warbler and reed warbler. In addition to the Pool and Marsh there are also attractive meadows, particularly immediately E of the marsh. Species include lady's smock, ox-eye daisy, spiny rest harrow and devil's bit scabious.

Wyken Slough, Coventry

The N boundary of the site is formed by the M6 motorway. Much woodland planting has taken place on the motorway embankments and alongside the motorway in recent years. Several acres of new woodland are now well on the way to becoming established.

Management   Coventry CC.
Interpretation   Information leaflet available.
Access   Open at all times.
Contact   Coventry's Countryside Project and Warwickshire NCT.

Further information

Coventry Countryside Project, Coventry City Council, Department of Economic Development and Planning, The Tower Block, Much Park Street, Coventry CV1 2PY (0203 833333).
Coventry City Council, Leisure Services Department, Fleet House, Queen Victoria Road, Coventry.
Warwickshire Nature Conservation Trust, Montague Road, Warwick CV34 5LW (0926 496848).

Acknowledgement   Text written by Peter Hunter, Senior Planner, Coventry CC.

DUDLEY

1 Castle Hill

Between the Broadway and Castle Hill Road (SO 948905).
Dudley MBC. 17ha.

Approach Within 15 minutes' walk of Dudley town centre.

Summary Castle Hill is of enormous local value to both wildlife and the community. With the zoo and the Black Country museum nearby, it is part of a major recreational and educational resource in the borough. The presence of certain plant species suggests that Castle Hill is ancient woodland and in addition it has a number of important geological features.

History Castle Hill, where the Normans built their castle to control the route towards the River Severn, is an area of Silurian limestone and has been extensively quarried in the past creating a complex of cliffs, slopes, pits and mounds along the hill.

Nature interest The Hill is dominated in the main by sycamore woodlands, although ash is abundant in places with most of the larger trees clustered around the edges of the pits from the pre-quarrying days. Dog's mercury forms a carpet throughout the woodland with occasional patches of bluebell, celandine and wood anemone. There is plenty of fallen timber which provides homes and food for birds and insects and a substrata for mosses and fungi.

Management Nil.

Interpretation Nil.

Access Open at all times.

Contact Dudley Leisure Services.

2 Fens Pools

Stourbridge Road (SO 915885).
Dudley MBC. 45ha.

Approach Buses from Birmingham to Pensnett, and from Dudley to Dudley Road.

Summary A great diversity of habitat types is present here, including many valuable marshes and wetlands. There is also the largest area of open water in the borough which attracts and supports a wealth of wildlife that is unparalleled in the Dudley district.

History In 1775 an Act of Parliament authorised the construction of the first canal to bring the rich and busy Pensnett Chase into the quickly developing national system of canals. Three reservoirs were set up—the Grove, the Middle and the Fens—whose waters pumped from neighbouring mines would feed the canal system.

Nature interest The dominant habitat type over much of the Fens Pools is grassland which is host to an abundance of butterflies including the uncommon green hairstreak. Typical grassland species include yellow oat grass, crested dogstail, yarrow, knapweed and tansy. There is also a large colony of the rare adder tongue fern scattered among the long grasses. The fen's wetland supports typical canalside vegetation dominated by reed sweet grass, reedmace, lesser water parsnip and branched bur-reed. This type of flora supports a wealth of freshwater life including pike, tench, breeding populations of smooth newt and common frog, several species of

dragonfly and large numbers of water spider—an uncommon species in urban areas. The Pools frequently attract migrating waterbirds and are consequently of special interest to birdwatchers.
Management British Waterways Board and Dudley Leisure Services.
Interpretation Nil.
Access Open at all times.

3 The Leasowes

Between Mucklow Hill and Manor Lane (SO 980840). Dudley BC. 60ha.
Approach Buses along Manor Lane and Mucklow Hill.
Summary An area of principally wet woodland supporting a variety of rich woodland flora and a diverse bird population.
History Formerly part of the estate of the poet William Shenstone, the Leasowes was landscaped in the 18C but it is now largely given over to Halesowen golf course.
Nature interest The woodland at The Leasowes is restricted to a narrow ribbon along the streams, springs and ponds. Little of the original oak/ash tree layer remains, and many planted trees such as beech, yew, hornbeam, common lime and horse chestnut now provide the dominant tree cover. There are artificially created pools ranging in size from a mere widening of the stream, to the large Breaches pool used for fishing. The pools are rich in aquatic flora, with angelica, marsh thistle, lady smock, brook lime and white water lily occuring in places. Breaches pool is the only pool at The Leasowes large enough to support waterfowl, with an abundance of coots, moorhen and mallard.
Management Maintained by Dudley Leisure Services.
Interpretation Nil.
Access Open at all times. Most of the former parkland is a well maintained golf course with restricted access, although the woodland walks are open to the public.
Contact Leisure Services.

4 Lutley Gutter

Lutley Lane off the Stourbridge Road.
Dudley MBC. 18ha.
Approach Buses from Stourbridge or Birmingham to Stourbridge Road. Five minutes' walk along Lutley Lane off the Stourbridge Road.
Summary A strip of woodland follows the Lutley Gutter forming an important wildlife corridor, connecting the open Worcestershire countryside with the Halesowen urban area.
History Remnants of ancient woodland are now surrounded by an urban area yet still retain their character.
Nature interest A strip of mixed broadleaved woodland runs all along the main stream and parts of the side stream. There is an excellent variety of trees and shrubs with no single dominant species. Crack willow, alder, sycamore, oak, ash and beech are frequent and locally dominant in the tree canopy. The most common understorey shrubs are hazel, holly and wych elm. Bluebell, bugle, wood sorell, yellow archangel and wood speedwell are found all

along the main stream, these wildflowers being frequently indicative of ancient woodlands.

Management   Leisure Services.
Interpretation   Nil.
Access   Open at all times.
Contact   Leisure Services.

5   Saltwells LNR

Saltwell Lane, Saltwells Road, Brierley Hill, DY5 (SO 934874). Dudley MBC. 70ha.

Approach   Though accessible from many points around its perimeter, the reserve's main car park is as above.

Summary   Perhaps Britain's most diverse urban wildlife reserve, it occupies the Blackbrook Valley and includes mature woodland, wetland, grassland and the deep Doulton's Claypit, a geological SSSI.

History   Part of the Pensnett Chase hunting forest in Norman times, the valley has for centuries been exploited for industrial purposes. Coal was mined here from the 1600s, iron production expanded greatly following the introduction of the blast furnace system in the 1750s. Clay extraction for ceramics produced the massive claypit, the workings ceased as recently as the 1940s. The Dudley canal which encircles the reserve before disappearing into a tunnel under Netherton Hill is a remarkable example of 18C engineering.

Nature interest   The claypit was an early SSSI designation for its

Bridge over Dudley Canal, Blackbrook Valley

geological interest, displaying an unusually clear section of the productive coal measures. Saltwells Wood, a late 18C plantation, is one of the finest woodlands in the West Midlands conurbation. The Black Brook offers a sequence of wetland habitats, while grazed fields are an adiitional element of this exceptionally varied reserve.

Management   A warden heads a small team based at a nature centre at the rear of Saltwells House, accessible by footpath from the car park.

Interpretation   Trail leaflets are obtainable from the nature centre, while a full history of the genesis of this showpiece reserve, *The Blackbrook Valley Project: a review* (NCC 1988), is also available.

Access   Open at all times. The Saltwells Inn at the end of Saltwells Lane is a convenient starting and finishing point for tours.

Contact   Warden (0384 261572).

Further information

Dudley MBC, Leisure Services, Ednum Road, Dudley, DY1 1HL (0384 456000).
Urban Wildlife Group (see Birmingham).

SANDWELL

1 Galton Valley Canal Park

(SP 080290).
Sandwell MBC; BWB. Approx. 3km.
Approach   Buses from West Bromwich to Brasshouse Lane; train to Sandwell and Dudley station.
Summary   A short walk along the canal will reveal a good display of both the historical and natural habitats of this stretch of the Birmingham canals. Together with the walls and bridges, hedgerows and trees, this broad green belt forms a unique glimpse into the flora of a lost heathland.
History   Originally the area was called the 'Birmingham Heath' but the demands of the Industrial Revolution meant that a more suitable route for transport, particularly to the Black Country coalfields, had to be found. James Brindley recommended that a canal should be built, and in 1826 Thomas Telford constructed the 'mainline canal'. He also built the Galton Bridge, a spectacular feat of engineering, the largest single span cast iron bridge in the world. Over the last 200 years the heath has completely disappeared under a tide of building, but not before many of the plants were able to colonise large areas of the canal embankments.
Nature interest   Heath plants which may be seen include wavy-hair grass, cowberry, gorse and heather. A wide variety of mosses make their home in the numerous walls and bridges. Many species of birds may be seen and during the summer months visiting butterflies such as red admiral, peacock and tortoiseshell are attracted.
Management   BWB owns the canals and has the responsibility of operating and maintaining them. In addition it owns or controls a substantial amount of other land. Sandwell council maintains the remaining land and buildings.
Interpretation   The Toll House, Smethwick High Street, acts as a main information centre with a ranger service offering information and guided walks. Wayside boards and trail leaflets are available.
Access   Open at all times.
Contact   Sandwell Leisure Services.

2 Haden Hill Park

Haden Hill Road (SO 960856).
Sandwell MBC. 97ha.
Approach   Buses from Birmingham or Halesowen to Haden Hill Road.
Summary   Set back from the main road, its holly-lined paths zig-zag through the park between mature trees and dip down into small clearings. Squirrels can often be seen darting between the trees and shrubs searching for food, and the Victorian rose garden on the hillside provides an unexpected splash of colour.
Nature interest   The park has a wide variety of plants including coltsfoot, creeping buttercup and ground elder. The small areas of woodland contain wild raspberry, wood arens, dog's mercury, hedge woundwort and wood millet. A wide diversity of bird species includes stock dove, willow warbler and spotted flycatcher while Canada geese breed on some of the lake islands.

Management   The site is administered by Sandwell MBC.
Interpretation   A nature trail has been laid out and an explanatory booklet is provided. The wide, smooth paths enable easy access to the site for disabled people.
Access   Open at all times.
Contact   Sandwell MBC.

3   Holly Wood

Queslett Road, Great Barr, B22 (SP 054945).
Sandwell MBC. 54ha.
Approach   Buses from Walsall or Birmingham to Walsall Road, or from West Bromwich to Newton Road.
Summary   An attractive broadleaved woodland adjacent to a wet grassland area is a community nature park well used by local residents and schools. Despite its relatively small size, the wood has many secret nooks and glades and also has an overgrown quarry. During the spring, the wood is carpeted with bluebells.
History   The wood originally formed part of the Scott family estate, later taken over by the health authority. When the M6 motorway was constructed it cut off Holly Wood from the main body of the woodland. UWG became involved with local residents when they wanted help in managing the wood and an adjoining area of wet meadow.
Nature interest   There is a great mixture of trees, including oak, birch, lime, ash and sweet chestnut. The wet meadow next to the woodland is also a valuable home for butterflies and wildflowers including some rare species such as bog pimpernel, marsh stitchwort and marsh arrowgrass. Owls appear to be common visitors to the area as are foxes.
Management   These grounds are now managed as a private reserve by the Walsall Group of the Staffordshire Nature Conservation Trust, through the Friends of Holly Wood Management Committee.
Interpretation   A noticeboard at the entrance to the park highlights some of its special features.
Access   Open at all times.
Contact   Sandwell MBC or the UWG.

4   West Bromwich Parkway

(SO 8999).
4km.
Approach   Buses from Dudley or Birmingham to Swan Village. From Oldbury to Whitehall Road. From Walsall or Bilston to Greets Green Road.
Summary   The Parkway runs along a now disused line of the Great Western Railway. As well as providing all the natural features of a grassland, woodland and wetland area, its historical significance promises a fascinating walk.
History   The past influence of steam can be seen throughout this stretch of natural habitat, including features such as the Sandwell Colliery Engine House and the impressive brick-built arches which span the walkway.
Nature interest   Apart from its industrial relics, the walkway has many interesting natural aspects with a superb sandstone cliff and a

rich grassland area. Unusual plants to be seen include purple toadflax, mat-grass and bristly ox-tongue. Many butterflies and moths are attracted to the area.

Management   Sandwell MBC.

Interpretation   The Parkway has access for cyclists and a 'trim-trail' and exercise equipment are provided.

Access   Open at all times.

Contact   Sandwell Recreation and Amenities Dept.

Further information

Sandwell MBC, Recreation and Amenities Department, Town Hall, West Bromwich, B70 (021 569 2200).

Urban Wildlife Group (see Birmingham).

STOKE ON TRENT

The decline of the mining and pottery industries in the 'Five Towns' around the upper valley of the Trent has left a considerable area of dereliction. Among other early environmental improvement initiatives was Hanley Central Forest Park. The most ambitious of recent greening projects was the 1986 Garden Festival on the site of Wedgwood's Etruria pottery works and part of the Shelton steelworks.

1 Ford Green Nature Reserve

Ford Green Road (SJ 889509).
Stoke CC.
Approach Buses from Burslem.
Summary A small tributary of the Trent flows through a valley with lakes and reedbeds.
History The valley was formerly followed by a railway. Ford Green Hall, Stoke's oldest house, adjoins the site. A former 16C timber-framed manor house containing furniture and other household items, it is now a museum.
Nature interest There is a good range of wildfowl plus herons and other waterbirds. For a couple of weeks in September there is a roost of some 20,000 swallows each night .
Management Stoke CC.
Interpretation Information boards.
Access Open at all times.
Contact Parks department.

2 Hem Heath Wood

Trentham Road, Hem Heath (SJ 885411).
Stoke CC. 8ha.
Approach Opposite main entrance of the Hem Heath Colliery.
Summary Plantation woodland managed as a nature reserve.
History Planted around 1860, the woodland includes a wide range of trees.
Nature interest Some 35 bird species have been recorded here, including woodpeckers, treecreepers and nuthatch. The network of rides and ditches is also good for plants, while a small pond adds variety. The reserve's value is enhanced by an adjacent block of woodland (40ha) in private ownership.
Management A Staffordshire Nature Conservation Trust reserve, it is being managed to introduce understorey and coppicing.
Interpretation A leaflet (50p including p&p) is available from the SNCT.
Access Open at all times.
Contact SNCT.

3 Hanley Forest Park

Bryan Street, Hanley (SJ 886489).
Stoke CC. 40ha.
Approach A short walk from Hanley centre.
Summary A not altogether successful attempt to improve a colliery area in the heart of the Potteries has produced a rather scraggy-looking park.

History   This high spoil tip is dramatic evidence of the scale of industrial usage right in the centre of the Potteries and now provides a vantage point for those energetic enough to reach its summit.
Nature interest   Tree planting provides some shelter and its lake supports a good variety of wildfowl.
Management   Stoke CC.
Interpretation   None on site.
Access   Open at all times.
Contact   Parks department.

4   Park Hall Country Park

Hulme Road, Weston Coyney (SJ 932440).
Staffordshire CC. 150ha.
Approach   About three kilometres from the centre of Longton.
Summary   A site restored after coal mining, sandstone quarrying and tipping.
History   High heathland used as a deer park until the 17C, it was later agricultural land before its exploitation for minerals extraction. Post-war gravel digging and tipping ravaged the land, before the local authorities bought it for a country park.
Nature interest   While ornamental planting and seeding is the prevailing result, parts of the park are developing wildlife interest.
Management   A ranger service operates from a small information centre.
Interpretation   Leaflets are available from the centre.
Access   Daylight hours.
Contact   Ranger service (0782 331889).

5   Parrots Drumble

A500, near Talke Pits (SJ 81666524).
Newcastle-under-Lyme DC.10ha.
Approach   A lay-by on the westbound side of the road allows access via a stile.
Summary   A wooded valley surrounding a stream.
History   Old coal mines are adjacent, with a disused railway running to the W of the site.
Nature interest   Woodland birds are numerous, while the flora of this area includes displays of bluebells and wood anemones in season.
Management   An SNCT reserve.
Interpretation   Nil on site
Access   Open to the public at all times.
Contact   SNCT.

6   Westport Lake

Canal Street, Newcastle Street, Longport (SJ 855503).
Stoke CC.
Approach   One mile from the centre of Burslem.

Summary   This large lake surrounded by industry supports an unusually varied range of wildfowl.
History   In the valley of Fowlea Brook, the lake is a reservoir adjacent to the Trent and Mersey canal.
Nature interest   Up to 40 swans are usual, with goosander and other migrants visiting in the winter. Away from the main lake, an area of scrub, wood, marsh and grassland is more secluded and ideal for casual observations.
Management   Parks departments.
Interpretation   From parks department.
Access   Open at all times.
Contact   Parks department.

Further information

Staffordshire Nature Conservation Trust, Coutts House, Sandon, Staffordshire ST18 0DN (08897 534).
Stoke City Council, Leisure and Recreation Department, Hanley Park, Cleveland Road, Stoke on Trent ST4 4DX (08897 202312).
Acknowledgement   Text written by John Drewett of SNCT.

TELFORD

Telford New Town has emerged gradually over the last quarter of a century, incorporating into its structure the small towns and villages of the area. The NW market town of Wellington lying within the shadow of the Wrekin and Ercall hills borders the Shropshire plain. It is flanked by towns and villages which had their heyday during the Industrial Revolution, towns such as Oakengates, Donnington, Dawley, Hadley and Madeley. Extensive mining of coal and ironstone in this part of Shropshire during the 18C was linked with the technique of smelting iron ore with coke perfected by Abraham Darby at Coalbrookdale. The River Severn, flowing through the Gorge to the S of the New Town at Ironbridge, was the most notable feature of this development, with its now famous iron bridge.

By the time Telford New Town was initiated many of the industrial scars had been hidden under wooded hills and heather and gorse covered banks. Many pools associated with the pits, foundries and canals were abandoned and over the years have become havens for wildlife. Some of these woods, banks and pools have been allowed to remain, together with pockets of older woodland, giving the new town of Telford its green network.

1 Benthall Edge

(SJ 670032).

Telford Development Corporation.

Approach   Over the Iron Bridge, or by car to the central car park, Ironbridge.

Summary   Sloping steeply down to the banks of the River Severn, on the opposite side to Coalbrookdale and Ironbridge, this tranquil wood provides a wonderful opportunity to escape from the man-made environment of the New Town, while affording fascinating glimpses of the historic town at its base, and—less attractively—Ironbridge Power Station at its W edge.

History   Although small remnants of ancient woodland may have survived unaltered through the ages, much of Benthall Edge has been affected by the industrialisation of previous centuries. The exploitation of the resources of Benthall Edge started during Norman times when coal was first extracted. Many of the trees of the wood were coppiced for charcoal during the 18C and 19C and only a few larger trees were left. Limestone and clay became the most important resources to be mined from the mid- 18C to early 20C. Signs of this industrial activity can be found within the woodland. Many of the paths were once tramways and inclines, and the remains of adit mines and abandoned limestone quarries can be seen.

Nature interest   The complex geology of Benthall Edge is reflected in the diversity of plant and animal life, recognised in its SSSI designation. On the Silurian limestone there are many plants such as yew, ash, spindle, wild service tree, dogwood and spurge laurel, which prefer calcarious soil. The ground flora also reflects this with abundant sanicle, sweet woodruff and yellow archangel. More acidic woodland of oak, birch and bilberry is found on the E edge over the coal measures. Many species of mammal have been recorded here including fallow deer and the smaller muntjac, and around the woodland edge and more open quarry areas many species of butterfly can be seen.

Management   A coppice management regime has been implemented in part of the woodland to encourage a greater variety and more diverse habitats, and to maintain it as an important landscape feature. Some of this wood is used by the Green Wood Trust which promotes new and traditional uses for small diameter, unseasoned timber.

Interpretation   There are two nature trails in the woodland, both of which can be obtained from the Tourist Information Centre in Ironbridge. One follows the route of the former Severn Valley Railway along the side of the river and is an easy, flat walk. The other trail winds up into the woodland, and is rather steep in parts, and can be very muddy so boots are necessary.

Contact   Information Centre, Ironbridge.

2   The Ercall

(SJ 638093).

Wrekin DC; private.

Approach   From A5, Wellington, along Ercall Lane.

Summary   The Ercall is an attractively wooded hill on the outskirts of Wellington. Public footpaths lead to view points on the summit, the Shropshire Plain stretching to the N and W, the Wrekin golf course and Limekiln woods to the E.

History   There is evidence that the Ercall has been quarried over many centuries. The most recent and extensive quarrying for Wrekin quartzite has just finished. Coppicing of the woodland ended during the last century.

Nature interest   Designated an SSSI for both its biological and geological interest, The Ercall is of great importance in the interpretation of Lower Cambrian stratigraphy in Britain. The deciduous woodland is dominated by sessile oak, characteristic of thin acid soils. The ground flora of wavy hair grass, heather and bilberry has the uncommon climbing fumitory associated with it. Wood warblers breed here.

Contact   Wrekin DC.

3   Granville Country Park

(SJ 720125).

Wrekin DC.

Approach   Off the Eastern District Road, along Granville Road.

Summary   This is an area of wooded banks, meadows, pools and marshes. Recently excavated industrial relics provide a theme for the park which is soon to be declared a Local Nature Reserve.

History   The area has been extensively mined for coal and ironstone, and the former pit banks, now attractively wooded hills, are evidence of this. Industries related to the mining of coal and ironstone needed a transport system, and many of the pathways through the Park follow former routes of mineral railways or canals. The site of the last colliery to be worked in Telford, in production until the 1960s, is situated near the country park, and gives it its name.

Nature interest   Many wildflowers are to be found along the path edges and open grassy areas of the park. Some of the grassland areas have regenerated naturally since industry declined, and have produced an interesting mixture of formerly common wild flowers, including yellow rattle, knapweed, ox-eye daisy, rest harrow, vetches and many others. Early marsh orchids are found in the wetter parts. Many butterflies feed on these open areas on sunny days. The pitbanks show the characteristic oak dominated woodlands of many of Telford's pitmounds, and some heather banks are at an earlier stage of revegetation. A marsh, more accurately called a sedge fen, has recently been declared an SSSI, and forms a habitat for some less well-known plant species and many birds, including reed buntings and sedge warblers.

Management   Wrekin council manages the park for its industrial archaeology and for nature conservation. Work has been done to clear pools of overhanging vegetation and to remove silt where necessary. Paths have been regraded both for walkers and as bridleways. Future management will keep the grassland clear of scrub so that the variety of wildflowers can be preserved.

4   Limekiln, Black Haves and Short Wood

(SJ 655097).

Wrekin DC; British Coal.

Approach   Limekiln Lane.

Summary   Although extensively mined in the past for coal and limestone, these woods are now quiet and secluded.

History   As far back as 1255 limekilns were recorded in the woodland; the central spine of limestone has the remains of many quarries. The whole of Limekiln Woods was originally mixed coppice woodland. Short Wood has suffered mining most recently and, like Black Hayes, was planted in part with sweet chestnut in the latter half of the 19C.

Nature interest   The habitat of many less common lime-loving plants such as heliborines and orchids, the woods offer a secluded sanctuary for many birds. Areas of open grassland add to the variety of species. Short Wood in springtime is a breathtaking sight with bluebells intermingled with yellow archangel and greater stitchwort.

Management   The open grassland habitat is regularly cleared of scrub to maintain species diversity.

5   Loamhole and Lydebrook Dingle

(SJ 667049).

Telford Development Corporation; CEGB; private.

Approach   From the Ironbridge Gorge Museum of Iron car park, Coalbrookdale.

Summary   Walk up from the Museum of Iron in Coalbrookdale and into the secluded dingle woodland. The path follows the stream for some way, then ascends from the valley along the Rope Walk, an old green country lane which is part of the Shropshire Way. Longer walks, further up the valley, overlook the ravine of Lydenbrook Dingle.

History   The stream has provided water for a series of pools to power the Coalbrookdale Company ironworks for hundreds of years. Sandstone has been quarried in Lydenbrook Dingle.

Nature interest   An SSSI, the Upper Furnace Pool, although heavily silted, provides a habitat for water birds. The ancient semi-natural dingle woodland has a variety of tree species, and includes wild service tree, wild cherry and field maple. The ground flora is very varied.

Management   A coppice cycle has been reintroduced in a hazel area. A boarded walkway has been constructed over the wet area, and the footpaths are maintained. Tree felling along the footpath allows light to reach the ground flora and so help preserve its diversity.

Interpretation   The Loamhole Dingle trail leaflet and the Coalbrookdale Water System trail leaflet are available from the Ironbridge Gorge Museum Trust shops.

6   Severn Gorge Woodlands

(SJ 670039).

Telford Development Corporation; private.

Approach   From the Ironbridge Gorge Museum Trust Visitor Centre.

Summary   The historic town of Ironbridge is surrounded on all sides by the wooded slopes of the Severn Gorge. The valley of Coalbrookdale, with formerly coppiced woodlands on either side, meets the Gorge above Ironbridge. There are many walks to be taken along the river and in the woods on either side. The most accessible areas are described here, but there are also many footpaths through Captain's Coppice, Lloyds Coppice, Dale Coppice and also from Blists Hill to Great Hay. On the S side of the river, the Severn Valley Way runs from Ironbridge to Coalport. A steep sided climb will give a panoramic view of Ironbridge from the summit of Lincoln Hill. The path is well marked, and steps lead up the hill to the Rotunda. From there descend to the picnic site in Coalbrookdale.

History   These woods became an amenity in the early 19C when ironmaster John Reynolds acquired them to continue his sabbath walks around Coalbrookdale for the benefit of his workers. Previously there were many charcoal hearths and limestone quarries and caverns.

Nature interest   The mixed deciduous woodland contains a large Atlas cedar, a mature false acacia and fly honeysuckle, relics of the sabbath walk planting. Old man's beard and spindle are characteristic of this limestone woodland. Some remnants of limestone grassland exist in the open areas of the hill, in the fields around Paradise and in the churchyard.

Management   Improvements to the woodland structure are planned.

7   Silkin Way

(SJ 633140–N) and (SJ 697025–S).

Summary   It is possible to walk or cycle from Bratton in the NW of Telford to Coalport in the SE along the Silkin Way, which affords an intimate view of the New Town. The N part passes through Apley Park and Hadley Castle, skirting Middle Pool. The S part of the route between the Town Park and Coalport is better known and easier to follow, passing Madeley Court and the Open Air Museum at Blists Hill.

History   Named after Lord Silkin, champion of the post-war new town movement, the S part of the Silkin Way follows the route of the Coalport Branch of the LNWR railway, which gives a gentle gradient from the Town Park to Coalport. Apley Park is the grounds of the former Apley Castle, and Middle Pool has been created from two former industrial pools. Madeley Court in the S, an Elizabethan manor house, stands among the wooded pitmounds of later development.

Nature interest   Silkin Way passes through a wide variety of scenery, agricultural, new industrial and former industrial land which has revegetated naturally. It includes a wide variety of habitats.

8   The Town Park and Hinkshay Field Studies Area

(SJ 700080 and SJ 695072).
Wrekin DC; Telford Development Corporation.

Summary   The Town Park offers a contrast between a formal and semi-natural landscape. The N end of the park adjacent to Telford shopping centre has an extensive children's adventure playground, and is landscaped with formal pools and gardens. Southwards, the park opens out into semi-natural scrub and woodland with several pools. The Hinkshay Field Studies Area, soon to be declared an LNR, is based around a canal basin and reservoir, and a short length of the former canal, framed by wooded pitmounds. Silkin Way passes through the Park.

History   As with many other open spaces in Telford, the Town Park lies in an area once humming with industrial activity. Most of the pools were canal reservoirs to feed the branch of the Shropshire Canal, which was superceded by the railway, now the route of the Silkin Way. The Blue Pool was excavated to provide clay for Randlay Brickworks. The remains of furnaces can still be found near Stirchley Chimney, which stands as a landmark in the centre of the Park. Many of the present pathways were once routes of mineral railways between the pits and furnaces.

Nature interest   It is easy to forget that the Park is in the heart of a new town. There are a variety of habitats, some undisturbed since they were abandoned at the turn of the century. Pool edge gives way to woodland, gorse and heather to rough grassland. Hidden away are marshy areas where orchids and ragged robin flourish. Even the most recently reclaimed central grassy area provides food for winter visitors, such as redwing and fieldfare. Kingfishers can be seen feeding at the pool during the winter months.

Interpretation   Town Park Rangers have an information cabin near the Town Centre, adjacent to the children's play area, where leaflets relating to the park may be obtained.

9   Wrekin, Ercall and Limekiln Woods

Wrekin DC; private.

Approach   From M54, junction 7.

Summary   The Wrekin, Ercall and Limekiln Woods are remnants of the once extensive forest of Mount Gilbert. The Wrekin, formed of pre-Cambrian acidic rock, some of volcanic origin, stands out from the Shropshire Plain, a landmark for many miles. The smaller hills of the Ercall and Lawrence lie in its shadow to the NE, with Limekiln and Short Wood beyond. The walk to the summit of the Wrekin, over 300 metres high, gives an unimpeded view of the countryside in every direction.

History   Near the summit are the remains of a hill fort, easily recognised on the ascent as the path passes through Hell's Gate and Heaven's Gate, the inner and outer fortifications. The Needle's Eye and the Cuckoo's Cup, rocky outcrops at the top, are famous landmarks.

Nature interest   Mixed deciduous woodland, dominated by sessile oak, clothes the N end. The S slopes have extensive conifer plantations. At the summit of the Wrekin are areas of heathland, with heather and wavy-hair grass. On the lower ground to the NE are wet meadows. Birds breeding here include sparrowhawk, woodcock and all three British woodpeckers.

Further information

Wrekin DC, Malinesee House, Malinsgate, Telford (0952 202100).
Shropshire Wildlife Trust, Old St George School, New Street, Shrewsbury SY3 8JP (0743 241691).
Telford Branch (SWT), Upper Forge, Coalbrookdale, Telford TF8 7DT (0952 452545).
Acknowledgement   Text written by Jean Rapson of the Telford Branch of SWT.

WALSALL

1 Hay Head Wood

Longwood Lane, Walsall (SP 041990).
Walsall MBC. 7.6ha.
Approach   Buses from Walsall to Sutton Road or Aldbridge Road.
Summary   Hay Head is largely oak woodland with a good diversity of trees including contrasting areas of wet woodland. The Rushall Canal adds to the wetland interest. Parts of the oak wood are over 200 years old.
History   Much of Hays Head's present character derives from the Industrial Revolution as by the late 18th century the site was being intensively mined for its Silurian limestone. Known locally as 'Great Barr' limestone this was widely used for smelting iron in the district's many blast furnaces. A canal was built to transport the limestone from Catshill (Brownhills) down to the Hay Head Works. In 1813 James Brindley used the lime to make underwater cement, much of which was used to construct Birmingham's numerous canals. The mine was eventually abandoned in about 1870 and since then the workings have been largely removed and the canal has gradually silted up, leaving nature to heal the industrial scars.
Nature interest   Because of its historical background many plants and wild animals make their home among the remains of the limeworks, and over 50 species of bird have been seen. These include blackcap and yellowhammer, which feed on the abundant insect life and nest in the hawthorn thickets. Wildflowers provide an attractive display, with wood anemone, wood sorrel and the creamy white sprays of meadowsweet which flower during the spring and late summer. The canal is also a well-known frog and toad breeding site.
Management   Maintained by Walsall MBC as a nature reserve.
Interpretation   A trail has been devised comprising a circular route of nearly a kilometre and a half and it is waymarked by numbered green discs. A nature trail guide is available.
Access   Open at all times.
Contact   Walsall Recreation and Amenities Department.

2 Park Lime Pits

Between Aldridge Road A454 and Bosty Lane, SW9 (SP 030999).
Walsall MBC. 32ha.
Approach   Bus from Walsall to Lichfield Road or Bosty Lane.
Summary   An area of mixed habitats includes woodland, wetland and pools all rich in wildlife. Paths, causeways and bridges lead across the area. There are extensive views from the land above the lime pits.
History   The pools have formed in lime workings which have now been abandoned for over 150 years. The Daw End Branch of the Rushall Canal links up with the lime pits.
Nature interest   Mature beech and hornbeam line the banks of the pools and the flowers and grasses such as burnet saxifrage, rough hawkbit and devilsbit scabious are typical of limestone areas. The trees and hedges support many birds and sparrowhawks and tawny owls can be seen here. The wetlands beside the pools boast such rarities as bulrush and mare's tail. Park Lime Pits forms part of the Beacon Regional Park.

Management Walsall MBC.
Interpretation There are interpretive panels around the Lime Pits.
Leaflets are available from Walsall Council Recreation and Amenities
Department.
Access Open at all times.
Contact Walsall MBC Recreation and Amenities Department.

3 Rough Wood

Between Bloxwich Road North and M6, WV12 (SJ 984009).
Walsall MBC. 27ha.
Approach Bus from Walsall to Wood Lane/Bentley Lane or from
Bloxwich to Bentley Lane.
Summary Rough Wood forms part of a large country park. The
broad leaved woodland is very atmospheric with glades, pools and
many old oaks.
History The wood has grown up on the site of a former colliery,
although some of the oaks are several hundred years old and predate
the coal mining. The floor of the wood is pitted by large hollows which
are the remains of shallow coal scrapes once dug by the local
residents.
Nature interest Along with the established oaks there are also
birch, elder, alder, aspen and many large holly bushes. Pools have
formed in some of the bigger hollows and these are very attractive to
amphibians. The wood has some interesting fungi and fly agaric,
Jews ear and sulphur tuft can be found. In the spring the wood is
carpeted with bluebells.
Management Walsall MBC.
Interpretation There is a large notice board at the entrance to the
wood. A nature trail guide is available from Walsall Recreation and
Amenities Department.
Access Open at all times.
Contact Walsall MBC.

Further information

Walsall MBC, Recreation and Amenities Department, Gorway Road,
Walsall, WS1 3BB (0922 26418).
Urban Wildlife Group (see Birmingham).
Acknowledgement Text by Peter Seccombe of the Amenities
Department.

WOLVERHAMPTON

A country town in Norman times, its abundance of coal and iron ore made it a major manufacturing centre in recent centuries. Following the decline of the 'smokestack' industries, several former industrial sites have been recognised for their wildlife interest, including Ladymoor Pool, Ladymoor Road, Coseley; Peascroft Wood, Peascroft Lane, Bilston; and the Valley Park which follows the Staffordshire and Worcestershire Canal to the W of the city.

Further information

Staffordshire Nature Conservation Trust (see Stoke).
Wolverhampton City Council, Department of Planning, Civic Centre, Wolverhampton WV1 1RG (0902 27811).

EAST MIDLANDS

CAMBRIDGE

A Roman settlement on the Cam, then called the Granta, developed during the 13C into a university town which has also been the location for a surprising amount of light industry during this century. On the edge of the Fen country, its formally recognised wildlife sites include a riverside meadow where the Cam enters the city and a former chalkpit north of the Gog Magog Hills.

1   Cherry Hinton Chalk Pits

Limekiln Road, Cherry Hinton (TL 484556).

Lime Kiln Close Reserve, Cambridge

Cambridge CC. 3ha.
Approach   Buses to Cherry Hinton.
Summary   Three large chalk pits supporting an abundance of chalk flowers have been a botanical attraction for at least three centuries.
History   The pits were dug to provide lime and clunch, a chalk stone used for building. The original village derives its name from the cherries that grew here, the wild cherry tree or gean having been recorded in 1685.
Nature interest   A rarity, the carrot-like herb *seseli libanotis*, was first recorded here by the 17C naturalist John Ray and has been visited by flower spotters ever since. Surveys by the 19C Professor of Botany CC Babington, which identified other unusual plants including perfoliate honeysuckle, provide a good basis for study of natural regeneration on abandoned chalkland.
Management   Management by the Cambridge Wildlife Group of the Cambridgeshire Wildlife Trust (CWT) includes measures to prevent excessive scrub growth.
Interpretation   Entry in CWT nature reserves guide, the Trust's HQ being in the neighbouring village.
Access   Only the pit known as The Spinney, nearest to the crossroads, is open to the public, via the caravan park entrance.
Contact   CWT.

2   Paradise

Barton Road, Newtown (TL 448575).
Cambridge CC. 9ha.
Approach   By foot from The Fen Causeway, car park off Barton Road.
Summary   As the Cam, or Granta, enters the city from the S it passes an area of marsh, scrub and young woodland known as Paradise, below which is Coe Fen.
History   Paradise was acquired by the city council in 1961 as public open space.
Nature interest   Paradise is a patch of wet meadow and marshland with belts of willow and alder scrub on the W bank of the River Granta above Coe Fen. It is rich in bird and plant life typical of riversides and wet land.
   Coe Fen (formerly Cow Fen) and Sheep's Green have been common grazing land for the townspeople of Cambridge for several hundred years. The regular grazing of cows, horses and sometimes sheep preserves a natural balance of the vegetation.
Management   City council and CWT.
Interpretation   Two booklets, *Paradise Nature Trail* and *Coe Fen* from which the above extracts are taken, are available from CWT.
Access   Open at all times.
Contact   CWT.

Further information

Cambridge City Council, Amenities and Recreation Department, Cambridge.
Cambridge Wildlife Trust, 5 Fulbourn Manor, Manor Walk, Fulborn CB1 5BN (0223 880788).

DERBY

On the Derwent above its junction with the Trent, the city was the site of a Roman fort and later a flourishing country town. Its industries developed during the 18C and 19C, but following the decline of the railway workshops and other factories since the last war, large areas are being redeveloped. Nature.conservation interest centres on the River Derwent and the wildlife potential of its formal parks.

In 1989 the city council launched 'Project Riverline' which includes the protection of open space along side the River Derwent south of the city. Already protected is a 25 acre woodland nature reserve owned by Courtaulds at their Spondon works. Details of educational and other arranged visits are available from the company at PO Box 5, Spondon, Derby DE2 7BP (0332 66071).

Further information

Derby City Council, Planning Department, Council Offices, Corporation Street, Derby DE1 2SS (0332 293111).
Derbyshire Wildlife Trust, Elvaston Castle Country Park, Derby DE7 3EP (0332 756610).

LEICESTER

Leicester is a city with strong Roman connections. It became a prosperous industrial town during the last century, prodominantly through the knitwear and hosiery industry which developed around the river and canal system which bisects the city. City Wildlife Project was formed in 1983 and has helped to pioneer urban nature conservation within the city. CWP has developed and/or manages over 40 nature sites in the city and has a vigorous programme of environmental education including walks, talks, publications and work with over 70 schools. Leicester is now one of the most ecology-conscious cities in Britain with nature conservation fully integrated into the city council's policies.

1   Anstey Lane Meadow Nature Reserve

Anstey Lane, LE4 (SK 567067).
Leicester CC. 0.8km.
Approach   Buses along Anstey Lane.
Summary   The wide verges forming this site provide a profusion of wild flowers by a busy main road, much visited by butterflies on sunny days.
History   In times gone by, Anstey Lane was a drovers' track and cattle were fattened by being grazed on the verges before they were sold at market. In recent times the verges were used for horse grazing, but the grazing rights are now leased by the CWP and the site is managed as a hay meadow.
Nature interest   Anstey Lane meadows constitute the best remaining example of calcareous grassland in the city. Since CWP has been managing the site, horse grazing has been stopped and a diverse flora has flourished. Species include betony, agrimony, pepper saxifrage and greater burnet saxifrage.
Management   A 'summer meadow' mowing regime is carried out, and a hay crop is taken in early autumn. The site is fenced but access is permitted by way of gates at the N and S ends. The boundary hedge has been laid in the traditional manner.
Access   Open at all times.

2   Aylestone Meadows

Between Aylestone Road and Great Central Way, LE2 (SK 575018).
Leicester CC. 100ha.
Approach   Buses along Aylestone Road, access via Aylestone Mill lock, Canal Street or Middleton Street.
Summary   A wonderful area of wetland and herb-rich grassland between the Rivers Biam and Soar. There are ponds, marshes, scrub and wide expanses of open grassland, providing a rich and varied landscape. Views of industrial areas of the city add to the character of the place rather than detracting from it.
History   The land has been variously used for pasture land, sports grounds and a tip. Its tendency to flood has limited its usefulness for these purposes.
Nature interest   Aylestone meadows provides one of the best wildlife habitats in the city. It supports a wide variety of grasses, sedges, rushes and many damp-loving herb species such as arrow-

head, cuckooflower and meadowsweet. Species of butterflies which can be seen here include orange tip, brimstone, meadow brown, common blue, small heath, wall brown, small copper and large and small skipper. The large and varied bird population includes water rail, snipe, yellow wagtail and kingfisher as well as large numbers of reed buntings, meadow pipits and yellow hammers.

Management   Aylestone Meadows forms part of the Riverside Linear Park, developed by the city council and running the 13 kilometre length of the city.

Interpretation   The Aylestone Meadows Nature Trail is managed by CWP with board walks, signposts and interpretative boards along the way. The booklet *Aylestone Meadows Nature Trail* by the CWP and published by Leicester city council is available free from the council or CWP.

Access   Open at all times.

3   Freeman's Common

Islington Street, LE2 (SK 589027).
Leicester CC. 1ha.

Approach   Within easy walking distance of the city centre or buses along Aylestone Road.

Summary   A raised area of wilderness surrounded by industry and backing onto a railway line. There are dense areas of scrub and brambles among unmanaged grassland. The ground is uneven.

History   The last remnant of Leicester's ancient common land, the site is now leased by the BBC for the siting of a transmitting mast and is currently being sublet to CWP for development as a nature park.

Nature interest   The flora is extremely diverse, with almost 100 species of flowering plant recorded. Notable among these are primroses which provide a bright yellow carpet in the spring.

Management   CWP is developing the site as a nature park.

Access   Open at all times.

4   Gilroes Spinney

Anstey Lane, LE4 (SK 564068).
Leicester CC. 2ha.

Approach   Buses along Anstey Lane.

Summary   The Spinney is next to the Anstey Lane Meadow and provides an attractive background to the meadow and a valuable woodland habitat.

History   The Spinney grew from trees planted as a screen for the Smallpox Hospital which used to be at the centre of the site. Since the demolition of the hospital the area has been untouched apart from the building of a transmitter in the centre.

Nature interest   The Spinney is noted for its abundant and diverse birdlife, including spotted flycatchers, all three native species of woodpecker and nesting tawny owls. Regular sightings of sparrowhawks have also been made. The ground flora includes sweet violet, wild basil and dog's mercury.

Management   A number of the more dangerous black poplars have been felled and about 800 wildflowers planted by local residents.

Access   Open at all times.

5   Grange Spinney

Ambleside Way, LE2 (SP 572992).
Leicester CC. 1.5ha.
Approach   Buses along Ambleside Drive, access via Ambleside Way.
Summary   The Spinney, with its mature canopy, provides a popular area for recreation.
History   The Spinney was planted at the turn of the century.
Nature interest   The canopy includes pedunculate oak and ash, the natural woodland trees of this area, and its ground flora includes bluebell, honeysuckle and sweet violet.
Management   Woodland management techniques have been employed, including coppicing, to allow for the growth of a more extensive ground flora and scrub layer and to give it a more ecologically sound woodland structure. A number of gravel paths have been laid and access points have been constructed. Local community groups have been involved in the management.
Access   Open at all times.

6   Highway Spinney and Meynells Gorse

Hinckley Road (SK 546035 and SK 541038).
Leicester CC. 4.82ha and 3.63ha.
Approach   Buses along Hinckley Road. Access via Hinckley Road and Braunstone Lane.
Summary   Two large, attractive woodlands bisected by the busy Hinckley Road constitute valuable habitat, given Leicestershire's paucity of ancient woodland in general.
History   The two sites are pockets of ancient woodland, being remnants of the old Leicester Forest.
Nature interest   As would be expected of such woodland there is a great diversity of species. A large number of birds nest in both areas, including woodpeckers, treecreepers and rooks. Insect species include hawkmoths and a large number of butterflies. Wood anemone, goldilocks buttercup and enchanter's nightshade are among the flora.
Management   Dangerous trees have been removed. The hedges surrounding the sites have been laid by CWP and new aggregate paths have been constructed. Invasive species such as sycamore and Norway maple have been selectively thinned to encourage a better ground flora.
Access   Open at all times.

7   Humberstone Park

Humberstone Park, LE5 (SK 621051).
Leicester CC. 600m.
Approach   Buses along Humberstone Road.
Summary   This is a section of the disused Tilton railway line, with a dense scrub embankment. It is adjacent to and overlooking Humberstone Park and provides a contrast with the park's open spaces.
Nature interest   The area provides a haven for songbirds, dunnocks, robins, goldcrests and the tit family.
Management   The site has only recently been acquired by the city council following a public inquiry which prevented its loss for housing development. Access is restricted.

Interpretation   CWP hopes to develop a nature trail in the near future.
Access   Contact CWP prior to visit.

8   Knighton Spinney

Knighton Park, LE2 (SK 605009).
Leicester CC. 3ha.
Approach   Buses along Welford Road or London Road.
Summary   Following the meandering path through the spinney gives the feeling of being in a wood considerably larger than a mere three hectares. Its cool, shady quietness makes it a pleasant place to linger on summer days.
History   The spinney was planted in the early 19C. It is thought that the reason for the planting was the increased demand for timber brought about by the industrial revolution, although no timber was taken because by the time it was mature the price had been undercut by imports from the expanding empire. It was also used for game cover, being drawn by the Fernie Hunt.
Nature interest   The woodland is the best in Leicester: flora includes wood anemone, dog violet and yellow archangel and over 70 bird species have been seen. Birds include greater and lesser spotted woodpeckers, blackcaps, spotted flycatchers and sparrow-hawks.
Management   The site is managed by CWP and some coppicing is undertaken. This ancient form of woodland management involves harvesting timber from blocks within the woodland on a rotational basis.
Interpretation   The site is wardened with an easy access nature trail for the disabled and the visually handicapped with listening posts, a tapping rail and a three-dimensional model of the site. A taped nature trail and personal cassette players can be hired from the CWP, and a written nature trail is also available.

9   Orchards Nature Park

Groby Road, LE4 (SK 566063).
Leicester CC. 2.66ha.
Approach   Buses along Groby Road.
Summary   The Orchards Nature Park is a quiet retreat from the busy Groby Road, with a series of paths laid through sometimes dense scrub.
History   Until recently the site was an area of allotments in which a large number of fruit trees were planted. After the allotments became disused these trees and other plants were left to grow wild.
Nature interest   This is a good area for nesting birds and small mammals, as the scrub provides plenty of cover. Kestrels frequently hunt across the park.
Management   It is hoped to create a mosaic of woodland edge habitats and attract species of birds normally found in this environment. To help this, boundary hedges have been planted, coppicing has been carried out and glade areas cleared. Access has been created by a system of footpaths.
Access   Open at all times.

10 Piper Way Nature Area

Piper Way, New Parks LE3 (SK 561035).
Leicester CC. 1ha.
Approach   Buses along Aikman Avenue.
Summary   Scrub, young trees, meadows and a pond make this area well liked and used by local people.
History   The site was once an elm spinney, all but destroyed by Dutch elm disease, and was used for some time as a tip. Landscaping was carried out by CWP with the help of a grant from Leicester council and hard work from local residents. A pond has been constructed from an enormous liner sandwiched between pieces of old carpet, collected locally, to prevent it from beingpunctured.
Nature interest   The site now represents an important reserve for wildlife in the area and as the trees, scrub and pond become better established its value should improve even further.
Management   Informal management agreement with CWP. The development of the site has been an attempt to involve urban residents with nature at first hand. An intensive community involvement exercise was undertaken by CWP during the design and construction of the site.
Access   Open at all times.

Piper Way Nature Area, Leicester

11   The Rally Nature Garden

Between Tudor Road and Richard III Road, LE3 (SK 579045).
Leicester CC. 0.2ha.
Approach   Within 10 minutes' walk off Leicester High Street.
Summary   The Rally is a peaceful little garden in the middle of a busy city.

A mixture of native and exotic plants provide interest, colour and shelter. At one end of the garden a reconstruction of West Bridge station platform, looking out onto what was once the historic Swannington railway line, enhances the atmosphere of the garden.

History   The site was once part of one of Britain's oldest railways. It fell into disuse and the nature garden was created from a wasteland site when a road building programme threatened the area. Two murals nearby portray the site as an early railway and as a butterfly haven.

Nature interest   The garden is divided into small areas of spring and summer meadow, ornamental shrubbery, rockery and woodland blocks. Its main interest is that of a butterfly haven; 20 species of butterfly can be regularly seen including comma, painted lady, orange tip, brimstone, meadow brown, gatekeeper, wallbrown, small copper, common blue and large and small skipper.

Management   The site has been managed by CWP as a demonstration of wildlife gardening, but this management is being handed over to the city council.

Interpretation   There are interpretative boards on site and an information leaflet about the nature garden is available free from CWP. A full colour poster depicting the butterflies of the site is available from CWP.

Access   Open at all times.

12   Spinney Hill Nature Area

Spinney Hill Park, LE5 (SK 607046).
Leicester CC. 0.2ha.

Approach   Buses along East Part Road.

Summary   The nature area forms a small corner of Leicester's most popular park, used by joggers, cricketers, dog-walkers, children and older people; the atmosphere of the park is friendly and cosmopolitan.

History   Spinney Hill Park celebrated its centenary in 1986. The nature area was added at that time by CWP and is now managed by the CWP, principally as a demonstration of ecological landscaping.

Nature interest   The area contains a created pond, spring and summer meadows and a woodland block.

Management   The site is managed and wardened by the CWP.

Interpretation   There is a nature centre building on site with various displays, widely used by school parties and members of the public. There are interpretative boards and two leaflets are available free from CWP.

13   Watermead Ecological Park and Wood

Oakland Avenue, LE4 (SK 598080).
Leicester CC. 1.5ha.

Approach   Buses along Melton Road. Access via Oakland Avenue.

Summary   Woodland, aquatic and meadow habitats provide plenty of scope to see nature in action.

History   The woodland area was planted by Severn Trent Water Authority around 1940 as a screen for the Belgrave pumping station. The park area was developed from disused grazing land by CW in 1983.

Nature interest   The central feature of the ecological park is a large pond, supporting populations of smooth newts, frogs and dragonflies. The pond is surrounded by areas of meadow and new woodland. An established small ash woodland adjoining the site provides additional interest and more woodland will soon be leased to enlarge the park further. Great burnet, meadow vetchling and meadowsweet grow in the meadows, and kingfishers, bullfinches and sparrowhawks are frequently seen.

Management   The wide variety of habitats makes for an ideal educational resource, and the site is much used by local schools. There is wheelchair access around the pond and a platform for viewing and pond-dipping. The park is cared for by a site warden.

Access   Open at all times.

Further information

Leicester City Council, New Walk Centre, Leicester (0533 549922).
City Wildlife Project, Parkfield, Weston Park Hinkley Road, Leicester LE3 6HX (0533 856675).
Leicestershire and Rutland Trust for Nature Conservation, Leicester City Group, 1 West Street, Leicester LE1 6UU (0533 553904).

Acknowledgement   Text written by Dave Nicholls, Project Director of CWP.

LINCOLN

From its origins as a Roman garrison town, Lincoln grew up along its waterways and later its railways. Hence, green spaces extend alongside these linear features right into the heart of the city and it is quite possible to see kingfishers, toads and hares in the most built-up areas—Lincoln Cathedral harbours roosting bats and nesting kestrels. There are several large public open spaces within the city where a wide variety of wildlife can be seen.

1 Hartsholme Country Park

Skellingthorpe Road, Lincoln (SK 945695).
Lincoln CC. 64ha.
Approach   Buses along Skellingthorpe Road.
Summary   A very varied site with a large lake and areas of grassland and woodland.
History   The lake was the original water supply reservoir for Lincoln. The rest of the park formed the grounds of Hartsholme Hall, built in Victorian times and demolished when it became derelict after the Second World War, when it had been used as army quarters.
Nature interest   The formal gardens around the Hall can still be made out, but most of the park has a wild feel to it. The lake is open and attracts wintering wildfowl. Along the edges there is much damp willow woodland, while elsewhere the woodland is more mixed: noctules roost in the beech trees and pipistrelles and

Fly agaric (Amanita muscaria), *Hartsholme Country Park*

Daubenton's bats can be seen feeding. Areas of dry acid grassland have species like heath bedstraw and tormentil. Barn owls, herons, woodcock and great spotted woodpeckers have all nested in the park. The common lizard may be seen as well as a variety of butterflies.

Management   Management of the park is overseen by a park ranger.

Interpretation   Various display are on shown in a visitors' centre.

Access   Open at all times.

Contact   The Park Ranger, Hartsholme Country Park, Lincoln.

2   South Common

St Catherine's, Lincoln (SK 975695).
Lincoln CC. 81ha.

Approach   Buses to St Catherines, Cross o' Cliff Road.

Summary   Grassland on the limestone ridge overlooking the centre of Lincoln.

History   One of two large areas of common land in Lincoln, grazed by horses and with a golf course and football pitches.

Nature interest   The calcareous grassland is rich in plant species, including devils-bit scabious, meadow saxifrage and lady's bedstraw, and the twayblade orchid has been recorded. Hawthorn scrub supports typical breeding warblers such as blackcap and willow warbler. Among the variety of mammals present, water shrews have been found in the ponds on the common.

Management   Grazing is administered by the city council in consultation with the Lincoln Commons Horse Association.

Interpretation   Nil.

Access   Open at all times.

Contact   Recreation and Leisure Deptartment.

3   West Common

Saxilby Road, Lincoln (SK 962722).
Lincoln CC. 48ha.

Approach   Buses to Carholme Road/Hewson Road.

Summary   Open grassland rising gently, with some ponds and marshy areas.

History   One of the city's two large areas of common land, West Common is also the site of Lincoln's racecourse, a golf course and football pitches, and is grazed by horses.

Nature interest   A very open site, the grassland is heavily grazed with just a few large trees around the ponds and some more recent plantings. The rough grassland is too heavily grazed to provide much interest, but marshy areas along the W boundaries of the site support such plants as Norfolk reed, water plantain, marsh bedstraw and celery-leaved buttercup. The birds to be seen are typical of grassland populations with large numbers of gulls, rooks and starlings in winter. Great crested newts have bred in a pond in the past.

Management   Grazing is administered by the Lincoln Commons Horse Association.

Interpretation   Nil.

Access   Open at all times.

Contact   Recreation and Leisure Department.

Further information

Recreation and Leisure Department, City Hall, Lincoln (0522 511511). Lincolnshire and South Humberside Trust for Nature Conservation, Lincoln City Wildlife Unit, c/o Wildlife Giftshop, 3 Castle Hill, Lincoln. *Acknowledgement* Text written by Andrew Heaton of the Lincoln City Wildlife Unit.

NORTHAMPTON

Located where two branches of the River Nene are crossed by a Roman road from Watling Street (A5) to Bedford, the town became a centre of the shoe industry in the 18C. The marshy valley, followed by a branch of the Grand Union canal, prevented much development southwards until the building of industrial estates by the town corporation. The town's nature sites range from riverside walks to woodland and a 'rescued' pond.

1   Billing Arbour's Wood

Billing Brook Road, Northampton (SP 793638).
Northampton BC. 10ha.
Approach   Buses along Lumbertubs Way or Billing Brook Road.
Summary   Broadleaved woodland with good shrub layer, and ground flora. A small lake on the E side provides additional habitat.
Nature interest   The wood is situated in the middle of an area of housing development. Two schools are located nearby and the wood provides a good educational opportunity as a refuge for wildlife in an urban environment. The wood is predominantly ash with frequent occurrance of sycamore and some oak. A well- developed shrub layer consisting of elder, wild cherry and some rowen provides good structure/habitat for a variety of birds and insects. The ground flora is very varied with herb robert, enchanter's nightshade, meadowsweet and creeping buttercup among the plants to be seen.
Interpretation   Nil.
Access   Open at all times.

2   Lings Wood Nature Reserve

Lings Way, Billing Lings, Northampton, NN3 4BE (SP 802638).
Northampton BC. 56 acres.
Approach   Buses along Lings Way or Blackthorn Road (short walk via Lark Rise).
Summary   Previously an area of heather and gorse heathland, combined with clumps of silver birch, and areas of grazed common land.
Nature interest   Nowadays, it consists of mixed woodland and acid grassland surrounding Lings House, the headquarters of the Northamptonshire Trust for Nature Conservation (NTNC). A good mix of tree species can be seen with sweet chestnut, larch, ash, Scots pine and silver birch among them. This Trust reserve is situated on the edge of Northampton in an area of recent housing development. Extensive conifer plantations in the N of the wood are surrounded by a band of hardwoods which extend into a narrow strip of woodland in the S. Two ponds provide habitat for a wetland flora including soft rush, water forget-me-not and reed sweet-grass.
Management   Management work in the wood (rhododendron control, willow coppicing, footpath maintenance) is undertaken by local volunteers and members of the Trust.
Interpretation   Leaflets, display room at Lings House. Guided walks can be arranged.
Contact   Lings Wood Warden, c/o NTNC, Lings House.

Dew Pond, Lings Wood, Northampton

3 River Nene at Barnes Meadow

Bedford Road, Northampton (SP 770597).
Northampton BC.
Approach Buses along the Bedford Road or a 15 minute walk from the town centre.
Summary Redundant arm of the River Nene with adjacent grasslands.
History Previously part of the main channel of the River Nene which has been rerouted prior to the construction of a new road.
Nature interest The relatively sheltered nature of this site combined with the slow flow gives the area a special significance for breeding birds and fish. A 'wildlife schedule' by local field naturalists gives extensive lists of flora and fauna recorded at the site. For further details contact either the NTNC or the Northamptonshire Natural History Society. Butterflies to be seen include meadow brown and gatekeepers. The common blue damselfly is another common sight during the late spring. The river itself is a prolific breeding ground for a number of fish species. Mammals recorded include fox, water vole, rabbit, bats (noctule and pipistrelle) and shrews (common and pygmy).

The site is a haven for a range of birds. Over 60 species have been recorded including little owl, kingfisher and great crested grebe. A good mix of aquatic, marginal and terrestrial flora includes brooklime, marsh woundwort, Gibbon's duckweed and shepherd's purse.
Interpretation Nil.
Access Open at all times.

4 River Walk at Kingsthorpe Mill, New Bridge

Mill Lane, Kingsthorpe (SP 746628).
Approach Any bus into Kingsthorpe from town centre. Alight at Cock Hotel.
Summary A riverside walk with nearby ponds, rough grasslands and scattered shrubs/trees.

History   Horse-grazed grasslands and a nearby mill once used the river's flow to provide power for grinding corn.

Nature interest   A stretch of the River Nene with a pleasant mix of aquatic and terrestrial habitats. Recently constructed footpaths, bridges and outdoor furniture provide easy access and enable visitors to enjoy the site in comfort. A good wetland flora exists with large amounts of emergent vegetation. Species include lady's smock, brooklime and fool's watercress. Such plants attract dragonflies, damselflies and other insects. These in turn are fed upon by a variety of birds and fish. Moorhen and snipe have been recorded as have 10 species of fish.

Access   Open at all time.

Interpretation   Nil.

5   Ransome Road Pond and Grassland

Ransome Road, Delapre, Northampton (SP 764594).
Northampton BC.

Approach   Buses along the London Road or 15 minute walk from town centre.

Summary   A large pond with adjacent areas of rough grassland situated on the fringe of an industrial estate, close to a large lake. Dense aquatic vegetation with areas of open water and nearby mature hedgerows.

History   This previously neglected pond was choked by emergent vegetation and rubbish. Labour supplied by the Northampton Urban Wildlife Group and other volunteers cleared an area of open water and removed rubbish and debris.

Nature interest   There is an excellent range of flora and fauna, with at least nine species of butterfly including ringlet, small heath and large skipper. Grey squirrels, moles, rabbits and water vole have all been recorded. The luxuriant growth of aquatic and marginal vegetation provides both food and cover for a large number of freshwater invertebrates. The common darter dragonfly and a variety of aquatic beetles are examples. A very diverse wetland flora includes marsh marigold, soft rush, gypsy wort and water-forget-me-not. The nearby tall hedge contains hawthorn, dogwood, alder and sycamore.

Management   The site was derelict when 'discovered' by the NUWG. A project day spent clearing the pond and some help from the Anglian Water Authority have helped increase the site's potential for wildlife.

Interpretation   Nil.

Access   Open at all times.

Contact   Northampton Urban Wildlife Group.

Further information

Leisure Services Department, Northampton BC, Town Hall, NN1 (0604 29033).

Northampton Urban Wildlife Group, Northamptonshire Trust for Nature Conservation, Lings House, Billing Lings, Northampton NN3 4BE (0604 405285).

Acknowledgement   Text written by Nick Barnes of NTNC.

NORWICH

In many respects Norwich differs from the large conurbations of the nation's industrial areas because it lacks many of the habitats commonly associated with these urban areas. Many sites of nature conservation value are in fact remnants of the countryside engulfed by the expanding city. Extensive areas of wildlife habitat are concentrated in the two river valleys and there are also woodlands that remain from once large country estates now surrounded by houses. The city council has begun to look at these open spaces with a view to developing their nature conservation and community potential through its Green Plan. This strategy provides a framework within which detailed policies are being formulated to protect and improve urban wildspace. Strong emphasis is placed on involvement from local groups, such as the Norwich Wildlife Group which, since its inception in 1984, has established itself as a provider of expert advice as well as fulfilling the role of a pressure group. The sites listed below represent the range of wildlife habitats from derelict land to remnant countryside. *City Safari Walks*, published by the Norwich Wildlife Group, is available from The Norwich Tourist Information Centre, The Guildhall, Gaol Hill, Norwich (0603 666071).

1 City Station

Heigham Street (TG 225096).
TNLS; various owners. 5ha.
Approach   Buses along Heigham Street or Drayton Road. Easily accessible by foot from city centre.
Summary   Until recently this area, on the site of a former station, was far more neglected than it is today and access was difficult. A path has now been created through the wood and the area greatly improved with some landscaping and conservation work undertaken to give it a more cared-for look. It is now a popular area for informal recreation. This is a typical urban wildlife site comprising a narrow strip of damp woodland lying between the now disused M&GN railway line and the River Wensum.
History   The railway line was abandoned in 1959 and since then the site has been derelict with the adjacent land being developed as an industrial estate. The railway line soon began to scrub over and the land between it and the river developed as woodland. The site became a convenient place to dump rubbish and soon attracted the attentions of road planners. Despite the threat of a road still hanging over it, the city council has in recent years undertaken many improvements to the site to make it more attractive. The railway line is now an official cycle path and continues as a long distance path into the countryside. There is also a footpath along the river edge and the whole area is now a popular recreation area.
Nature interest   The alder woodland is particularly good for birds with a variety of wetland and woodland species throughout the year. Long-tailed tits, treecreepers and jays can be seen all year round, whereas willow warbler, chiffchaff, blackcap and spotted flycatcher are summer visitors. During the winter months the woods are often alive with colourful finches, such as redpoll and siskin, feeding on the seeds of alder and birch. On the river and along its banks moorhen, coot and in winter the diminutive little grebe can be seen. The bankside vegetation resounds to the call of reed and sedge warblers

and occasionally the rare grey wagtail. The walk along the riveredge provides access to a host of wetland and aquatic plants, many of these find refuge in areas especially created by volunteer conservation workers. In one marshy clearing there is fools water cress, water parsnip, gypsywort and celery-leaved buttercup.

Along the railway line there are areas of wasteground that have a wide variety of wildflowers, many of them established from garden rubbish. In a short space of time it is possible to find over 100 species. Among them are bugloss, cotton thistle, blue fleabane, toadflax, tansy and birdsfoot-trefoil, the foodplant of the common blue butterfly. The interesting selection of garden escapes includes soapwort, sweet pea, evening primrose, American marigold, and these together with the ubiquitous buddleia are a rich source of nectar for numerous butterflies.

Management   Besides the creation of footpaths and bridges to open up the area, volunteers have created a series of marshy areas to encourage wetland plants and small areas of sallow scrub have been coppiced to provide dense cover for breeding birds.

Interpretation   None envisaged.

Access   Open at all times.

2   City Wall

Norwich CC.

Approach   Easily accessible by foot from city centre with main sections along Chapel Field Road and Carrow Hill.

Summary   The City Wall may not appear a very obvious place to look for wildlife but there are a number of features that make it particularly attractive to those interested in urban wildlife. Firstly, it is easily accessible with footpaths running along the entire length. Secondly, the surviving stretches are located in parks, some formal and some informal, that have their own wildlife interest. Thirdly, they are home to a number of interesting species not easily seen in more natural places in the city.

History   Henry III granted a licence to the city to build a ditch and pallisade to protect it and to levy tolls on traders who entered. By the late 13C to early 14C the *fossa* as it was known had been improved with flint and stone walls and was fortified with towers. These towers were used variously as prisons, homes for plague victims, snuff mills and as boom towers to protect the city from waterborne approach. A murage was levied on the inhabitants of the city for repairs to the walls but since the Middle Ages much has been destroyed. About 600m survive in scattered locations.

Nature interest   The wall provides a dry, sunny environment with ample crevices for plants to gain a foothold. Many of the plants found on the wall are introduced to this country. The Oxford ragwort, originally from the Mediterranean, escaped from the Oxford Botanical Garden during the 1790s, and ivy-leaved toadflax, probably escaping in the 16C, came from Italy. Other introduced species include rosebay willowherb, feverfew and along the most impressive stretch of wall on Carrow Hill there is yellow corydalis, wallpepper and wallflower. Among the native species are ferns such as male fern, polypody and hartstongue as well as pellitory-of-the-wall. Associated with the wall are sandy paths with areas of bare ground that harbour a fascinating selection of wasteland plants adapted to these conditions, including several species of speedwell, whitlow grass, shepherd's purse and the intriguingly named Venus's-looking glass.

Management   The walls are maintained as a historical monument with little concern for the plant life they hold and it is perhaps surprising that any plants survive at all. Undoubtedly, many species have been unable to establish themselves because of the regular repair work but those that do epitomise the tenacity required by plants in the urban environment and their colours add greatly to the attraction of the wall.

Interpretation   None envisaged.

Access   Open at all times.

Contact   Tourist Information Centre.

3 Kett's Heights

Kett's Hill (TG 242092).

Norwich CC. 1ha.

Approach   Buses along Kett's Hill or Riverside Road.

Summary   The site has been turned into a wildlife garden by the Norwich Wildlife Group. There are woodlands on the steep slopes and areas of mown grass and scrub. Volunteers have also planted hundreds of trees and introduced dozens of species of wild plants to attract more wildlife. The network of paths leads to a viewpoint that commands probably the best view of the centre of Norwich.

History   One of the garden's attractions is the historical associations dating back to the 11C. First, the area was the site of St Michael's Chapel, the remains of which can still be seen. Then Robert Kett set up his headquarters here in 1549 during the Norfolk Rebellion when he besieged Norwich. During the Victorian era it was laid out as a formal garden and during the Second World War it was turned over to an allotment. Finally, the site became derelict before being adopted by the Norwich Wildlife Group in 1984.

Nature interest   Many common species of wildflower have been introduced such as ox-eye daisy, tansy and primrose. These have joined those flowers left over from the time when the area was a garden, such as columbine, American golden-rod and bluebell. The most prominent plant, however, is alexanders which carpet much of the steep slopes and forms a bright green backcloth to the site in the first half of the year. For such a small site there is a good selection of common birds including blackcap, willow warbler, spotted flycatcher and mistle thrush. The view from the top enables close views of feeding swifts in the evenings and the occasional kestrel. The many wildflowers now attract meadow brown, small skipper and comma butterflies.

Management   Following the Norwich Wildlife Group's efforts to establish the garden, management is now shared with the city council. The site attempts to reconcile the needs of wildlife and people on a small site, for example, dense scrub areas have been planted to provide cover for birds while adjacent grassland is mown grass for recreation. A programme of gradual improvement to the site by introducing more wildflowers and tending young trees is continuing.

Interpretation   A guide to the history and natural history is available from the Tourist Information Centre.

Access   Open at all times.

Contact   Tourist Information Centre.

4   Marston Marshes

(TG 218056).
Norwich CC. 24ha.
Approach   Buses along Ipswich Road or Church Lane.
Summary   The Yare Valley Walk runs through this marshland site and there is a convenient circular walk of about two kilometres. The marshland comprises grazed paddocks intersected by dykes all set in an attractive valley landscape of farmland, hedgerows and small woods, right on the edge of the city. The site is often wet and may be under several metres of floodwater during the winter. Summertime sees a drop in water levels and it is possible to walk the site in stout footwear.
History   For many years the area was grazed by cattle and the dykes were maintained as water-filled field boundaries. In recent years this grazing, so vital to the survival of the area's rich wildlife, has ceased because of the difficulties of finding livestock to graze such a small, isolated area. Many features of the area's past exploitation can be found, including pollarded willows and the remains of wind pumps used in past drainage attempts.
Nature interest   The site has a wonderful array of both common and scarce marshland plants such as marsh marigold, water violet and cuckoo flower alongside less familiar bogbean, frogbit and flowering rush. The birdlife reflects the wet nature of the site with breeding reed warbler, sedge warbler and snipe. In the scrubby and woodland edge areas there is a wide variety of small birds including many warblers, redpoll and green woodpecker. In early spring the dykes hold large numbers of frogs and toads, whereas in late summer the site is noted for the distinctive banded demoiselle damselfly.
Management   A detailed management plan has been prepared for the site which includes a programme of regular maintenance of the six kilometres of dyke to maintain open water and the digging of ponds in less interesting areas. The key to the site's survival is the reinstatement of grazing or, failing that, mowing and the maintenance of the high water level through a system of sluices.
Interpretation   To date there is no interpretive material but the management plan calls for improvements in access, the creation of a marshland garden with facilities for schoolchildren and interpretive leaflets.
Access   Open at all times.

5   Mousehold Heath

Gurney Road (TG 243101).
Norwich CC. 75ha.
Approach   Buses along Mousehold Lane, Heartsease Lane and Sprowston Road.
Summary   Mousehold is a remnant of heathland and woodland totally surrounded by housing and providing a vital open space in the N of the city. In the intensively farmed landscape of Norfolk it offers city dwellers the opportunity to experience a wild environment.
History   The Heath was conveyed to the city in 1880 by the Dean and Chapter of Norwich cathedral to be used for 'lawful recreation'. Over the centuries the Heath has attracted many artists to its open landscape. Today, however, due to lack of management the open heath is very restricted and much of the area has reverted to woodland.
Nature interest   The heathland areas remaining are now small but

are an attractive feature in late summer with the mauve heather and other associated species such as bell heather, gorse and western gorse, a dwarf species more commonly found in the W of the country. Dependent on these open areas are common lizards and birds such as yellowhammer and linnet. Most of the woodland comprises birch with areas of mature oak wood. These hold many bird species such as great and lesser spotted woodpecker, willow warbler and redpoll and occasionally the distinctive trilling sound of the wood warbler can be heard above the roar of passing traffic. The woodlands are also a good place to look for fungi including fly agaric, wood blewit, tawny grisette and penny bun.

Management   Despite the many pressures on the site there has been minimal management of the open heath with the result that scrub and bracken has spread rapidly, controlled only by accidental fires. Local voluntary conservation groups have now begun management in a demonstration area which will aim to restore heather and diversify the young woodland. The results of this management will then be applied to other areas on the Heath.

Interpretation   An interpretive leaflet is available from the Tourist Information Centre or Amenities offices.

Access   Open at all times.

Further information

Norwich City Council, Amenities Department, Elliot House, 130 Ber Street, Norwich NR1 3EH (0603 622233).

Tourist Information Centre, Guildhall, Gaol Hill, Norwich NR2 1NF (0603 620679).

Norwich Wildlife Group, c/o 69 Bethel Street, Norwich (0603 664327).

Acknowledgement   Text written by Reg Land of the Norwich Wildlife Group.

NOTTINGHAM

The River Trent flows to the S of the city. Through the W side of the city flows the River Leen which meets the Trent just S of the city, having entered Nottingham in the suburb of Bulwell. Large sites within the city include Wollaton Park where the Hall contains a natural history museum. Main industries of the city have included lace and bicycles and now are tobacco, telecommunications and pharmacy products. The urban section of the Nottinghamshire Trust for Nature Conservation (NTNC), the Nottingham Urban Wildlife Scheme (NUWS), manages several sites within the city.

1 Broxtowe Country Park

Nuthall Road.
Nottingham CC.
Broxtowe Wood   (SK 528431). Approx 6ha.
Approach   Access gained by turning off the A610 near Babbington Colliery and driving along a rough track.
Summary   An ancient woodland with hazel coppice, magnesian-limestone grassland and a small marsh.
History   The woodland has no doubt been used as a source of timber in the past. Dumping of colliery waste from nearby Babbington Colliery has also taken place, evidence of which may be found in the wood and on the N embankment.
Nature interest   Surveys have shown that Broxtowe Wood has a rich and valuable flora. Local rarities such as giant bellflower and yellow rattle can be found. Among 33 species of birds recorded are jays, great spotted woodpecker, brambling, willow tit and grey wagtails. Frogs and grey squirrels have been seen and there are signs that foxes, rabbits and moles are present. Woodmice are also common.
Management   The site is managed by the city recreation department in consultation with NUWS. A large area of the wood was once maintained as hazel coppice but this has fallen into neglect. Some attempt has been made at coppicing the sycamore in the S part of the wood.
Interpretation   None.
Access   Open at all times.
Contact   City Recreation Department and NUWS.

2 Bulwell Hall Park

Squires Avenue, Bulwell.
The Park, bought by Sir Albert Ball in 1908 and acquired by the city council thereafter, contains three sites of wildlife interest.
Homewood   (SK 532469). 3ha.
Approach   From Camberley Road, Bulwell.
Summary   A mature sycamore and ash plantation.
History   In 1881, which is as far back as maps exist, the wood was called Black Wood and contained both deciduous and coniferous trees. A stream entered from an underground pipe and flowed across open fields and woodlands. By 1915 the wood was called Home Wood and it was the same shape and size as today. A thin strip was bordered by a metre-high hedge. By this time the golf links and nursery bordering the wood had been established. The sewage works had

been built by 1930 on the path of the stream flowing into the wood and the stream channelled underneath this. By 1949 the adjacent airfield had been established to the NE and fenced off from the wood.

Nature interest   The site is a sycamore and ash plantation with a ground flora dominated by dog's mercury. Also contained are several species of local interest including nettle-leaved bellflower and yellow archangel making Home Wood an important site for the city.

Management   Some years ago an area of wood was clear-felled to remove a large number of dead elms and to sell timber for cash. An area was coppiced, but was then left to regrow.

Interpretation   None.

Access   Open at all times.

Contact   City Recreation Department.

Barkers Wood   (SK 537465). 2.5ha.

Approach   From Camberley Road, Bulwell.

Summary   A mixed oak woodland with a dense scrub layer.

Nature interest   Barkers wood is a mixed woodland comprising areas of oak, ash, birch and sycamore. Oak and ash are dominant. There are some 14 vegetation types to be found including interesting local species such as wood sedge and wood melick, and it is one of the few sites within the city in which wood sorrel grows. It is one of only two good oak woodland sites inside the city boundary.

Management   City Recreation Department.

Interpretation   None.

Bulwell Park Meadow   (SK 536469). 0.5ha.

Approach   Camberley Road.

Summary   Old calcareous hay meadow on magnesium limestone.

Nature interest   The grassland is dominated by tor grass with the low growing herbaceous species yellow rattle, agrimony and common restharrow. A number of local species typical of calcareous and ancient grassland occur at the site, including dropwort, sweet vernal grass, quaking grass, glaucus sedge and crested dog's tail.

Management   City Recreation Department and NUWS.

Interpretation   None.

3   Chilwell Dam Plantation

(SK 517429). Approx 2ha.

Approach   By foot through Broxtowe Country Park; also off Shanwell Close, Broxtowe, via a footpath.

Summary   An area of mixed secondary woodland with a series of old fish ponds.

History   Shown as three ponds with sluice gates running into Broxtowe Wood on the first Ordnance Survey map (1832–38), Chilwell Dam Plantation is marked, indicating it was planted rather than natural woodland. Thomas Webb Edge, who lived at Strelley Hall, was responsible for this. From a woodland census in 1920 it was found that all land adjacent to the plantation was improved agricultural land. A new Nottingham loop road was slightly rerouted to by-pass the wood following local pressure.

Nature interest   The wetland flora includes horsetail, marsh marigold, willow and sallow. In the woodland can be found dog's mercury, wood anemone, yellow archangel and both nettle-leaved and clustered bellflower. Great spotted woodpeckers, jay, turtle dove and sparrowhawk inhabit the site. Small mammals found are woodmouse, bank vole and fox among others.

Management   City Recreation Department and NUWS.
Interpretation   None.
Access   Open at all times.
Contact   City Recreation Department and NUWS.

4 Colwick Park and Nature Reserve

Colwick Road (SK 605395).
Nottingham CC. Approx 3ha.
Approach   Along Colwick Road (B686) or via Racecourse Road or Mile End Road off Colwick Road.
Summary   Colwick Country Park is a large recreational area which contains a small nature reserve. This consists of woodland enclosing an interesting wetland area.
History   Colwick Country Park originated from former gravel workings just four kilometres to the E of Nottingham city centre. It was jointly developed by Nottingham council and Severn Trent Water Authority with assistance from the Countryside Commission and Sports Council. Work began in 1976 and the park was opened in 1979.
Nature interest   Colwick Park nature reserve consists of a sycamore woodland which has developed around an area of open water known as The Loop. The site contains some interesting wetland features and supports several local species including marsh foxtail, greater pond sedge, yellow iris and skullcap. The reserve is an important site for the city as it contains a diverse range of plant communities from mixed woodland to wetland. These provide habitats for sedge warblers, swallows, coots, moorhens and tufted ducks. The reed swamp also provides a spawning area for fish, frogs, toads and newts. The largest areas of open water within the park support large numbers of migrant waterbirds, particularly winter wildfowl.
Management   The council is ensuring further planting within the area.
Interpretation   The site is run by wardens and there is easy access to the nature trails. Pamphlets on the trail can be obtained at Colwick Park or the city council.
Access   Open at all times.
Contact   City Recreation Department.

5 Fairham Brook

Green Lane, Clifton (SK 559337).
Nottingham CC. Approx 10ha.
Approach   Various access points.
Summary   A linear wetland reserve with areas of reedbed and scrub.
History   The reserve was originally established as an educational resource for the adjoining school, but this use has lapsed over the years.
Nature interest   Fairham Brook comprises a strip of lowland fen, with reedbeds and scrub. Clumps of blackthorn and hawthorn occur on the bank of Fairham Brook which forms the N boundary, and along Farnborough Road there are also areas of willow scrub. There is a pond in which frogs spawn. Owing to lowering of the brook, the

middle section of the site is now dry meadow and plants include meadow cranesbill, great burnet, yarrow, meadowsweet, knapweed, tufted vetch, lady's bedstraw and devil's bit scabious. The brook itself contains a good selection of invertebrates as well as chub, sticklebacks and bullheads. Birds include heron and kingfisher.

Management   The site is managed by NTNC which seeks to improve local awareness of the status of the reserve.

Interpretation   Fact sheet available from NTNC.

Access   Open at all times.

Contact   Local Warden, 390 Farnborough Road, Clifton, Nottingham, NG11 9AD or NTNC.

6   Harrison's Plantation

Old Coach Road, off Wollaton Road (SK 530403).
Nottingham CC. 2ha.

Approach   Also approachable via Martin's Pond.

Summary   A mixed ash and sycamore woodland containing a willow holt and a fishing pond.

History   The plantation is around 200 years old and resulted from natural regeneration on a series of 'stew ponds' and willow plantations associated with the medieval fishery at the adjacent Martin's Pond. The fishing pond is of more recent origin (it does not feature on Sanderson's Map of 1835) and may have been excavated as a source of blue clay for bricks, or to provide a puddling agent for the nearby Nottingham Canal. More recently the plantation assumed a recreational use as an amenity woodland for local residents.

Nature interest   This site is a mixed willow, ash and sycamore wood. Ten vegetation types occur and it is the only city location for broad-leaved helleborine. Nettles and brambles dominate the ground flora. The plantation supports a variety of typical woodland bird species including great spotted woodpecker and nuthatch. Treecreeper occurs in the winter months. Several riparian species occur around the fishing pond including kingfisher in autumn/winter. Typical woodland mammals (grey squirrel, wood mouse) also occur. The fishing pond and the other damp areas of the plantation provide an excellent habitat for amphibians with common frog and common toad both present. Several species of fish occur in the pond.

Flora includes mixed beds of fool's water cress and lesser water parsnip; rich tall-grass/herb communities; mixed scrub and hedgerows of hawthorn and blackthorn willow and an understorey herb layer dominated by dog's mercury.

Management   The site is licensed to the NTNC and managed by NUWS.

Access   Open at all times.

Contact   NUWS.

7   Martin's Pond

Russell Avenue, off Russell Drive, Wollaton (SK 527401).
Nottingham CC. 4ha.

Approach   Buses from city centre.

Summary   An artificial wetland containing areas of open water and stands of emergent aquatic vegetation. It is an excellent site for birdlife.

History   Possibly one of three ponds referred to in the Nottingham Canal Act 1792; possibly a fish pond associated with the original Wollaton Hall. The site is a Local Nature Reserve, the first declared in the city as the council's contribution to European Wetland Year 1976.

Nature interest   The site is an urban wetland, comprising a large area of open water, reed swamp and a small central wooded island. Breeding birds include willow, sedge and reed warblers, great crested and little grebes and ruddy duck. Small numbers of common wildfowl occur in winter and spring, as do water rail and snipe. Pied wagtails and yellowhammers sometimes roost. There are few waders in general owing to the lack of muddy areas. Frogs and toads spawn annually and smooth and palmate newts are present. Other vertebrates include water shrew and water vole, other voles, mice and fox. Invertebrates include swan and pea mussels, dragonflies, mayflies, flatworm and leeches. One of the most important features of the reserve is the large stand of the uncommon lesser reedmace which is being infiltrated by the common reedmace.

Over 150 flowering plants have been recorded, none particularly rare except in the context of the city location, including water mint, water figwort, fool's water cress, sweet-flag and marsh arrow grass.

Management   The site is managed by the council and NTNC for its wildlife interest.

Interpretation   Fact sheet available from NTNC.

Access   Open at all times.

Contact   City Recreation Department.

8   Moorbridge Pond

Bulwell (SK 546468).

Nottingham CC. Approx 2.5ha.

Approach   Hucknall Road and Bestwood Road, these roads forming the sites boundaries to the W, S and E.

Summary   A small but diverse wetland site on the boundary of the city.

History   Before the Second World War a concrete revetment wall was built around what is thought to mark the position of the original 'Bull-Well'. At the same time a pipe was laid under Moorbridge Pond, probably circumventing the marshland, to the nearby dye works. Prior to the 1930s a stream arose at the Bull-Well and flowed across what is now the wetland of the pond. This used to be a popular venue for Nottingham residents to bathe and for 'dayoutings'. The stream was also used by a local dyers and finishers works.

Nature interest   Moorbridge Pond is a very diverse wetland which supports all the known horsetail species found within the city and lady fern which is rare in urban areas. Other locally uncommon species are slender tufted sedge, ivy leaved duckweed and skullcap. It is also valuable for its reptiles including common lizards and adders. This is also an important breeding site for wetland birds, reed warblers, reed buntings, teal, snipe and kestrel have been seen here.

Management   The site is licensed to NTNC from the city council and is managed by NUWS.

Interpretation   Fact sheet available from NTNC.

Access   By arrangement with·the NUWS.

Contact   NUWS.

9   Parish Boundary Hedge, Broxtowe

Nottingham CC and Broxtowe BC (SK 523431).
Approach   Runs along the N and W borders of Broxtowe Country Park adjacent to Broxtowe Wood.
Summary   An ancient parish boundary hedgerow that still retains the old double ditch system in places.
History   Part of the hedge is thought to be over 800 years old. On the W side of the hedge, before recent housing development, was Assarts Farm, formed by clearance of a wood long before the Enclosures Acts. Assarts Farm was leased out as a source of revenue to the owner during the reign of Richard I (1189–99). The hedge marks the boundary between Nuthall and Bilborough parishes.
Nature interest   Among the wildlife can be found moles, hare, fox, bank voles, and long-tailed field mice. Meadow pipit, greenfinch, bullfinch, linnet, great tit and blue tit are among the 23 species of birds sighted. Many varieties of herbs include herb robert, red campion, lady's mantle, white bryony and yellow archangel.
Management   Broxtowe BC and Nottingham CC in collaboration with NUWS.
Interpretation   None.
Access   There is unlimited access to the whole length of the hedge from Broxtowe Country Park which is on the S and E side of the hedge.
Contact   NUWS.

10   Quarry Holes Plantation

Nuthall Road (SK 537433).
Nottingham CC. Approx 2ha.
Approach   May be approached from Nuthall Road or Tilbury Rise or from the disused line which can be reached via Broxtowe or Bells Lane.
Summary   A small mixed secondary woodland on the site of a former limestone quarry.
History   The Quarry Holes site has been used for quarrying since the 15C. 'Basford' stone taken from the site was used to repair the Trent Bridge in the city. The quarry was used for local house building too, but that ceased about 100 years ago.
Nature interest   A green island surrounded by housing contains a mixture of ash and sycamore with a limited woodland ground flora.
Management   The site is licensed to NTUC by the city council and is managed by NUWS under licence to the NTNC. Its proximity to the Cinderhill housing estate and to several schools such as William Crane School and Basford Hall College makes it a potentially valuable reserve for educational and recreational activities.
Interpretation   None.
Access   Open at all times.
Contact   NUWS.

11   Sellers Wood

Sellers Wood Drive, Bulwell (SK 524454).Nottingham CC. Approx 15ha.
Approach   Off the outer loop road.
Summary   An area of ancient woodland and heathland containing several small ponds and with a pleasant nature trail.

History Once part of Sherwood Forest, it provides a refuge for wildlife within the urban area. Sellers Wood was declared an LNR in 1981 having been purchased from Richard Sankey & Son Ltd in 1967. The trail was the first to be developed by Nottinghamshire county council in conjunction with the NCC, Countryside Commission, NTNC and neighbouring local authorities.

Nature interest A diverse ground flora contains a number of species which are indicative of ancient woodland, including giant bellflower, early purple orchid, yellow archangel and wood anemone. There are several well-vegetated ponds, which contain a wide range of aquatic fauna, and which provide drinking areas for woodland birds and mammals. Birds include most of the common woodland species and kingfishers have been seen.

Management Managed by Nottingham CC jointly with NTNC.

Interpretation A leaflet is available from the City Recreation Department.

Access Open at all times.

Contact NTNC.

12 Thompson's Wood

(SK 528388). 6ha.

Approach Through Wollaton Park around lake.

Summary An acidic woodland including damp marshy areas.

Nature interest Part of the Wollaton Hall Estate, Thompson's Wood is an acidic woodland that runs along the W boundary of the park. The centre of the wood contains an area of marshland that has developed under the influence of outflow water from the adjacent ornamental lake.

The site is rich in wildlife including badgers, grey squirrels and field mice. The wetland contains local species such as celery-leaved buttercup, skullcap, ragged robin, bog bean and false fox sedge. The site is important for both the city and the county as it contains the rare urban vegetation types, common club rush and wood club rush. The site also contains the best examples within the city of willow and alder woodland on damp soils.

Management The city recreation department aims to encourage the re-establishment of ground flora after the construction of a concrete embankment along the edge of the lake.

Interpretation None.

Contact City Recreation Department.

13 Wollaton Park

Wollaton Road.

Nottingham CC. Approx 170ha.

Approach Vehicle entrance on Wollaton Road; pedestrian via Wollaton Road, Middleton Boulevard, Derby Road and Parkside.

Summary An extensive area of parkland with an ornamental lake and patches of woodland including Thompson's Wood described above.

History Sir Richard Willoughby acquired estates in Wollaton through marriage and the family eventually settled in the Manor House near the church in the 13C. The Hall was rebuilt around 1588 and became the home of Baron Middleton in 1711. In 1925 the Hall and Estate were sold to the Nottingham Corporation for £200,000. 1926 saw the opening of the city's Natural History Museum, and in 1970 an Industrial Museum.

Nature interest The main attraction of the park are the herds of fallow and red deer. Tawny owls, great crested grebe and little grebe are found around the wooded areas and the lake. From October to mid February there is a large rook roost. Within the grounds there are also four species of bats: noctule, long eared, whiskered and pipistrelle.

Management The park is managed by the council which employs groundsmen and a gamekeeper whose main task is to care for the deer.

Interpretation There are many walks around the park, with well laid out paths and signed routes to follow. More information on these are available at Wollaton Hall.

Access Open during daylight hours.

Contact City Recreation Department.

Further information

Nottingham CC, Recreation Department, Woodthorpe Grange, Nottingham.

Nottinghamshire Trust for Nature Conservation, 310 Sneinton Dale, Nottingham NG3 7DN (0602 588242).

City Group (NTNC), c/o Elizabeth Palmer, 1 Rathmines Close, Lenton, Nottingham NG7 2LS (0602 783278).

Botanical Survey of the City of Nottingham by J.O. O'Reilly and S.E. Page (James Davies and Partners, Nottingham).

Acknowledgement Text written by Niall Machin and colleagues on the Nottingham Urban Wildlife Scheme (NUWS) of Notts TNC.

GREATER MANCHESTER

Greater Manchester is a compact county; some 1300 square kilometres in extent and only 35 kilometres from N to S and 55 kilometres across. It is located in the upper reaches of the River Mersey basin and rests against the Pennines Chain. It has a very varied landscape from remote moorland and wooded cloughs to gently rolling plain and mossland. Ten districts range around the cities of Manchester and Salford at the heart of the conurbation.

The Pennine Hills sweep around the N and E of the county, encircling Bolton, Bury, Rochdale, Oldham, Tameside and Stockport. In many places they reach 460 metres and are incised by steep-sided valleys and gorges. Mainly of millstone grits, alternating hard and soft rocks have caused great staircases up the valley sides. The hills are topped by peat moor.

Below these hills flow the large rivers Irwell, Tame, Medlock, Irk and Roch on their way to the Mersey. This is where the major cotton towns grew up. The terraced flood plains of the Lower Irwell and Mersey rivers are largely open and, swelled by its upper tributaries, the Mersey runs wide and slow.

Different again is the well-treed, rolling land to the S through which flows the River Bollin, the edge of Stockport, Manchester and Trafford districts.

Over the rest of Greater Manchester, covering the whole of Wigan, coal-bearing rocks have formed an almost flat landscape. It is enriched by woodland cover and the large lakes and reed beds caused by subsidence from former deep mining. The River Douglas flows from here, not to the Mersey, but NW to the Ribble estuary.

BOLTON

1   Bradshaw Brook and Jumbles Country Park

3km N of Bolton (several sites N and S of SD 735140).
Bolton MBC.

Approach   By train from Bolton to Bromley Cross or by car via A676 and B6391.

Summary   Part of the larger Croal/Irwell Valley, and linking with the West Pennine Moors, this attractive tributary valley holds several woodlands and reservoirs.

Nature interest   There are good deciduous woodlands with bluebell carpets and other flowers, scrubs, water areas and associated reedbeds and marsh. Kingfisher, grey wagtail and dipper are regularly seen. Jumbles Reservoir near the head of the valley is famous for its breeding and wintering waterpool, notably grebes, swans, coot and many duck.

Management   Nature conservation interests are managed here alongside farming, recreation and water catchment interests.

Interpretation   At Jumbles Country Park there is an information centre (0204 853360) and information boards.

Access   Open at all times.

Contact   West Pennine Moors Ranger Service (WPMRS) and Croal Irwell Valley Warden Service (CIVWS).

2 Doffcocker Lodge

Moss Bank Way, Doffcocker BL1 (SD 685103).
Bolton MBC. 10ha.
Approach Buses along Chorley Old Road from Bolton and also by car from A58 Bolton Ring Road (Moss Bank Way).
Summary Attractive water area located on the edge of the town below Smithills Moor.
Nature interest Among the best sites in the county for wintering waterfowl, it has large numbers of duck including rare visitors. Tufted duck, pochard, goldeneye, wigeon and teal congregate in large numbers, while breeding birds include mallard, Canada geese, coot, moorhen and grebes.
Management Managed as a nature reserve.
Access Open at all times.
Contact Bolton Recreation Section.

3 Moses Gate Country Park

Hall Lane, Farnworth, BL4 (SD 742065).
Bolton MBC. 100ha.
Approach By train on the Manchester to Bolton line to Moses Gate station. By bus from Bolton towards Little Lever. By car from M61 and A666 (St Peters Way).
Summary/history Once mill ponds and industrial waste tips, the area has been reclaimed to become an attractive valley with the River Croal flowing through it.
Nature interest The ponds and reedbeds are excellent for water birds including swans, geese, ducks, grebes and visiting kingfishers and herons. The reedbeds, scrub and young woodland attract many warblers.
Management Being a country park, this area is managed to balance the needs of recreation and nature by the warden service.

Moses Gate Country Park, Croal-Irwell Valley

Interpretation   There is an information centre in the country park.
Access   Open at all times.
Contact   CIVWS.

4 Nob End

Prestolee Road, Radcliffe M26 (SD 750064).
Bolton MBC. 11ha.
Approach   Via Moses Gate Country Park (above) or by car from
Radcliffe or Little Lever and Prestolee Road.
Summary/history   A triangular site at the confluence of the rivers
Croal and Irwell and bounded by the Manchester Bolton and Bury
canal, a former alkali waste tip from the turn of the century has since
naturally colonised.
Nature interest   The lime flora is very attractive and species-rich,
with many uncommon plants such as blue fleabane, carline thistle
and blue-eyed grass and huge colonies of fragrant orchids and several
species of marsh orchid. There is also common broomrape. The best
'industrial' site in the county, it has great scientific and educational
value and its plant ecology has been described in several scientific
papers and books. It is currently under consideration as an SSSI, and
good for butterflies and moths, especially the common blue and five
spot burnet.
Management   A warden service manages the site, mainly for
nature conservation.
Access   Open at all times.
Contact   CIVWS.

5 Rumworth Lodge

New Tempest Road, Lostock BL6 (SD 677078).
Bolton MBC. 17ha.
Approach   Close to junction 5 of M61 from the A58 Bolton Ring
Road and along Lock Lane.
Summary   Attractive water area within farmland to the SW of
Bolton.
Nature interest   Pochard, shoveler, tufted duck and whooper
swans are among the winter visiting waterfowl. The surrounding
grasslands attract winter thrushes and in summer the reedbeds and
marsh provide cover for breeding reed and sedge warblers. Snipe and
lapwing visit in large numbers.
Management   No organised management.
Access   Can be viewed from surrounding roads and paths at all
times.
Contact   No special contact point.

Further information

Bolton MBC, Environmental Services Department, Recreation
Section, Wells Spring, Victoria Square, Bolton (0204 22311).
West Pennine Moors Ranger Service (0204 694880).
Jumbles Country Park Warden (0204 853360).
Croal Irwell Valley Warden Service (0204 71561).
Greater Manchester Countryside Unit, West End Offices, Jowetts
Walk, Ashton-under-Lyne, Tameside OL7 0BB (061 343 3134).
Lancashire Trust for Nature Conservation, Manchester Office, c/o

Environmental Institute, Greaves School, Bolton Road, Swinton, Bolton M27 2UX (061 794 9314).

LTNC Bolton Group, c/o Hall i'th' Wood Museum, Bolton, BL1 8UA (0204 22311).

Acknowledgement Text of this and the other Greater Manchester district sections were written by the Greater Manchester Countryside Unit.

BURY

1 Chesham Woods

Chesham Road, Bury BL9 (SD 815125).
Bury MBC.
Approach By bus along Walmersley Road and then along Chesham Road.
Summary Four blocks of woodland on the outskirts of Bury, planted in grounds of a now-demolished mansion.
History The woodlands fell into disrepair following demolition of the house and have been the subject of a number of development proposals. In the light of this a number of bodies have undertaken the upkeep and improvement of the woods.
Nature interest There are small numbers of woodland plants and birds. Bats also occur in the area.
Management Managed by the local authority, LTNC, Bury & District Conservation Volunteers, BTCV, local residents and, very recently, Community Task Force. Dry stone walling, hedge laying, treeplanting and erection of bat boxes have already been carried out. Future tasks include creation of paths and planting of wildflowers.
Access Open at all times.
Contact LTNC Manchester office.

2 Gollingrod Wood, Broadhey and Woodhey Woods

Between Nuttall Hall Lane, Ramsbottom (SD 784158) and Woodhey Road, Holcombe Brook, Ramsbottom (SD 798152).
Bury MBC. 42ha.
Approach By car from A676, by bus from Bury to Holcombe Brook and Ramsbottom.
Summary On the Irwell as it flows S from the W Pennine Moors is Gollinrod Wood, an area of oakwood with willow scrub and to its SW is Broadhey and Woodhey woods. These are steep and narrow cloughs comprising ancient or long-established woodland and fast flowing streams.
Nature interest This is an area of general wildlife value with an attractive understorey and rich ground flora locally, including bluebell carpets, dogs mercury, wood sorrel and great woodrush. Common spotted orchids and unusual plants occur on the lime waste of a former chemical works.
Management Management seeks to control bank erosion by the fast flowing stream and to bring rejuvenation to this mature woodland.
Access Open at all times.

3 Kirklees Brook

Garside Hey Road, Bury, BL8 (SD 783130).
Bury MBC. 29ha.
Approach By bus from Bury towards Ramsbottom along Brandlesholme Road (B6214).
Summary This brook flows from the Edgeworth Moors to join the River Irwell at Bury and the valley contains several mill ponds.

Nature interest   Noted for its wide and interesting range of industrial and semi-natural habitats, the brook includes water areas which support a very rich flora and fauna, such as breeding newts, sticklebacks, molluscs, dragonflies and damselflies. Wild flowers of note are common valerian, meadowsweet, common spotted orchids, ragged robin and yellow flag. There are breeding kingfisher, wagtails and warblers.

Management   The local authority is attempting to extend management and accessibility further into this valley.

Access   Open at all times by various paths.

Contact   CIVWS.

4   Manchester Bolton and Bury Canal

Wellington Street, Bury BL5 to Nob End in Bolton (S from SD 793010). BWB. 8km.

Approach   A few minutes' walk from Bury town centre. The towpath forms part of The Irwell Valley Way walk.

Summary/history   Water traffic finally ceased in 1966 leaving an attractive rural walk alongside an interesting water habitat, within the Croal Irwell Valley.

Nature interest   It is noted for its aquatic flora containing several uncommon plants and marginal marsh communities are also of interest, including spiked water-millfoil, frog-bit and local arrowhead. Several species of pondweed are present including rarities such as wrack-like pondweed, and flat-stalked pondweed. Marsh plants include skullcap, marsh pennywort, purple loosestrife and royal fern in a few places. Freshwater jellyfish have been recorded.

Management   Negotiations are under way with BWB for local authority acquisition or to enable it to manage the canal as a recreation and natural history resource.

Access   Open at all times.

Contact   CIVWS.

5   Mere Clough

Clifton Road, Prestwich, M25 (SD 799038). Bury MBC. 40ha.

Approach   By bus along Bury New Road, (A56) between Bury and Manchester.

Summary   Bradley Brook runs through a narrow wooded valley to join the River Irwell. This is only four kilometres from Manchester city centre.

Nature interest   This is a long established mature woodland which offers a good range of other wildlife habitats. Predominantly sycamore with oak, birch and beech, and rich in willows, hazel and other shrubs. Wet areas support giant horsetail, meadowsweet, angelica and spotted orchids. Water fern is to be found on one pond.

Management   Management seeks to control bank erosion by the fast flowing stream and to bring rejuvenation to this mature woodland.

Access   Open at all times along public footpaths.

Contact   CIVWS.

Further information

Bury MBC, Planning Department, Craig House, Bank Street, Bury (061 705 5000).
Croal Irwell Valley Warden Service (0204 71561).
Greater Manchester Countryside Unit (address under Bolton).
LTNC Croal-Irwell Group, 338 Ringley Road West, Radcliffe, Bury (061 724 6289).

MANCHESTER

1 Abbey Villa Park

Pencroft Way, Hulme, M15 (SD 844964).
Manchester Science Park.
Approach Buses along Lloyd Street North, then via Burlington Street and Pencroft Way.
Summary A habitat creation site on formerly derelict land.
History A plot of derelict land within Manchester Science Park, originally thought to have been housing. The area was developed in 1984 by NPK Landscapes (on behalf of Landlife) creating a variety of habitats, using money from Manchester CC's Community Initiatives Fund.
Nature interest A variety of habitats include a pond with a marshy margin, neutral grassland and developing scrub. The site attracts a variety of wildlife, including a thriving frog population.
Management Managed by the LTNC with the help of local community groups and schools.
Access Open at all times.
Contact LTNC Manchester office.

2 Blackley Forest and Heaton Vale Reservoirs

Blackley New Road, M9 (SD 840035).
Manchester CC. 15ha.
Approach Buses between Manchester and Middleton along Middleton Road (A576).
Summary On valley side of River Irk and near Heaton Park.
Nature interest Woodland and reservoir offer a wide range of wildlife habitats: alder, birch and oak with colonies of wood anemone, lesser celandine, marsh marigold and butterbur. Reservoirs contain water violet. There is abundant ladies' smock in places.
Access Open at all times.
Contact Manchester Recreation Department.

3 Boggart Hole Clough

Rochdale Road, Blackley, M10 (SD 865025).
Manchester CC. 33ha.
Approach Buses between Manchester and Middleton along Rochdale Road (A664).
Summary A large open area deep within the conurbation and part of the Irk Valley.
Nature interest Remnant clough woodland of oak and birch with colonies of bluebells. Many woodland birds and swifts, swallows and house martins occur in open spaces. Tufted duck and other waterfowl are on the pond.
Access Open at all times.
Contact Manchester Recreation Department.

4 Fletcher Moss

Millgate Lane, Didsbury, M20 (SJ 847902).

Manchester CC. 5ha.

Approach   Trains from Manchester to East Didsbury station. Buses from Manchester and by car off A34, on to A5145 (Wilmslow Road).

Summary   Part of a larger area open to the public—the Mersey Valley.

Nature interest   An attractive wildlife area within a bend of the Mersey, it is important for its ponds, marsh and wet willow woodland which has a rich insect and bird population: sedges, greater reedmace, yellow flag, marsh marigold, angelica, marsh woundwort and purple loosestrife. Ponds contain abundant frogs and introduced newts.

Management   Managed for recreation and wildlife.

Interpretation   None at present.

Access   Open at all times.

Contact   Mersey Valley Warden Service (MVWAS).

5   Moston Railway Sidings

Williams Road, Failsworth, MIO (SD 883016).
Private.

Approach   By bus along The Broadway or St Mary's Road and then via The Fairway or by train to Dean Lane Station.

Summary   A base-rich marsh situated between housing and a main rail link some three kilometres from Manchester city centre. The site is used casually by children, but there is great scope for more formal educational use and community involvement.

History   This is unclear, but the marsh appears to have developed following construction of the railway. The adjacent housing was developed on the former Failsworth golf course.

Nature interest   The base-rich clay has been colonised by a variety of marsh species, including southern marsh orchid, common spotted orchid, marsh ragwort, sneezewort and adder's tongue fern as well as many sedges and bryophyte species. Frogs and smooth newts breed in substantial numbers and several bird species are found on the site, including the occasional snipe.

Management   The site is managed by LTNC under an informal agreement with the owners. The Trust hopes to develop the site as a reserve in the future.

Interpretation   None at present.

Access   Open at all times.

Contact   LTNC Manchester office.

6   Sunbank Wood

Sunbank Lane, Thorns Green, Altrincham (SJ 799841).
Manchester CC. 15ha.

Approach   By car from junction 6 of M56 with A538.

Summary   Attractive area of mature woodland in the Bollin Valley.

Nature interest   An oak and sycamore woodland, it is noted for its rich woodland floor plant communities and birdlife. Bluebells, wood anemone, lesser celandine, ramsons, yellow archangel, lords and ladies and drooping sedge.

Management   The warden service is managing the wood for recreation and wildlife and ensuring renewal of oak.

Interpretation   None.

Access   Open at all times.

Contact   Bollin Valley Warden Service (BVWS).

Further information

Manchester City Council, Recreation Department, Alexandra Centre Offices, 2 Southcombe Walk, off Moss Lane East, Manchester M15 5NW (061 226 0131).
Mersey Valley Warden Service (061 491 1647).
Bollin Valley Warden Service (0625 534790).
Greater Manchester Countryside Unit (address under Bolton).
LTNC Manchester Office (see under Bolton).

OLDHAM

1 Daisy Nook Country Park

Newmarket Road, Ashton-under-Lyne OL7 and Stanneybrook Road, Failsworth, M35 (SD 920007).
Oldham/Tameside MBC. 19ha.
Approach   By car from A62 at Failsworth along either Ashton Road West and East or Mersey Road North. Also from Oldham/Ashton Road (A627) along Newmarket Road and into Stannybrook Road.
Summary   In the heart of the Medlock Valley is a country park offering both recreation and wildlife interest.
Nature interest   Oak and ash woodlands with varied wildlife habitats with hawthorn, bramble, guelder rose and holly, colonies of common spotted orchids, centuary and angelica. Crime Lake with its water fowl is nearby.
Management   The warden service manages this area to balance recreation and wildlife needs.
Interpretation   Visitor centre at the country park.
Access   Open at all times.
Contact   Medlock Valley Warden Service (MVWS).

2 Huddersfield Narrow Canal

From Uppermill in Oldham (SD 996060) to Stalybridge in Tameside. BWB. 13km.
Approach   From A670 at Uppermill (buses from Oldham) and many other access points through to Stalybridge where the canal starts near the town centre at the junction of Mottram Road (A6019) and Huddersfield Road (B6175).
Summary   Running through the Tame Valley, the canal towpath is an attractive walk.
Nature interest   The canal has developed a surprisingly rich and varied aquatic flora and fauna including many unusual species and rarities to the county. It has just been notified as an SSSI. Abundant arrowhead, floating water plantain, perfoliate pondweed, flat-stalked pondweed, wrack-like pondweed. Also flowering rush and royal fern. Animal life includes freshwater sponge, dragonflies, fish, amphibians and snails. Kingfishers and grey wagtails are seen.
Management   As canal boat traffic increases, natural history is being protected.
Access   Open at all times.
Contact   Tame Valley Warden Service (TVWS).

Further information

Oldham MBC, Leisure Services Department, Civic Centre, West Street, Oldham, OL1 1XN (061 624 0505).
Medlock Valley Warden Service (061 330 9613).
Tame Valley Warden Service (061 344 3306).
Greater Manchester Countryside Unit (address under Bolton).
LTNC Oldham and Rochdale Group, 11 Hazeldene Road, Manchester 10 (061 681 7444).

ROCHDALE

1 Alkrington Woods

Alkrington Hall Drive, Manchester New Road, M24 (SD 862051).
Rochdale MBC. 37ha.
Approach   From either A576 or A664 Manchester to Middleton
Roads and within easy walking distance from Middleton town centre.
Summary   Within the Irk Valley and offering variety of habitat.
Nature interest   Noted for its mill ponds and deciduous woodlands,
it offers a wide spread of natural history interests. On the water are
coot, moorhen, ducks and grebes. Kingfisher and sand martin visit.
Plants include spotted orchids, marsh marigold, yellow flag and
greater reedmace.There are local patches of sphagnum moss and
cotton-grasses. Woodpeckers and owls are found in the oak
woodlands.
Management   Managed to balance wildlife and recreation and
woodland rejuvenation.
Access   Open at all times.
Contact   Rochdale Community Leisure Department.

2 Healey Dell

Shawclough Road, Rochdale (SD 880159).
Rochdale MBC; Rossendale BC. 62ha.
Approach   From Rochdale via A671 towards Whitworth and from
B6377 Shawclough Road.
Summary   An attractively wooded valley and LNR are based on the
River Spodden as it flows S from the moors into Rochdale.
Nature interest   This is one of the best remnant clough woodlands
in the county and its habitat diversity is increased by colonisation of
industrial areas such as mill ponds and railway tracks. Predominantly
oak, there are also areas of ling and bilberry heath. Boggy areas
support sphagnum mosses and cotton-grasses. Colonies of spotted
orchids. Breeding woodpeckers and a large rookery are part of its rich
birdlife.
Management   Managed by its own warden service to balance
needs of wildlife and recreation.
Interpretation   There is a visitor centre at the reserve.
Access   Open at all times.
Contact   Healey Dell Warden Service (0706 250459).

3 Hollingworth Lake Country Park

Smithy Bridge Road, Littleborough (SD 935149).
Rochdale MBC. 48ha.
Approach   By train from Manchester or Rochdale to Smithy Bridge
station. By bus from Rochdale. By car from junction 21 of M62 via
A663 or from Rochdale via A58 towards Littleborough and then via
B6225.
Summary/history   Originally built as a compensation reservoir for
the Rochdale canal, it is now a popular recreation area and country
park set in the folds of the Pennine fringe.
Nature interest   Among the best waterfowl areas in the region, it

features wintering wildfowl including whooper and mute swans, mallard, pochard, teal, wigeon and goldeneye. Migratory birds and shore waders include snipe, ringed plover, dunlin and terns. Breeding birds include great crested grebe, little grebe, coot and tufted duck. These can be seen from the lakeside trail.

Management   Although a venue for sailing, fishing and other recreation, the lake has a cordoned nature reserve.

Interpretation   Visitor centre where considerable literature is available.

Access   Open at all times.

Contact   Hollingworth Lake Warden Service (0706 250459).

Further information

Rochdale MBC, Community Leisure Department, Royle Works, Royle Road, Castleton, Rochdale, OL11 3ET (0706 341226).
Greater Manchester Countryside Unit (address under Bolton).
LTNC Oldham and Rochdale Group (address under Oldham).

SALFORD

1 Blackleach Reservoir

Hill Top Road, Worsley, M28 (SD 739040).
British Coal. 8.7ha.
Approach   Buses along Bolton Road, then walk down Hill Top Road.
Summary   The S basin is the largest water body in Salford, apart from the Docks. The old N basin, now filled in, is developing interest as grassland, wetland and scrub. The site is used a great deal by local people for walking, fishing, birdwatching etc. and there is growing use by schools for field work.
Nature interest   The S basin is important for wintering and breeding wildfowl, especially pochard, tufted duck, mallard and great crested grebe. Large numbers of frogs, toads and smooth newts breed here. The marginal vegetation is also of interest.
Management   None at present, but the LTNC is involved in developing plans for the site along with the local residents and it is hoped that the site will become a nature reserve in due course.
Access   Open at all times.
Contact   LTNC Manchester office.

2 Oakwood and Clifton Marina

Clifton House Road, off Manchester Road, Clifton, M27 (SD 775038).
Salford CC. 32ha.
Approach   By car from junction 15 of M62 along A666 (Manchester Road) and with buses between Farnworth and Salford along Manchester Road.
Summary   Woodland located on the slopes of the Irwell Valley and a large water area created from digging to supply gravel for the nearby motorway construction.
Nature interest   A varied woodland and grassland habitat offers oak, birch and sycamore woodland over bluebell carpets. Adjacent marshy habitats support spotted orchids. The water area is good for coot, tufted duck and wintering waterfowl.
Management   Managed by a warden service as a recreation and nature area.
Interpretation   A visitor centre is being created at Clifton House Farm.
Access   Open at all times.
Contact   Croal Irwell Valley Warden Service.

3 Worsley Woods

Greenleach Lane, Worsley M28 (SD 753010).
Salford CC. 36ha.
Approach   From junction 13 of M62 and A572 (Worsley Road).
Summary/history   A small wooded valley, site of an early deep coal mine from which the Bridgewater Canal took coal to Manchester.
Nature interest   General wildlife interest in a complex of mature plantations includes local bluebell carpets. Interesting ponds support

breeding frogs and newts. Aquatic and marginal plants include water violet, yellow flag and marsh marigold.

Management   Located as it is in a built up area, these woods are a popular recreation area and there is a strict management regime to protect the woodland habitat from over use.

Access   Open at all times.

Contact   Salford Recreation Department.

Further information

Salford MBC, Recreation Department, Crompton House, 100 Chorley Road, Swinton, Salford M27 2BW (061 794 4711).
Croal Irwell Valley Warden Service (0204 71461).
Greater Manchester Countryside Unit (address under Bolton).
LTNC Walkden Group, 11 Stoneysvile Avenue, Walkden, Salford.

STOCKPORT

1 Etherow Country Park

Compstall Brow Compstall Marple (SJ 973916).
Stockport MBC. 53ha.

Approach   By car from Stockport via A560 and Romiley or via A626 and Marple, on to B6104 (Compstall Brow/Compstall Road).

Summary   This country park is located in the Etherow Valley, where the river is flanked on each side by mature woodlands. The reservoir, feeder and weir were all originally constructed for the nearby mill.

Nature interest   Much of this extensive area of woodland is mature oak with a particularly rich understorey and many woodland flowers. Part of the site, with the adjacent Roach Wood, is an SSSI and has excellent all-round wildlife interest and is particularly good for birds. Plants include bluebells, wood sorrel, yellow archangel, ramsons, golden saxifrage, enchanter's nightshade and, locally, moschatel and wood avens. Birds include all three woodpeckers, tree creeper, nuthatch, blackcap, woodcock, white-throat, wood warbler, sparrowhawk, sandpipers, wagtails, teal, wigeon and geese.

Management   As a busy recreation area, the management regime particularly seeks to protect the woodland and its wildlife. There is a nature reserve within the park.

Interpretation   There is a visitor centre where information and many leaflets are available.

Etherow Country Park, Stockport

Access   Most of the area is open at all times and there is restricted access to the nature reserve.
Contact   Etherow Goyt Valley Warden Service (EGVWS); Cheshire Conservation Trust.

2   Gatley Carrs

Brookside Road, Gatley SK8 (SJ 842889).
Stockport MBC. 3ha.
Approach   By train from Manchester or Wilmslow to Gatley station and walk along Gatley Road (A560).
Summary   This is an interesting area sandwiched between the M56 and Gatley, and lying within the Mersey Valley.
Nature interest   An area of reed bed and marsh with an attractive variety of plants alongside Gatley Brook, including meadowsweet, ragged robin, valerian, butterbur, ramsons, yellow flag and marsh bedstraw. Good for birds such as snipe, reed bunting, warblers.
Access   Open at all times.
Contact   Medlock Valley Warden Service (see Tameside).

3   Kirk and River Wood

Chadkirk Road, Romiley, SK6 (SJ 942901).
Stockport MBC. 21ha.
Approach   By car from Stockport via either A560 or A626 and then A627 (Otterspool Road/Dooley Lane).
Summary   Located in the Goyt Valley, E of Stockport and between the river and the Peak Forest canal.
Nature interest   An attractive mature woodland with a rich aquatic flora and fauna in the canal features oak, sycamore, bluebells, dog's mercury, ramsons, drooping sedge, wood avens, wood sorrel, wood anemone, yellow archangel. The uncommon toothwort is present. Birds include grey wagtail, dipper, kingfisher, nuthatch, owls and woodcock.
Access   Open at all times.
Contact   EGVWS.

4   Poise Brook and Goyt Valley

Marple Road, Offerton, SK2 (SJ 925896).
Stockport MBC. 25ha.
Approach   By car from Stockport via A626 (Marple Road) and also from Woodbank Park off New Zealand Road, Stockport.
Summary   A long walk is possible through the wooded slopes of the tributary Poise Brook Valley and the main River Goyt Valley ending in formal parkland. This is part of the Etherow Valley Way walk.
Nature interest   This is mature deciduous woodland with good bird life and woodland flowers. Locally abundant bluebells, colonies of ramsons and wood sorrel. Local celandine, wood anemone, golden saxifrage and drooping sedge. Birds include kingfisher, grey wagtail and sand martins.
Management   Most of the woodland is managed to balance wildlife and recreation and to bring rejuvenation of the woodland.
Interpretation   None at present.

Access Open at all times.
Contact EGVWS.

Further information

Stockport MBC, Leisure Services Department, Stopford House, Piccadilly, Stockport (061 427 4949).
Etherow Goyt Valley Warden Service (061 427 6937).
Mersey Valley Warden Service (061 491 1647).
Greater Manchester Countryside Unit (address under Bolton).
Cheshire Conservation Trust, Marbury Country Park, Northwich, Cheshire CW9 6AT (0606 781868).

TAMESIDE

1 Eastwood and Acre Clough

Hough Hill Road, Stalybridge (SJ 971974).
RSPB. 22ha.
Approach Within walking distance of Stalybridge town centre via Cheetham Park and Hough Hill Road.
Summary Interesting and attractive area located on the edge of the town.
Nature interest Important for its oak woodland birds, the area has a diversity of habitats including scrub, grassland and marshland. Abundant bluebells and wood sorrel with common spotted orchid, ragged robin and meadowsweet. Birds include warblers and finches.
Management This area is managed as a nature reserve by an RSPB warden.
Access Restricted access from the warden.
Contact RSPB warden (061 303 7449).

2 Hollinwood Branch Canal

Lumb Lane, Droylsden M35 (SJ 911996).
Tameside MBC. 1km.
Approach By car from Ashton via A635 towards Manchester and the A662 to Droylsden and along Market Street, then Moorside Street and Lumb Lane.
Summary Situated in the Medlock Valley and linking to Daisy Nook Country Park.
Nature interest An SSSI, it is probably the best site in the county for aquatic plants such as water soldier, floating water plantain, arrowhead, frogbit, spiked water-milfoil and various pondweeds. It is also a good site for molluscs.
Management Care is being taken to prevent recreation uses harming the canal's natural value.
Interpretation Visitor centre at Daisy Nook Country Park.
Access Open at all times.
Contact Medlock Valley Warden Service.

2 Hulme's and Hardy Woods

Hulme's Lane, Stockport Road, Denton (SJ 927936).
Tameside MBC. 10ha.
Approach By bus between Ashton and Stockport along Stockport Road (A6017).
Summary Attractive woodland walk alongside the river in the Tame Valley.
Nature interest This mature woodland supports many plant species including abundant bluebells and enchanter's nightshade. Common helleborine, common valerian, purple loosestrife and marsh hawksbeard are also present.
Access Open at all times.
Contact Tame Valley Warden Service.

Further information

Tameside MBC, Recreation Department, Council Offices, Wellington Road, Ashton-under-Lyne, OL6 6DL (061 330 8355).
Medlock Valley Warden Service, Medlock Valley Visitor Centre, The Stables, Park Bridge, Ashton-under-Lyne (061 330 9613).
Tame Valley Warden Service, Council Offices (as above) (061 344 3306).
Greater Manchester Countryside Unit (see under Bolton).

TRAFFORD

1 Dunham Park

Charcoal Road, Altrincham (SJ 740870).
National Trust. 92ha.
Approach   By car from junction 8 of M56 along A56 towards Manchester and left into Charcoal Road (B5160).
Summary   This is a deer park and historic landscape around Dunham Hall, the park being located within the Bollin Valley.
Nature interest   The woodland, designated an SSSI, consists of very old beech and oak important for its rare beetles and flies. Birds include great spotted woodpecker, Canada geese, coot, moorhen, mallard and other ducks. Grey squirrels abound.
Management   The National Trust manages the park to balance wildlife, landscape, deer herd and recreational interests.
Interpretation   Visitor information point near Dunham Hall.
Access   Open at all times.
Contact   Bollin Valley Warden Service.

2 Trafford Ecological Park

Mosley Road, North Trafford Park, Stretford M17 (SJ 793974).
Trafford Development Corporation. 4ha.
Approach   By car from junction 4 of M63 on to A5081 and then along Tenax Road and Trafford Park Road.
Summary   A former tip in an area of heavy industry which was formerly part of the ground of a country house has been developed as the first ecological park in the NW.
Nature interest   Four types of woodland, meadow, wetland and lake are being created. The old lake is a wildlife reserve for many water birds such as moorhen, coot, mallard, great crested grebe, heron, Canada geese, snipe, golden plover and gulls, plus wagtails and swallows. The surrounding area has a fine show of orchids in June.
Management   This area is being managed as a nature reserve and an educational resource.
Interpretation   There is a site warden and visitor centre which includes classroom facilities.
Access   Restricted access; contact the warden.
Contact   Trafford Ecological Park warden (051 873 7182).

Further information

Trafford MBC, Leisure Services, PO Box 15, Warbrick House, Washway Road, Sole, M33 1AH (061 872 2101).
Bollin Valley Warden Service (0625 534790/1).
Greater Manchester Countryside Unit (see under Bolton).

WIGAN

1 Astley Moss

Rindle Road, off East Lancashire Road (SD 696975).
LTNC. 26ha.
Approach   Through Astley Green and along Rindle Road.
Summary   Remnant peat mossland, it represents one of the last examples of its type in the area because of pressures from agricultural development and peat extraction. A wonderfully wild place considering its proximity to industrial Salford and Leigh.
History   This area was once part of a very large expanse of peat bog which covered SW Lancashire. Drainage and fragmentation of the surrounding areas have resulted in invasion by birch scrub, bracken and purple moor grass, which in turn has dried the Moss to a much greater extent than previously.
Nature interest   Important for its ornithological value, Astley Moss attracts many breeding birds, including snipe, curlew and tree pipit. Nightjars have bred in the past. Wintering species include short eared and long eared owls, hen harrier, merlin and various finches. A wide variety of invertebrates are present, including several dragonfly and damselfly species and locally scarce moth species such as the large emerald and wood tiger. The site is botanically interesting with localised marsh orchid colonies.
Management   The site is managed by the LTNC, the owners since 1986 following purchase from British Coal. A management plan has been prepared, the principal aim of which is to restore part of the site to active peat bog through the damming of drainage ditches and raising of the water table.
Interpretation   None at present.
Access   Open at all times.
Contact   LTNC Manchester office.

2 Borsdane Wood

Pennington Green, Hindley, Wigan (SD 625060).
Wigan MBC. 31ha.
Approach   By car from Wigan via either Aspull (B5238) or Hindley (A577) and along Hall Lane/Ladies Lane to a track opposite Hindley Golf Club.
Summary   On the boundary between Wigan and Bolton, the wood covers both sides of a valley.
Nature interest   An old oak woodland, good for birds and plants, accommodates woodpeckers, jay, tawney owl, sparrowhawk, kingfisher and abundant bluebells and local wood sorrel.
Management   Managed for recreation and wildlife.
Access   Open at all times by public footpaths.
Contact   Wigan Countryside Warden Service (WCWS).

3 Dean Wood

Upholland in the Douglas Valley (SD 532069).
Wigan MBC. 35ha.
Approach   From Gathurst railway station on Gathurst Road (B5206) and by a track by Hillside under the M6.

Summary   This woodland follows the valley of a stream marking the county boundary.

Nature interest   A long established oak woodland valuable for its plants and birds. Masses of bluebells can be seen with wood anemone, ramsons, moschatel, wood sorrel, dog's mercury and yellow pimpernel. Woodpeckers and warblers breed here.

Management   Managed to balance wildlife needs and recreation pressures.

Access   Open at all times.

Contact   WCWS.

4   Haigh Plantations

Haigh Hall Country Park, Haigh (SD 600080). Wigan MBC. 84ha.

Approach   From Wigan, off B5239 (Red Rock Lane) towards Aspull or on A49.

Summary   Mature plantations lying between the Leeds–Liverpool Canal and the River Douglas.

Nature interest   A range of birdlife can be seen and there are interesting plants and amphibia, too. Woodpecker, owls, sparrow-hawk, nuthatch, woodcock, blackcap, chiffchaff breed in the area. Plants include bluebell and wood sorrel. There are frogs, toads and newts in the ponds.

Management   For recreation and wildlife.

Interpretation   Information centre at country park (0942 832895).

Access   Open at all times.

Contact   WCWS.

5   John Pitt Woods

Shevington (SD 552086).
Wigan MBC. 34ha.

Approach   By car from junction 27 of M6, E on A5209 then right on B5206 (Shevington Lane), turning left into Parkbrook Lane.

Summary   Woodland flanking a stream running into the Douglas.

Nature interest   Large oak/birch woods with a good natural history interest particularly for birds and fungi. Woodpeckers and warblers are common. Bluebells, wood sorrel and celandine occur.

Management   For recreation and wildlife.

Access   Open at all times.

Contact   WCWS.

6   Pennington Flash Country Park

St Helens Road, Leigh (SJ 635990).
Wigan MBC. 263ha.

Approach   By car from the A580 or from Leigh and A572 (St Helens Road).

Summary/history   This large lake (104 hectares), which has been formed from mining subsidence, is the focus of a country park.

Nature interest   The flash is noted for its wintering waterfowl and migrant visitors. Over 200 species of birds have been recorded in the country park, including mallard, pochard, tufted duck, coot and grebes. There are occasional Iceland and glaucous gulls, while turnstone, oyster catcher, knot, grey plover and terns visit in passage.

Management   Management for the protection of wildlife gets considerable attention here because of the pressure of recreational activities, and there is a nature reserve within the country park.
Interpretation   Visitor centre at the country park.
Access   Open at all times.
Contact   WCWS (0942 605253).

7   Wigan Flashes

Ince in Makersfield (SD 583035).
Approach   From Wigan by Poolstock Lane (A5106).
Summary/history   An area over two square kilometres of former industrial land includes a network of water areas created by coal mining subsidence including Scotman's Flash and Pearson's Flash, and industrial waste tips with the Leeds–Liverpool canal running through the centre. Part of the area is in the Douglas Valley.
Nature interest   The flashes and reedbeds are a haven for waterfowl and small wetland birds. Several rare plant species have been found and there are large colonies of wild orchids in the marshy areas and on industrial waste. Also marsh helleborine and cotton-grasses. Wintering tufted duck, pochard and coot visit. Swans, grebes, ducks, gulls, terns and waders can be seen in passage, along with occasional osprey and bittern.
Management   It is hoped that much of the area will become a nature reserve for both protection and improvement.
Access   Open at all times along canal towpath and other paths.
Contact   WCWS.

8   Worthington Lakes Reservoir

Worthington in the Douglas Valley (SD 583108).
North West Water. 25ha.
Approach   North of Wigan along Chorley Lane (A5106).
Summary   Former industrial reservoirs fed by the River Douglas.
History   Built originally for water supply, these reservoirs are now used for recreational purposes.
Nature interest   The reservoirs attract many water birds, some of which breed on the site, including grebes, wintering diving ducks, coot, moorhen, terns and waders. Herons and kingfishers are often seen.
Management   Managed for both recreation and wildlife. The N part includes the Arley nature reserve.
Interpretation   Information centre at the country park and Worthington Lakes (0257 425550).
Access   Open at all times.
Contact   WCWS.

Further information

Wigan MBC, Leisure Department, Station Road, Wigan (0942 44991).
Wigan Countryside Warden Service (0942 828116).
LTNC Leigh Group, 8 Leigh Road, Atherton, M29 0NA (0942 891570).
Greater Manchester Countryside Service (see under Bolton).

MERSEYSIDE

The meanders of the River Mersey, as it leaves Manchester across the Cheshire plain, twist through Warrington before squeezing through the Runcorn Gap gorge between Widnes and Runcorn. Below the bridge the tidal mudflats of the estuary are a giant feeding ground for birdlife, with the unspoilt meadows of the N shore between Widnes and Liverpool providing roosting areas.

Liverpool's densely populated territory has been the location of pioneering urban nature conservation initiatives, while it also preserves a few older habitats as in the splendid Croxteth Park. Next door Knowsley's Knowsley Park is private, but the district—including the towns of Kirby, Huyton and Prescot—retains agricultural land around these centres. Intruding further into the Lancashire countryside, the glass-making town of St Helens is making efforts to protect the wildlife that has colonised its many derelict industrial sites including the St Helens canal in the Sankey Valley and clusters of mill ponds and waste tips. Sefton, stretching N along the coast to Southport, boasts a famous dunes system, while on the other side of the Mersey the Wirral peninsula offers a network of country parks as well as remnant mossland near the heart of Birkenhead.

KNOWSLEY

1   Acornfield Plantation

Kirby L32 (SJ 436977).
Knowsley MBC. 12ha.
Approach   Small car park at SE corner, on Spinney Road.
Summary   An attractive woodland site next to an industrial estate. On acid, peaty soils, the grassland in the more open areas has a healthy feel to it.
History   Probably planted in the early 19C, the wood was certainly present in 1829 and many of the beech and oak probably date from this time. Despite being on the edge of an industrial estate and subjected to pollution from an adjacent aluminium smelting plant for many years, the woodland is still attractive and interesting.
Nature interest   A 'moss woodland' of oak, sycamore, beech, sweet chestnut and hornbeam on acid, peaty soils. There is only a sparse shrub layer and the ground flora was dominated until recently by bracken. Its control has led to the spread of species such as foxglove, red campion and bluebell, while in the acid grassland areas heathy species such as tormentil and heath bedstraw can still be found.

The relatively large number of trees which are dead or dying (from the pollution which occurred until recently) provides for a diverse fungal community of which 29 species have been recorded.

The marsh in the centre of the woodland consists mostly of soft rush and sphagnum and provides some extra variety. In addition there is a small pond on the N boundary with water starwort, flote grass and soft rush.
Management   The neglected look of the wood when it was being affected by pollution led to some vandalism and regular fires which speeded up the bracken and rhododendron encroachment which were already a problem. A scheme to improve the wood was

implemented in 1983 and half the area has since been replanted with trees. The site is managed by Knowsley Parks and Countryside Service.

Access   Open at all times.
Contact   Knowsley Parks and Countryside Service.

2   Halewood Triangle Country Park

Halewood (SJ 848442).
Knowsley MBC.

Approach   Main access points Higher Road in SW corner, Okell Drive on E side, Lydiate Lane at N end and Stanford Crescent on W side. Extends N onto the Liverpool Loop Line (see separate entry).

Summary   Former railway land oak woodland, willow and birch scrub, grassland, heathland and ponds.

History   The triangle was formed by the construction of the Cheshire Lines Railway, opened in 1879, and providing a link from the main Liverpool–Manchester line to Southport. Farming was severely disrupted, with the present grassland areas continuing to be cropped until at least 1945 and grazed until the early 1960s. Passenger services on the Cheshire Lines continued until 1964 and the tracks and ballast were removed in 1976. The site was purchased by Knowsley MBC in 1982 and developed as a country park with the assistance of Merseyside County Council as part of Operation Groundwork.

Nature interest   This is a large site with a surprising diversity of both habitats and species. Semi-mature oak woodland, occupying more than one-third of the park, has an interesting ground flora which includes remote sedge, broad buckler and male ferns, wood horsetail and red-veined dock. A large area of dense birch and willow scrub has developed on the disused tracks and sidings in the past 15 years. A small area of heather heath has developed on acid sandy soil, surrounded by woodland on the E fringe of the park. The extensive areas of former agricultural grassland contain a good range of herbaceous species including wild angelica, sneezewort, zig-zag clover and an increasing number of common-spotted orchids. Five ponds add further interest and provide a home for all three British species of newts. The whole site supports at least 21 species of breeding birds, including redpoll and blackcap, and is visited by many others over the winter months and during migration.

Management   The site is managed by Knowsley Parks and Countryside Service in accordance with a management plan prepared in 1985. In recent years the central area of grassland has been cut once a year to encourage the growth of the more attractive herbaceous species. A programme of selective felling in some areas of scrub is designed to extend the area of mature woodland.

Interpretation   None in advance of the development of a visitor centre within the next two years.

Access   Open at all times.
Contact   Knowsley Parks and Countryside Service.

Further information

Knowsley MBC, Parks and Countryside Service, Blacklaw House, Roby Road, Huyton, L36 4HA (051 443 3627).
Joint Countryside Advisory Service, Metropolitan Boroughs of Know-

sley, St Helens and Sefton, Bryant House, Liverpool Road North, Maghull, Merseyside, L31 2PA (051 520 1606).
Lancashire Trust for Nature Conservation, Cuerden Park Wildlife Centre, Shady Lane, Bamber Bridge, Preston, PR5 6AU (0772 324129).

LIVERPOOL

The strategic importance historically of a thriving port complex on the W side of the country with immediate access to Ireland and the W trading routes is well known. The port and port-related industries and services led to a rapid growth and imigration into the area but went into rapid decline in the 1960s. Damaged by bombing raids in the Second World War, many new estates were built in open countryside to rehouse families and provide new facilities for people moved from overcrowded areas. To the E of the area traditional industries of coal mining and glass making have been centred on St Helens.

Despite the once seemingly inexorable outward spread of the urban areas attention is now being drawn into improving their facilities and character. Wildlife conservation is seen as an integral part of this and many exciting new initiatives are being planned to safeguard important wildlife sites, to bring them to the attention of the public and to allow access where possible.

1   Childwall Woods

Woolton Road, Childwall (ST 413883).
Liverpool CC. 11ha.
Approach   Buses from city centre currently include 73, 78, 81, 173.
Summary   This lively wood is the survivor of an area that was once open and rural. Black Wood (five hectares) on the other side of Woolton Road is part of the same complex.
History   Acquired by the council in 1913, the land formerly formed the grounds of Childwall Hall, demolished in 1953 to make way for the present college of education. Black Wood was purchased in 1939.
Nature interest   Surrounded by housing and with a field to one side, the wood is dense oakwood with many rabbits and nesting kestrels. Rhododendrons dominate the ground floor layer. The bird list includes woodcock, swift, stock dove and willow warbler. Black Wood is ideal for birdwatchers with a great concentration of nuthatches, tawny owls, little owls, gold crest and many others. The great spotted woodpecker and the treecreeper nest here in the winter. This is a dense shady woodland much like Childwall Wood, but devoid of ground shrubbery. Bank voles, wood mice, stoats and weasels feed on the rich diversity of insects found here.

There was once a corn grinding mill at Little Woolton, situated very close to Childwall, that was obviously for the use of a manor family. There are also herbs such as bluebell, deadnettle, mustard, raspberry and many others, as well as an extensive fungi list.
Management   This wood is managed by Liverpool CC. In the future the council will be clearing old and dangerous trees that are threatening to fall and block paths and damage the wood.
Interpretation   None.
Access   Open at all times.
Contact   Recreation and Open Space Directorate (051 724 2371).

2   Cressington Docks

Dock Road, Garston, L9 (ST 397843).
Freightliners Ltd. 25ha.
Approach   Buses to Speke, off at Dock Road, down to the waterfront, towards the road to the right leading toward the wooded area.

Summary Amid the concrete and brick of the waterfront is the Cressington Dock area with woodland and heath caught between private housing and a disused railway embankment. The area is used by local residents to walk dogs and as a getaway from the city.

History The most upstream of Liverpool docks, at one time the dockland was used as a goods yard of which the tracks and foundation still stand. The area behind and to the S of the docks still houses a few industrial workshops.

Nature interest Cressington has great potential as a nature reserve, being an important wintering site for the grey partridge and associated birds such as kestrel and lapwing. Thick stands of silver birch saplings are in abundance along the E edges of the woodland and heath. In the summer months butterflies swarm throughout the area. Marsh orchids and common spotted orchids have been found living among great willow shrubs. In moist patches of the woodland are moss and fungi.

Management None.

Interpretation None.

Access Open at all times.

Contact Freightliners Ltd, Dock Road, L19 (051 427 7941).

3 Croxteth Country Park

Croxteth Hall Lane, Croxteth (ST 410945).

Croxteth Park Trust. 210ha.

Approach By car or bus to Muirhead Avenue. Presently bus 18 from city centre or Pierhead.

Summary The parkland surrounding Croxteth Hall includes several areas of wildlife interest including the Mull Wood LNR, Dam Wood, Craven Wood and Main Hey.

History In 1972 Viscount Molyneux, 7th and last Earl of Sefton died, and his widow gave the people of Liverpool 540 acres of the family's original 1,000 acre manor farm, the rest becoming land for the housing which now surrounds the estate.

Nature interest There are three wooded areas and a 50 acre nature reserve all of distinct ecological interest. The woodlands are managed on a semi-commercial basis, for the planting and usage of timber trees, but primarily for amenity purposes. Mull Wood (20 hectares), a former pheasant-shoot, is now a Local Nature Reserve. Dam Wood (10 hectares) derives its name from the damming of the River Alt, which flows N to the sea at Formby, to provide water power for the estate's mill. Craven Wood (11 hectares) is the site of a proposed woodland centre.

The walled garden and the home farm are remnants of Victorian times. In the home farm rare breeds such as the threatened Irish moiled cow are kept alongside sheep, pigs, poultry, cattle, goats and horses.

There are 37 ponds here, of which some are left to nature, others maintained as duck pits. It is proposed that more ponds are dredged and stocked with perch, rudd and roach. Many fish can be found in the River Alt.

Management A long-term woodland management plan is in force, with a permanent nature reserve and proposals for a woodland centre to raise timber and process it. The use and teaching of woodland crafts is expected to flourish in the future with an increased demand and interest from the public to maintain and learn traditional pursuits at Croxteth. 150 acres of land is used for grazing, 150 is mown (including

the 40 acres around the Hall) and 240 is woodland.
Interpretation   Various leaflets from the Visitor Services Department in the Hall.
Access   Open at all times.
Contact   Croxteth Country Park (051 228 5311).

4   Fazakerley Brook and Park

Longmoor Lane, Fazakerley (ST 378970).
Mersey RHA. 4.7ha.
Approach   Higher Lane, Fazakerley.
Summary   This haven for local residents, hospital staff and patients is threatened by development.
History   Fazakerley is believed to be an Anglo-Saxon word meaning 'meadowland with a border or boundary field'. The cottages on Longmoor Lane, built in 1887–89, are now listed buildings. Originally there were 21 cottage blocks (accommodating 584 units) surrounded by gardens and a playing field, built to house deprived children, cared for by foster parents in charge of each unit. The Health Department acquired the homes in 1958 and converted them into a mental health centre. In 1960 this became known as New Hall, Britain's largest training centre for mentally-handicapped people. The park and brook are directly behind this.
Nature interest   A very large area of woodland and grassland lies behind the hospital with the small, clean brook running through it. In the meadow are buttercups, dandelions, daisies, forget-me-nots and other wildflowers. Many herbs grow in this large grassland area including pineapple mayweed, sealfheal, rosebay and bristly ox-tongue. There are many grasses and sedges from the common bentgrass to the wavy hairgrass and a good variety of birds.
Management   Unmanaged. The Mersey Regional Health Authority planned to develop the land S of Fazakerley Hospital.The application was successful and the Authority gave permission to build residences, a supermarket, a public house, extend Brookfield Drive and landscape a public open space. Mersey HA then sold the land to a private developer. An appeal is pending.
Interpretation   Nil.
Access   Open at all times.
Contact   Liverpool Health Authority, Orleans House, Edmond Street, Liverpool 3 (051 227 4300).

5   Loopline

Halewood to Aintree.
BR and Sustrans. 18km.
Approach   From Halewood in the S and Aintree in the N via Knotty Ash.
Summary   An unofficial linear park has the potential to be an official nature area with much to offer to the surrounding communities in the way of nature trails, cycling paths and wildlife preservation.
History   The loopline follows the Liverpool Outer Areas Rail Loop owned by Cheshire Lines which closed in 1964. Many of the old railway stations are still standing and with wildflowers and plants growing wild around them they have become nature havens. West Derby station is the best known and most attractive.
Nature interest   The area is of significant ecological value with an

incredible diversity of flora and fauna. The Loopline is generally divided into 10 sections when surveyed by ecology and conservation teams. They are Halewood Triangle (a conservation area), Woolton, Gateacre, Childwall, Broad Green, Knotty Ash, West Derby (home of Croxteth Country Park), Norris Green, Walton and Walton Triangle. Surveys done on all 10 sites prove that the Loopline is 'locally rare' in that species and habitats are only found here in the Liverpool area. Semi-permanent pools at Knotty Ash are rich with reeds, yellow flag, willow species and rushes, all wetland plants. The rare emerald damselfly has been spotted here as well as three other species and four other species of dragonfly.

Halewood Triangle houses wetland plants, mosses and a good butterfly habitat. The section adjacent to West Derby station consists of sheer two metre sandstone walls covered with lichen, fern, ivy, liverwort and moss. The royal fern still survives from the days when it was planted at the station as an ornamental plant. The smallest mammal in the country lives along the Loopline—the pygmy shrew, the size of a big beetle.

Management   In 1986 Sustrans Ltd, a registered charity designed to create pedestrian and cyclist routes, purchased Loopline land from British Rail. Other projects they have undertaken include the Bristol path. For the Loopline, Sustrans is building a 16 kilometre cycle and footpath. A voluntary management committee has been formed to consider the needs of the communities around the Loopline, members include Operation Groundwork, Friends of the Earth, West Derby Conservation Group, Merseyside Environmental Trust, Lancashire Trust for Nature Conservation and Landlife Urban Wildlife Unit. Landlife's objective is to present to Sustrans a proposal that will incorporate the needs of the community with the desire for a safe, pleasant walkway/cycle path, and the need to preserve the wildlife along the Loopline.

Interpretation   A booklet titled *The Liverpool Loopline*—a guide to walks and wildlife is available from Landlife.

Access   Open at all times.

Contact   Landlife.

6   Oglet Shore

Hale to Garston Foreshore (ST 440815).
7km.

Approach   Speke bus to Dungeon Lane or by car along Hale Road.

Summary   An SSSI for the range of plants and animals on the Mersey foreshore.

History   At one time fishing and boat building dominated the area, Oglet being a famous shrimping village like Marshside at Southport and Parkgate at Wirral. Oglet women trudging to the Garston market, their baskets laden with shrimps, were once a common sight. Hale Lighthouse at Hale Head is the most S edge of 'old' Lancashire. Hale is now within Cheshire, and the lighthouse closed in 1958 when shipping on the Upper Mersey diminished.

Nature interest   Oglet shore is the home of 36% of Britain's pintails and 15% of the European total. 8.5% of all British teal live here. Both birds graze on the vegetation of the salt marshes and the sea invertebrates in the mud flats of Dungeon Banks. Sand leek grow on the coast, bristly ox-tongue on the cliffs and glass worts, in the salt marshes. Streams with shrubby herbaceous borders run from the fields into the Mersey, and swallows and swifts are attracted to the hedges in summer.

Management A ranger service operates here with six rangers. The goal is to create a cliff top walk from Spike Island in Widnes via Garston Docks and Otterspool promendade to Liverpool, completing the Mersey Way. The section at Oglet is already complete, problem areas being at Rams Brook where a bridge is needed and Garston Docks which are privately owned and inaccessible.

Interpretation The ranger service offers conducted tours for schools and interested parties.

Access Open at all times.

Contact Head Ranger, Oglet Shore Ranger Service (051 425 4121).

7 Stanley Sidings Pond

Prescot Road (SJ 384916).
Liverpool CC. 0.1ha.

Approach The reserve is situated on a disused railway sidings behind the Stanley Abattoir. Access is via a service road to Cathedral Memorials, a monumental masons situated to the W and rear of the abattoir. The site can be approached on foot.

Summary A small reserve which is one of the few sites of biological interest in urban Liverpool was previously under threat of development.

History The pond was to have been lost during the council's development programme, but the site became a reserve after local people brought it to the attention of the Lancashire Trust for Nature Concervation (LTNC).

Nature interest It has the largest and only significant breeding colony of the smooth newt in Liverpool.

Management Licensed to and managed by the LTNC.

Interpretation Nil.

Access Apply for the key from the LTNC Croxteth group.

Contact LTNC.

8 Stockton's Wood

Speke Hall, The Walk, L24 1XD (SJ 423828).
National Trust. 3ha.

Approach Buses to Speke Hall Avenue, walking down the Walk to Stockton's Wood on the left, or drive to the estate and park.

Summary The Wood lies within the grounds of Speke Hall overlooking the Mersey and surrounded by Liverpool airport. A large assemblage of deadwood-associated invertebrates substantiates the belief that Stockton's Wood is a long-standing, undisturbed woodland.

History Stockton's Wood stands on what was once the heathland of Speke. Surveys of the area indicate that part of it was probably ancient woodland.

Nature interest A 1981 report by the National Trust indicates that the fauna originated in the nearby ancient woodland which existed along the edges of the Mersey estuary, and in copses which existed near to the present site of Stockton's Wood. As these nearby sites were lost, the fauna moved across to Stockton's Wood which has probably always had a good proportion of dead and dying trees, due to the waterlogged nature of the site.

Craneflies, mothflies, damselflies and dolochopodid flies flit among the flora. A good spider fauna live among the woodlice, snakefly and millipedes. Typical woodland birds are seen here and sparrowhawk, tawny owl and kestrel occasionally nest.

Management   Work has already begun to develop a good drainage system for the poorly drained soils, and to maintain the present drainage channels which include roughly 2,500 metres of channel.

Interpretation   The National Trust is aiming to involve local schools in the management of Stockton's Wood with informal tours designed to encourage appreciation of the wood and Speke Hall. The Trust has extensive literature on the geology, physiography, soils and biology of the area and wood.

Access   Open all year.

Contact   Head Warden, National Trust, Speke Hall, The Walk, Liverpool L24 1XD (051 427 7231).

9   Walton Park Cemetery

Rawcliffe Road, off Rice Lane, Walton (ST 355955).
Liverpool CC. ha.

Approach   A train from Liverpool Central Station on the Ormskirk line to Walton, or drive to Rawcliffe Road, Current buses 20, 68, 341.

Summary   Pass through the lodge gates and city farm buildings and to the left you are met by a curtain of green that shields the cemetery from the outside world.

History   For many years this ancient burial ground was the pauper cemetery of Liverpool. Today the cemetery is famous for the grave of Robert Tressel, author of *The Ragged Trousered Philanthropists*. The museum here is named after Tressel and contains a wealth of history.

Nature interest   Tombstones covered with ivy lie beneath a canopy of shade from sycamore, oak and lime. There is an abundance of bird life here including bullfinch, greenfinch, bluetit and great tit. Bats roost nearby in old farm sheds. An acid heath, much like peat, supports heathers. A variety of fungi grow on the ground, tombstones and deadwood.

Management   Rice Lane Farm next door houses sheep, pigs, goats, donkeys and geese.

Interpretation   Literature available from the farm.

Access   Cemetery open at all times.

Contact   Rice Lane Farm (051 530 1066).

Further information

Liverpool City Council, Recreation and Open Space Directorate, Mansion House, Calderstones Park, Allerton, Liverpool 18 3JD (051 724 2371).

Landlife, The Old Police Station, Lark Lane, Liverpool L17 8UU (051 728 7011). Its Urban Wildlife Unit is at Innovation Centre, 131 Mount Pleasant, Liverpool L3 5TF (052 709 1013).

Literature produced by Landlife includes *A Guide to Walks and Wildlife* series, with booklets describing Priory Wood, Mill Wood and Sefton Park.

Acknowledgement   The above text is by Jan Findlater of Landlife based on research by colleagues including John Eves, Stephan Bodnar, Neil Roberts, Ian Brown, Sue Atherley, Alison Slade, Paul Weightman, Jane Martin and John Benson.

ST HELENS

St Helens is a relatively modern town owing its existence to the industrial revolution. The rapid expansion of the town during the late 18C and 19C from a collection of small hamlets to a population of 85,000 in 1901 was due to the local availability of coal and sands suitable for glassmaking, together with the opening in 1757 of the Sankey Navigation or St Helens Canal linking St Helens to the coast and Liverpool. This combination of local fuel together with the ability to import additional raw materials and export the finished product led to the expansion of the chemical, glass and metal refining industries. The existing ecological interest of St Helens is very closely linked to this industrial history of the town and in particular to the canal system and to the waste products generated by the coal, glass and chemical industries.

1 Carr Mill Dam

Carr Mill Road, St Helens (SJ 524978).
Private. 30ha.
Approach   Small car park at SW corner of Carr Mill Road. Access on foot from Sankey Valley Park to the SE, from Goyt Hey Wood to the NE.
Summary   A large mill dam with a good marginal vegetation providing cover for nesting birds including great crested grebe, and surrounded by interesting woodland and grassland.
History   Originally a mill dam but enlarged in the 1820s to provide water for the St Helens Canal system, using Black Brook as a feeder stream.
Nature interest   Like many other stream-fed lakes, the shallower areas around the influx of the two streams on the N—the Black Brook and the Goyt—provide the most interesting habitats. The marginal vegetation includes water plantain, yellow flag, water parsnip, hemlock water-dropwort and reed canary grass, merging into alder and willow carr on the landward side. This vegetation provides cover for breeding coots, moorhens and great crested grebes. The open water at the head of the Black Brook arm supports abundant broad-leaved pondweed. Areas of acidic grassland on the N bank and oak woodland extending up the Goyt Valley are also of considerable interest.
Management   No formal management.
Interpretation   Guided walks, slide talks and local walk leaflet available from the Ranger Service.
Access   Open at all times.
Contact   St Helens Ranger Service (0744 39252).

2 Clinkham Wood

Lorton Avenue, Moss Bank (SJ 514980).
St Helens MBC. 7ha.
Approach   Just N of the East Lancashire Road (A580), street parking along Lorton Avenue/Windermere Avenue.
Summary   An unusually large urban wood in a small clough with a spring-fed stream and marshes.
History   The wood appears on a tithe map of 1808 as a plantation with a boundary very similar to the present one. The N section of the

wood was temporarily cleared to make way for a small roof-tile quarry in the mid-18C, becoming recolonised by the early years of the present century. More recently, small scale residential development has extended across the N end of the wood, creating a small outlier in part of the wooded quarry. The whole site is now enclosed by urban development.

Nature interest   The present tree cover is mostly of oak, sycamore and ash but with some birch in more acidic areas and alder and willows in wetter areas. The ground layer is impoverished in some parts of the wood due to a combination of trampling, fly tipping and the presence of dense rhododendron scrub, but elsewhere includes bluebells, ramsons, wavy-hair grass and wood sage—the latter being rare in St Helens. The stream and marshes support a good range of wetland species including yellow flag, great hairy willowherb, flote grass and remote sedge.

Management   Little in recent years, but following an initiative by Landlife (St Helens), the council proposes future management as a community woodland by a group representing local residents, with technical support from the local authority's Community Leisure Department.

Interpretation   None.

Access   Open at all times.

Contact   St Helens Ranger Service.

3   Glass House Close Wood

Blackbrook (SJ 532972).

St Helens MBC. 4ha.

Approach   On foot along the Sankey Valley from Blackbrook visitor centre to the E or from Carr Mill Dam (under A580) to the W.

Summary   A species-rich oak woodland on the edge of the Sankey Valley Park with alder and willow carr occupying wetter areas in the valley bottom.

History   An old woodland which is shown on a tithe map of 1848 in nearly identical outline. Two large wet hollows in the wood may have originated as clay pits. The lower section of the wood contains the remains of an old waterway, pre-dating the St Helens Canal, which used to carry iron 'bullets' from a foundry at Carr Mill to a slitting mill at Stanley Bank.

Nature interest   A mature oak woodland on relatively steep slopes above the Blackbrook. The drier upper slopes are fairly acidic with a ground layer which includes wood anemone, woodsorrel, bluebell and quite extensive stands of bracken. The damper more nutrient-rich lower slopes grade into willow and alder carr in the valley bottom. Here the vegetation includes ramsons, wild angelica, marsh marigold, yellow flag and butterbur on the river bank.

Management   None at present.

Interpretation   Guided walks, slide talks. Woodland leaflet available from St Helens Ranger Service.

Access   Open at all times.

Contact   Ranger Service.

4   Havannah Flashes

Cooper's Lane, Haydock (SJ 548957).

Private. 5ha.

Approach   Car park on S side off Havannah Lane, off Newton Road. Pedestrian access along Sankey Valley from E and W, and along Cooper's Lane from N.

Summary   A subsidence flash with a rich aquatic and marginal vegetation and an extensive reedbed supporting breeding sedge and reed warblers.

History   The flashes started to appear in the last quarter of the 19C. Two ponds formed at first near to the St Helens Canal. These eventually grew and flooded the wooded valleys of two streams flowing down from the fields S of Haydock. The most probable cause of the land sinking was the opening of two deep coal mines at Havannah (1891) and Southport (1893) Pits with galleries extending N under the canal towards Haydock.

Nature interest   The flashes support a rich variety of aquatic and marginal vegetation including broad leaved pondweed, water forget-me-not, brooklime and skull cap. The W arm has an extensive stand of common reed which supports breeding sedge and reed warblers. Water quality is extremely good and the flashes contain a rich variety of aquatic insects including the water scorpion and several species of damselflies and dragonflies. Fish present include roach, tench, chub, carp and pike.

Management   Leased by Collins Green Angling Club which stock the flashes and regularly removes excess water weed.

Interpretation   Leaflet available from Ranger Service.

Access   No formal access. Can be viewed from Sankey Valley footpath which runs alongside (open at all times).

Contact   Ranger Service.

5   Sankey Valley Park

Visitor Centre, Blackbrook Road (SJ 535966).
St Helens MBC. 8km.

Approach   Open access on foot for most of its length. Car parking available at Blackbrook Visitor Centre—off Blackbrook Road, Havannah Flashes—off Newton Road, Wharf Road—off Common Road, Red Brow Wood—off Wargrave Road, Old Hey—off Wargrave Road.

Summary   A linear park with extensive wetland, grassland and woodland habitats extending from close to the centre of St Helens SE towards Warrington.

History   The construction of the St Helens canal (1755–57), the first in England, provided the main stimulus to the development of the town as a major centre for the coal, glass and chemical industries. With the coming of the railway in 1830, however, the importance of the canal declined; the Ravenhead branch closed by 1898, the whole of the canal beyond Newton Common lock was abandoned by 1932 and the remainder finally abandoned by 1963. The scars of 200 years of industrial history were then compounded by the extensive use of the valley for industrial and domestic waste disposal, with large sections of the canal itself being filled. In 1977 St Helens borough council, Merseyside county council and the Countryside Commission joined forces in a major land reclamation scheme to create the Sankey Valley Park. Sections of the canal were re-excavated, rubbish tips and spoil heaps landscaped and thousands of trees planted. In 1979 the St Helens Ranger Service was established to help manage and interpret the newly created countryside area. Access was improved, new footpaths laid and visitor facilities provided including a visitor centre at Blackbrook.

Nature interest   Much of interest can be found along the entire length of the Park, but attention is drawn here to the wetland habitats in three remnant sections of the canal at Blackbrook, Broad Oak and Old Hey. Parts of the Blackbrook section near the visitor centre are becoming silted and have large stands of common reed and great reedmace. Other species present include yellow flag, water plantain, water mint, curled pondweed and broad-leaved pondweed. A rich invertebrate fauna, including the water spider, has also been recorded. Two short sections of the canal at Broad Oak (E of the sewage works) support a good range of marginal and aquatic plants including common spike-rush, sweet flag, broad-leaved pondweed and spiked water milfoil. (The surrounding grassland here includes alkaline patches with purging flax, yellow-wort and eyebright present). At the E end of the park, the Old Hey section lying S of Wargrave, supports many of the same wetland species, together with horn-wort and purple loosestrife.

Management   Routine habitat management includes the control of emergent vegetation along canal banks and the mowing of some grassland areas to create spring and summer wildflower meadows. In future, some sections of the canal will need de-silting to retain their open water character. Woodland management is carried out with the help of volunteers.

Interpretation   Visitor centre at Blackbrook open daily; guided walks and slide talks, local and natural history leaflets and booklet available.

Access   Open at all times.

Contact   Ranger Service.

6   Sherdley Park

Marshalls Cross Road (SJ 516930).
St Helens MBC. 120ha. (including golf course).

Approach   Car parking off Elton Head Road or Marshalls Cross Road.

Summary   A large urban park on the S side of St Helens containing several plantation woodlands with associated wetland and grassland habitats.

History   Formerly part of a private estate acquired by the borough in the 1940s and developed as a formal park. In addition, to some excellent woodlands, the park contains an 18 hole golf course, formal walled gardens, play area, pets corner and plant sales.

Nature interest   Delph Wood, lying next to the golf driving range, is a plantation of oak, sycamore and birch with a large marsh supporting willow carr and large stands of yellow flag. Other less common marsh plants include bur-marigold, water forget-me-not, marsh willow herb, marsh pepper and cuckoo flower. Dobb's Wood on the W edge of the golf course occupies a small stream valley. A series of marshes along the stream support a good variety of wetland plants including wood horsetail, hemlock water dropwort, water mint and hemp agrimony. The steep valley sides also support acidic grassland containing heath bedstraw and tormentil. Dam Wood in the SE of the park is a plantation of oak, sycamore and rhododendron. The dam has been drained and is now a marsh, notable for the presence of wild angelica and marsh bedstraw among a good range of wetland species.

Management Little management of wildlife habitats at present, apart from a mowing regime to encourage spring flowers in Delph Wood Meadow. Future work planned includes footpath improvements and a programme of woodland management.

Interpretation Information base, leaflets, guided walks on local and natural history available through the ranger service.

Access Open at all times.

Contact Ranger Service.

7 Sutton Mill Dam

Clockface Road (SJ 524923).

St Helens MBC. 5ha.

Approach From Clockface Road, Marshall's Cross.

Summary A partially silted dam with a large reed canary grass swamp, with some sallow carr also present.

History One of a series of dams on the Sutton Brook providing—until recently—water for the production of cellophane by British Sidac. First recorded on local maps in 1845 when it provided power for a corn mill. Siltation increased in the early 1960s as a result of mining subsidence at the head of the dam.

Nature interest Reed swamp complements the open water and now occupies half the original dam area. Reed canary grass is the dominant species but reedmace, great hairy willowherb and yellow flag are also present. Willow carr is developing in the swamps and the site supports a good variety of breeding birds including reed bunting.

Management A current scheme by Groundwork (Knowlsey/St Helens), in association with the council and Sutton Mill Dam Action Group, aims to establish a wildlife park. Works include provision of safe public access, fishing platforms, protection of wildlife areas, tree and shrub planting and protection of open water quality using the reed bed as a biological filter. There are plans to introduce wildfowl at a later stage.

Interpretation A nature pack has been produced for the Sutton Mill Dam Action Group by the Groundwork Trust, and there are plans for nature trail and signboards in future.

Access Open at all times.

Contact St Helens Community Leisure Department.

Further information

St Helens MBC, Community Leisure Department, Century House, Hardshaw Street, St Helens WA10 1RN (0744 24061).

Acknowledgement Text by Mick Brummage of the Joint Countryside Advisory Service, with additional information from Keith Walker of the St Helens Ranger Service.

SEFTON

Seaforth Nature Reserve

Pumping Station Compound, Royal Sefton Dock, Bootle, Merseyside (SJ 315970).
Mersey Docks and Harbour Company. 40ha.

Approach   Eight kilometres N of Liverpool centre at the mouth of the Mersey. Access by foot is through the Freeport entrance off Crosby Road South.

Summary   This is an outstanding example of a man-made ecosystem. Two large pools were reclaimed in 1961 from beach and derelict sand dune habitats and the reserve consists of a mixture of habitats from a saltwater and freshwater pool, colonised and bare dumped rubble, dry calcareous grassland, marshy grassland and dry sandy areas.

History   The reserve was established in 1983 by the Lancashire Trust for Nature Conservation with the permission of Merseyside Improvements Limited and the Mersey Dock and Harbour Company.

Nature interest   Over 190 species of bird have been reported and the site is on the migratory route along the W coast. The reserve is one of the most important roosts for gulls in Britain and particularly notable for the nationally significant spring flock of little gulls. It is a centre for bird watching, especially of the spring and autumn seabird passages. In addition, the reserve has an interesting diversity of plants and invertebrates characteristic of coastal and ruderal habitats.

Management   The site is leased to and managed by the Lancashire Trust for Nature Conservation (LTNC).

Interpretation   There is a visitors' centre with various displays to be used by school parties and members of the public. Some interpretative material is available in the hides. An educational trail is being developed and a leaflet about the site is being produced.

Access   Open at all times.

Contact   LTNC, Seaforth Nature Reserve, Pumping Station Compound, NW Seaforth Dock, Liverpool L21 1JD.

Further information

Sefton MBC, Civic Offices, Bootle, Merseyside (051 922 4040).

WARRINGTON

North Cheshire between Liverpool and Manchester contains a wide variety of habitats. Centuries of industrialisation around the towns of Runcorn, Warrington and Widnes have by no means obliterated the traditional landscape of farms and small woodlands. In fact industry has increased the diversity with old quarries, waste tips, waterways, reservoirs and artificial marshlands of dumping grounds for slurry and dredgings. Natural wetlands survive in relics of lowland peat bogs and saltmarsh of the estuary.

1   Risley Moss

Risley Moss, Ordnance Avenue, Birchwood, Warrington (SJ 668923). Cheshire CC. 89ha.

Approach   From the A574 between Warrington and Junction 11 of the M62, follow the signs to Risley Moss at Birchwood.

Summary   One of the few remaining areas of mossland in the NW, a mixture of woodland and regenerating mossland also includes grassed glades and ponds.

History   Cut for peat until the 1930s, Risley Moss was effectively isolated when it became part of a wartime ordnance factory. As part of Warrington New Town, the site was developed as an educational nature reserve and a place for peaceful recreation. Cheshire county council took over the control of the site in the early 1980s.

Nature interest   The regenerating peat bog has a patchwork of sphagnum mosses and purple moor grass. The birch woodlands have a wide variety of fungi; the mounds of clay have a different flora including orchids. The site is notable for its dragonfly and damselfly species and it attracts a range of birds of prey through the year. Both woodland and mossland have hides for birdwatching.

Management   The site is managed by a ranger service based at the visitor centre. Controlled drainage has led to the regeneration of the sphagnum bog, and woodland and water bodies are managed to ensure a variety of wildlife habitats.

Interpretation   There is a visitor centre with an exhibition and an audio-visual show. The rangers organise talks and guided walks as well as special events and an environmental education programme. Leaflets are available from the visitor centre and the hides and observation tower also have information boards on wildlife and the local landscape.

Access   Open daylight hours, except Fridays and Christmas Day.

Contact   Visitor centre (0925 824339).

2   Rixton Claypits

Warrington BC. 10ha.

History   Rixton Claypits is a naturally colonised site developed from abandoned clay workings last dug in the mid-1960s. It has been saved from several development threats, having been designated an SSSI in 1979, and provides an island of refuge for wildlife in a predominantly industrial and intensive agricultural landscape. The site has been managed since 1986 by Warrington council's ranger service and is promoted as a much needed educational resource.

Natural history   The main interest lies in the huge number of species of plants (c200), birds (c100), insects and fungi to be found in a relatively small area due to the site's varied topography and base-rich soils. Notable species include N marsh orchid and S marsh orchid, common spotted orchid, yellow wort, common centuary and stoneworts. Among the fauna are willow warblers, willow tits, sedge warblers, white-throat and ruddy duck; nine species of dragonfly breeding on site and common, pygmy and water shrew.

Management Various grassland management techniques are used aimed at maintaining or increasing floristic diversity of plant species and the prevention of willow and silver birch scrub invasion. There is also a habitat improvement programme to attract a greater number and diversity of bird and insect species. A programme of monitoring surveys assesses the effects of different management techniques.

Interpretation Rixton Claypits most readily lends itself to use as an educational resource due to its wide range of and increasingly rare habitats and is visited regularly by local schools, colleges and universities. There is a varied guided walk and activities programme for the general public as well as events and activities for children in school holidays. Guided walks for groups, trusts and societies can be arranged as can illustrated talks and lectures on specific topics. There is also a series of leaflets, guides, worksheets and checklists available.

Access Daytime.

Contact Warden (via Head Ranger 0925 601617).

Further information

Merseyside Valley Partnership, Camden House, York Place, Runcorn, Cheshire WA7 5BD (09285 73346). The Partnership consists of the Warrington and Runcorn Development Corporation, Warrington Borough Council, Halton Borough Council and Cheshire County Council.

Cheshire Conservation Trust, Marbury Country Park, Northwich, Cheshire CW9 6AT (0606 781868).

Acknowledgement Text of this and the Widnes and Runcorn section written by Dave Potts of The Mersey Valley Partnership.

WIDNES AND RUNCORN

1 Mersey Way

The Mersey Way at Hale, near Widnes, Cheshire (SJ 472809).
Rights of way on privately owned farmland. 6km.
Approach   On foot from Hale village, down Church Lane to the lighthouse.
Summary   Clifftop and shoreline footpaths between Widnes and Liverpool with views over developing saltmarsh and mudflats of the Mersey, feeding grounds for ducks and waders.
History   This is a section of the Mersey Way, a network of footpaths along the N bank of the River Mersey across Cheshire, a distance of 45 kilometres.
Nature interest   The Mersey estuary (an SSSI) has international significance as a feeding ground for ducks and waders. From the Mersey Way at Hale mallard, pintail, wigeon and shelduck can often be seen, as well as curlews, oystercatchers and smaller waders. Raptors, including harriers, visit in the winter and sparrowhawks and kestrels may be seen in the nearby farmland all year round. Saltmarsh and shore plants here include glasswort, sea aster, thrift, sea sandwort and scurvy grass.
Management   The Mersey Way is being developed by the Mersey Valley Partnership. At Hale, BTCV helps to maintain the footpath and steps to the shore and combat erosion of the sandstone and clay cliffs. The NCC is involved in controlling the invasion of the spartina grass on the saltmarsh.
Interpretation   A booklet of three walks is available from the Mersey Valley Partnership.
Access   Open at all times.
Contact   Mersey Valley Partnership.

2 Pickerings Pasture

Pickerings Pasture, Mersey View Road, Widnes (SJ 488837).
Halton BC. 16ha.
Approach   By car or bus between Widnes and Hale Village to Halebank. At the Mersey View Hotel down Mersey View Road to the end.
Summary   Wildflower meadows on the edge of the Mersey Estuary (SSSI), the site also offers views over saltmarsh and shore, with a wide variety of bird life to see all year round.
History   After 30 years of waste tipping the site has been restored as public open space with a wildlife theme.
Nature interest   Wildflower-rich grassland of different types and young woodland attract a wide variety of insect and bird life. The bird species list stands at over 100 (residents and visitors). Hares are also to be seen here, particularly in the spring. Cheshire Conservation Trust has a hide overlooking a scrape, and a beach on the edge of the marshes.
Management   The Mersey Valley Partnership and Halton BC work together to diversify this site. Cutting at different times of year and at different heights, and extensive planting has produced spring meadow, summer meadow, wildflower lawn, cornfield and wetland, as

well as newly planted woodland and woodland edge habitats.

Interpretation   A ranger service monitors the progress of the site and organises walks, talks, slide shows and practical conservation tasks. Wildlife and historical information is available on site and leaflets can be obtained from the Mersey Valley Partnership.

Access   Open at all times. There is a daytime car park.

Contact   Mersey Valley Partnership.

3   Runcorn Hill

Runcorn Hill, Highlands Road, Runcorn (SJ 508818).
Halton BC. 14ha.

Approach   By bus between Runcorn Railway Station and Shopping City, to the Cenotaph on Greenway Road, then a short distance up Highlands Road past the post office. The car park is also on Highlands Road.

Summary   Woodland walks through quarry bottoms and high sandy heath with views across the Mersey estuary to N Wales. Breeding birds, winter visitors and the varied landscape make this an attractive site at all times of the year.

History   Large sandstone quarries abandoned at the turn of the century have returned to nature. Formerly a common, the site came under local authority control in the 1930s. A small part became a formal park but most was allowed to remain as urban wilderness.

Nature interest   The poor sandy soils have been colonised by birch and pine woodland and by heathland plants such as gorse, broom and heathers and the rarer heath bedstraw and heath cudweed. There is an interesting variety of insects, fungi and birds, including sparrow-hawk and little owl. The site includes a birdwatching area with a hide and a butterfly garden.

Management   The Mersey Valley Partnership and Halton borough council work together with BTCV to manage the site. The aim is to minimise erosion damage and extend the diversity of the habitats.

Interpretation   A ranger service organises events such as walks, talks and practical environmental education sessions. Leaflets are also available.

Access   Open at all times.

Contact   Mersey Valley Partnership.

Further information

Mersey Valley Partnership (see Warrington).
Cheshire Conservation Trust (see Warrington).

WIRRAL

The peninsula between the Dee and Mersey is an interesting mixture of countryside including the built up area of Birkenhead and Wallasey and large industrial plants around Port Sunlight. At the N tip, the Birkett stream feeds the Float which became the focus of the Birkenhead docks. Birkenhead Park, famous as the model for Victorian parks throughout Britain and the USA, is now somewhat threadbare. Former private parks such as Arrowe Park and that at Bromborough now include public nature reserves, and at Eastham Ferry a country park has been created around the Eastham Woods. The Wirral country park is one of the country's most unusual, being a 19 kilometre stretch of former railway from West Kirby S along the Dee shore. The mudflats at Gayton are prime birdwatching territory.

Small Copper (Lycaena phlaeus), *Wirral Country Park*

1   Arrowe Park

Arrowe Park Road, Birkenhead (ST 277858)
Wirral MBC. 160ha.
Approach   Buses along Arrowe Park Road.
Summary   Arrowe Park serves as a conventional urban park, with a golf course, pitch and putt course, tennis courts and bowling greens, but it also has several woodland areas and a beautiful lake and stream which attract many species of wild life.
History   The Park became famous as the site of the Boy Scouts World Jamboree in 1929.
Nature interest   The mature woodland alongside the stream holds a variety of plants and provides good breeding and roosting

territory for a wide range of birds including tawny owl and sparrowhawk.

Management The site is wardened by park rangers.

Interpretation Visitors can obtain information about the park and its facilities at Ivy Farm, situated within the park.

Access Open at all times.

Contact Department of Leisure Services and Tourism.

2 Bidston Hill

Bidston, Birkenhead (ST 288894).
Wirral MBC.

Approach Buses to Hoylake Road or Upton Road.

Summary A sandstone ridge rising to over 75 metres above sea level, Bidston Hill contains a wide variety of natural habitats, including wet and dry heathland, coniferous and deciduous woods, exposed sandstone outcrops and open grassland.

History The hill has for centuries been an important route in the area and has been the site of a windmill, lighthouse and observatory since the 1800s.

Nature interest The heathland areas have diverse plant species with many wild flowers. The variety of habitats also benefits small animals, such as stoat, weasel and squirrel, and a wealth of birds including over 60 species of breeding birds.

Management The site is wardened by Wirral council rangers.

Interpretation Educational facilities and a Rangers Centre are provided at Tam O'Shanter's Cottage on the slopes of Bidston Hill.

Access Open at all times.

Contact Department of Leisure Services and Tourism.

3 Bidston Moss

Bidston Link Road, Wallasey (ST 288912).

Access Bidston Station, or buses along Hoylake Road.

Summary This small area of nature reserve has an interesting mixture of ponds, lowland moss and scrub land on an area of tipping. The site attracts passage and wintering birds.

History Bidston Moss was an extensive area of lowland moss which has been slowly reduced in size. The reserve, set up in 1983, protects the last remnants of the moss.

Nature interest The shallow ponds and boggy areas support good examples of flora and fauna of lowland moss. In winter, these areas are used by wintering ducks and waders; during periods of migration more unusual birds are commonly recorded.

Management The reserve is wardened by Wirral Park Rangers.

Interpretation No facilities.

Access Open at all times.

Contact Department of Leisure Services and Tourism.

4 Dibbinsdale Local Nature Reserve

Spital, Bromborough (ST 345838).
Wirral MBC. 35ha.

Approach Buses along Spital Road, Bromborough.

Summary The reserve comprises ancient woodland, meadows, reed beds, parkland and amenity grassland, set in the valley of the Dibbin.

History The amalgamation of part of a private woodland estate and a small local authority park in 1981 established the reserve which, with careful management, has now improved its habitat, diversity and interest.

Nature interest The woods lining the valley side of the Dibbin form the largest remaining block of semi-natural woodland in Merseyside and have been relatively undisturbed since the Ice Age. The reserve is rich in plant life, including an area of river meadow, and animal life, with more than 60 species of breeding birds recorded.

Management Wardened by Wirral council rangers.

Interpretation The former Woodslee Cottages have been converted to provide a small display area for use by schools and the general public. A leaflet is available and organised events are held at certain times during the year.

Access Open at all times.

Contact Department of Leisure Services and Tourism.

5 Eastham Country Park

Eastham, Wirral (ST 365816).
Wirral MBC. 28ha.

Approach Buses to Eastham Ferry.

Summary Set on the banks of the Mersey with unique views across the estuary, the woodlands contain fine stands of beech, birch, oak and sweet chestnut, together with a magnificent rhododendron and azelia dell. A fine nature trail along the cliff top and through the woods is popular with visitors.

History Eastham Woods has been a place for leisure and recreation since the early 1800s. Historical features include a bear pit and the site of an ancient river crossing, Job's Ferry.

Nature interest Apart from the woodland species, the park contains many interesting species of flowers including wood anemone, woodsorrel, celandine, red campion, white campion, yellow loosestrife and Solomon's seal. Birds include three species of woodpecker, warblers and sparrowhawk.

Management The park is wardened by Wirral council rangers.

Interpretation There is a visitor centre with interpretation facilities and a craft workshop. The rangers hold regular events in the park.

Access Open at all times.

Contact Department of Leisure Services and Tourism.

Further information

Wirral MBC, Department of Leisure Services and Tourism, Westminster House, Hamilton Street, Birkenhead L41 5FN (051 647 2366).
Wirral MBC, Planning and Estates Department, Town Hall, Brighton Street, Wallasey L44 8ED (051 638 7070).

Acknowledgement Text written by staff of the above departments.

SOUTH YORKSHIRE

BARNSLEY

Some 2,500 years ago, it is thought, an Iron Age fort was the first settlement here. By the time the Normans arrived in 1066, 'Berneslai' as it was then known, was an insignificant little village. The Cluniac monks at Pontefract who owned the village decided that they might profit from a market and fair where they could sell their own produce. From 1249, when the royal charter granting a market and fair was bought from Henry III, Barnsley became the major township of the district. Coal was first won in the area in the 15C and the Barnsley seam was to become one of the richest in Yorkshire. In 1620 wire drawing was a thriving industry. The manufacture of linen was introduced to Barnsley in 1744, and the town's hand loom weavers went on to produce some of the finest linen in the world. As the linen trade declined due to cheaper Irish linen, the arrival of the railways in the 1840s allowed the rich coal seams to be exploited. The mining industry still employs over ⅓ of all working men in the borough. The borough has an excellent range of wildlife habitats from the high moorlands in the W, which form part of the Peak District National Park, to the river valleys and low land of the E where fields and woodlands abound.

1 Broomhill Flash

Broomhill (SE 413028).
Yorkshire Wildlife Trust (YWT). 12ha.
Approach It is best approached from the A635 by leaving this road about ½ a kilometre E of Darfield at the junction for Wath-upon-Dearne. Follow the Wath-upon-Dearne direction and after one mile turn right at The Railway public house and the nature reserve appears on the right hand side after about ½ a kilometre. There is parking for 12 vehicles, and the approach path and viewing hide have been adapted to accommodate wheelchairs.
Summary The reserve is one of many mining subsidence 'flashes' which were created, mainly between 1950 and 1965, along the largely industrialised Dearne Valley.
History Most were subsequently drained but, by an unusual agreement between the Trust and the Wombwell Gun Club which originally leased the site, the Trust took over overall control in 1982 and prevented the loss of the area. The Gun Club's activities are now carefully limited by agreement.
Nature interest This seemingly uninteresting site comprising about four hectares of open water with little marginal vegetation, surrounded by eight hectares of grazed pasture, attracts a wide variety of birdlife. Notable are the waders which migrate along the Dearne Valley but llso large numbers of waterfowl collect, mainly in winter. The prolific fishlife contributes considerably to the presence of many bird species. Herons are usually present while great crested grebes, red breasted mergansers and goosander are just some of the birds regularly attracted by the fish stocks. The pastures around the Flash are very attractive to large numbers of passing golden plovers and lapwing, the latter species also breeding, as do redshank and snipe.

Management YWT and the Wombwell Gun Club maintain the site to enhance its wildlife value.
Access Open at all times. A large viewing hide overlooks the Flash. Groups of more than half a dozen should book with the hon. warden.
Interpretation YWT produces a site leaflet plus a pamphlet guide to its S Yorkshire reserves (see **Further information**) from which this and other YWT site descriptions have been taken with slight adaptation.

2 Carlton Marsh Local Nature Reserve

Shaw Lane, Carlton, Barnsley (SE 378104).
Barnsley MBC. 30ha.
Approach Off Shaw Lane, adjacent to Shaw Dike.
Summary The reserve includes marsh, wetland, dry grassland, damp grassland, ponds and a disused railway embankment. These different types of habitat provide an interesting and diverse flora and invertebrate fauna with some notable plant rarities.
History Designated as a local nature reserve in 1978.
Nature interest Its interest is mainly ornithological with 117 species of birds being recorded in 1986, but interesting marsh plant communities include species such as southern marsh orchid, common spotted orchid and adder's tongue fern. Two public viewing hides are available and there are specially designated ponds for schools' use in the study of freshwater ecology.
Management Barnsley Department of Leisure and Amenities together with the Carlton Marsh Reserve management committee.
Interpretation Various display panels and occasional open days and guided walks. A full report is published each year.
Access Open at all times.
Contact Leisure and Amenities Countryside Section.

3 Wath Ings

Broomhill (SE 413028).
Yorkshire Water Authority. 25ha.
Approach The reserve lies about one mile N of Wath and is approached from the B6273 between Brampton and Darfield. Visitors must park by this road near the gated entrance to British Coal land (SE 419025) and proceed to the reserve on foot. The site is near to Broomhill Flash (see above).
Summary Early records show the general area being occasionally used for grazing and hay cropping. During the 19C drainage works improved the agriculture and much of the wildlife was lost. This process has been reversed in recent years with the occurrence of mining subsidence which brought water back onto the Ings. The area soon became noted for its ornithological value.
History It was the original intention of the Yorkshire Water Authority to carry out a further scheme which would render the area completely dry. However, the YWT was able to promote an alternative approach with the authority resulting in the maintenance of the wetland habitat and the declaration of a nature reserve in 1976. Since that time the Trust has artificially extended the area of open water and mud providing additional habitat for the waterfowl and wading birds.
Nature interest Covering rough pasture, marshland and open

water, Wath Ings forms one of the few pieces of wetland in the area which is protected from major disturbances like illegal shooting and trespass. The reserve's main interest lies in its attraction to migrating birds—particularly waders—which use it as a feeding and resting place on their spring and autumn journeys. During the summer the water level drops and, by the autumn, large areas of mud are exposed holding rich food for the wading birds. Some of these areas of mud are very close to the hides and at that time of year spectacular views of the commoner waders like snipe, redshank, greenshank and dunlin are practically guaranteed. Outside the migration period, there is still much to see. In winter, large flocks of visiting wildfowl gather on the main pool. Most of the commoner duck can be seen and they are often joined by birds like pintail and gadwall as well as whooper and Bewick's swans.

The wintering flocks disperse in spring but many of their number remain to breed in the reedgrass marsh. Summer also sees redshank and reed bunting nesting in the rough pasture and the hedges become alive with small birds. Kingfishers nest nearby and are often feeding on the reserve, as are little ringed plover which choose to breed on the adjacent coal spoil heaps.

Management   YWT maintains the site in close collaboration with the Yorkshire Water Authority.

Access   Access to the reserve may be gained by means of a Trust membership card or for non-members by means of a permit issued by the management committee. There are three viewing hides affording views of the main water bodies.

Interpretation   A site leaflet and the S Yorkshire reserves booklet are available from YWT.

Contact   YWT or hon. warden (0226 82940).

4   Wilthorpe Marsh

Barnsley (SE 333086).
Barnsley MBC.

Approach   Five-minute walk from Huddersfield Road bus routes. Car park by canal, Smithies Lane.

Summary   Excellent wetland site within three kilometres of the town centre, between the River Dearne and a remnant of the Barnsley canal. Subsidence flashes provide open water with large expanses of lowland marsh.

History   Low-lying flood plain with clay substrate used for low intensity grazing.

Nature interest   One of the few remaining natural marshes in S Yorkshire, with a rich and varied flora and fauna, it includes a lowland acid bog with cotton-grass, yet has calcicolous plants elsewhere. Almost 300 species are recorded. Birds are mainly passage, with some winter wildfowl. Heron and kingfisher are regular, and two raptors breed. The insect fauna is interesting, with many dragonflies.

Management   The canal has been cleared by Barnsley Trades Council. It is hoped that a management agreement can be drawn up for part of the marsh.

Interpretation   None.

Access   Open at all times by public footpaths.

Contact   Barnsley MBC.

5 Worsbrough Country Park

Worsbrough Bridge, Barnsley (SE 345035).
Barnsley MBC. 100ha.
Approach   Off the A61 Barnsley to Sheffield road.
Summary   The park is situated in an attractive section of the valley of the River Dove and its feeders Rockley Dike and Brough Green Brook. It provides a contrasting range of habitats and hence a wealth of wildlife. The habitats include redundant reservoir, willow carr, landscaped grassland, mixed deciduous woodland, redundant canal, arable farmland and traditional hay meadows.
History   Worsbrough Country Park is a former industrial area that has now become a haven for wildlife. Within the Park lies Worsbrough Mill Museum, a working 17C water-powered corn mill, and several areas of industrial archaeological interest. These include two ancient pack horse bridges, an old horse-drawn tramway railway, a redundant canal header reservoir and canal basin. Close to the park and linked by public footpaths are the remains of Rockley Iron Furnace, built about 1652, and Rockley Engine House, built in 1813 to drain local ironstone workings.
Nature interest   The site is particularly important for bird species. All three species of woodpecker, kingfisher, sparrowhawk, kestrel, tawny owl and little owl are regular breeders and wintering wildfowl are of special interest. The creation of traditional hay meadows together with disused railway embankments provide a wealth of wildflowers. The various aquatic habitats contain interesting invertebrate species as well as the three British species of newt. Fox and badger are found within the park and the small mammal population includes water shrew.
Management   Leisure and Amenities Countryside Section.
Interpretation   An interpretative ranger and interpretative farm manager arrange year round programme of guided walks and activities. School and visitor reception area.
Access   Open at all times. Worsbrough Mill Museum, during normal daylight hours Wednesday to Sunday.
Contact   Countryside Section.

Further information

Barnsley MBC, Department of Leisure and Amenities, Countryside Section, Phase III, Court House Site, County Way, Barnsley S70 2TL (0226 733272).
Barnsley MBC, Department of Planning, Central Offices, Kendersley Street, Barnsley S70 2TN (0226 733222).
Yorkshire Wildlife Trust, 10 Toft Green, York YO1 1JT (0904 659570).
The booklet *Visiting Nature Reserves in South Yorkshire* by Roger Mitchell, the Trust's chairman, is available free in return for an sae sent to the above office. As with other voluntary organisations, the sending of a donation—or better still, a membership subscription—is desirable.
Acknowledgement   Text for council sites written by Steve Tivey, Countryside Officer, Leisure Services.

DONCASTER

Sited to the E of the Pennines, Doncaster has a long history of being a major transport centre. Road, rail and canal have all contributed to the town's growth and economic development. Apart from transportation, the extractive industries of coal, limestone and aggregate have had a marked effect on both the economy and landscape of the borough. While arable agriculture extends over much of the rural landscape of Doncaster there are many sites rich in natural history interest.

1 Campsall Country Park

Campsall (SE 546138).
Doncaster MBC. 32ha.
Approach   Buses along Churchfield Road and Campsall Village.
Summary   A varied mixture of habitats in a large area of open access countryside.
History   Previously a neglected estate which was used as game covert with woodland walks and ornamental lakes, the site has been developed to allow visitors to get close to nature.
Nature interest   The complex geology and topography of the site provides a wide variety of habitats which is reflected in the rich flora and fauna of the site. There are over 230 species of flowering plant including yellow iris, green alkanet and bogbean. The two main lakes hold a large population of waterfowl with great crested grebe and little grebe breeding regularly.
Interpretation   A full time ranger provides an interpretative service for local schools and other interested groups. The site is used for numerous events and guided walks.
Management   The council's site management plan is in operation and is directed towards the enhancement of habitats, especially grassland.
Access   Open at all times.
Contact   Amenities and Leisure Services.

2 Cusworth Hall Country Park

Cusworth (SE 547038).
Doncaster MBC. 40ha.
Summary   Perched on top of a limestone ridge, this old estate provides spectacular views of the town centre and surrounding countryside.
History   Created as landscaped ground in the mid-18C, the area contained many elements of formal parkland. The grounds now display a mixture of formal and semi-natural habitats.
Nature interest   Woodland, grassland and wetland flora are well represented. The mature beech and limes provide roosts for a large colony of noctule bats.
Interpretation   There are no permanent on-site rangers, but Cusworth is a popular venue in the countryside activities programme.
Management   Amenities and Leisure Services.
Access   Open at all times.
Contact   Amenities and Leisure Services.

3 Howell Wood Country Park

South Kirkby (SE 437095).
Doncaster MBC. 30ha.
Approach   Buses along Common Road or by public footpath from Clayton Village.
Summary   A woodland containing a wide variety of trees and woodland types, with streams and several small pools providing aquatic habitats.
History   Formerly part of an estate and used as game cover. Recent fires destroyed several hectares of mature oak woodland. This area has been replanted with hardwoods.
Nature interest   Noted for its variety of woodland birds, the site has a large resident population of breeding birds plus numerous passage migrants and vagrants such as crossbill, siskin and firecrest. Plant and insect species are particularly abundant along the stream courses.
Interpretation   A full-time ranger provides a visitor service, as well as guiding school parties and organised groups. There is a 0.5kilometre disabled trail.
Management   Amenities and Leisure Services in accordance with management plan proposals.
Access   Open at all times.
Contact   Amenities and Leisure Services.

4 Kings Wood

Bawtry (SK 652945).
Doncaster MBC. 15ha.
Approach   Buses along Bawtry Road, one mile N of town centre.
Summary   A woodland comprising mainly oak and sweet chestnut.
History   An ancient woodland, Kings Wood shows evidence of having been used for coppice. The council has recently purchased the site from British Rail to preserve the woodland and provide an informal amenity site close to a main trunk road.
Nature interest   The age and maturity of the woodland is the main base for its natural history interest. Though poor in flora the wood is well-known for its insect life and wide range of fungi.
Interpretation   At present the site is provided with interpretative panels and is used occasionally for countryside activities.
Management   Amenities and Leisure Services in accordance with management plant proposals.
Access   Open at all times.
Contact   Amenities and Leisure Services.

5 Potteric Carr

Carr Hill Industrial Estate, Balby Carr.
BR. 140ha.
Approach   Lying nearly five kilometres S of Doncaster between Balby and Bessacarr, this large reserve can be approached via Carr Hill from the A630 (Doncaster–Sheffield road) or from the A6182 which connects Balby Carr to Junction 3 of the M18 motorway. (Car park SE 590007).
Summary   Before the 17C the land to the S of Doncaster formed a large impenetrable area of reedfen and marsh; a wilderness in the true sense. By the end of the 19C this had been converted by drainage

into rich agricultural land and little remained of the once abundant wildlife. The coming of the industrial era, somewhat surprisingly, improved the prospects for wildlife in the area. The railways, constructed about the turn of the last century, created new habitats on the embankments and cut land off from modern farming practices. Later, during the 1960s, mining subsidence caused water once again to flood some of the land, allowing the old communities of reedfen and marsh to reassert themselves.

History   In 1968 the YWT came to an agreement with British Rail to tenant Low Ellers Marsh. From that time the reserve has been extended to include other areas affected by mining subsidence as well as woodland, grassland and disused railway embankments. Located on the outskirts of a large centre of population, the reserve has had to face a number of threats, from motorway and railway proposals to a major drainage scheme. Now these threats no longer exist, the area and its wildlife are benefiting from careful management.

Nature interest   The large areas of open water and reedfen form the most immediate attraction of the reserve. In winter large numbers of the commoner wildfowl like mallard, shoveler, teal, pochard and tufted duck collect here, often with smaller numbers of wigeon and gadwall, while one may occasionally see a more unusual bird such as a pintail, goldeneye, goosander or scaup. The reedbeds provide superb protection for breeding birds and many of the commoner wildfowl, together with great crested and little grebe, and uncommon water rail and reed warbler, regularly nest here.

It is the variety of habitats, however, that makes Potteric Carr so interesting. The woodland, pastures and scrub-invaded railway embankments support a thriving population of owls, woodpeckers, finches, warblers and tits. On a fine day in spring it is possible to see over 70 different bird species. The habitats also support a large number of plants, insects and other wildlife. The disused railway embankments are particularly important for their lime-loving plants and grass snake, common lizard and dingy skipper butterfly populations. Other areas support unusual plants such as marsh stitchwort, water violet and purple small reed as well as insects like the brimstone butterfly.

Management   YWT.

Access   Access to the reserve is in two parts. The W Bessacarr and Balby Carr nature walks may be visited by means of Trust membership card or, for non-members, by means of a permit issued by the management committee. The remaining areas of the reserve require a BR walking permit, issued through the Trust, to enable certain operational railway lines to be crossed at prescribed points. The Trust's obligations to BR require a strict enforcement of these arrangements.

There are five viewing hides on the Balby Carr Nature Walk and three elsewhere, together with a large network of footpaths. The field centre is usually open for part of most weekends and during the week.

Interpretation   A site leaflet and the S Yorkshire reserves booklet are available from YWT (see Barnsley).

Contact   YWT or hon. warden (0302 5364660).

6   Sprotbrough Flash

Sprotbrough.
British Coal; private. 72ha.

Approach   The reserve adjoins the River Don in the Don Gorge approximately five kilometres W of Doncaster. Access via the A1(M) is obtained by using the A630 turn-off (follow signs for Rotherham). At first traffic lights (Cecil Hotel on left) turn right onto Mill Lane follow this road and after crossing the River Don turn left immediately at the former bridge toll house. Limited parking is available between the toll house and The Boat Inn. Access to the reserve can be made by following the towpath for approximately 200 metres upstream.

The reserve itself covers approximately 12 hectares but the Yorkshire Wildlife Trust also enjoys access arrangements over substantial areas (60 hectares) of the adjoining woodlands through a management agreement with Steetley Minerals Ltd. Car park (SE 538015).

Summary   At the turn of the century the area known as Sprotbrough Flash comprised alluvial meadows but by the mid-1920s coal working had created subsidence in the area which eventually became permanently flooded by water from the adjoining River Don. The raising of the water level in the River Don in the 1940s and again in the 1960s resulted in the creation of a large water body some 3/4 mile long and two metres deep.

History   At Sprotbrough the River Don cuts through a magnesium limestone escarpment creating an area of great scenic and wildlife attraction, an area thought to have inspired Walter Scott's 'Ivanhoe'. The reserve lies at the centre of this area, which is of great historical interest ranging from one of the earliest known water engines dating from approximately 1700, which pumped water from the River Don to Sprotbrough Hall, to the lime kilns of the now demolished village of Levitt Hagg, once the main source of employment in the valley.

Nature interest   The varied emergent and riparian vegetation on the reserve has provided ideal feeding and nesting conditions for waterbirds. Coupled with large fish stocks this has provided breeding habitat for up to seven pairs of great crested grebe; also little grebe, mallard, tufted duck and pochard. The reserve's location in the Don Valley attracts many migrant birds, particularly warblers and, inevitably, there have been some rarities among the 150-plus species recorded such as spotted crake and barred warbler. But of greater importance is the value of the reserve and adjoining woodlands as a breeding area of approximately 60 species of birds, including several which are locally uncommon.

The adjoining woodlands, situated on the outcrop of the upper magnesium limestone, are rich and varied. S-facing, in a sheltered valley, their wildlife is more typical of S downlands than of Yorkshire. In particular, the ground flora in these ancient woods is of great interest: bee, fly and pyramidal are three of eight orchid species occurring here and many locally rare species are represented.

Management   YWT.

Access   Open at all times. There are three viewing hides located between the Flash and the River Don. Groups of more than six should book with the hon. warden.

Interpretation   A site leaflet and the S Yorkshire reserves booklet are available from YWT (see Barnsley).

Contact   YWT or hon. warden, c/o 26 Hyman Close, Warmsworth, Doncaster.

7 Thorpe Marsh

Marsh Lane, Bentley–Barnby Dun Road.
CEGB. 60ha.

Approach   Adjacent to Thorpe Marsh Power Station near Barnby
Dun, the reserve is approached from the Bentley–Barnby Dun road.
Car parking is available just outside the power station at the end of
Marsh Lane—the second turning right after leaving Barnby Dun. Car
park (SE 602095).

Summary   The reserve is situated on land owned by the CEGB and
was developed in close co-operation with them and the former S
Yorkshire county council. It is an example of how, with foresight and
planning, industrial activities can accommodate wildlife interests.

History   The area around Thorpe Marsh has been used for grazing
and hay cropping for many centuries as the 'ridge and furrow'
drainage system, still clearly visible on the reserve, suggests. Much of
the present reserve was bought by the Board for use as an ash disposal
site. Following representations from the YWT and a review of its
long-term ash disposal requirements, the Board was able to accept
proposals for the development of a nature reserve. A large amount of
fill material was required for the construction of perimeter
embankments to the ash disposal site. This was obtained from
adjacent land of low ecological interest and it was possible to design
the excavations to produce a lake with maximum wildlife potential.
Thorpemere, as it is now known, forms an important part of the
reserve and is overlooked by the field centre and three hides.

Nature interest   The ancient grassland makes up the bulk of the
reserve. Having been undisturbed for so long, many plants, some by
no means common, have come to grow there. Pepper saxifrage,
tubular water dropwort and greater burnet can be found here while
broad-leaved helleborine grows in one corner beneath dense scrub.
The grassland has become invaded by hawthorn scrub and the area is
surrounded by dense hedgerows. These provide nesting sites for
many small birds, particularly the warblers and finches in summer,
while in winter redwings and fieldfares gather in large flocks.

Dense scrub has also become established along much of the disused
railway embankment which runs through the reserve. Goldcrests and
long-tailed tits are often observed here. Where the scrub opens out
wild flowers such as common spotted orchid, wild carrot and cowslips
are seen among the rough grass. Some of the best areas for butterflies
and other insects are found along this embankment. The new lake,
Thorpemere, with its young reedbeds and newly-established
adjoining areas of native trees, has quickly become an attractive area
for waterbirds and waders. Mute swan, heron, mallard, tufted duck,
pochard and teal are regularly seen, while less frequently such birds
as goldeneye or shelduck are recorded. In autumn, whooper swans
are regular visitors.

Management   YWT.

Access   Access to the reserve may be gained by means of a Trust
membership card or, for non-members, by means of a permit issued
by the management committee. There are five viewing hides, a field
centre and a specially equipped classroom for use by schools.

Interpretation   A site leaflet and the S Yorkshire reserves booklet
are available from YWT (see Barnsley).

Contact   YWT or hon. warden (0302 883404).

Further information

Doncaster MBC, Directorate of Amenities and Leisure Services, Corke Street, Bentley, Doncaster DN5 0DB (0302 873401).
Yorkshire Wildlife Trust (see Barnsley).
Acknowledgement   Text for council sites written by Peter Bromley of the Amenities Department.

ROTHERHAM

Situated on the middle coal measures of the carboniferous period, with Permian limestone on the E, Rotherham's history is bound up with its geological resources. A Roman fort was established here to protect crossings on the River Don and River Rother, and the College of Jesus made the town a centre of learning in the Middle Ages.

Agriculture was the main activity until the canalisation of the River Don in the 17C opened up the mineral resources to wider markets, a process which continued with the expansion of the railway system in the next century. Rotherham has been an important producer of coal and steel ever since, though industrial diversification has followed the recent rundown in these heavy industries.

1   Anston Stones Wood

North Anston (SK 531831).
Anston Parish Council. 38ha.
Approach   The Rotherham–Worksop bus service passes the wood. There are long lay-bys along the A57 for car parking.
Summary   A magnificent woodland in a gorge of magnesian limestone has associated areas of scrub and grassland. Public footpaths run through the wood from North Anston and Lindrick.
History   Ancient woodland managed commercially until the mid-18C, it supplied oaks to Chatham Dockyard.
Nature interest   Rich in most aspects of wildlife, it includes flowering plants, mosses and liverworts, fungi, insects, spiders, snails and birds. Cowslips and orchids occur in the grassland and nettle-leaved bellflower in the shade. Ash and lime are the dominant trees now that the wych elms have been killed by disease, though areas of mature beech and sycamore plantation occur.
Management   Anston parish council is managing the wood for its wildlife and amenity value.
Interpretation   Leaflets from Rotherham MBC.
Access   Open at all times.
Contact   Anston Parish Council, 35 Wentworth Way, Dinnington, Sheffield S31 7SY.

2   Catcliffe Flash

Situated between the villages of Catcliffe and Treeton, near Rotherham (SK 425882).
Rotherham MBC. 16ha.
Approach   By bus from Rotherham; by the link road from the Sheffield Parkway direct link to the M1.
Summary   Situated in the shadow of Orgreave Chemical Works, a semi-urban/industrial area, a rich subsidence flash of open water has become colonised by aquatic plants. Common reedmace and common reed form the fringe vegetation with the drier parts colonised by willows. Views over the water area can be made from a lay-by at the side of the road from the comfort of your car in cold, wet conditions. There is a footpath around the whole area, but the main interest is on the open water.
History   Mining of coal caused subsidence of the land, and as it was close to the River Rother the hollows became waterfilled so

creating the 'flash'. Originally the area of water was much larger with the main road running around the edge. Due to severe flooding which occurred regularly in Catcliffe, an area was filled through the middle of the flash and the road built along the route as it is today. Catcliffe Flash was almost lost to wildlife when the then owners applied for permission to fill it with refuse. The then S Yorkshire county council intervened, and after negotiations purchased the more interesting part of the flash and gave permission for the other side to be filled in, followed by tree planting which has almost been completed.

Nature interest   Mainly ornithological, it is attractive to certain breeding birds including sedge and reed warblers, moorhen, coot, little grebe, great crested grebe, mallard and tufted duck. During spring and autumn passage, mud is exposed and a wide range of waders is attracted with notable records of greenshank, spotted redshank, wood sandpiper, curlew sandpiper, ruff and little stint. It is during the winter months that Catcliffe has become more important due to pressures put upon other local areas of water, with records of whooper and Bewick's swans as well as mute, mallard (200), tufted duck (80), pochard (120), teal (50) and coot (120). Other visitors have included shoveler, wigeon, pin tail, ring-necked duck, long-tailed duck, scaup and ruddy duck. Occasionally, there is a long-eared owl roost in the willows, well away from the road.

Management   No formal management has been undertaken at the present apart from some tree and hedge planting at the roadside, and the erection of a gate (which is closed and locked) to a footpath. The current owner is Rotherham council and future management plans are being considered.

Interpretation   Nil.

Access   Open at all times.

Contact   Countryside Management Service.

3   Chesterfield Canal

Thorpe Salvin (SK 535815).
BWB; Rotherham MBC.

Approach   Kiveton Park BR station is at the W end of this section. By bus to Kiveton Park from Rotherham, Holbrook and Worksop.

Summary   This disused canal is bordered by mature woodlands for most of the length in Rotherham. Running through an agricultural area, it is an attractive area at all times of year.

History   Dug in the 1770s to link Chesterfield with the coast, the canal has been disused since the summit tunnel collapsed at the beginning of this century. Canal enthusiasts are hoping to restore the Rotherham section for pleasure craft in co-operation with BWB.

Nature interest   The canal and banks, together with the woods, quarries and grasslands alongside, form a rich wildlife corridor. Grass snakes can sometimes be seen swimming in the canal, kingfisher is occasionally seen and the woodlands have plenty of bird life.

Management   Some of the woodlands are being managed for the wildlife interest by Rotherham Countryside Management Service, and the Chesterfield Canal Society is promoting the amenity use of the waterway.

Interpretation   Leaflets from Rotherham MBC and Canal Society; notice boards at Turnerwood.

Access   Towpath and footpaths through woodlands open at all times.
Contact   BWB, 24 Meadow Lane, Nottingham, HG2 3HL, Chesterfield Canal Society (see below).

4   Denaby Ings

Dearne Bridge, Mexborough (SE 498008).
British Coal. 32ha.

Approach   The Mexborough–Marr road runs through the reserve, and the field station and adjacent car park are situated on this road near the point where it crosses the new course of the River Dearne. There is a second car park on the road to Cadeby (SE 505007).

Summary   The designation of the reserve in 1967 reflected its improving wildlife value following mining subsidence and the creation of enlarged water bodies. Today the site's value is based on the continuity of riparian habitats dominated by crack willows and their associated insect populations, and the more recent ornithological interest resulting from mining subsidence. It is thus an example of the type of marshland community which once covered large parts of the Dearne Valley coupled with the development of a more recent habitat, comprising large open water bodies fringed by reed sweet grass.

History   A part of the reserve was destroyed in 1974 when British Coal, against vigorous opposition from YWT, gained planning permission to extend the Hull and Barnsley Tip which serves Cadeby Colliery. This resulted in the loss of half the water area of Cadeby Flash. To their credit, British Coal financed a modest W extension of the Flash as compensation, but its overall reduction in size reduced its ornithological interest. Paradoxically, Cadeby Colliery closed in 1986. Could this have been foreseen, the tipping on the reserve would not have been necessary.

Nature interest   There are three hides giving excellent views of the large variety of waterbirds that can be seen. The Cadeby Flash hide is specially adapted for handicapped people in wheelchairs and can be reached by a wide and level tarmac path running directly from the car park to the door of the hide.

Species of waterbirds that can usually be seen include mallard, shoveler, teal, great crested grebe, little grebe, pochard, tufted duck, mute swan, coot and moorhen. Whooper and Bewick's swans are among the winter visitors, as are wigeon, pin tail and goldeneye. Kingfisher and heron are seen from time to time throughout the year. The reserve includes an area of pasture and two disused railway embankments. The embankments are well wooded and provide an excellent habitat for small birds, mammals and woodland plants. More than 300 species of wild flowers and over 40 different grasses have been recorded.

The insect life is outstanding and a very wide variety has been recorded. Indeed, it was among the crack willows at Denaby Ings that the beetle, *Acrotrichis henrici*, was first found in Britain. Many butterflies can be seen, including the orange tip, common blue, wall brown, peacock, red admiral and painted lady. In summer, dragonflies, mayflies and lacewings are common.

Management   YWT.

Access   Open at all times. Groups of more than six should book with the hon. warden. During a visit to the reserve you must keep to the main path down the side of the pastures and to the top of the two railway embankments, except for the steps down to the two hides. British Coal do not allow any access along the top of the embankment separating Cadeby Flash from their colliery spoil tip. The field station is open for part of most weekends, or by arrangement.

Interpretation A site leaflet and the S Yorkshire reserves booklet (from which this entry is taken are available from YWT (see Barnsley).

Contact YWT or hon. warden (0709 894249).

5 Roche Abbey

Maltby (SK 5489).
Sandbeck Estates. 60ha.

Approach Buses to Outgang Lane, Maltby, then walk either via Blyth Road and Gypsy Lane or along public footpaths through Nor Wood.

Summary Excellent woodlands in the valley of the Maltby Dyke surround the ruins of the Abbey. The footpath from Maltby to Laughton-en-le-Morthen passes through these woods.

History The Cistercian monastery was dissolved by Henry VIII and used as a 'quarry' for building stone. The area was landscaped by Capability Brown.

Nature interest Several plants introduced by the monks can still be found including alpine currant, monkshood, elecampane and leopard's bane. The woods are on magnesian limestone and contain a rich flora of flowering plants, mosses and fungi, which in turn support an exceptionally rich insect fauna. The woods are also excellent bird watching areas with nuthatch, marsh tit and hawfinch and the Dyke has grey wagtail.

Management Parts of the site are used for forestry and game rearing.

Interpretation Leaflet from Rotherham MBC.

Access Public footpath open at all times.

Contact Sandbeck Estates, Sandbeck Hall, Maltby, Rotherham.

6 Thrybergh Country Park

Thrybergh (SK 475960).
Rotherham MBC. 21ha.

Approach The Rotherham to Doncaster bus service passes the entrance of the country park.

Summary A country park at a reservoir used for water sports and other recreational activities during the summer months, acts as a wildfowl refuge in the winter. A circular walk around the reservoir is open during the summer only.

History Thrybergh Reservoir was created by damming the Silverwood Brook in 1880 but was taken out of commission in 1982.

Nature interest The areas of grassland and water edge have interesting plants and insects, but the main interest is the bird life. The wintering wildfowl and a large gull roost can involve thousands of birds, and passage migrants have been particularly studied.

Management The country park staff manage the area as a recreational facility and nature reserve.

Interpretation Leaflets from Rotherham MBC. An annual report on

wildlife is produced by the Rotherham and District Ornithological Society.
Access   Open at all times.
Contact   Thrybergh Country Park, Thrybergh, Rotherham.

7 Wentworth Park

Wentworth (SK 4097).
Fitzwilliam Estates. 275ha.
Approach   The Rotherham to Barnsley bus service passes both the SE and NW entrances to the main right of way which bisects the area.
Summary   The former seat of Earl Fitzwilliam is set in magnificent countryside between Rotherham and Barnsley. The footpath from Greasbrough to Wentworth passes between the ornamental lakes and through the deer park, other paths giving access to the lake sides.
History   Wentworth Woodhouse has the longest frontage of any stately home in England and has been the home of the Fitzwilliams until recently. The park was landscaped and the lakes constructed in the 17C.
Nature interest   A herd of red deer, about 100 strong, shares the deer park with cattle and can often be seen from the footpath. The ornamental lakes are important wintering areas for waterfowl and smaller numbers can be seen in summer. The lake margins have a variety of plants, fungi and insects.
Management   Part of the park is farmed, the lakes are fished and the woods used for game rearing.
Interpretation   Leaflet from Libraries, Museum and Arts Department.
Access   Public footpaths open at all times, discretionary footpaths ditto.
Contact   Fitzwilliam (Wentworth) Estates, Estate Office, Wentworth, Rotherham, S62 7TD.

Further information

Rotherham MBC, Libraries, Museum and Arts Department, Biological Records Centre, Clifton Park Museum, Clifton Lane, Rotherham S65 2AA (0709 382121).
Rotherham MBC, Countryside Management Service, Recreation Offices, Grove Road, Rotherham S60 2ER (0709 382121).
Rotherham MBC, Development and Planning, Norfolk House, Walker Place, Rotherham S60 1QT (0709 382121).
Rotherham Urban Wildlife Group, c/o 6 Hill Close, Brecks, Rotherham S65 3JE.
Chesterfield Canal Society, c/o Bridge House, 33 Sheffield Road, Creswell, Derbyshire (0909 721418).
Acknowledgement   Text written by Bill Ely of the Biological Records Centre; additional assistance provided by David Wood, countryside officer in the Planning Department.

SHEFFIELD

Sheffield began as a small settlement on the River Sheaf (from which it takes its name) in Anglo-Saxon times. The Normans built a castle there and many years later Mary, Queen of Scots spent a large part of her captivity in the castle. Sheffield is built on the coal measures and its geology has played a large part in its development into an industrial city. It has been famous for centuries for its cutlery (one of Chaucer's pilgrims carried a Sheffield 'thwistel' or knife in *The Canterbury Tales*) and later as a centre for mass production of steel. Local iron ore and coal provided the raw materials for these industries and the coal measure sandstone provided the grinding wheels used in the production of cutlery. Water power to drive the grindstones was available in abundance in the form of many small streams flowing off the high moors W of the city, through wooded and deeply cut valleys, down into the River Don. These wooded valleys still remain, being generally too steep for building development, and now form green corridors connecting the inner city with open country. The city is also well-endowed with parks and areas of woodland. Although the city's heavy industrial base has been greatly reduced, Sheffield is now experiencing a revival in prosperity and large areas of land in the industrial 'East End' are being redeveloped.

1 Blackbrook Wood

Between Manchester Road and Redmires Road (SK 295867).
Sheffield CC. 24ha.
Approach Can be reached from the 51 bus route, over the Hallamshire Golf Course.
Summary The wood contains a wide range of plants and birds in a number of different habitats. It is quiet and unspoilt, giving a feeling of remoteness and naturalness.
Nature interest The wood lies to the W of Sheffield, on the grits and shales of the coal measures, and is situated on the N facing slope of the Rivelin Valley. The wood is a sessile oak, rowan and birch wood, with a varied ground flora, ranging from typical woodland species such as bluebells to elements of the upland flora such as cowberry. The steeper dry slopes are dominated by wavy hair grass, while the wetter lower slopes are covered by creeping soft grass. A line of seepage has resulted in the presence of wet flushes with sphagnum, bog asphodel and marsh violet.

The oldest part of the wood is along the stream, where the largest trees and a number of plants restricted to this area including yellow archangel and greater woodrush can be found. Around 60 species of bird have been recorded including woodcock, tawny owl, green and great spotted woodpecker. The wood is remarkably free from alien species such as sycamore, and a healthy cycle of regeneration and decay is taking place. This itself, through the presence of dead and dying wood, provides valuable habitats for fungi and insects.
Management None.
Interpretation Nil on site.
Access Open at all times.
Contact Sheffield CC.

2 Bowden Housteads Wood

Sheffield (SK 3986 and SK 3987).
Sheffield CC.
Approach   Bowden Housteads Wood is a deciduous woodland less than 3km E of the centre of Sheffield. It is bisected by the Sheffield Parkway, the main link into Sheffield from the M1 motorway.
Summary   The woodland is mainly oak and sweet chestnut with birch and holly, with a number of small streams flowing N to the River Don, the main water course being Car Brook.
Nature interest   Some grassland and playing fields form part of open space to the W. Most of the commoner birds—jay, wood pigeon, jackdaw—frequent the woods, and meadow pipits, gulls, rooks and skylark can often be seen on the playing fields.
Interpretation   Nil on site.
Access   A number of paths cross the N end of the wood from Darnall and a footbridge over the Parkway to join with other paths in the S wood, one of which follows the Car Brook upstream. Here some wet areas of rushes and hairy willow herb expand the habitat for botanists and entomologists as well as providing pleasant walking for the general naturalist with some good views across Sheffield.

3 Harleston Street Urban Wildlife Zone

Adjacent to Sutherland Road and Petre Street, Pitsmoor S4 (SK 365888).
Sheffield CC.
Approach   Buses along Ellesmere Road from city centre.
Summary   High density housing and a church were demolished in 1976 and the site has regenerated naturally. It became well known to local naturalists, and when a landscaping plan threatened the wildlife interest in 1987, the Sorby Natural History Society proposed an alternative management plan, which was accepted.
Nature interest   The site has good numbers of common butterflies and day-flying moths. Dragonflies from neaby wetlands rest and feed here. Overgrown brick rubble forms an 'urban scree' providing a habitat for a community of ground invertebrates. A scarce woodlouse is common here, and a number of rare ground beetles have been recorded. The flora is only of average interest but species support a wide range of smaller flying invertebrates. The bird life has yet to be studied in detail, but skylarks and partridges are known to breed here and kestrels are regular visitors seeking the resident field vole population. Harleston Street is a valuable site as few abandoned areas have survived since the mid-1970s when the major housing demolition took place in Sheffield.
Management   The site is managed jointly by Sorby Natural History Society and the owner, Sheffield CC, as an urban insect reserve. The aim is to maintain maximum diversity and populations of invertebrates typical of an inner city site. Ruderal vegetation is to be maintained by rotational disturbance, and some experimental areas are being left to develop.
Interpretation   Guide notes are being prepared, and an interpretation/study building is being planned.
Contact   Sorby NHS.

4 **Kelham Island**

Sheffield S3 (SK 352882).
Sheffield CC. 4ha.

Approach Buses along West Bar, Shalesmoor and Nursery Street; within 15-minute walk of Sheffield city centre.

Summary Adjacent to Kelham Island Industrial Museum, on the banks of the River Don, Kelham Goit and the small islands of the Don are surprisingly rich in wildlife for a site in the heart of Sheffield's industrial area.

History Kelham Goit is probably the oldest mill race in Sheffield, dating back to the 12C. The construction of Kelham Weir altered the water flow of the River Don, allowing sediment to build up into an island, now well-wooded with a regenerated population of alder, sycamore, willow and hawthorn. Kelham Island itself is now the site of an industrial museum, but the neglected areas have evolved into interesting habitats.

Nature interest The Goit has a rich freshwater invertebrate fauna, including a locally scarce leech. Damselflies are abundant in summer. The River Don at this point is oxygenated by the weir, and supports a thriving population of minnows, as well as the more ubiquitous three-spined sticklebacks. Roach and brown trout are occasionally seen. The banks of the River Don and the smaller islands are rich in flying insects and include a rare solitary wasp and wetland hoverfly. Over 30 species of birds have been recorded at the site, including frequent sightings of kestrel and kingfisher. The rich invertebrate fauna is a reflection of the diverse vegetation. Over 80 species of flowering plants are known including tufted loosestrife, gypsywort and marsh woundwort.

Management The site is managed by Sheffield City Museums as an industrial museum site, but with a sympathetic attitude to the natural heritage.

Interpretation A nature trail is being planned.

Access There is limited access to the goit and riverside. Further access can be obtained by arrangement with Kelham Island Industrial

Kelham Island, Sheffield

Museum. The River Don can be freely viewed from Ball Street bridge.
Contact   Sorby NHS.

5   Limb Valley, Whirlow Brook Park and House

Between Houndkirk Road (near Round House, Ringinglow) and
Ecclesall Road South (A625), S11, main entrance at SK 311827.
Sheffield CC. 35ha.

Approach   Suburban fringe, SW of city within 7km of city centre.
Bus to Dore passes nearest entrance; a less frequent service to
Ringinglow gives access to the upper end of Valley.

Summary   An attractive wooded valley with mill pond and stream
gives access to open country, with panoramic views of the city from
the upper edge of the wood. It is noteworthy for its variety of habitats
which, apart from deciduous, coniferous and mixed woodland,
includes dry and wet pasture, heathland and a landscaped park with
water features and ornamental borders.

History   Though the site of former industry—coal winning, lead
smelting and copper production—records of woodland extend back
300 years with intermittent clear felling and replanting. Woodland
and adjoining Whirlow Brook Park was presented to the public by the
J.G. Graves Charitable Trust between 1938 and 1946. The House was
formerly the home of Sir Walter Benton Jones, a renowned Sheffield
industrialist.

Nature interest   About 200 species of flowering plant occur in the
Valley including wood anemone and yellow archangel. The park has
many interesting cultivars and a varied collection of conifers including Caucasian, Austrian and Swiss stone pines. Some 60 species of
bird occur regularly including local species such as redstart, nuthatch
and wood warbler. Interesting mammals and reptiles include badger
and common lizard. The variety of habitats attract a diverse population of butterflies and moths. Both species of common grasshopper
occur. Among the beetle population there are several indicators of old
woodland.

Management   The footpath through the Valley forms part of the
City Round Walk. The park and most of the woodland are managed
by the Recreation Department in consultation with the Moorlands and
Woodlands Advisory Group and the Sorby NHS.

Interpretation   The wildlife in the Valley has been surveyed intensively for 10 years by sections of the Sorby NHS and the results have
been published annually in the Society's Journal, *The Sorby Record*,
since 1978. Copies are available from the City Museum.

Access   Open at all times.
Contact   Sorby NHS.

6   Loxley Valley

Main area of interest runs from Malin Bridge (SK 325893) to Damflask
Reservoir (SK 285906).
Sheffield CC.

Approach   Buses from city centre to Malin Bridge (nearest access
point to city).

Summary   A rich and varied river valley stretching well into the city
includes Little Matlock Wood, an area of ancient woodland.

History   Formerly an industrialised valley, the remains of some of
its many water powered wheels and their dams can still be seen.
Mining for ganister and fireclays was carried out from the early 1800s

until 1963. Legend has it that Robin Hood was born in the area.

Nature interest   Little Matlock Wood (Acorn Hill), is an ancient woodland on the S bank of the river. It has a variety of trees of varying ages with fairly open canopies and well-developed shrub layers. It is botanically rich and includes such old woodland indicators as yellow archangel and dog's mercury.

There is also a variety of ferns and grasses including oak fern and wood fescue. There are also areas of marsh, heath and meadowland, resulting in a very varied flora, and aquatic habitats in the old mill dams. The invertebrate fauna is correspondingly rich, especially for its lepidoptera, hoverflies, beetles and molluscs. 76 species of bird have been recorded in the woodland. The dams provide suitable conditions for amphibians. Palmate newt, smooth newt, common frog and common toad all occur in the valley. Six species of bat have been recorded in the valley and its mammal population includes the water shrew along the river.

Management   Sheffield CC.

Interpretation   Nature trail along part of valley—Malin Bridge to Stacey Bridge, leaflet available from Recreation Department.

Access   Open at all times.

Contact   Sheffield CC.

7   Sheffield Botanic Gardens

Clarkehouse Road (SK 335863).

Sheffield CC. 8ha.

Approach   Buses 33, 81, 82, 83 along Ecclesall Road from city centre. Other entrances from Brocco Bank and Clarkehouse Road.

Summary   A delightful open area near to Sheffield city centre is a sanctuary for both people and wildlife from the bustle of the city.

History   The Botanical Gardens were created 150 years ago. The Victorian glasshouses, bear pit and formal gardens still remain, together with an interesting plant collection and large informal areas of woodland gardens crossed by a range of pathways. An ideal refuge from the city to stroll, or sit quietly and watch wildlife.

Nature interest   Observe quietly for a few minutes and you can almost be guaranteed to see grey squirrels foraging and all of the common garden birds in abundance. You may be lucky enough to see more unusual species such as nuthatch, tree-creeper or willow warbler or winter flocks of fieldfare feeding on the profusion of berries. The ponds provide a breeding site for frogs, toads and newts, and tawny owls, hedgehogs and bats search for food after the gates close for the night. The curator is keen to encourage wildlife and a small demonstration wildlife garden has been created by Sheffield Friends of the Earth in a corner of the gardens.

Management   Recreation Department.

Interpretation   Regular demonstrations and tours of the gardens take place covering a wide range of horticultural subjects and pro-moting the educational aims of the Botanic Gardens. Many local soci-eties participate in staging events and displays—programme inform-ation from Sheffield Civic Information, Central Library.

Access   Open daytime all year. Easy wheelchair access.

Contact   The Curator.

Further information

Sheffield CC, Recreation Department, PO Box 151, Meersbrook Park, Sheffield S8 9FL (0742 556244).

Ecology Unit, Natural Sciences Section, City Museum, Weston Park, Sheffield S10 2TP (0742 760588).

Central Library, Union Street, S1 (0742 734760/1).

Sorby Natural History Society, 81 Greystones Close, Sheffield S11 7JT (0742 661562).

Sheffield City Wildlife Group, c/o 26 Wincobank Lane, Sheffield S4 8AA (0742 431466).

Acknowledgement   Text written by members of Sorby NHS.

WEST YORKSHIRE

BRADFORD

Often unkindly stereotyped as a forbidding Victorian monument to industrial growth, Bradford contains a large number of green areas. Of course, the woollen mills have left an indelible mark on the structure of the city, a mark attractively portrayed in the Industrial Museum. Coal mines and ironworks also once dotted the locality. The local millstone grit has been used to good effect in the predominantly sand-coloured stone buildings of the city. It also accounts for the relative acidity of the soil in this basically moorland environment. Though it was never a transport or communications centre, the River Aire and Leeds–Liverpool Canal run close to the city (the Bradford Cut once brought the canal right to the City Hall). These and the disused railways (the two survivors of which fail to meet in the city centre!) contribute to the variety of settings of nature interest.

1   Heaton Woods

On the N edge of Heaton and W of Frizinghall, about five kilomteres from City Hall (SE 143364).
Bradford CC.
Approach   Buses along Keighley Road (walk up Redburn Road) or Bingley Road (via Weather Royds Wood).
Summary   A pretty wooded glacial valley is bounded by residential areas and a golf course on the N edge of the Yorkshire coalfield.
History   Coal was mined locally in the 17C, using horizontal day-holes, the hollows still being visible, and ceased in the 19C. Shale and clay were used in a brickworks, whose chimney still stands, and the hill above the valley is a quarry spoil tip.
Nature interest   A variety of deciduous trees grace the valley, including alder (by the stream) willow, oak, elm, silver birch and sycamore. Several rough (hawthorn) hedgerows add to the habitats used by birds, which include many common species plus the occasional dippers, treecreepers, nuthatches, greenfinches, goldfinches, jays and sometimes great spotted woodpeckers. Grey squirrels and foxes frequent the woods. There is a wide range of flowers and grasses, plus an interesting crop of autumn fungi, including fly agaric and varieties of *russula*. A fascinating feature is the orange-coloured Red Burn containing iron oxide. An unfortunate one is that storm sewage outflows render the main stream, Red Beck, a health hazard.
Management   Heaton Woods is owned mainly by Bradford council, which works alongside the Heaton Township Association on its upkeep.
Interpretation   The Heaton Township Association has a forthcoming publication, *Heaton Woods History and Natural History*.
Access   Open at all times.
Contact   Heaton Township Association, c/o 108 Highgate, Heaton, Bradford.

2 Jockey Beck

Near the junction of Allerton Road and Thornton Road (SE 135335).
Bradford CC.

Approach   From Bull Royd Lane and Olive Grove.

Summary   A neglected section of a stream flowing from the better-known Chellow Dene reservoirs is also known as Chellow Dene Beck.

Nature interest   Despite its position between houses and its use for rope swings and children's dens, many birds, flowers and trees may be found here. Alder, ash, hazel, oak, willow, poplar, willow, elm (some diseased) and beech occur, along with remnants of hawthorn hedgerow. There are resident bullfinches along with other common birds. Sparrowhawks and kestrels hunt in the valley. Some plants have escaped from gardens and grow wild, mixing happily with others that were there long before the gardens were planted.

Interpretation   Nil at present.

Management   Slight.

Access   Open at all times.

Contact   Nil at present.

3 Judy Woods

A series of connected wood and farm lands lies between Norwood Green, Wyke, Low Moor and Shelf (SE 153284).
Bradford MBC.

Approach   Buses along Halifax Road or Station Road, Wyke.

Summary   A two-mile section of green belt between Bradford and Halifax, comprising Royds Hall Great Wood, Old Hanna Wood, Low Wood and Jagger Park Woods, is bounded on two sides by housing estates and touched by the Calderdale Way. A favourite walk with children, it has much interest and fine views.

History   Low Moor Ironworks and Shelf Ironworks, established 1786, used to own most of the area which accounts in part for the lie of the land and also for features such as an artificial cutting through which the Blackshaw Beck passes at one point. Judy Brig carries across the beck one of the only remaining sections of the 18C packhorse route from the Piece Hall, Halifax, to that in Bradford.

Nature interest   The most significant feature is the extensive deciduous woodland comprising oak, silver birch, chestnut, ash and the ubiquitous sycamore, several of which date back to the 18C. Different seasons give opportunity to see flowers, from anemone, lesser celandine, lungwort and wild garlic in spring to summer's pink purslane, speedwell, Himalayan balsam and butterbur. Autumn brings numerous fungi, including the more unusual stinkhorn, puffball, and wood urchin. Grey squirrels are present, along with foxes plus a number of field and woodland birds (but no cuckoo!).

Management   Bradford council own the site, but in places it shows signs of fairly long-term neglect and vandalism. The beck, once polluted by sewage and cleaning fluids, now has rubbish tipped into it near the Woodside Estate. More resources and monitoring are required to maintain this lovely area as a public amenity.

Interpretation   Nil at present.

Access   Open at all times.

Contact   Bradford CC.

4 Northcliffe Woods

Northcliffe Woods, Shipley, Bradford (SE 140360)
Bradford CC. 8ha.

Approach   Any bus along the A650 into Saltaire from the town centre alighting at Cliffe Gardens.

Summary   A pleasant walk along well-defined footpaths passes through mature oak woodland. A small beck runs across the valley floor where the woodland opens out into rough grassland. A model railway track has been built here.

History   The oakwood was bought by Shipley MP Norman Rae in 1919 and was subsequently donated to Bradford council.

Nature interest   The mature oak woodland supports an interesting and varied fauna and flora. Nesting birds include greater spotted woodpecker, nuthatch, treecreeper, wood warbler and several species of tits. Greater woodrush, wood sorrel and wavy hair-grass flourish on the acidic soil while damper areas support plants such as lady's smock, common valerian, meadowsweet, wood speedwell and lemon scented fern. Other interesting herbs scattered throughout the wood include bluebell and dog's mercury.

Management   Bat boxes plus a few bird boxes have been dispersed throughout the wood.

Interpretation   Nil.

Access   Open at all times.

Contact   Parks Department.

5 Queensbury Triangle

Near Yew Trees Green, below Clayton Edge, between Queensbury and Thornton (SE 105310).
Private.

Approach   Along Cockin Lane from Thornton Road or easy approach down Station Road from Sandbeds Queensbury crossroads.

Summary   An abandoned railway site consists of old platforms, cuttings, viaduct and tunnels.

History   A remnant of important railway station and goods yard adjoins the junction of lines joining Bradford, Halifax and Denholme.

Nature interest   The site is an excellent botanical oasis in land that is otherwise of semi-moorland origins. Railway ballast and rubble provide some basic nutrients normally lacking in an acidic habitat. Over 90 species of plants are present on the site showing good examples of different stages of natural succession. A notable species is the wood vetch, not normally found in the Bradford area.

Management   This area is owned by a farmer and, although at present people roam freely, plans are afoot to turn it into a horse-riding arena.

Interpretation   Nil at present.

Access   At all times.

Contact   Nil.

6 Undercliffe Cemetery

Undercliffe Lane, B03 (SE 175342).
Bradford CC. 10ha.

Approach   Buses up Otley Road.

Summary   A Victorian cemetery contains strikingly large

monuments and the graves of both well-heeled worthies and forgotten paupers.

History   Opened in 1854, it was maintained with formal flower beds and cut grass until income from burials began to decline. The cemetery company was liquidated in 1975, following which vandalism and neglect took their toll. In 1984 Bradford council declared it a conservation area, acquired it in 1985 and an MSC scheme began to restore it as a public amenity in 1986.

Nature interest   The three main habitats of the site are tall and short grasslands plus a 'sycamore copse and mature hedgerows containing other trees such as ash, elder, lime and holly, providing bird and animal cover. Only four or five elms remain after Dutch elm disease. The more unusual plants found in the cemetery include nipplewort, shepherds cress, lesser meadow-rue, bog pimpernel, common pennycress, common figwort, great burnet and slender water cress. A dozen or so species of bird nest here, and woodcock, chiffchaffs, spotted flycatcher, redpolls and pipits are also seen passing through.

Management   Hopes are high that this ecological resource will continue to figure in priorities established for the site.

Interpretation   There is an ecological adviser on site on weekdays who will arrange guided walks. A minibeast tick chart has been constructed for children, who are encouraged to discover insect life on the site.

Access   Open at all times.

Contact   Site warden (0274 642276).

Further information

Bradford CC, Department of Recreation, Provincial House, Bradford BD2 1NP (0274 752653).

West Yorkshire Ecological Information and Advisory Service (WYEIAS), Cliffe Castle, Keighley (0535 64184).

Bradford Urban Wildlife Group, c/o 4 Wagon Lane, Bingley, West Yorkshire (0274 569358).

Acknowledgement   Text written by David Lyon of Bradford UWG.

CALDERDALE

Calderdale, centred on Halifax, is W Yorkshire's most westerly district, stretching across the Pennines to the Lancashire border. Halifax itself is one of the Yorkshire wool towns currently undergoing a transformation as its mills and famous Piece Hall are cleaned up and adapted to modern uses. Its wildlife sites are also now receiving protection, with the council operating a countryside service which pays particular attention to the educational possibilities of its urban schools.

1 Jerusalem Farm

Jerusalem Lane, Luddenden, Halifax (SE 038277).
Calderdale MBC. 14ha.
Approach   From Halifax on A646 turn right at Luddenden Foot to Booth, through village and sharp left to farm after quarter of a mile.
Summary   Jerusalem Farm is being developed as a Countryside Training and Resource Centre where the demonstration of good countryside management in its widest sense will be its prime function.
History   The farm has been in local authority ownership for many years and has been used for informal activities and camping.
Nature interest   Jerusalem Farm and the adjacent Wade Wood SSI have always been popular, not just for recreation but also for the high ecological interest of the area. Some of the plants to be found here are indicative of an ancient woodland flora including species rare in the county. Good and extensive marshy flushes adjoining Luddenden Brook are ecologically sensitive and activities have been directed away from these areas. An oak and birch dominated woodland gives a varied fauna throughout most of the area. This valley has long been regarded as one of the most important sites in Calderdale.
Management   Managed by Countryside Service.
Interpretation   Leaflets, boards and displays.
Access   Grounds open at all times, camping at all times by arrangement, Centre by arrangement.
Contact   Centre Manager (0422 883246) or Countryside Service.

2 North Dean Nature Centre

Clay House, West Vale, Halifax (SE 098214).
Calderdale MBC.
Approach   4km S of Halifax on A629, turn right on to B6112 to Clay House Park. Car park near traffic lights.
Summary   North Dean Nature Centre contains an exciting new exhibition about the natural history and countryside of Calderdale. Linked to the adjacent North Dean Wood and the wide open spaces of Norrland Moor, the Centre makes an excellent venue for a day out in the country.
Nature interest   North Dean is recognised as a representative habitat type and is designated an SSSI. Within the woods are to be found many different areas from thick tree cover of beech, oak and sycamore to open glades of heather, birch and bilberry. There are also damp parts and rocky outcrops and this variety of habitats gives an interesting lower part and scattered quarrying activities. These areas,

now long disused, have also become valuable for the plants and animals to be found in them.

Management Managed by the Countryside Service as a countryside recreation site.

Interpretation Interpretation leaflets, boards and nature trail.

Access Centre open every day except Monday (excluding Bank Holidays). Weekends only November to Easter. Woodland open at all times.

Contact North Dean Nature Centre (0422 74014) or Countryside Service.

3 Ogden Water

Causeway Foot, Keighley Road, Halifax (SE 066309).
Calderdale MBC. 70ha.

Approach 6.5km N of Halifax, turn left off A629 at Causeway Foot Inn along Ogden Lane to car park.

Summary Ogden Water is an area of reservoir, mixed semi- mature woodlands and open moorland criss-crossed by many footpaths. Parts of the area have been used for over a century for walking, picnics, and nature studies.

Nature interest Ogden Water is a totally artificial landscape yet, through the building of the reservoir and planting of trees at the end of the last century, it has become a well- loved area for naturalists to visit. Though predominantly a pine plantation, there are also a number of deciduous trees to be found which, with the water, support a good cross section of birds and animals. Many interesting and rare plants and insects have been found, although with unrestricted sheep grazing for many years the plants have diminished. Now, with careful control, perhaps we will see again a greater variety than exists at present in this beautiful area.

Management Managed by the Countryside Service as a countryside recreation site.

Interpretation Leaflets, boards.

Access Open at all times.

Contact Site manager (0422 249136) or Countryside Service.

Further information

Calderdale MBC, Leisure Services, Countryside Service, Wellesley Park, Halifax, West Yorkshire HX2 0AY (0422 59454).

Acknowledgement Text written by Ian Kendall of Leisure Services.

KIRKLEES

Kirklees is an amalgam of various former borough councils in the old West Riding of Yorkshire, formed at local government re-organisation in 1974. Largest of the towns is Huddersfield and others include Dewsbury, Batley, Mirfield, Meltham and Holmfirth. Kirklees takes its name from Kirklees Hall, on the site of a former nunnery where legend says Robin Hood died and is buried.

For a metropolitan borough Kirklees is remarkably rural, containing much unspoilt countryside. The area S of Huddersfield is very well wooded for N England, the Holme Valley in particular contains many fine deciduous and mixed woodlands clinging to the valley sides. The most industrialised area is the heavy woollen district of Dewsbury and Batley, which also contains the most intensive agriculture. However, even in this area there are urban and rural sites with a rich variety of wildlife.

1 Bradley Quarry Wildlife Area

Upper Quarry Road, Bradley, nr Huddersfield (SE 172204).
Kirklees MBC. 2ha.
Approach   Buses available from Huddersfield along Leeds Road (A62) to Bradley.
Summary   An attractively wooded site, situated within the green belt at the E end of Huddersfield.
History   The site was extensively quarried for stone until it was bought by the council in 1897 for use as a refuse tip. The tip was never really used for its original purpose and by the process of succession gradually became colonised by a range of trees and shrubs. Early in 1985 it was proposed that the site be developed into a nature reserve, where native plant species would dominate, thus providing a natural habitat for local wildlife and also a facility for educational purposes.
Nature interest   The trees which can be found around the site are those which have self-seeded, the dominant canopy species being oak, birch and sycamore. The shrub layer consists of dog rose, bramble and elder. Other trees include alder, elm and rowan. Along the sides of the woodchip paths a variety of plants, including woodsage, foxglove, bluebells and red campion, can be found. Jays and blue tits can be seen feeding on oak buds, while kestrels prey on the large population of voles and wood mice. Foxes and hares are also quite common, although not easily seen.
Management   The site is managed as a wildlife area by the Kirklees Countryside Service. The main aim is to diversify the woodland habitat and promote its use as a recreational and interpretive resource, while minimising any possible disturbance. A management plan is being written in line with this aim.
Interpretation   The site is covered by the Countryside Link series of leaflets. It is intended to produce an interpretative plan for the site as part of the management plan.
Access   Open at all times.
Contact   Countryside Service.

2 Gledholt Woods

Gledholt Bank, Paddock, Huddersfield (SE 133167).
Kirklees MBC. 2.65ha.

Corporation in 1920.

Nature interest The woods are planted with a mixture of syca-more, beach and oak, together with some hornbeam, whitebeam, horse chestnut and sweet chestnut. The shrub layer consists of holly, hawthorn, wild raspberries, brambles and rhododendrons. Bluebells flower in profusion in the spring and lily of the valley also

Approach Within easy walking distance from Huddersfield town centre, follow Greenhead Road W.

Summary A most attractive cool and shady woodland very close to the centre of a large industrial town.

History Early records show the woodlands were part of Sir John Ramsden's Greenhead Estate in 1848. It was acquired by Huddersfield grow in the less shaded areas.

The stream flowing through the woods has been dammed at some time to form a large pond, and also an interesting boggy area of ground which provides a suitable habitat for horsetail, the great willowherb and flag iris. The aquatic fauna includes perch, roach, bream and carp. Also present are freshwater mussel and cray fish. Despite the larger fish, frogs use the pond for spawning and many tadpoles can be seen in the spring. The ornithological interests include blackbird, song thrush, robin, chaffinch, tree creeper and greater spotted woodpecker. Warblers and flycatchers may be noted during the summer months.

Management The site is managed by the Countryside Service and Kirklees Forestry Service. A management plan is to be pro-duced for the site.

Interpretation The site is covered by the Countryside Link series of leaflets. It is intended to produce an interpretative plan for the site as part of the management plan.

Access Open at all times.

Contact Countryside Service.

3 Golcar Appleyard Picnic Site

Station Lane, Golcar, nr Huddersfield (SE 101153).
Huddersfield CC. 2ha.

Approach Buses to Golcar and Linthwaite from Huddersfield.

Summary An intimately wooded site, providing easy access to the Colne Valley circular walk and the Huddersfield Narrow Canal.

History The site is adjacent to the Golcar viaduct which is part of the Leeds, Manchester, Liverpool railway line. The Golcar area has had long associations with the woollen textile industry and several remnants of the old industry in the area can be seen—for example, weavers' cottages, 'taking-in' doors, pulleys and bridges and 'wuzzing holes'. The site was originally a sewage works and was reclaimed prior to local government re-organisation in 1974 and opened as a picnic site in 1982.

Nature interest The trees on the site are a mixture of existing remnant woodland and those which have been introduced. Species include ash, sycamore, oak and non-native introduced species such as red horse chestnut and pink flowering hawthorn. Unfortunately, the main areas of grass consists of typical amenity mix sown in imported top soil. The path by the stream running into the canal leads through a woodland where bluebells can be found in spring.

Nearer the water the vegetation changes to that typically found in wet areas. Bistort and woody nightshade are common in damp areas, whereas bulrushes and mares-tail grow in wet areas.

Management The picnic site is managed by the Countryside Service. The aim is to diversify the site for the benefit of wildlife and promote its use as a recreational and interpretative resource, while minimising any possible disturbance. A management plan is being written in line with this aim.

Interpretation There are two on-site interpretation boards and the site is covered by the Countryside Link series of leaflets.

Access Open at all times.

Contact Countryside Service.

4 Lower Spen Wildlife Area

Park Road, Ravensthorpe, nr Dewsbury (SE 228209).
Kirklees MBC. 3ha.

Approach Buses from Dewsbury and Huddersfield to Ravensthorpe.

Summary An interesting wetland site in a very industrialised area attracts a variety of migrating wading birds in autumn.

History The site was previously part of the now defunct Ravensthorpe sewage works. The area has long been frequented by migrating wildfowl and waders, which can still be found in the depleted wetland habitat along the Calder and Spen valleys.

Nature interest The River Spen flows through the wildlife area. Although of poor quality it supports a wide range of wildlife owing to the shallow and stony stream bed and well- vegetated margins. Rough grazing pasture and hedgerows increase the diversity of the site. There is a good variety of plants, which include Himalayan balsam, hemlock and reed grass growing on the streamside. Celery leaved buttercup and persicaria can be found growing in muddy areas and around the pond. Other flowering plants include melilot, weld, winter cress and wild lettuce. Unusual to this area is a small colony of wild plum, which can be found growing by the streamside. Resident breeding birds are linnet, greenfinch and reed bunting, with several pairs of moorhen along the River Spen. During autumn, migrating waders on their way S from the N breeding grounds can be seen, including common sandpiper, dunlin, ringed plover and greenshank. Winter visitors include grey wagtail, common snipe and teal. Thrushes, field fares and redwings from Scandinavia feed on the berries of hawthorn and elderberry, while mixed flocks of finches are attracted by the abundance of seedheads. Mammals present include water voles and weasels, but there are no records of amphibians. Butterflies present include common blue, small skipper and small copper. Dragonflies include the large brown hawker.

Management The site is managed as a wildlife area by the Countryside Service. The main aim is to create a wetland habitat with a diversity of wildlife which can be used as a recreational and interpretative resource with a minimum of disturbance or damage. A management plan is being written in line with this aim.

Interpretation The site is covered by the Countryside Link series of leaflets. It is intended to produce an interpretative plan for the site.

Access Open at all times.

Contact Countryside Service.

Lower Spen Wildlife Area, Kirklees

Further information

Kirklees MBC, Countryside Service, PO Box B95, Civic Centre, Huddersfield, West Yorkshire HD1 2NA (0484 22133).

Acknowledgement   Text written by Neil Windett of the Kirklees Technical Services Department.

LEEDS

Situated on the River Aire where it emerges from the Pennines into the Yorkshire plain, Leeds owed its initial growth to its position as the marketing centre for the Yorkshire woollen industry. Later, with the introduction of steam power, woollen manufacture became more important and, later still, the ready-made clothing industry. Engineering has also been an important contributor to Leeds' prosperity since the industrial revolution, partly because of the ready availability of coal to power the new factories.

1   Bramley Fall Wood

Leeds and Bradford Road, LS13 (SE 245365).
Leeds CC. 24ha.
Approach   Buses along the Leeds and Bradford Road, or from the Leeds–Liverpool canal towpath.
Summary   A mainly oak woodland growing on the S slope of the Aire Valley. Some exotic trees have been planted recently by the council.
History   Part of the woodland appears to be based on abandoned coppice, and the remainder to be natural regeneration on the sites of worked out quarries.
Nature interest   The woodland supports a good population of woodland birds. Lesser spotted woodpecker has been seen, and the great spotted woodpecker is normally present. Blackcap and other warblers are present in the breeding season. The woodland has a good fungus flora.
Management   Managed as a public park by Leeds CC.
Interpretation   A leaflet, *Bramley Fall*, published by Leeds CC gives historical information and is a guide to footpaths and access.
Access   Open at all times.
Contact   Parks Department.

2   Clayton Woods

Low Lane, Horsforth, LS18 (SE 255385).
Private. 20ha.
Approach   Buses along Low Lane or Silk Mill Drive.
Summary   An apparently natural woodland which, although much reduced by quarrying and other developments, provides extensive woodland habitats and a wide variety of woodland birds.
History   The land use history appears to be quite complex. Parts of the woodland seem to have developed naturally on abandoned agricultural land.
Nature interest   Most of the common woodland birds may be found here. In particular, all three species of woodpecker breed most years, as well as nuthatch, treecreeper and several species of warbler. The range of species is extended by the presence nearby of Oil Mill Beck which attracts a number of water birds. There are some interesting ponds in the neighbourhood.
Management   Little active management.
Interpretation   Nil.
Access   Open at all times.

3 Meanwood Valley

The valley begins on the N outskirts of the city, following the course of a stream known variously as Marsh Beck, Adel Beck, Meanwood Beck and Sheepscar Beck leading eventually to junction with the River Aire at the site of the origin of Leeds, just to the E of the present city centre. The stream is culverted from Buslingthorpe Lane to the Aire. Most of the areas of natural history interest are now in the ownership of Leeds CC (from SE 266416 to SE 296360).

Approach   Buses along Meanwood Road; buses along Otley Road; from the Leeds Ring Road (A6120) at SE 269375.

Summary   The Valley offers a succession of habitats stretching for about 6.5 kilometres , from the mainly open grassland-with-scrub of Sugarwell Hill in the E, to the alder carr and woodland of Breary Marsh (SSSI) in the NW. Between these extremes are several wooded areas, with parkland-type woodland at Meanwoodside and parts of The Hollies, and more natural woodland at Adel Woods, Scotland Wood and Meanwood Woods.

History   The valley has a long history of industrial development based on the water power provided by the beck. Industry has gradually declined with the availability of other forms of power, but many relics of the past in the form of mill streams and mill ponds can still be found. The valley slopes are in many places too steep and stony for agricultural use, and woodland and other habitat has grown up here, including places where earlier cultivation has been abandoned. Many notable naturalists have lived in the valley, and its natural history, and in particular its botany, has a long and detailed record.

Nature interest   All the woodland birds of the Leeds area can be found in one or other of the woodlands. The wood warbler has its only regular Leeds breeding site in Adel Woods and five or six other species of warbler can be found in most years. All three species of woodpecker breed in the valley, together with all the common birds of woodland. The stream provides breeding sites for kingfishers, dippers and occasionally grey wagtails—species which are also present outside the breeding season. The seeds of the streamside alders are taken by siskins, which are regular winter visitors, and other birds. The open habitats of Sugarwell Hill have birds of open country such as skylark, meadow pipit and partridge, and it provides the best site for observing the passage of migrants such as wheatear, whinchat and some of the warblers which use the valley. There are many species of wildflowers, some relics of old hay meadows, and the woodlands support a very varied fungus flora.

The Grove Lane pond is a former millpond, half of which was filled in as part of a council landscaping scheme. It now supports a large population of frogs and some smooth newts. The water supply and management of the pond is organised by the Leeds Urban Wildlife Group. There are lakes at Adel Dam, Golden Acre Park and Breary Marsh.

Management   Management of the council-owned land varies from the intensive, crowd attracting cultivation of Golden Acre Park to the (welcome) neglect of some other areas. Management is not generally directed to wildlife conservation except at Adel Dam (20 acres) which is owned and managed by the Yorkshire Wildlife Trust.

Interpretation   The council maintains a visitor centre at Means-woodside. The Meanwood Valley Trail leaflet published by the council gives details of the footpath links and points out some of the sites of historical interest.

Access   Council-owned areas are open at all times. Entry to Adel Dam is restricted, enquiries to YWT.

4   Roundhay Park

Prince's Avenue, LS8 (SE 330380).
Leeds CC. 245ha.
Approach   Buses along Prince's Avenue and Street Lane.
Summary   This large public park contains a number of visitor attractions and stages many events during the course of the year. There are two lakes which attract some wildfowl and other water birds, and areas of woodland.
History   The park, the history of which can be traced back to the 13C, was formerly the grounds of a private house, which still stands, and was acquired by the council in 1872.
Management   The park is managed by the council and large numbers of people visit the various attractions provided.
Nature interest   The large size of the park enables a good variety of birds to survive in the mature deciduous woodlands in spite of the considerable visitor pressure. Of particular interest is the lesser spotted woodpecker which breeds here most years. The lakes attract a wide variety of water birds, but disturbance usually prevents them from remaining very long.
Interpretation   Nil.
Access   Open at all times.
Contact   Parks Department.

Further information

Leeds City Council, Leisure Services Department, Parks Division, 19 Wellington Street, Leeds LS1 4DG (0532 46300).
Leeds Urban Wildlife Group, c/o 26 Kingsley Drive, Leeds LS16 7PB.
Acknowledgement   Text written by Peter Larner of Leeds UWG.

WAKEFIELD

Capital of the old West Riding and until recently the HQ of the now disbanded West Yorkshire county council, the city serves as a regional centre. Wool was its staple for centuries before and after the industrial revolution, but mining and other heavy industries have now been supplemented by commercial services. The present metropolitan district also includes venerable towns such as Pontefract, and its variable character encompasses sites of wildlife interest in areas ranging from former medieval centres to mining towns. The council has an active greening programme which is intended to protect such sites and to link them into a green network with the district.

1 Anglers Country Park

Haw Park Lane, Wintersett, Wakefield (SE 369154).
Wakefield CC. 64ha.
Approach   Signposted from the A61 and A638.
Summary   Aquatic and meadow habitats along with young tree plantations.
History   The country park was created as part of a restoration scheme carried out after opencast coal mining. Works completed in 1984 included the creation of a 30 hectare lake.
Nature interest   The park is already an important site for winter wildfowl attracting a variety of species. The meadow areas during the summer provide nesting areas for birds such as skylarks and attract a variety of insects.
Management   Wakefield Countryside Service with the emphasis being on nature conservation, informal countryside recreation, environmental education and interpretation.
Interpretation   There is a small visitor centre, from which rangers organise countryside events which are open to the public as well as for visiting school groups.
Access   Open all year round but times vary.
Contact   Visitor Centre (0924 863262).

2 Bretton Country Park

Huddersfield Road, Haigh, Barnsley (SE 295124).
Wakefield CC. 39ha.
Approach   Just off J38 of the M1.
Summary   Open parkland with mature trees and grassland renowned for its high landscape value.
History   The area which now comprises the park was formerly the Deer Park of Bretton Hall estate which has a very rich and varied history. The unusual underground deer shelter can still be seen.
Nature interest   A haven for wildlife attracting a wide variety of birds, insects and mammals.
Management   Wakefield Countryside Service with the emphasis being on nature conservation, informal countryside recreation, environmental education and interpretation.
Interpretation   A small visitor centre offers leaflets on a variety of topics. Countryside events are open to the public, as well as for visiting school groups.

Access   All year round but opening times vary.
Contact   Visitor Centre (0924 830550).

3   Newmillerdam Country Park

Barnsley Road, Newmillerdam, Wakefield (SE 331157).
Wakefield CC. 100ha.
Approach   A61.
Summary   Aquatic and woodland habitats with a small area of grassland.
History   The lake at Newmillerdam was once used to drive the waterwheels of the local cornmill and was part of the Chevet Park estate.
Nature interest   The lake is home to a wide variety of wildlife, including swans, grebes, dragonflies and damselflies. The large areas of broadleaved and coniferous woodland also support a wide variety of wildlife including squirrels and woodpeckers.
Management   Wakefield Countryside Service with the emphasis on nature conservation, informal countryside recreation, environmental education and interpretation.
Interpretation   The ranger organises countryside events, which are open to the public, as well as activities and visits for school groups.
Access   From 8am until dusk all year round.
Contact   Ranger Service (0924 296203/4).

Further information

Wakefield City Council, Planning Department, Newton Bar, Wakefield, West Yorkshire WF1 2TX (0924 370211).
Acknowledgement   Text written by Jonathan Hall of the Planning Department.

NORTHWEST

Coverage of the Lancashire boroughs of Blackburn, Hyndburn, Lancaster, Preston and Rossendale is followed by that of the industrial towns of the Cumbria coast. Blackburn, Hyndburn and Rossendale lie in the Pennines N of Greater Manchester. Lancaster and Preston were formerly busy ports as well as manufacturing centres—the latter also taking over from the former as the county's administrative centre. The historic county, now shorn of Greater Manchester and Merseyside, remains the area served by the Lancashire Trust for Nature Conservation (LTNC), based outside Preston.

Pleasington Old Hall, Blackburn

BLACKBURN

Pleasington Old Hall Wood and Butterfly Garden Nature Reserve

Pleasington (SD 646270).
Blackburn BC. 4ha.
Approach   The reserve lies 4km WSW of Blackburn town centre by Tower Road off the A674, adjacent to Pleasington Cemetery and Crematorium.
Summary   The reserve consists of a woodland and small wetland with an attached butterfly garden, and will be developed as an educational/interpretational and recreational resource.
History   The idea for a reserve was promoted by the former Mayor and Mayoress of Blackburn on behalf of LTNC as a joint project with Blackburn council.
Nature interest   The wood has a rich diversity of tree species and is a mixed semi-natural woodland. The wood is a refuge for locally rare plants such as touch-me-not and many woodland bird species can be seen here. The butterfly garden has been planted with species to attract adult butterflies and act as larval food plants.
Management   Managed by Blackburn BC with advice from LTNC to whom it is to be leased.
Interpretation   An information leaflet is available.
Access   Open at all times.
Contact   Reserve Manager, 3 Avondale Road, Darwen, Blackburn, Lancashire (0254 772524).

Further information

Blackburn BC, Leisure Services, Town Hall, King William Street, Blackburn BB1 7DY (0254 55201).
Lancashire Trust for Nature Conservation, Cuerden Park Wildlife Centre, Shady Lane, Bamber Bridge, Preston PR5 6AV (0772 324129).
Acknowledgement   Text of this and other Lancashire entries was written by members of LTNC.

HYNDBURN

1   Foxhill Bank Reservoir

Oswaldtwistle (SD 736280).
NW Water. 8ha.
Approach   Close to Oswaldtwistle town centre.
Summary   Foxhill Bank reservoir is situated in a shallow valley through which flows Tinker Brook, a tributary of the river Hyndburn. A wide range of habitats is represented from broadleaved woodland and scrubland to wetland which have colonised three disused and partially drained lodges—Heart Lodge, Sludge Lodge and Foxhill Bank Lodge.
History   Within the urban area of E Lancashire, the site is extremely rich and diverse. The site was brought to the attention of LTNC by a local action group concerned about the site which was threatened with drainage. An ecological survey has been accepted by NWW and Hyndburn council and the threat of drainage lifted.
Nature interest   The shallow lodges—or mill ponds—are reverting to fen and have an interesting and important emergent population, with large numbers of frogs, toads, and smooth and great crested newts. Various warblers, water fowl, passage migrants, dragonflies and a variety of insects can be seen. Adjacent to these lodges are well-developed areas of scrub and plantation woodlands. Future links with the remainder of the reservoir systems in the area are to be explored.
Management   The site will be managed as a reserve by LTNC and the Foxhill Bank local group following the proposed sale of the site to Hyndburn BC.
Interpretation   None at present.
Access   Open at all times.
Contact   Foxhill Bank local group (LTNC), c/o 4 Devon Avenue, West End, Oswaldtwistle, Lancashire.

Further information

Hyndburn BC, Leisure Services, Gothic House, 50 James Street,Accrington BB5 1EZ (0254 33521).
Lancashire Trust for Nature Conservation (see Blackburn).
Ribble Valley Group (LTNC), c/o Little Beck, Eaves Hill Lane, West Bradford, Chittern, Lancashire (0200 23954).

LANCASTER

The Roman town, whose fortifications and bath house can still be seen, overlooked the crossing of the River Lune. The present castle still dominates the scene, surrounded by residential slopes on one side and industrial sites on the other.

Canal, river and green fingers penetrate the city, which has grown with textile, cabinet making and laminate industries among others. An increasing tourist target, Lancaster is within easy reach of Morecambe Bay and the Lake District and enjoys a surprising amount of ecological activity for a town of 45,000 people, plus interesting industrial sites in the neighbouring towns of Carnforth and Heysham.

1   Bowerham Nature Pond

Cranwell Avenue (SD 488608).
Lancaster CC.
Approach   Buses to Bowerham from city centre.
Summary and history   Created in 1984–85 by Landlife from a relict area of impeded drainage and surrounded on three sides by houses, the pond is not large enough to incorporate amenity areas.
Nature interest   The water in the pool is clean, supporting a wide range of aquatic invertebrates plus frogs, toads and palmate newts. Reed buntings, snipe, grey wagtails and moorhen can be seen regularly while kingfishers and dippers fly across the stream which flows along one side. Some of the plants have been rescued from local developing industrial sites, such as the flowering rush. Others, brought from Leighton Moss, include flag iris, great water dock, water plantain, burr-reed and water crowfoot.
Management   Landlife. Regular weeding is necessary to stop clogging by flote grass and oxygenators.
Interpretation   Contact Landlife.
Access   Open at all times.
Contact   Landlife.

2   Hest Bank Shore

(SD 467664).
Private.
Approach   By car off the A5105. Buses between Morecambe and Carnforth.
Summary   This saltmarsh and mudflat area has always been an excellent spot to view vast numbers of waders, especially in winter, and also shelduck, pin tail along the coast to the S.
History   Has always been saltmarsh and mudflats.
Nature interest   Knot, dunlin, oystercatchers, curlew, bar-tailed godwits, ringed plover, golden and grey plovers, lapwings and sanderling can all be seen here. The huge circling flocks of knot are one of the most spectacular sights in the Morecambe Bay area. Visit halfway up a rising tide.
Management   None.
Interpretation   Contact LTNC.
Access   Open at all times.
Contact   LTNC.

3 Heysham Nature Reserve

Heysham Village (SD 599407).
CEGB. 2ha.
Approach   Car park at observation tower. By bus to Heysham
power station.
Summary   A small reserve, although due for considerable expansion in the 1990s, it contains many different habitats including pond,
stream, derelict land, scrub, grassland and bush and glade. The site
will be undergoing change for a long time to come. Part of the site
includes a sea watch hide at Red Nab, accessible through the power
station perimeter.
History   Heysham power station was built on the site of the former
Heysham lake, a site well known for wintering wildfowl and waders.
The CEGB intends to reinstate and diversify the natural habitats, at
the same time practising creative ecology on the totally artificial parts.
Nature interest   The sea watching hide is best October to March.
The sea wall and jetty are also good for sea watching—for the
hardened birder perhaps, at high tide in storm conditions.

The reserve site itself can be viewed from the observation tower.
While footpaths provide access to certain parts, access to the main
habitats is only possible with guidance from LTNC staff or volunteers,
as the small size of the area creates a delicate state of balance.

Three species of orchids, broomrape, haresfoot, Danish scurvy
grass, greater knapweed, marsh pennywort and other notable plants
are easy to see. The plant list in 1987 stood at 240 species, remarkable
for so small a site.

The invertebrate fauna includes the snail *Cernuella virgata* and the
spider *Agalena labyrinthica*, with damsel and dragonflies, many
species of moths including the drinker and eyed hawk, and butterflies
including small copper, small heath, common blue and wall brown.

Birds on the site include nesting sedge warblers, white-throats and
blackcaps, with reed buntings and moorhen lower down nearer the
water. This is the main site in the district for ringing and other
migration monitoring. Every year some rarities appear, including
recent firecrests, yellow-browed warblers, a bee-eater, barred warbler and great grey shrike. Birds to be seen from the sea watch points
include sandwich tern, black tern, gannets, little gulls, petrels,
shearwaters and many other seabirds and many species of waders
including regular purple sandpipers. Visit preferably on a rising tide,
above 8m.
Management   CEGB, LTNC.
Interpretation   LTNC has several booklets available. There is a site
cabin used for visiting groups if required.
Access   Approx. 10am to 5pm for main site (observation tower gates
open and close at these times). The hide is accessible at any time, the
key being obtained from the Stage 2 security cabin on Princess
Alexandra Way.
Contact   LTNC.

4 Lundsfield Quarry

Bolton-le-Sands (SD 497687).
Private.
Approach   From the Nether Kellet road to the W of the M6, drive N
a short way on the track then use footpaths. Cross marshy field to W of

path onto plateau area.

Summary   Old quarry waste flora.

History   Used for many years as a quarry, this site is only part of a complex of tips and hollows, criss-crossed by footpaths leading to neighbouring villages and farms. Left to its own devices for some time, it supports an interesting flora.

Nature interest   The most spectacular displays of orchids can be seen here, from the early purples through to common spotted in profusion, N marsh, early marsh, hybrids and other interesting species. Other rough grassland herbs, sedges and rushes surround the central pond, which is habitat for damsel and dragonflies, frogs and newts. The edges of the site have shrubs, trees and scrub. Many goldfinches, greenfinches and linnets can be seen at most times of the year.

Management   LTNC has management plans for the site.

Interpretation   Contact LTNC.

Access   Open at all times.

Contact   LTNC.

5   Lune Industrial Estate

Lune Road (SD 458615).
Private. 10ha.

Approach   Buses from the city centre to the marsh; on foot along the quay, Lune Road and Willow Lane; it can also be reached from the Lancaster-Glasson Dock cycleway.

Summary   Much ground flora with many wildflowers, butterflies and moths. Edged by trees, mostly sycamore. Rough underfoot. It is only the factories to one side which indicate the former use.

History   The Lune Industrial Estate has been progressively declining for many years. Problems of lorry access and an increase in the number of houses nearby have increased this trend. Most of the flora is growing on great thicknesses of linoleum and laminates as this used to be a dumping area for waste materials from local industries. One small area is still an unvegetated sea of broken glass.

Nature interest   Many large stands of willowherbs, melilots and ragwort, and many other species such as purple, yellow and small toadflaxes, knapweed and mixed grassy floras with vetches and trefoils. The paucity of much of the soil has led to a profusion of flowers, which attract such butterfly species as common blue, small copper, small heath, wall browns, meadow browns, vanessids and whites. Snipe, partridge and pheasant can be seen regularly. Parts of the site ignite spontaneously throughout summer from the heat generated underground.

Management   None. The site will, however, be part of a regeneration area in the city council's 10 year local plan, 1988-98. This would mean a loss of the main nature interest.

Interpretation   Contact Landlife.

Access   Open.

Contact   Landlife.

6   Priory Fields

Between castle and quay (SD 473619).
Lancaster CC.

Approach On foot by walking past the castle and priory church, or up from the quay.

Summary/history The landform is the remains of the old Roman fortifications whose wall lines and gateways can still be detected. Since Roman times a moorland/heathland flora has established itself, and this remains although cut regularly under an amenity grassland regime. The old railway track at the bottom has been converted into a pleasant walkway.

Nature interest The plants, such as sheep sorrel, bedstraws, moorland sedges, grasses and mosses share the area with cuckoo flower and, on the old railway, ladies' mantle, yellow vetchling, knapweed and toadflax. Tawny owls, sparrowhawks, kestrels and even peregrines are seen here, the first three nesting nearby. Large areas of ragged robin and other species have been planted recently by the council.

Management Lancaster CC.

Interpretation Contact Landlife.

Access Open at all times.

Contact Landlife.

7 Skerton Weir

Ladies Walk Sidings (SD 481633).

Approach From car park, or on foot along the river from the quay.

Summary Mainly popular with anglers, birdwatchers and walkers, the weir area includes a small wooded island and a fish-ladder.

History The present configuration of the weir was created quite recently. All the old islands were piled together to make the single feature which now divides the flow just below the weir. On certain tides a small bore can be seen coming up river past the quay and Maritime Museum, but does not often reach this far up.

Nature interest Grey wagtail, cormorants and kingfishers are regular, with goldeneye, tufted duck and mergansers in winter. Goosanders, which breed up river, are present throughout the year and can be watched at quite close range diving among the downflow and outwash.

In recent years, night heron, black tern and little grebe have been on the site, while many species of waders pass on spring migration and to a lesser extent in autumn. There is often a sizeable heron roost, while salmon, trout, flatfish and eels can be seen easily. Look out for siskins in the nearby alders.

Management Fish and water movements are monitored by the river and angling authorities. Otherwise unmanaged.

Interpretation Contact Landlife.

Access Open at all times.

Contact Landlife.

8 Steamtown

Carnforth (SD 497708).

Steamtown railway museum.

Approach By rail to Carnforth. By car, signposted off the Carnforth–Warton road.

History Carnforth used to be a major rail junction. The area of sidings W of the present buildings contains an artificially created limestone grassland, much of the ground material being limestone chippings. Steamtown is on the geological boundary between the limestone and the millstone grit to the S.

Summary   Part of the site is a rich limestone grassland with many interesting species of flowering plants. Steamtown is a working railway museum, visited by thousands of people. There is an admission charge to the whole site.

Nature interest   The exceptional limestone grassland contains many grasses typical of the area to the N, such as Warton Crag, plus flowering species such as orchids, blue fleabane, knapweeds, scabiouses, vetches, trefoils and centaury.The associated fauna is reflected in the butterflies and moths attracted to the site, which include vanessids, small heath, common blue, small copper, wall brown and poplar hawk moths.

Management   Steamtown and LTNC.

Interpretation   Contact LTNC.

Access   Phone Steamtown for opening times (0524 734220).

Contact   Steamtown or LTNC.

9   Williamson Park

Wyresdale Road (SD 4961).

Lancaster CC.

Approach   Buses to Moor Hospital from city centre; it is only one mile from the centre but uphill all the way.

Summary   Much of the planting is mature. The wild areas are small but secluded and it is usually possible to find a corner of tranquility. The views are fantastic (the memorial in the park is built on the highest point in Lancaster) whether it is of sunset over the Lakeland fells, of the Isle of Man on a clear day or a glimpse of Blackpool Tower.

History   Created in Victorian times by Lord Ashton. The council is introducing a theme park concept, with the memorial being rendered safe and augmented by a butterfly house.

Nature interest   No rare native plants survive but the remaining patches of woodland flora and old lichen-covered birch trees clinging to the gritstone outcrops give a natural feel. The variety of types and height of vegetation, plus the water features, attract many birds including great spotted woodpecker, wood warbler, spotted flycatcher and sparrowhawks.

Management   Lancaster CC.

Interpretation   Guide booklets from Lancaster Curriculum Development Centre, Storey Institute, Lancaster.

Access   Closed to vehicles at dusk.

Contact   As above.

Further information

Lancaster City Council, Town Hall, Lancaster.

Landlife, Lancaster Branch, Lancaster Enterprise Workshops, White Cross, Lancaster LA1 4XH (0524 67462). It sponsors the Lancaster Educational Nature Areas Project (LENAP), based at Moorside School, Bowerham, Lancaster (0524 62062), among other projects.

Lancaster Group (LTNC), c/o North Lancashire Naturalists, Holly House, Hornby, Lancashire.

Acknowledgement   Text written by Chris Whitehead of Landlife and LTNC with assistance from Jennifer Newton of LTNC.

PRESTON

1 Brockholes Wood

Lower Brockholes, Preston (SD 575305).
Preston BC. 20ha.
Approach   On the E suburbs of Preston between the Farrington and Moor Nook estates, the wood stretches from the A59 to the M6.
Summary   Approximately 50 acres of semi-natural woodland with a diverse ground flora, which will be managed for conservation, education and access with the support of local people.
History   This woodland had suffered from dumping, and the residents expressed a desire to see the wood improved and managed. During the European Year of the Environment the Lancashire county council offered financial support to the local residents' group through NACRO, the managing agent, for managing the woodland.
Nature interest   Semi-natural ancient woodland, some parts of which are dominated by oak, which is regenerating, with a diverse ground flora. Other parts are dominated by sycamore with little undergrowth and a poorer ground flora.
Management   A management committee is composed of representatives from LTNC, BTCV, Preston council and the local residents' group.
Interpretation   Nil.
Access   Open at all times.
Contact   LTNC.

2 Preston Dock

Penwortham, Preston (SD 506295).
Preston BC.
Approach   Along the N side of the Ribble close to the Albert Edward Dock in the Penwortham area of Preston.
Summary   Preston council's Riversway development is intended to embrace the maritime, industrial and natural heritage of the former dock estate.
History   There has been a port near Preston since the 14C. With the growth of industry in the 18C the use of the River Ribble by shipping increased and in 1883 the Ribble Navigation and Preston Dock Act allowed the development of the present dock. The dock has ceased to be commercially viable and, under Preston council's Riversway development, the area will be rejuvenated.
Nature interest   The wildlife of the Ribble and estuary is being encouraged. Many of the habitats have been created recently, close to the riverside track consisting of three main habitat types—woodland, wildflower-rich grassland and areas of disturbed ground.
Management   Preston council with advice from LTNC.
Interpretation   The Riversway Preston Dock Trail Guide is available from Preston council and was produced by LTNC in partnership with the council during the European Year of the Environment.
Access   Open at all times.
Contact   Preston BC Docks and Marine Officer, Ashton on Ribble, Preston, Lancashire.

Further information

Preston BC, Leisure Services, Guildhall, Lancaster Road, PR1 2RL (0772 2113456).
Lancashire Trust for Nature Conservation (see Blackburn).
Fulwood Group (LTNC), c/o 30 Yewlands Avenue, Fulwood, Preston PR2 4QR (0772 717281).

WEST CUMBRIA

BARROW

Situated at the tip of the Furness peninsula, Barrow started life as a small port under the protection given by the elements of Walney Island to the S and W. Exploitation of the local iron ore and the construction of the Furness Railway in 1846 began Barrow's rapid growth. By 1860 establishment of a major iron and steelworks gave huge impetus to its expanding population. In only a few years Barrow grew from a small hamlet to a Victorian boom town.

The iron and steelworks have now gone and large areas of derelict land are being reclaimed. The shipyard, which specialises in building nuclear-powered submarines, remains the town's major employer. New light industries are being encouraged by the provision of small industrial parks. Over ⅓ of the borough is designated an SSSI. Although a large part of this is intertidal mudflat and sand, also included are the extensive dune systems of Walney Island and Sandscale Haws. The Cumbria Trust for Nature Conservation (CTNC) manages three reserves in the borough—North Walney NNR, South Walney and Foulney Island.

1 Abbotswood

To the E of Furness Abbey; on the approach to Barrow, just off the A590 (SD 220718).
Barrow BC. 8ha.
Approach   The entrance is on Manor Road which leads from either Rating Lane or Abbey Approach, which in turn lead from the A590 on the NE edge of Barrow.
Summary   Abbotswood is a semi-natural woodland forming a backdrop to Furness Abbey. A series of footpaths have been created in recent years by the council and the area has been set aside as a nature reserve.
History   Park Wall, which runs through the wood, is an ancient monument, and dates from the 15C. It used to define the boundary of the abbey precinct. Abbotswood House was built in the wood in the 1850s for Sir James Ramsden, one of the founding fathers of Barrow, but was damaged during the last war. It was demolished in 1960 and a control centre built on the site. This still remains although it is not now apparently suitable for use during a nuclear war.
Nature interest   Despite its small size Abbotswood is important in a borough deficient in woodland, in that it is an ancient woodland site and has a good number of mature trees. The ground flora has bluebells, dog's mercury, primroses and abundant ramsons, while the understorey is well developed with hazel, holly and hawthorn. A large number of exotic trees were planted in Ramsden's time including holm oak, Japanese red cedar, Crimean pine, Portuguese laurel and Swedish whitebeam. Native trees include yew, sessile oak, rowan, birch and ash. Animal life includes badgers, roe deer, foxes, rooks, jays, tawny owls, woodpeckers and bats.
Management   Minimal woodland management has taken place since the war, although in recent years there has been some control of rhododendron. A network of footpaths has been created, together

with some fencing and tree planting by community programme teams.

Interpretation   Numerous interpretative boards are on site and a nature trail leaflet has been produced by CTNC and Barrow council.

Access   Open at all times.

Contact   CTNC (Urban Wildlife Project) or Barrow council.

2   Cavendish Dock

On the S edge of Barrow (SD 215683).

Associated British Ports. Over 50ha.

Approach   Cavendish Dock can be approached from Salthouse Road (NE corner) and Cavendish Dock Road (NW corner).

Summary   Its importance lies in being one of the largest areas of coastal freshwater in the NW of England. The site is very important for wintering waterbirds and has recently been designated an SSSI.

History   Built in 1878 the dock was not used for shipping, but as a 'header' for the rest of the dock system of the port of Barrow. The water level is maintained by freshwater entering from the Poaka Beck. Until recently the water was also used for cooling for the nearby Roosecote power station (now closed), which resulted in the dock waters being warmed.

Nature interest   Vast numbers of wintering waterbirds can be seen here, particularly in bad weather. Nationally important numbers of red breasted mergansers have been recorded, as well as large numbers of tufted duck, widgeon, goldeneye, cormorant, coot and dabchick. The dock is also very important for swans during moulting, over 200 having been seen at one time.

Management   No management for wildlife, although the effect of the closure of the power station is being investigated.

Interpretation   The dock features in the *Westfield Nature Trail* leaflet produced by Barrow council and CTNC.

Access   Access is sometimes possible with the permission of Associated British Ports.

Contact   CTNC (Urban Wildlife Project) or Associated British Ports, Ramsden Dock Road, Barrow.

3   Hawcoat Quarry

N edge of Barrow, E of Schneider Road (SD 198716).

Barrow BC.

Approach   From Schneider Road or Quarry Brow.

Summary   An old sandstone quarry, part of which was used until the 1960s as the corporation tip. The quarry floor has since been grassed over, while the face has become colonised with a variety of vegetation.

History   It is possible that stone used in the later stages of Furness Abbey came from the quarry, but it was certainly the source of stone for the nearby Ormsgill Farm, dating from around 1605. A branch line of the Furness railway was built in 1863 to carry the stone to the docks both for their construction and for export. Production peaked in 1878 when the quarry was worked on three levels and plant included steam derricks as well as manually-operated cranes. The older parts of Barrow are all built from this attractive red sandstone, including the town hall.

Nature interest   Although most of the quarry floor was covered

with topsoil and seeded with a rye grass-clover mix, some areas have
retained their original grassland flora. Thus one can still find knapweed, wild carrot, wild parsnip and meadow vetchling, especially
around the edges and on the top of the quarry. The quarry face itself
has now been colonised by whitebeam, holly and gorse, with
sycamore, hawthorn and wych elm at the base. Other parts of the
quarry are developing into scrub, aided by tree-planting, and these
rougher areas are attractive to a wide range of birds, especially
finches and thrushes.

Management   The site is managed by the council as open green-
space, with some tree-planting around the margins.

Interpretation   The quarry features in the CTNC's urban trail
leaflet. Events are organised here regularly, including wildflower
introduction and tree-planting.

Access   Open at all times.

Contact   CTNC (Urban Wildlife Project) or borough council.

4   Ormsgill Reservoir

N edge of Barrow, between Walney Road and Schneider Road (SD
195707).
Barrow BC. Over 10ha.

Approach   Access is possible from Schneider Road or Devonshire
Road.

Summary   A sheltered reservoir, only three metres at its deepest,
and with a narrow perimeter path, it is surrounded by housing, industry and a tip, but excellent for waterbirds, especially in winter. It is
stocked by the Furness Anglers who also lease the banks.

History   Built to provide cooling water for the nearby steelworks, it
was at one time the largest in Europe. The steelworks have gone, and
the reservoir is now one of Barrow council's sites of local natural
history interest.

Nature interest   Great crested grebe nest every year as well as one
or two pairs of swans. Large numbers of coot and tufted duck spend
the winter here, as well as pochard, mergansers and goldeneye. The
reservoir is stocked with coarse fish including bream, carp and tench.
Water plants include common reed, yellow iris, and the locally
uncommon hornwort.

Management   CTNC has set up a management committee and has
co-ordinated work such as tree planting and footpath improvements.
The Furness Anglers carry out work on site and manage the fishery.

Interpretation   Regular activities have been organised by CTNC to
promote the site, and the reservoir features in CTNC's urban nature
trail leaflet for Hawcoat and Ormsgill. A more detailed leaflet is in
preparation.

Access   Open at all times.

Contact   CTNC (Urban Wildlife Project) or Barrow BC.

5   Westfield Nature Trail

From the S edge of Barrow at Cavendish Dock (SD 217688) SW
towards Rampside (SD 234660).
Private.

Approach   The trail can be joined from the Salthouse Road in
Barrow. Other entry points are either near Roose Hospital or at St

Mary's Church on the Rampside Road, or at Rampside near the Concle Inn or by the Clarkes Arms.

Summary   A series of public footpaths on the outskirts of town lead past important wildlife sites, including Cavendish Dock and Roosecote Sands and areas of semi-natural landscape with plenty of good wildlife habitats including ponds, old hedgerows and unimproved grassland.

History   Part of the trail follows the route of the old railway line that led from Barrow to Roa Island (before the docks, Barrow's only deepwater berth). The trail also passes by some of Barrow's more recent industry including Roosecote power station, the British Gas Onshore Terminal for Morecambe Bay, and Roosecote sand and gravel quarry.

Nature interest   Both Cavendish Dock and the Roosecote Sands are SSSIs for water birds—the former providing food and shelter for wintering birds, while the latter is an important year-round feeding ground, particularly for waders such as dunlin, sanderling and plovers. A wide range of habitats can be seen along the trails; fields where lapwing, snipe and curlew breed, gorse scrub with stonechats, and ponds with frogs, dragonflies, warblers and mallard.

Management   Barrow council undertakes footpath improvements and maintenance.

Interpretation   A detailed colour leaflet was produced in 1985 as a contribution to Europe's Water's Edge campaign, prepared by Barrow council and CTNC (from whom it is still available), supported by British Gas and the CEGB. Activities are organised by CTNC to promote the trail.

Access   Open at all times from public footpaths.

Contact   CTNC (Urban Wildlife Project) or Barrow BC.

Further information

Barrow BC, Parks Department, c/o Town Hall, Duke Street, Barrow-in-Furness, LA14 2LD (0229 25500).

Cumbria Trust for Nature Conservation, Church Street, Ambleside, Cumbria LA22 0BU (05394 32476).

Urban Wildlife Project (CTNC), c/o CTNC Ambleside.

Barrow Support Group (CTNC), c/o NW Corner, Greenscoe, Askam-in-Furness, Barrow.

Acknowledgement   Text written by Paul Kirkland and Chris Squire of CTNC.

CARLISLE

Cumbria's cathedral city and a major industrial and market place, Carlisle has enjoyed prominence since its days as a Roman administrative centre and fort (the largest on Hadrian's Wall). Sited in the borders, it was here that Bonnie Prince Charlie proclaimed his father king in 1745. A successful port from Elizabethan times until the 1800s when Whitehaven came into prominence, the town was also an important centre for weaving and at one time had the largest cotton mill in England. But in the early 1800s a decline in fortunes led to unemployed weavers rioting—who were apparently pacified by being paid to do environmental improvements! The advent of the railway assured Carlisle's future due to its location, and by 1876 the town was a terminus for seven railway companies.

1 Durranhill Pond

To the E of the city between Harraby and Botcherby (NY 422549).
Cavrays Ltd.
Approach   The site lies just W of the link road between the A6 and A69.
Summary   A small piece of land was spared by the developers when a large area of scrub and wetland was bulldozed and cleared for redevelopment for industrial use. The Carlisle Wildlife Group (an umbrella group of conservation organisations in the city) was allowed to create a pond to try to retain some of the wildlife of the area.
History   Durranhill sidings originally belonged to the Midland Railway and lie adjacent to the Leeds–Carlisle line.
Nature interest   Wildlife that once inhabited the sidings is being encouraged to recolonise the area set aside. A variety of pondlife has been reintroduced from nearby sites.
Management   More species will be introduced in an attempt to recreate the habitats that existed prior to the clearance.
Interpretation   Used by Inglewood Junior School as a study area, it features in a leaflet produced by the CarlisleWildlife Group, covering several of Carlisle's wildlife sites.
Access   Not open to the public but interested groups can obtain a key from CWG.
Contact   CTNC (Urban Wildlife Project) or Carlisle Wildlife Group c/o Carlisle city council planning department.

2 Engine Lonning

On the W edge of Carlisle, N of Newton Road. (NY 383563).
Carlisle CC. 10.5ha.
Approach   From the city centre, take the B5307 due W towards Kirkbridge (Newton Road). Turn right about ¼ mile past the Infirmary, opposite Newton School. This track leads down to Engine Lonning.
Summary   A large area of disused railway land, to be developed as public open space for recreation, the site contains some good semi-natural habitats as well as areas that have become recolonised with an interesting variety of wildlife.

View from Engine Lonning across River Eden, Carlisle

History   The area was previously owned by the Waverley line which closed in 1968, and was mostly occupied by engine sheds. A Roman rampart, part of Hadrian's Wall, runs through the site.

Nature interest   Much of the area has retained its wildlife interest near streams and on steep banks, thus there are many old grassland plants with some rarities such as the parasitic lesser broomrape. Other species include lesser twayblade, celery-leaved buttercup and common spotted orchids. There are small wooded areas which have several mature English elms. Many plants, however, were brought in with railway ballast including several coastal plants such as sand sedge and common centaury. Birds recorded include spotted fly-catcher, long-tailed tit, kingfisher, sedge warbler, snipe and tawny· owl.

Management   To be developed for recreation with sports pitches, playgrounds and wildlife areas.

Interpretation   None as yet.

Access   Open at all times.

Contact   CTNC (Urban Wildlife Project) or Carlisle Wildlife Group.

3   Kingmoor Nature Trail

N of Carlisle between Kingstown and the River Eden (NY 388580). Carlisle CC.

Approach   The trail starts from Kingmoor Road, 2.5 kilometres NW of the town centre. From Carlisle, take the A7 (Scotland Road), turning left at the first traffic lights into Etterby Street. This continues as Eden Place, Etterby Scaur and finally Kingmoor Road where the trail starts.

Summary   A linear trail leads through a thin strip of mixed woodland and along a disused railway line, over former common land, on the edge of the city.

History   The area was part of King's Moor, once an expanse of moss and scrub, granted to the people of Carlisle by Edward III in 1352.

Local people had grazing and peat-cutting rights, but by the 18C the corporation had begun to enclose and lease off the land. Many legal battles ensued unsuccessfully. The trail largely follows the old racecourse, used as such for many years until about 1850.

Nature interest   Predominantly oak/birch woodland, but also with beech, sycamore, Scots pine, Douglas fir and larch. The ground flora is not particularly rich, but due to the acidic soil has species such as heather, bilberry and gorse. Birds recorded include pied woodpeckers, coal tits, treecreepers and a wide range of warblers. Roe deer and foxes are also frequent visitors.

Management   The footpaths are maintained by the council, but the woodland is largely unmanaged.

Interpretation   A leaflet has been produced by the council.

Access   Open at all times.

Contact   Leisure Services Department or CTNC (Urban Wildlife Project).

4   Kingmoor Sidings Local Nature Reserve

NW of Carlisle alongside the main railway line to Scotland (NY 388572).

Carlisle CC. 8ha.

Approach   Via the access road which runs down from Etterby Road to Balmoral Court. It is hoped to create an additional footpath link to Kingmoor Road to link with the Kingmoor Nature Trail.

Summary   A disused sidings, the site has been colonised by birch scrub and also has several ponds and marshy areas.

History   Formerly a site for engine sheds, once part of the Caledonian railway.

Nature interest   Over 60 bird species have been recorded, with around 25 breeding, including the lesser white-throat. Other birds which may be seen include snipe, lesser redpoll, finches and warblers. Several butterflies occur, the dingy skipper being one that is locally uncommon. The flora is rich with over 170 plants recorded, including good numbers of N marsh orchid.

Management   To retain a mixture of open areas, wetland, and scrub, while creating and improving footpaths. More ponds are being excavated.

Interpretation   Large display boards on site and a leaflet describing the natural history.

Access   Open at all times.

Contact   Leisure Services Department or CTNC (Urban Wildlife Project).

5   Upperby Park

On the edge of Carlisle (NY 403534).

Carlisle CC.

Approach   Off Durdar Road, about 1 mile S of the city centre.

Summary   A traditional park, with a small boating lake called Hammond's Pond, was recently extended, part of which is set aside as a 'wildlife area'.

History   The recent history of the area is as the site of an old brickworks. The land has been given by Laings to the city to extend

Upperby Park.

Nature interest   As a habitat creation site with little inherent interest, wildflowers have been introduced from other sites due to be destroyed.

Management   The aim is removal of dominant perennials and encouragement of a variety of species, plus tree planting.

Interpretation   Nil on site.

Access   Open during park hours.

Contact   CTNC (Urban Wildlife Project) or Carlisle Wildlife Group.

Further information

Carlisle CC, Civic Centre, Carlisle (0228 23411).

Cumbria Trust for Nature Conservation (see Barrow).

Acknowledgement   Text written by Paul Kirkland of CTNC.

MARYPORT

Maryport was a Roman garrison town from AD 120 and the remains of its fort, Alvana, are situated on Sea Brows, cliffs immediately to the N of the town. The nearby 19C battery is to be converted into a museum to house the considerable number of Roman artefacts found in the area. The original name of Alnefoot was changed by Humphrey Senhouse to honour his wife Mary. The seat of the Senhouse family was Netherhall, which has been left relatively undisturbed to form a semi-natural park close to the centre of town, of interest for its mature trees and woodland flora.

The harbour was central to the development of the town, fishing dating back well over 2,200 years, when oysters were one of the main catches. The coal and shipbuilding industries greatly influenced the growth of the town which experienced a period of affluence until the end of last century when loss of the old industries led to a steady decline. Recent attempts to bring new light industries into the town have produced extensive developments planned to turn the dock into a marina and maritime museum. The grassland which developed on the derelict land around the docks is botanically very rich, and local conservationists have been successful in securing a part of this to remain while reclamation takes place nearby.

1   Netherhall Park

Off the main road through Maryport on the E side of town (NY 041365).
Private.
Approach   Main entrance is via the lodge on the A596.
Summary   An unmanaged parkland, now more natural in appearance.
History   Nether Hall was the seat of the Senhouse family, and the original 14C pele tower still stands.
Nature interest   The Hall grounds are dominated by mature trees, mostly oak, which provide nesting sites for owls, woodpeckers and pigeons. Bats and red squirrels are also regularly seen. The main floral interest lies in the garden plants that have become naturalised. These include winter heliotrope, dog's tooth violet and large bellflower. Many species of old woodland are present such as wood brome and ramsons. A small pond is now much overgrown, but royal fern and bamboo persist.
Management   None.
Interpretation   None.
Access   Although private, the grounds are well used by locals with the permission of the owners.
Contact   CTNC (Urban Wildlife Project).

2   River Ellen Walk

The walk leads from Maryport to the village of Dearham along the footpath on the S side of the river (NY 041363; NY 066366).
Private.
Approach   Access is gained near the railway bridge at Netherton, Maryport, or at the Crosby turn off near Dearham Bridge.
Summary   A pleasant riverside walk, passing through a variety of habitats.
History   The area has a long history of coal mining, with a series of

old sites visible along the river. The water power was once used by corn mills, which have now been converted into houses. The ruins of Nether Hall can be seen on the edge of Maryport.

Nature interest   An old cut off section of the River Ellen provides an interesting area of reedbeds, known locally as the Dog Gravey. Birds to be seen include heron, water rail and white-throat. Cherry Wood, an ancient woodland site, has a very rich ground flora, including dog's mercury, sea-wort, primrose and enchanter's nighshade. Several herb-rich meadows adjoin the river, along with patches of marsh and fen. A wide variety of birdlife can be seen along the river, including dipper, merganser and goosander.

Management   Improvements to the paths are being made by CTNC in conjunction with BTCV and Groundwork.

Interpretation   A leaflet is being drawn up by CTNC.

Access   Open at all times through public footpaths.

Contact   CTNC (Urban Wildlife Project).

3   Sea Brows

The sea cliffs to the N of Maryport (NY 040378).
Allerdale DC.

Approach   Proceed N from the harbour and join the footpath which leads to Bank End Farm.

Summary   The sea cliffs have been subjected to quarrying in the past, but the area has been left undisturbed for many years.

History   The cliffs are of St Bees sandstone, laid down about 20 million years ago. The stone was used for building by the Romans and much of the town is also of this material. A large quarry was opened in 1880 to provide stone for Senhouse Dock. The Roman fort, Alvana, is sited above the cliffs and the nearby 19C battery is to be opened as a museum to house the large number of Roman artefacts that have been found locally.

Nature interest   The cliffs are now well vegetated except where some erosion occurs on the steeper slopes. Large stands of bracken and rosebay willowherb provide cover for a wide range of small mammals. Birds regularly seen among the gorse, hawthorn and willow include yellowhammer, linnets and warblers. The grassland is herb rich with common spotted and N marsh orchids, and six species of fern. Part of the cliffs are covered with a coastal heath community dominated by heather. In the wet hollows, ragged robin, angelica, and valerian occur, and the natterjack toad has been seen in some of the shallow pools.

Management   Steps and footpath improvements have been carried out by pupils of Netherhall school and other groups, and some tree planting and fencing work is done by the council.

Interpretation   Guided walks are occasionally organised and a leaflet is in preparation by CTNC.

Access   Open at all times via public footpaths.

Contact   CTNC (Urban Wildlife Project) or the council.

Further information

Allerdale DC, Parks Department, Holmewood, Cockermouth (0900 823741).

Cumbria Trust for Nature Conservation (see Barrow).

Allerdale Support Group (CTNC), c/o 'Rosslynn', Crosby, Maryport.

Acknowledgement   Text written by Paul Kirkland and Anne Riddell of CTNC.

WHITEHAVEN

The port of Whitehaven was once ranked third busiest in Britain, and the former wealth of the town is still evident in the fine Georgian houses, many now sadly neglected. The coal industry developed spectacularly during the 17C. Due to Sir John Lowther in particular, an important trade grew up with the American colonies, bringing in sugar, tobacco and rum. The town was planned on a grid system based upon Sir Christopher Wren's plans for rebuilding London after the Great Fire, and this is still evident today, despite later in-filling.

By the end of the 19C, coal was a major industry, with shipbuilding and iron foundaries flourishing. Improved engines built locally meant that mining could be carried out for a considerable distance under the Irish Sea. But following a steady decline since Victorian times, the last deep mine, Haig Pit, finally closed in 1986. Plans are now under consideration for a new mine to develop on the S side of the town. A flourishing fishing fleet still sails from the harbour but the main user of the port is the company Albright and Wilson (Marchon), the major employer in the town, which produces detergents. A recreational area has been developed on S beach by reclaiming a former colliery site. Pleasant coastal walks extend in both directions from the town, with industrial remains adding to the considerable botanical, ornithological and geological interest of the cliffs. Whitehaven is notable for its large areas of open space, much of which is owned by the council and left in a semi-natural state. Extensive woodlands are present within the town boundary, the most interesting occupying a parallel series of gills on the E side. A large reservoir at Mirehouse, a remnant of the coal industry, is managed by the anglers of Haig Pit, and is an important refuge for a wide variety of wildlife.

1   Aikbank Wood

In a narrow gill adjacent to Aikbank Road (NX 984193).
Private.
Approach   Between Victoria Road and Aikbank Road, paths run through the site from both roads.
Summary   A small deciduous wood surrounded by housing.
History   One of the many gill-woodlands on ancient sites in the town, it was used for years as a play area by local children.
Nature interest   Predominantly an oak woodland with a good ground flora, it includes greater woodrush, wood sage, devil's bit scabious and several ferns. Animal life includes bats, red squirrels, tawny owls, tree creepers and rooks.
Management   Local people have adopted the area with the owner's permission and are carrying out small scale management work with the help of CTNC.
Interpretation   None at present.
Access   A public footpath passes through the wood.
Contact   CTNC (Urban Wildlife Project).

2   The Old Waggonway

The track runs at the base of the cliffs at Bransty, between Whitehaven and Parton (NX 972194).
British Coal.

Approach The route starts near the railway station at Whitehaven and joins the road through Parton village.

Summary A walk along the base of coastal sandstone cliffs with considerable industrial remains as well as features of wildlife interest.

History This was the route taken by the coal waggons in the last century, and the remains of the William and Harvey pits are still to be seen en route.

Nature interest The cliffs have good exposures of the coal measures with many fossils in evidence, even though friable. The cliffs provide nest sites for kestrels, and the scrub provides cover for white-throats and warblers. The vegetation is varied, with the N marsh orchid, wood vetch, everlasting pea, dyer's greenweed and greater horsetail being notable species.

Management None.

Interpretation A leaflet is in preparation by CTNC.

Access Open at all times.

Contact CTNC (Urban Wildlife Project).

3 Woodhouse Quarry

On Greenbank, below the Marchon works (NX 972165).
Private.

Approach A track leads up from the old brickworks adjacent to the cemetery. Access is also possible from the nearby housing estates.

Summary An old disused brickworks quarry, showing good outcrops of the coal measures series with associated fossils, although the rock is very friable.

History The quarry was worked for clay from the turn of the century, the clay being transported to the brickworks below by rail, but the brickworks closed in the 1970s.

Nature interest Nesting birds include kestrels. The wet area on the quarry floor has a large population of N marsh orchid. The old slag banks have been colonised by neutral grassland species such as ox-eye daisy, hawkweeds and cowslips.

Management Part of the quarry may be used in the future as a tip. CTNC will be working to ensure the best areas are spared.

Interpretation Nil on site.

Access Although privately owned it is well used by locals for walking (the quarry face is, however, rather unsafe).

Contact CTNC (Urban Wildlife Project).

Further information

Copeland BC, Planning Department, Catherine Street, Whitehaven (0946 31111).

Cumbria Trust for Nature Conservation (see Barrow).

CTNC, West Cumbria Office, 'Workspace', Cragg Road, Cleator Moor, near Whitehaven (0946 810910).

Whitehaven Support Group (CTNC), c/o 3 Landsdowne Grove, Whitehaven.

Acknowledgement Text written by Paul Kirkland and Anne Riddell of CTNC.

WORKINGTON

Situated on the estuary of the River Derwent, Workington developed as a small fishing village, forming part of an elaborate coastal defence system during the Roman period. The town grew rapidly, its deep water port being the only one between the Mersey and the Clyde. With the exploitation of local coal, the town prospered under the lords of the manor, the Curwens, with an export trade of iron, steel and coal. By the end of the 18C two major blast furnaces were in operation, together with a factory specialising in the production of cannon.

The Curwens were a powerful family, much involved in local and national affairs. The remains of Workington Hall can be seen in Curwen Park, an estate which was described as a fair park of fallow deer in the 17C. It still provides a natural environment close to the centre of town, with many pleasant walks along the river and through the ancient woodlands on the old river terraces.

The steel industry remains an important source of employment in the town, although as an Enterprise Zone many new industries are being encouraged into the area. Much reclamation of old industrial sites is taking place but many such areas remain and form important habitats for wildlife within the town, including sites for such national rarities as natterjack toad and peregrine. Siddick Pond, an SSSI and LNR, lies on the N outskirts of the town and is an important site for a wide range of birdlife. A second LNR is due to be set up at Harrington Reservoir, to the S of Workington.

1 Curwen Park

On the S bank of the River Derwent, on the NE side of Workington (NY 009289).
Allerdale DC.
Approach   The main entrances are through the gates guarded by unicorn heads—one next to the courts on the A596, and the other on Ramsey Bank on the A66.
Summary   A large park, partly laid out as formal gardens, partly left in a natural state, surrounding Workington Hall. The fields next to the Derwent are grazed and some are used for football pitches.
History   Workington Hall, seat of the Curwens, was inhabited until 1927. Part of the original 14C building can still be seen but much of the remains are of later construction.
Nature interest   The variety of habitats means that the park is full of interest. The steep sides of the old river terraces are wooded, with a good ground flora of ramsons, bluebells and lords and ladies. Owls are regular nesters, while swans, divers and herons can be seen near the river.
Management   Parks department.
Interpretation   Nature trail and leaflet in preparation by CTNC.
Access   Open at all times.
Contact   CTNC (Urban Wildlife Project) or Allerdale Parks Department.

2 Harrington Reservoir and Ellerbeck

Harrington, Workington adjacent to Moorclose Road (NX 995258).
Allerdale DC, English Estates (North).

Approach   Either from Moorclose Road, St Mary's church car park or the disused railway line at the S end of the site.

Summary   A very diverse though small site surrounded by council housing. It consists of a stream, the Ellerbeck, which flows into a reservoir with well-vegetated margins. The site is used as a short cut by local people and is popular with dog owners.

History   Harrington used to be a thriving village on the edge of Workington, with its own harbour and railway stations. The reservoir was built in 1863 to provide water for the local steel industry. Following the decline in steel production, the reservoir was used for sailing model boats and for skating.

Nature interest   The site, though small, is remarkable for its range of habitats. The marginal fen vegetation is dominated by reed canary grass, with marsh marigold, yellow flag and marsh wound-wort. The stream has dense stands of willow which provide good cover for birds, and wood anemone is abundant in the shade in the spring. A herb-rich wet meadow lies upstream with abundant common spotted and N marsh orchids, meadow sweet, angelica and saw-wort. A drier meadow, once grazed but now managed as a hay meadow, has greater burnet, ox-eye daisy and yellow rattle, with a small number of butterfly orchids. Over 75 species of bird are recorded, 22 of which regularly breed, including reed bunting, sedge and grasshopper warblers, white-throat and long-tailed tits. A pair of mute swans breed on the reservoir each year and are a local attraction.

Management   The site is a proposed LNR. The CTNC has set up a steering committee to promote local involvement, to help co-ordinate the work required to make the site safe and accessible, to collect information and to produce interpretative material. In addition a WATCH club is based here. A management plan has been pre-pared and the aim is to protect and enhance the wildlife value, while promoting the site for public enjoyment.

Interpretation   Signs and leaflets are in preparation by CTNC.

Access   Open at all times.

Contact   CTNC (Urban Wildlife Project) or Parks Department.

3   Siddick Pond

On the A596 Maryport road on the N outskirts of Workington (NY 002304).

Allerdale DC.

Approach   The entrance is on the A596. There is a bird hide inside the main gates.

Summary   Called a 'pond' but a fairly large lake, it and the fringing marsh occupy a depression which was once the delta of the River Derwent. The area is an SSSI and part is an LNR.

History   The Derwent now runs ½ mile to the S, and the pond is fed by the Ling Beck. This passes over alluvial deposits, causing deposition of sand and silt. The site once had a colliery, closed in the 1960s, and the water was used to cool the nearby ironworks. The site was designated an SSSI in 1952 for its birdlife and part became an LNR in 1981.

Nature interest   The water is base-rich and has a diverse aquatic flora including lesser water plantain. The fringing reed beds provide an excellent habitat for birdlife. Over 170 species have been recorded, with over 35 nesting regularly—including mute swan, dabchick, shoveler, pochard and tufted duck. Wintering birds include goldeneye, teal and whooper swan.

Management   The site is managed by the council, is overseen by the Siddick Pond Management Committee and has an honorary warden.

Interpretation   Information and records are kept at the bird hide near the entrance, and a booklet is available from the council.

Access   The reserve is normally locked but the key is available from the council.

Contact   CTNC (Urban Wildlife Project) or Allerdale parks department.

Further information

Allerdale DC (see Maryport).
Cumbria Trust for Nature Conservation (see Barrow).
Acknowledgement   Text written by Paul Kirkland and Anne Riddell of CTNC.

NORTHEAST

CLEVELAND

Cleveland is a largely urban county located either side of the Tees estuary although it also includes attractive countryside on the fringe. The area experienced rapid growth during the second half of the 19C following the discovery of workable deposits of ironstone in the Eston Hills. It quickly became a national centre for the manufacture of iron and steel and for ancillary industries such as shipbuilding and bridge building.

Much of this heavy industry has now disappeared and steel making has moved downstream to the mouth of the river leaving large areas of derelict land which are presently being reclaimed. Some of these derelict areas have been colonised by interesting plant communities, particularly on blast furnace slag, and some such areas are being retained and managed as wildlife sites.

Cleveland county council is committed to the countryside management approach and much of the county is covered by the Cleveland Urban Fringe Scheme (CUFS). Established in 1982, this very successful countryside management scheme has resulted in the development of a number of urban wildlife sites.

The Cleveland Nature Conservation Trust (CNCT), formed in 1981, manages a number of urban reserves and is keen to promote nature conservation in urban areas.

1   Billingham Beck Valley

Billingham (NZ 454221).
Cleveland CC. 28ha.
Approach   Bus to Norton Green. Car park off the Old Norton Road.
Summary   An extensive area of wetland sandwiched between the new and old A19 roads and the built up areas of Norton and Billingham. The area, which is the flood plain of Billingham Beck, can be viewed from the network of paths.
History   The land was water meadows and includes a former osier bed. The Norton water mill was located in the valley and the mill race remains. The area was much disturbed by the construction of the new A19 trunk road and has since been progressively acquired by the county council.
Nature interest   The site is one of the few remaining natural flood plains in Cleveland and retains its distinctive flora. It is rich in wildflowers including great burnet, marsh marigold, and yellowflag iris. Birds seen include kingfisher and heron.
Management   The site is managed through the warden service and the objective is to maintain the wetland character. Works include ditch management and several scrapes have been made.
Interpretation   There is a warden service which produces a regular newsletter and organises guided walks. A leaflet is available and an ecology park is being developed on an old tip.
Access   Open at all times.
Contact   Warden Service of the Department of Economic Development and Planning.

2 Charlton's Pond

Billingham, Cleveland (NZ 232473).
Stockton-on-Tees BC.
Approach   Car park along Cowpen Lane Estate, Billingham.
Summary   A large expanse of freshwater surrounded by woodland and a large bird sanctuary. There are two ponds with access around both.
History   Developed in an old brickworks' clay pit early this century. Stocked with fish before the First World War. Made a nature reserve in 1963 and bird sanctuary declared in 1968.
Nature interest   This is the only bird sanctuary in the county of Cleveland. The area is rich with bird and plant life. A wide variety of birds inhabit the sanctuary, including mallard, common tern, moorhen and coot. Plant life is very rich with species such as branched bur-reed, amphibious bistort and the very attractive great reedmace.
Management   The site is run by a board of management appointed by Stockton-on-Tees BC. The Angling Committee also helps in the management of Charlton's Pond.
Interpretation   The nature trail has been designed for everyone and there is easy access around the ponds up to the bird sanctuary.
Access   Access to Charlton's Pond can be gained by parking just off Cowpen Lane, Billingham. Charlton's Pond Nature Trail begins at this point. There is no access into the bird sanctuary, to prevent disturbance to breeding birds.
Contact   CNCT or Stockton-on-Tees BC.

3 Coatham Marsh

Redcar, Cleveland (NZ 584246).
British Steel Corporation. 54ha.
Approach   Along Tod Point Road, Warrenby.
Summary   An area of landscaped mounds, lakes and freshwater marsh, supporting an abundance of wildflowers and birds, all easily visible from footpaths and hides.
History   Until about 1850 the marsh extended W to the River Tees and was extensively used as saltings. Land reclamation and industrial development cut the area off from the river and only about 20 hectares remains as freshwater marsh. There is also about 34 hectares of newly mounded land and lakes, constructed in the late 1970s from a domestic refuse tip.
Nature interest   The flora is interesting and diverse, including freshwater species such as water plantain, branched bur-reed and water crowfoot. Some saltmarsh plants survive in pockets, including sea spurry and saltmarsh grass. The lime-rich slag tipping at the W end has allowed the establishment of species such as yellow-wort and stonecrop.
   Ornithologically, the area is probably the most important freshwater marsh in Cleveland S of the Tees. 31 species of wader, seven of geese, all three British swans and 19 species of duck, including up to 500 teal and 100 widgeon, have been recorded on the marsh. In addition, several notable rarities have occurred, such as little egret, white-winged black tern and short-toed lark.
Management   The site is managed by CNCT, whose aim is to protect the semi-aquatic nature of the marsh by a combination of water level control and grazing. The flora of some fields is maintained by mowing and grazing.

Interpretation   There is a site warden during working hours, a number of voluntary wardens at others and the footpaths are well signposted.
Access   Open at all times; permits available from CNCT office.
Contact   CNCT.

4   Cowpen Marsh

Between Billingham and Hartlepool, Cleveland (NZ 505255).
ICI. 65ha.
Approach   Along A178, Port Clarence–Seaton Carew road.
Summary   A large expanse of freshwater grazing marsh bissected by several 'fleets' and a smaller but very valuable area of intertidal saltmarsh.
History   Originally part of the intertidal Tees estuary, the area was long ago reclaimed to provide further industrial land. The 1740 sea wall still forms an important feature of the reserve, as do the remains of several medieval saltworkings.
Nature interest   The saltmarsh, the only significant area remaining between Lindisfarne and the Humber, supports an array of salt-loving plants, now unusual in this area. It is also an important feeding and nesting area for a considerable number of waders, particularly in winter.

The freshwater marsh, especially the fleets (slow-flowing, meandering streams, rich in plant life) are very attractive to waterfowl. The area also supports a number of breeding passerines, including reed buntings, and attracts various passage migrants.
Management   The area is managed by CNCT, so far as possible under the lease, to protect and enhance the wildlife value of the site. The water levels are, therefore, carefully controlled and an effort is made to ensure the fleets are as attractive to breeding, passage and overwintering waterfowl and waders.
Interpretation   The reserve is wardened during working hours, and voluntary wardens are present at some other times.
Access   The reserve is best viewed from the 'Blockhouses' on the 1740 wall or the modern sea wall. These are accessible outside the shooting season (1 February–31 August), as part of the area is also leased by ICI to wildfowlers and access is prohibited during the season.

At all times the saltmarsh and tidal creeks can be viewed from the Edgar Gatenby hide, accessible from the car park on the A178, as are hides overlooking the nearby Seal Sands and tidal pool.
Contact   CNCT.

5   Lazenby Bank

Lazenby (NZ 571195).
Cleveland CC; ICI. 100ha.
Approach   Bus to Lazenby village. Car park off A174 at Lazenby.
Summary   Lazenby Bank is on the S edge of the Teesside conurbation extending from Eston Nab to Wilton. It contains a variety of habitats from open moor to mature woodland and extensive remains of the ironstone mining industry.
History   The woodlands are mainly secondary, the earliest being planted during the 19C. The site was extensively disturbed by

Lazenby Bank, Cleveland

ironstone mining and many relics can be seen, including a large Guibal Fan House known locally as the SS Castle. Some areas disturbed by mining have been colonised with birch scrub and others have been planted with conifers.

Nature Interest   These woodlands, although mainly secondary, are important for birds and invertebrates. Most of the warblers breed in and around the woods and lesser spotted woodpeckers and hawfinches have been seen.

Management   The site is managed through CUFS and a warden service exists. Part of the site is managed as a nature reserve with restricted access.

Access   Part restricted and part open at all times.

Contact   Warden or Department of Economic Development and Planning.

6   Marton West Beck Valley

Middlesbrough, Cleveland (NZ 527140 to NZ 496177).
Middlesbrough BC and Cleveland CC. 44.7ha.

Approach   Car park at Slip Inn off Ludgate Lane (B1380). Buses along Emerson Avenue, Ludgate Lane and Gunnergate Lane.

Summary   Walking the 6.5 kilometres of this valley takes one from closely mown grassland and standard trees near the heart of the city, through natural grassland and scrub to mature woodland on the urban fringe. A superb wildlife corridor in which the visitor is often totally unaware of the urban surroundings.

History   The steep sides of much of the valley mean that it survived the ravages of agriculture virtually untouched. Two areas of the valley were affected by virtue of being in the grounds of the now demolished Tollesby and Gunnergate Halls. The beck is now used as a flood control system and has three impounding dams, one of which led to the creation of the Fairy Dell Lake.

Nature interest   The valley supports 240 species of flowering plants including hairy violet and imperforate St John's wort, both unusual in Cleveland. It is also one of the best butterfly sites in the county, particularly notable for the large numbers of orange tips on the wing in late spring. Over 70 bird species have been seen in the area, including frequent sightings of great spotted woodpecker, tawny owl, blackcap and grey wagtail.

Management   The site is managed as a conservation, recreational and educational resource by Middlesbrough council under a management plan drawn up by the Marton West Beck management group made up of council officers, and representatives of the county council, local conservation organisations and local residents.

Interpretation   Two nature trails have been developed and a research interpretation team and a team of rangers are based at Newham Grange Leisure Farm, Coulby Newham.

Access   Open at all times.

Contact   Middlesbrough BC, Recreation and Amenities Department.

7   Normanby and Ormesby Brickworks, 10 Acre Bank

Normanby (NZ 550166).
Cleveland CC. 28ha.

Approach   By foot from Normanby, car park off Flatts Lane at Normanby Brickworks.

Summary   A group of sites off Flatts Lane, Normanby, comprising woodland and grassland show stages of succession from recent scrub to mature semi-natural woodland.

History   The former Normanby and Ormesby Brickworks were reclaimed during the early 1980s, while Ten Acre Bank is an area probably of ancient semi-natural woodland disturbed by mining during the last century. It has been neglected in recent years and is now managed by the county council.

Nature interest   The woods contain a good variety of tree species and provide habitats for typical woodland birds. Ponds provide habitats for amphibians.

Management   The sites are managed through CUFS and woodland regeneration is being encouraged in some of the reclaimed areas. Local schools are involved in management.

Interpretation   A leaflet is available for the Normanby and Ormesby sites.

Access   Open at all times.

Contact   CUFS.

8   Rosecroft, Whitecliffe and Loftus Woods

Loftus (NZ 711183).
Cleveland CC. 20ha.

Approach   By foot from Loftus town centre.

Summary   Unspoilt woodland in steep stream valleys within a few minutes' walk of the centre of Loftus.

History   Probably ancient semi-natural woodland, although Rosecroft Woods show evidence of more intensive management and some planting of conifers has occurred. Loftus Woods contain the dam and leat of Loftus water mill which was closed in 1950 and is now a private house.

Nature interest   Whitecliffe Wood in particular is relatively undisturbed with a wide variety of tree species and contains a ground flora typical of ancient semi-natural woodland, including golden saxifrage, bluebell, wild garlic, wood anemone and wood sorrel.

Management   The woods will be managed traditionally through CUFS.

Interpretation   A leaflet, *Loftus Dam*, is available and one on Whitecliffe and Rosecroft Woods is in preparation.

Access   Open at all times.

Contact   CUFS.

9   River Tees Valley

Cleveland CC.

Approach   Access from the Quayside at Stockton and Transporter Bridge, Middlesbrough. Car park at Riverside Park, Middlesbrough.

Summary   A series of sites managed by the county council in the Tees Valley. Sites include former industrial areas such as the old Malleable Works at Stockton and semi-natural vegetation such as Bassleton Wood. Several sites are linked by the Tees Heritage Trail.

History   The River Tees became rapidly industrialised in the 1850s, but during the present century the main works have migrated to the mouth of the river leaving large areas of derelict land. Much of this land is now being reclaimed, although some naturally colonised areas are being retained.

Nature interest   There is a great diversity of natural history interest along the banks of the Tees. Where accumulations of old furnace slag occur there are many plants associated with limestone areas. Particularly rich are the banks at Malleable Works where plants such as biting stone crop, mouse ear hawkweed, rough hawkbit, toadflax and pearlwort are thriving. On the immediate banks of the river are many saltmarsh species including sea plantain, sea beet and sea aster, while areas such as Bassleton Wood contain remnants of a woodland flora.

Management   The sites are managed through CUFS, and a warden service operates.

Interpretation   The warden service provides a newsletter and organises guided walks. A leaflet, *Tees Heritage Trail*, describes the industrial and natural history of the area.

Access   Open at all time.

Contact   CUFS.

Further information

Cleveland CC, Department of Economic Development and Planning, Gurney House, Gurney Street, Middlesbrough, Cleveland TS1 1QT (0642 248155).

Teesside Development Corporation, Tees House, Riverside Park, Middlesbrough, Cleveland TS2 1RE (0642 230636).

Middlesbrough BC, Recreation and Amenities Department, Vancouver House, Central Mews, Gurney Street, Middlesbrough, Cleveland TS1 1QP (0642 245432).

Stockton-on-Tees BC, Municipal Buildings, Church Road, Stockton-on-Tees, Cleveland TS4 1LE (0642 670067).

Cleveland Nature Conservation Trust, Old Town Hall, Mandale Road, Thornaby, Stockton-on-Tees, Cleveland TS17 6AW (0642 608405).

Acknowledgement Text written by Dave Counsell of Cleveland CC and Lloyd Austin of CNCT.

DARLINGTON

County Durham's main towns, Darlington and Durham city, are ancient towns which became early beneficiaries of the railway age. Stephenson's 'Rocket', planned to haul coal from Darlington to Stockton's wharfside, was successfully put through its paces in 1825. Durham's position dominating the crossing of the River Wear was enhanced by the arrival of the rail route N to Newcastle. Today, wildlife sites are becoming part of their range of heritage features.

Skerne Valley Park

Rockwell, Darlington (NZ 297164).
Darlington BC.
Approach Buses to Albert Road, walk along Albert Road to the bridge over the river, bear left along river bank through Five Arch Bridge.
Summary Rockwell forms part of the newly created Skerne Valley Linear Park which follows the course of the River Skerne from Albert Road Bridge in the industrial N end of Darlington to the village of Great Burdon, a distance of just over three kilometres, on the N bank. By crossing the river at Haughton and returning via Albert Hill a round trip of six and a half kilometres can be made.

Rockwell itself can be reached by following the W bank of the Skerne from Albert Road Bridge for about half a kilometres passing under Five Arch Bridge, the viaduct carrying the main London–Edinburgh line. On passing through the bridge the conservation area occupies both sides of the river until the houses are reached.
History The area takes its name from an outcrop of glacial conglomerate which is now tucked away among a group of trees about 45 metres past the start of the houses and 30 yards N of the

Skerne Valley Park, Rockwell Conservation Site, Darlington

river bank. From the base of this outcrop emerges a fresh water spring, the Rockwell.

The entire length of this river bank on both sides at one time consisted of a series of springs, marshes and ponds created when the river course was altered many years ago. Also present were remnants of the old flood plain flora. Much of this was lost as a result of the building of Rockwell Pastures housing estate in the mid-1970s. In the early 1980s it was rumoured that the remaining area of flood plain was due to be filled with rubble from an old factory demolition, and that the area would be grassed to form part of the new park. Following several years of campaigning and negotiations with the borough council, five acres of flood plain were saved and in addition the S bank of the river and an area of wood running N from Albert Road Bridge were included in a management agreement with the Durham Wildlife Trust (DWT).

Nature interest   The flood plain consists mainly of *Glyceria* marsh, with good stands of the greater and lesser pond sedges. The ponds contain populations of great crested newt, smooth newt, frog and toad. Damselflies and dragonflies breed in the ponds along with many other aquatic invertebrates. The adjacent dry railway embankment supports a wide range of plant species and also provides the habitat for 16 species of butterfly and is also a good nesting and forage area for small birds. More than 60 bird species are recorded from the area and kestrel, sparrowhawk and tawny owl all hunt here.

Management   The site is managed by the Darlington group of the DWT which, with the co-operation of the local council, has planted trees, dug ponds and sown wild flower seed while at the same time retaining as much of the original marsh vegetation as possible. A low key grass cutting regime is carried out to prevent the development of rank vegetation.

Interpretation   Public access is encouraged provided that people observe a sympathetic attitude and remain on the paths to avoid disturbance to sensitive areas. Good paths are maintained on the site and access is possible even in winter or following floods.

Access   Open at all times.

Contact   DWT.

Further information

Darlington DC, Parks Department, Town Hall, Darlington.
Durham Wildlife Trust (see Durham).
Darlington Group (DWT), c/o 15 St Andrews Street, Darlington (0325 59577).

Acknowledgement   Text written by Dave Race of DWT.

DURHAM

Flass Vale

(NZ 266426)
Durham DC. 16ha.
Approach   Bus depot in Waddington Street.
Summary   Numerous paths traverse the Vale giving access to rough grassland, scrub, mature woodland and streamside. The variety of habitat provides refuge for numerous bird species and even for foxes and badgers. The large mammals, used to frequent human passage, are often seen in the open.
History   The Vale is continuous with Crossgate Moor and, until early in the present century, constituted rough grazing with woodland on the steep slopes. In the early years of this century sand was extracted from two pits, one at the back of Western Hill and the other on the S boundary, now occupied by Newton's haulage yard. The 1919 OS map shows a curling rink at the N corner and allotments to the E of the stream that runs down the middle of the Vale. The contours of the curling rink are still clearly visible and a bank of lupins now marks the site of the allotments which are still remembered by older Durham residents.
Nature interest   The presence of a number of diverse habitats, ranging from streamside and grassland through gorse and hawthorn scrub to mature oak wood, allows a great range of animal species to thrive within a relatively confined area. There is a variety of woodland birds, including the conspicuous tawny owl, great spotted woodpecker and woodcock, and also species of open habitat such as white-throat. There is a large badger sett and at least two breeding groups of foxes. The vegetation indicates considerable human influence, old fruit trees and roses intermingling with will-herb and gorse, but some of the woodland is of long standing and bluebells carpet the floor in the spring. There is a small number of N marsh orchids which are worth searching for.
Management   The area is managed by the parks department for the benefit of wildlife and informal leisure. The main paths and steps have recently been remade.
Access   Open at all times.

Further information

Durham CC, Parks Department, Barkers Haugh, Durham.
Durham Wildlife Trust, 52 Old Elvet, Durham DH1 3HN (091 386 9797).
Acknowledgement   Text written by Jenifer Butterfield of DWT.

GATESHEAD

Situated on the S bank of the River Tyne opposite Newcastle, this large conurbation has a history centred on the heavy industries of the late 19C and early 20C such as shipbuilding and coal. Much of this is now gone, but the borough is replacing them with modern industries while at the same time providing a pleasant environment for its citizens. Surprisingly, much of the S and W of the borough has a distinctly rural feel to it.

1   Derwent Walk Country Park

Between Swalwell and Rowlands Gill. Access via Thomley Woodlands Centre (NZ 178604) and Swalwell Visitor Centre (NZ 198620).

Gateshead MBC. 182ha.

Approach   Buses from Newcastle and Gateshead along A694 to Swalwell and Rowlands Gill. Car parks at both centres.

Summary   Part of the old railway line from Blaydon to Consett, winding through the lower Derwent Valley, it includes excellent riverside, meadows and ancient woodland habitats. Very popular with Tyneside residents, it attracts up to 300,000 visitors each year.

History   The railway closed in 1962 and was purchased by Durham county council as a long-distance footpath and bridleway. On re-organisation it passed to Tyne and Wear county council in 1974 and eventually to Gateshead MBC in 1986, by which time it had been designated as a country park. Areas of land surrounding the line have been added in recent years, including Lockhaugh Farm and Thornley and Paddock Hill Woods. This has resulted in a rich and diverse variety of habitats supporting an abundance of wildlife to be enjoyed by visitors as they travel through this green and attractive valley.

Nature interest   The ancient woodlands situated in the steeply-sided denes running off the main valley are dominated by sessile oak with birch, ash and wych elm. A rich shrub and ground flora exists beneath this canopy with bluebell, primrose and wood garlic in spring and cow wheat, wood sage and bilberry later in summer. Some of the meadows are herb rich with good displays of meadow buttercup, common spotted orchid and self heal. Birds present include sparrow hawk, woodcock, great spotted woodpecker, grey wagtail, dipper and kingfisher with a full complement of warblers in the summer and siskin and brambling in winter. The mammals are well represented with roe deer, red squirrel and badger present in the extensive woodlands. Insect life is both abundant and diverse with 17 species of butterfly and eight species of dragonfly recorded along with numerous mayflies, stoneflies and caddisflies present in the clean waters of the River Derwent.

Management   The country park is managed by the Countryside Management Team of the Department of Parks and Recreation for informal public recreation, landscape and wildlife conservation.

Interpretation   There is a warden and interpretation service based at the Thornley Woodlands Centre, Rowlands Gill. Trails have been constructed suitable for the disabled at both the Woodlands Centre and Swalwell Visitor Centre. Nature trail and local history guides books are available from the centres. A free newsletter is published quarterly and seasonal work books suitable for primary schools can be purchased. In addition a series of 'Exploring' books have been produced which examine the wildlife of woods, ponds and meadow in more detail.

Access   Open at all times.

Contact   Countryside Management Team.

2 Shibdon Pond Local Nature Reserve

Blaydon (NZ 195628).

Gateshead MBC. 12ha.

Approach   Buses from Newcastle and Gateshead stop in Blaydon shopping precinct; a short walk along Shipdon Road (B6317) brings you to Blaydon swimming baths, the Pond being behind paths where car parking facilities are available.

Summary   The nature reserve is a mixture of open water, marsh and herb-rich grassland on a site of an old coal mine and farm in an urban setting surrounded by local industry and housing.

History   The area, an SSSI, is part of the flood plain of the river Tyne and tends to be water-logged. Part of the site was Blaydon Main Colliery which closed in 1923. The pond formed soon afterwards, spreading quickly onto surrounding farmland. This process has continued until the present day and the marsh and damp grassland at the edge of the pond have formed as a result. The area was purchased by Blaydon UDC in 1968 and passed to Gateshead MBC in 1974, which leased it to the Durham Wildlife Trust (DWT) in 1979; they now jointly manage the site.

Nature interest   Open water areas support pond weeds such as water starwort and spiked water milfoil. Large stands of reed mace occupy the shallow margins of the pond. Those merge with tall fen containing reed grass, greater willowherb and water plantain. Both damp and dry grassland are herb rich, supporting a flourishing population of N marsh and common spotted orchids. The bird interest is divided between the wintering wildfowl and breeding summer visitors with over 160 species recorded so far, a splendid

Shibdon Pond, Gateshead

total for an urban site. Wintering wildfowl include tufted duck, pochard, teal and shoveler while sedge and reed warbler, whinchat and lesser white-throat can be found in summer. Resident birds such as water rail, reed bunting and mute swan may be found in the extensive areas of marsh. Passage migrants are well represented with green sandpiper and greenshank seen annually while real rarities such as laughing gull, firecrest and barred warbler are occasionally found. A surprisingly rich and varied insect life occurs on the reserve with 16 species of butterfly and nine species of dragonfly recorded among numerous other species associated with old damp habitats making this site one of the most important in the NE of England.

Management   Jointly managed by Gateshead MBC and DWT for its wildlife value and also for low-key informal public access via the nature trail.

Interpretation   There is a site warden and nature trail. Trail guides can be obtained either from the site warden or from the Thornley Woodlands Centre. A bird observation hide has been constructed in a protected area in the SE corner of the reserve. This is open when the warden is on site and keys can be obtained from the Thornley Woodlands Centre. The hide is suitable for wheelchair users.

Access   The nature trail is open at all times.

Contact   Countryside Management Team.

3 Ryton Willows

Ryton-on-Tyne (NZ 155650).
Gateshead MBC. 22ha.

Approach   By bus from Newcastle and Gateshead to Ryton Hotel public house then following signs through old village to the river. Limited car parking is available on Station Bank.

Summary   Mixture of haughland, pond, marsh and woodland on a steep scarp slope situated on the S bank of the River Tyne opposite the Tyne Riverside Park.

History   The Ryton Willows get its name from the fact that the haughland was at one time flooded regularly by the river giving rise to a willow scrub habitat. This ceased when the river was widened and dredged in the 19C. Of the three ponds, the two on the S side of the railway were formed as borrow pits and the material used to build the embankment which carries the Newcastle to Carlisle railway. The third pond, N of the railway, is the remains of an ancient meander of the Tyne. Much of Middle Wood consists of planted exotic trees such as monkey puzzle, American white oak and beech. This was undertaken in Victorian times when the land formed part of the local large house known as The Grove. Large parts of the Willows are registered common land and as such have been used by the local population for many years. Goose Fairs and the Ryton Hirings were regular events on the Willows after the First World War and the Gut pond was used as a boating lake.

Nature interest   The ponds and marsh, an SSSI, are very rich and varied containing a number of locally rare waterplants such as greater bladderwort and frog bit which reaches its northernmost point in Britain at this site. The grasslands have been colonised by large amounts of gorse and broom scrub while the riverbanks show parallel zones of vegetation, ranging from damp-loving species close to the high tide mark to drought resistant types on the top of the bank where the soils are dry and well drained. The mainly deciduous woodland is dominated by sycamore but fine specimens of beech, cherry and horse chestnut also occur. The wet flush communities which lead down to the ponds beneath the woodland canopy contain lesser celandine, wood horsetail and, close to the ponds themselves, yellow flag and marsh marigold. The river plays host to a large wintering population of goldeneye with smaller numbers of goosander and great crested grebe. Water rail, reed bunting and sedge warbler will be found in the marsh while the woods hold the usual assortment of warblers, woodpeckers and finches. The grassland supports skylark and meadow pipit and redpoll, linnet,and yellow hammer nest in the scrub areas. The pond life is abundant with large numbers of frogs, toads and newts present in the spring, and a full range of mayflies, caddisflies and crustacea can be found along with a healthy population of bank voles.

Management   Countryside Management Team.
Interpretation   Site warden and nature trail. The trail guide can be obtained either from the warden or from the Thornley Woodlands Centre.
Access   Open at all times.
Contact   Countryside Management Team.

4   Washingwell Wood

Sunniside (NZ 219599).
Gateshead MBC. 11ha.
Approach   Buses from Newcastle and Gateshead along A692 between Lobley Hill and Sunniside. Alight at Marquess of Granby public house. Car parking available at Fugar Bar.
Summary   Mixed conifer and deciduous woodland in steeply sided dene with open areas, streamside and grassland.
History   Most of the woodland was clear-felled by the NCB at the end of the Second World War and replanted with conifers. Little or no management was undertaken until the site was purchased by Gateshead in 1977. The presence of the adjacent Watergate Colliery blighted the area until it was closed in the early 1960s. The woodlands are much used by the local community who knew it by the name of Bluebell Wood. The reason for this name became apparent when a large area of conifers was cleared beneath the electricity power lines by the North East Electricity Board in 1985. The following spring produced an astonishing display of bluebells in the cleared area.
Nature interest   Much of the wildlife interest is confined to areas of deciduous woodland, open ground and streamside. For such a small site it contains a remarkable variety of plants and animals. Nearly all the spring flowering herbs are present with splendid displays of bluebell, wood sorrel and lesser celandine. Later in the year the locally rare climbing corydalis can be found alongside foxglove and heath bedstraw. Birdlife is abundant with the finches well represented including goldfinch, yellow hammer and linnet. In the winter months siskin, brambling and crossbill may be found feeding on larch and alder cones.
Management   Countryside Management Team.
Interpretation   Site warden and nature trail. The trail guide can be obtained from the warden or from the Thornley Woodlands Centre.
Access   Open at all times.
Contact   Countryside Management Team.

Further information

Gateshead MBC, Department of Parks and Recreation, Countryside Management Team, Thornley Woodlands Centre, Rowlands Gill, Newcastle-on-Tyne NE39 1AU (0207 545212).
Durham Wildlife Trust (see Durham).
The excellent Tyne and Wear Nature Conservation Strategy published by the NCC covers Gateshead and the other four districts within the region.
Acknowledgement   Text written by Trevor Weston of the Countryside Management Team.

NEWCASTLE UPON TYNE

As well as preserving its Town Moor at the heart of the city, Newcastle has found that its steep sided denes running down to the Tyne have provided resilient green corridors even in areas covered by 19C and 20C housing and factories. Location for various innovative nature conservation initiatives during the 1980s, the city now enjoys a network of natural sites ranging from country parks to small study areas adjacent to schools in the poorest districts.

1   Benwell Nature Park

Pipetrack Lane, Benwell, NE4 (NZ 217637).
Newcastle CC. 2ha.
Approach   Bus along Armstrong Road.
Summary   A site where schools and the local authority have been involved in habitat creation to provide an important site for environmental education.

Creating a pond edge at Benwell Nature Park, Newcastle

History   Formerly occupied by terraced housing, the site was reclaimed by the city council with all subsequent landscaping and planting works carried out by local children under BTCV guidance.
Nature interest   The variety of habitats includes a pond, woodland and limestone outcrops.
Management   The park is managed by the city's education department, with continuing involvement of local schools and the active Benwell Nature Club.
Interpretation   An education officer is based on site, where there are classroom/field study facilities.
Access   Normally open during school hours; outside these times, please phone to make arrangements.
Contact   Warden (091 273 2983).

2   Big Waters Nature Reserve

Sandy Lane, Brunswick, NE (NZ 230733).
Newcastle CC. 50ha.
Approach   Buses to Brunswick/Seaton Burn/Dinnington from Haymarket, Newcastle. Car park off Sandy Lane.
Summary   A 16 hectares mining subsidence pond has developed in the valley of the Hartley Burn, much of it now managed as a nature reserve. The main pond is clearly visible when travelling N of Newcastle on the A1.
History   The pond grew from pasture land over the past 60 years. Mine waste was tipped from Dinnington Colliery on part of the site, further impounding the burn. This land was reclaimed as a picnic site in 1969 when a road was built across the site, separating the much smaller Little Waters to the E.
Nature interest   The main pond, an SSS1, has large waterfowl populations, including wintering whooper swans and large flocks of coot. Breeding birds include great crested grebe, mute swan and grasshopper warbler, while the pond supports good invertebrate populations. The pond is fringed by rich fen communities, and an area of herb-rich ridge and furrow pasture.
Management   The nature reserve area is leased to the Northumberland Wildlife Trust (NWT), while the remainder is managed as a picnic site by the recreation department, with some fields let for grazing.
Interpretation   A Big Waters nature trail leaflet was produced by the former Tyne and Wear county council, and the city's ranger service and NWT can accommodate occasional organised parties. There are active voluntary warden groups covering the reserve and picnic site areas.
Access   The nature reserve is open to NWT members although much of the site is a sanctuary area. The picnic site is open at all times and there are good views of waterfowl from the public area.
Contact   Recreation Department, NWT.

3   Heaton/Armstrong Parks and Jesmond Vale

Heaton, NE6 (NZ 265656).
Newcastle CC. 28ha.
Approach   From Benton Bank or Heaton Park Road.
Summary   Two Victorian parks and a valley with a mixed amenity

and naturalistic landscape form an important S extension of the Ouseburn Valley wildlife corridor, as well as a popular recreational resource.

History   Heaton Park was once part of the Ridley Estate, while Armstrong Park was laid out by the eponymous Lòrd and presented to the city in 1880. Jesmond Vale retained a pastoral character into this century, although it is now surrounded by urban development.

Nature interest   Where Heaton and Armstrong Parks abut the Vale a strip of ancient oak woodland is retained, supporting a good ground flora including wood anemone. Tawny owls breed in Heaton Park, while kingfishers can occasionally be seen in the Vale.

Management   The sites are managed as public open space by the city's recreation department.

Interpretation   The Jesmond Dene ranger leads guided walks and school parties to these areas, although there is no written interpretation.

Access   Open at all times.

Contact   Recreation Department.

4   Jesmond Dene

Jesmond NE2 (NZ 262663).
Newcastle CC. 35ha.

Approach   Buses along Jesmond Road to Benton Bank.

Summary   This mature wooded valley is a successful blend of Victorian parkland and ancient woodland forming a very popular recreational site with significant wildlife interest only three kilometres from the city centre.

History   Once supporting a number of watermills, the dene was landscaped by Lord Armstrong in the mid-19C. Waterfalls were blasted out of the stream bed, and newly discovered exotic trees introduced, blending with fern banks and areas of natural vegetation. Designed as a private pleasure ground, it was given to the city in 1883, with an extension N to Haddricks Mill being purchased in 1950.

Nature interest   The dene forms a vital part of the important Ouseburn Valley wildlife corridor. Woodland flowers include pendulous sedge, while shaded sandstone outcrops support a relatively rich bryophyte flora. Birds include nuthatch, hawfinch, kingfisher and sparrowhawk.

Management   The site is managed as public open space by the city's recreation department, with areas set aside as wildlife sanctuaries.

Interpretation   A full time ranger is based at a temporary visitor centre at Pet's Corner; improved facilities are under construction in Millfield House. This 19C building will have exhibition rooms, a classroom, archive and AV facilities. Publications comprise a nature trail and history trail priced at 30 pence each.

Access   Open at all times.

Contact   Jesmond Dene Visitor Centre (091 281 0973).

5   Sugley Dene

Neptune Road, Lemington (NZ 191653).
Newcastle CC. 20ha.

Approach   Bus along Neptune Road.

Summary   A narrow, steep sided dene preserves an important fragment of ancient woodland in an area surrounded by housing.
History   Another city dene which has escaped clearance or infilling while post-war development spread around it.
Nature interest   The dene supports a good woodland flora, including pendulous sedge and opposite-leaved golden saxifrage, and allows birds such as white-throat and chaffinch to reach the centre of a large housing estate.
Management   The site is managed as a naturalistic open space with public access recently improved.
Interpretation   None.
Access   Open at all times.
Contact   Recreation Department.

6   Throckley/Walbottle Dene

Hexham Road, Throckley, NE15 (NZ 163665).
Newcastle CC. 30ha.
Approach   Buses to Throckley from Newcastle city centre.
Summary   One of the largest tracts of ancient woodland in the city, Walbottle Dene is vulnerable to vandalism and rubbish dumping, but forms an important wildlife corridor close to housing.
Housing   The course of Hadrian's Wall crosses the dene, whose steep slopes have avoided agricultural and urban development. The dene was acquired for public open space from the Duke of Northumberland, who owns a smaller section to the S.
Nature interest   On the Northumberland register of ancient woodland, its slopes are covered with mature oak woodland on an acidic substrate, with a ground flora of great wood rush and wavy hair grass. Damper, richer soils in the valley floor support drifts of wood sorrel, ramsons and wood anemone.
Management   Maintained as naturalistic open space by the city recreation department.
Interpretation   School visits and guided walks are undertaken by the Tyne Riverside Country Park Ranger.
Access   Open at all times.
Contact   Recreation Department.

7   Throckley Pond Nature Reserve

Tyne Riverside Country Park (NZ 150658).
Newcastle CC. 11ha.
Approach   Buses to Throckley Bank Top and walk via Coach Road or South Farm. Buses to Newburn and walk via Blayney Row. Car parking at Newburn riverside and Blayney Row.
Summary   A colliery pond, mixed plantation and abandoned pasture provide the richest area of wildlife interest within the Newburn section of Tyne Riverside Country Park.
History   The pond was formed between two spoil heaps of the Isabella colliery which closed in 1954. One heap was planted up with woodland soon after as game cover, and the other reclaimed by 1980. In 1982 the site was incorporated in the new Tyne Riverside Country Park.
Nature interest   The pond has a rich invertebrate fauna, including the only Tyne and Wear site for the beetle *Graptodytes pictus*. Amphi-

bians include smooth and palmate newt, while the aquatic flora includes whorled water milfoil. The woodland supports breeding goldcrest, blackcap and coal tit, occasional visitors include roe deer and red squirrel. An adjacent abandoned pasture has a good small mammal population.

Interpretation   Rangers at Tyne Riverside Country Park provide an interpretive service for organised groups, while a simple nature trail guide is available.

Access   Open at all times.

Contact   Newburn Visitor Centre, Tyne Riverside Country Park (091 264 8501).

8 Walker Riverside Park

Pottery Bank, Walker, NE6 (NZ 288630).
Newcastle CC. 17.5ha.

Approach   Buses along Walker Road; parking at Potter Bank.

Summary   A newly reclaimed site offering a good potential for environmental education close to the River Tyne.

History   Heavy industry along the riverbank included a tar works, leaving behind difficult problems of toxic wastes which needed to be overcome in the reclamation scheme, completed in 1988.

Nature interest   Much of the vegetation is immature, although the site provides a good vantage point for the River Tyne wildlife corridor. Cormorants, kittiwake and redshank can be seen from the park. A nearby disused railway retains a more natural flora, while the adjacent West Walker School is constructing a wildlife garden.

Management   Management of the site will be carried out by the city's recreation department, with a strong input from the local community.

Interpretation   A ranger will be based at a field study centre at West Walker School to develop the park's interpretation facilities.

Access   Open at all times.

Contact   Recreation Department.

9 Walkergate Wildlife Garden

Walkergate Junior School, Coutts Road, Walker, NE6 (NZ 283656).
Newcastle CC. 1ha.

Approach   Close to Walkergate Metro station.

Summary   This is an early and successful example of urban gap site regeneration using naturalistic techniques, with the involvement of the local community.

History   Formerly the site of a dairy, the site was developed by the school in 1981–82 with the help of BTCV.

Nature interest   A variety of 'mini-habitats' have been successfully created, including a woodland, pond and limestone rockery.

Management   Designed to be virtually maintenance free, the site is managed by the school.

Interpretation   Document available on using wildspace with children.

Access   By arrangement with the school.

Contact   Headteacher (091 265 5737).

Further information

Newcastle upon Tyne CC, Recreation and Leisure Department, 7 Saville Place, Newcastle upon Tyne, NE1 8DQ (091 232 8520).

Northumberland Wildlife Trust, Hancock Museum, Barras Bridge, Newcastle upon Tyne NEZ 4PT (091 232 0038).

Acknowledgement   Text written by Kevin Honour of the City's Recreation Department.

NORTH TYNESIDE

North Tyneside, between Newcastle and the N Sea coast, lies at the gateway to the ancient kingdom of Northumbria. Its seven kilometre coastline and numerous interesting ponds and wetlands, set within a patchwork of agricultural land and urban settlements, are all linked by an extensive network of disused waggonways leading from the open countryside of Northumbria through urban areas of the district to the Tyne.

1 Annitsford Pond

Front Street, Annitsford, NE23 (NZ 266742).
North Tyneside MBC. 1ha.
Approach   Buses to Front Street, Annitsford, then following signs to Annitsford Rest Home for the elderly. Pedestrian access to pond along footpath behind the rest home.
Summary   A small semi-urban pond between arable land and allotments, this site has a good amphibian and invertebrate fauna and some interesting breeding birds. The marginal vegetation is relatively well developed as the area is ungrazed.
History   Annitsford Pond is a small boulder clay subsidence pond caused by past coal mining activities in the area.
Nature interest   The pond is fringed by willow carr and interesting communities of wetland plants including bulrush, sedges, rushes and reed canary grass which provide a habitat for breeding populations of wildfowl such as little grebe, moorhen, mute swan, coot, tufted duck and mallard. The pond is known to provide a habitat for an extremely good amphibian population including the common frog, common toad and smooth newt.
Management   Jointly managed by North Tyneside council and the Northumberland Wildlife Trust (NWT) as a nature reserve. Access to certain areas of the pond is restricted to avoid disturbance to breeding waterfowl.
Interpretation   An information board is sited at the entrance to the nature reserve.
Access   Open at all times.
Contact   North Tyneside Countryside Interpretation Service.

2 Brierdene

The Links, Whitley Bay, NE26 (NZ 345738).
North Tyneside MBC. 5ha.
Approach   Metro to Whitley Bay. Buses to Whitley Bay Cemetery, then walk along links to entrance of the dene.
Summary   A peaceful coastal dene adjacent to the popular coastal links of Whitley Bay, Brierdene represents a site of considerable attraction for its herb-rich banksides.
History   A small coastal dene which has avoided agricultural and urban developments, the dene was probably once wooded but tree felling and replanting has occurred in the past.
Nature interest   The banksides of Brierdene provide one of the best examples of semi-natural neutral grassland in North Tyneside with small areas of flush meadow. Well over 100 plant species have been recorded including pepper saxifrage, burnet saxifrage, quaking

grass, agrimony, common twayblade and common spotted orchid. The site supports a number of common bird and butterfly species and foxes have been recently observed in the area.

Management   A management plan has been produced by the council and the area is maintained by the authority as an informal countryside area within the urban area of Whitley Bay.

Interpretation   Nil on site.

Access   Open at all times.

Contact   Countryside Interpretation Services.

3   Gosforth Park

Salters Lane, Gosforth, Newcastle, NE3 (NZ 256702).
Natural History Society of Northumbria. 37.3ha. (16.7ha. in North Tyneside).

Approach   Buses to Four Lane Ends Metro Station. Approximately 20 minutes' walk to entrance of nature reserve along A189 (Salters Lane). Cars along A189.

Summary   Situated about 6.5 kilometres from the centre of Newcastle, the site forms part of the Gosforth Park Nature Reserve and consists of a shallow man-made lake with associated reedswamp, herb-rich fen, willow carr, broad leaved woodland and remnants of heathy grassland. It provides a valuable refuge for wildlife on the N fringe of the Tyneside conurbation and is of importance for its invertebrate population and because it includes the largest reedbed in the E Northumberland area.

History   Much of the present landscape was laid out by the Brandling family during the 18C with the construction of a lake and the planting of the Gosforth Park woodland. The park was acquired by Gosforth Race Course Company in 1880 and the area was set aside as a nature reserve in 1929. It is thus the oldest nature reserve in the NE.

Nature interest   The reedbed comprises a fringe of bulrush surrounded by extensive stands of common reed which support breeding reedbunting, sedge and reed warblers, while areas of open water are frequented by moorhen, coot, mallard, teal and little grebe. Frogs, toads, common and palmate newts are also recorded as breeding. The areas of woodland support breeding sparrowhawk, tawny owl, woodcock and great spotted woodpecker and also provide a habitat for local populations of badgers, fox, red squirrel and roe deer. Carr woodland adjacent to the lake supports an interesting ground flora comprising of sphagnum and polytrichum mosses, star sedge, marsh pennywort and corolroot orchid.

Management   Woodland management programme and selective reedbed management have been implemented by the Natural History Society of Northumbria.

Interpretation   By arrangement with site warden and the Natural History Society of Northumbria.

Access   Restricted to members. Access for non-members by arrangement with site warden and the Natural History Society of Northumbria.

Contact   Site warden; Natural History Society of Northumbria, Hancock Museum, Barras Bridge, Newcastle upon Tyne NE2 4PT (091 232 6886).

4   Hadrian Park Pond

Addington Drive, Wallsend, NE28 (NZ 311696).
North Tyneside MBC. 1.5ha.

Approach   Buses to Hadrian Park Estate, Wallsend. Pond is located at N perimeter of estate adjacent to A1 Tyne Tunnel Road.

Summary   A small densely vegetated pond with excellent amphibian and aquatic invertebrate populations.

History   Hadrian Park Pond, unlike most other ponds in North Tyneside, is not a mining subsidence pond. It represents the last remaining fragments of the formerly extensive Longbenton Bogs system which originally occupied a strip of land across the whole of the borough. It is thus immeasurably older than the subsidence ponds in the area and appears to represent a relict lowland fen.

Nature interest   The pond is fringed with extensive communities of bulrush, sedge and rush species and is one of very few sites in Tyne and Wear holding a population of great crested newts as well as other amphibians. A rich aquatic insect fauna is present including dragonflies, damselflies and several rare species of water beetle.

Management   A management package which seeks to protect and enhance those features of considerable nature conservation interest has been drawn up by the council, NWT and Countryside Commission. The package includes sympathetic peripheral landscaping, construction of boardwalks to certain areas of the pond and the creation of a wildlife sanctuary area.

Interpretation   In preparation.

Access   Open at all times.

Contact   Countryside Interpretation Service.

5   Holywell Dene

Hartley Lane, NE25 (NZ 335755).
Duke of Northumberland. Approx 10ha. in North Tyneside.

Approach   Buses to Hartley Village, entrance to dene at SE of village along Hartley Lane.

Summary   A large wooded coastal dene at the N boundary of the district, Holywell Dene represents the only site of ancient semi-natural woodland and associated flora in the borough.

History   As with many other coastal denes, the area has escaped woodland clearance and agriculture, although significant proportions of the dene are used as winter grazing.

Nature interest   The area is of particular interest for the presence of a diverse woodland ground flora which includes species such as primrose, sanicle, bluebells, ramsons, wood sorrel, wood anemone and dog's mercury. Canopy species include introduced beech and sycamore together with remnants of pedunculate oak, ash and wych elm surviving on the steep valley sides.

Management   Lack of public ownership has restricted management, although some agreements have been made with the current tenant farmer to fence off selected areas of the dene to allow natural regeneration of the woodland and its ground flora.

Interpretation   Nil on site.

Access   Following routes of designated public footpaths through the dene, it is open at all times.

Contact   Interpretation Service.

6   Marden Quarry

The Broadway, Whitley Bay, NE30 (NZ 355715).
North Tyneside MBC. 6.6ha.
Approach   Buses to Whitley Bay Town Centre or Metro to Whitley Bay, then walk along the Broadway to park entrance.
Summary   This is virtually the only exposure of magnesian limestone N of the Tyne and is of interest as a N outlier of this series. The site holds an interesting limestone grassland flora and a valuable waterfowl pond.
History   The site occupies a disused limestone quarry and reservoir dating back to the late 17C, converted to an informal nature park and opened in 1977.
Nature interest   A mixture of natural and exotic plants provides colour and interest throughout the park. Of particular importance are several areas of limestone grassland, which are very rare within the borough. Characteristic plants include quaking grass, eyebright, burnet saxifrage and common spotted, N marsh and early purple orchids. The W of the site is characterised by scrub, dominated by mature and often senescent elder with occasional hawthorn and dog rose. The pond area represents an important site for waterfowl such as mallard, wigeon, gadwall, teal, pochard, tufted duck, goldeneye and mute swan.
Management   Maintained by the council as an informal nature park.
Interpretation   Nil on site.
Access   Open at all times.
Contact   Interpretation Service.

7   St Mary's Island and adjacent coastline

The Links, Whitley Bay, NE26 (NZ 347753).
North Tyneside Council. Approx 7km.
Approach   Buses or Metro to Whitley Bay, then buses to Whitley Bay Cemetery followed by walk along Trinity Road.
Summary   An island, St Mary's is linked to the mainland at low tide by a causeway over a wave cut platform. The area is of great geological, ornithological, botanical and marine interest.
History   Before the present lighthouse was built the island was a landing place for smugglers and the surrounding rocks were also the scene of many shipwrecks. This led to the demand for the construction of a lighthouse, which opened in 1898 and continued to operate until 1984.
Nature interest   St Mary's is a most unusual and exciting area because of the variety of wildlife and habitats that can be seen. The island itself, with its extensive area of rock pools, possesses a wide range of marine life. It is also a good vantage point from which to observe seabird movements, while the intertidal area is a favourite feeding and resting place for many waders, terns and gulls. Wet areas in the adjacent clifftop grassland are also favoured by waders, and the clifftop is an important landfall site for passage migrants in spring and autumn. The clifftop at Curry's Point is one of the few remaining semi-natural grasslands in North Tyneside and show some good examples of maritime flora. The area is also of great geological significance as the coastline between Tynemouth and Seaton Sluice forms the S part of the best exposed and complete section of upper carboniferous coal measure rocks in the whole of Britain and is thus of national importance.

Management   The council have acquired the island and associated buildings, which now accommodate a coastal interpretative/visitor centre.

Interpretation   Visitor centre (091 252 0853). A self-guided walk leaflet is in production.

Access   A notice board displaying the centre's operating times and tide times is located on the mainland at Curry's Point.

Contact   Coastal Information Officer, Interpretation Service.

8   Wallsend Dene

Rosehill, Wallsend, NE25 (NZ 307672).
North Tyneside Council. 4.5ha (Burn Closes pasture and Willington Gut Saltmarsh).

Approach   Metro to Wallsend or Hadrian Road, buses to Rosehill and Church Bank.

Summary   Wallsend Dene is a mosaic of unmanaged grassland and scrub, with grazed pastures and areas of more formal parkland and amenity use. The dene is a valuable wildlife corridor and contains two areas that are of high nature conservation value, namely the Burn Closes pasture and the Willington Gut Saltmarsh.

History   The history of the dene is as rich and varied as the wildlife it supports. The Burn Closes area has always been connected to the ancient townships of Willington and Wallsend and has remained relatively untouched by industrial and urban developments. The area has remained intact as a public amenity area and was recently the subject of an ambitious environmental improvement scheme.

Nature interest   The Burn Closes area of the Dene represents one of very few areas left in the district with ancient semi-natural grassland or meadow. Key species present include pepper saxifrage, dyer's greenweed, common fleabane, betony and cowslip. The site also represents the most N location in Britain of the bee orchid, a solitary plant being recorded in 1988. The Willington Gut area is the only remaining example of a characteristic middle saltmarsh community on the River Tyne and extends for approximately ½ mile inland along the dene. Typical species include sea milkwort, sea arrowgrass, sea plantain and sea aster.

Management   The site has been the subject of an environmental improvement project, and some maintenance is carried out by the council in specific locations within the dene.

Interpretation   Nil on site.

Access   Open at all times.

Contact   Interpretation Service.

9   Wallsend Swallow Pond Nature Reserve

Whitley Road, Benton, NE12 (NZ 300696).
North Tyneside MBC. 14ha.

Approach   Buses along A193 Whitley Road, Metro to Palmersville. Nature reserve located approx. 1/4 mile behind Benton hypermarket.

Summary   Swallow Pond is one of the two most important colliery subsidence ponds in Tyne and Wear and holds important populations of both breeding and winterng wildfowl, passage wading birds, marsh and fen plants and aquatic invertebrates.

History   The pond is one of the older mining subsidences ponds in the district, being formed around 1930–40. An old fence through the

Swallow Pond, Wallsend

pond illustrates the area's pastoral history while the surrounding plantation occupies a former mining and tipping site.

Nature interest   Swallow Pond has well developed emergent fen and carr vegetation including bulrush, greater spearwort, yellow flag, bottle sedge, spike rush and amphibious bistort. The area is one of the most attractive inland sites in Northumberland for passage waders such as ruff, spotted redshank, dunlin, greenshank, snipe and common sandpiper. Unusual visitors include black tailed godwit and little ringed plover, while national rarities and vagrants such as black winged stilt and pectoral sandpiper have also been recorded. Wigeon, teal, shoveler, mallard, pochard and tufted duck regularly visit or over winter on the pond; regular breeders include mallard, moorhen, mute swan, coot and little grebe. The pond site also holds populations of common toad, common frog and smooth newt, and mammals observed include foxes, rabbits, hares, water voles, shrews, hedgehogs, bats and mice.

Management   The site is managed as a nature reserve by NWT and maintenance is carried out by the council.

Interpretation   Leaflets available from NWT. The Rising Sun Countryside Interpretation Centre is located approx 1/4 mile N of the pond (091 266 3524 x132).

Access   Open at all times.

Contact   Interpretation Service.

Further information

North Tyneside MBC, Leisure and Tourism Department, Countryside Interpretation Service, Central Library, Northumberland Square, North Shields, NE30 1QU.

Northumberland Wildlife Trust (see Newcastle).

Acknowledgement   Text written by David Mitchell, Countryside Project Officer, North Tyneside Council.

SOUTH TYNESIDE

Around the valley of the River Don and its junction with the Tyne at Jarrow, South Shields and Jarrow have a history streching back to Roman times. In later years it was an important coal port for the Durham coalfield, and a shipbuilding area similar to its neighbouring borough on the N side of the river. Its territory encompasses a North Sea coastline with cliffs favoured by birdwatchers. Wildlife sites here include Harton Down and Marsden Old Quarry adjacent to the Marsden Bay nature reserve. Inland, the valley of the River Don is being developed as a green corridor.

Further information

Durham Wildlife Trust (see Durham).
South Tyneside MBC, Westoe Road, South Shields, NE33 2RL (091 427 1717).

SUNDERLAND

Outside the N of England the image of Sunderland, at the mouth of the River Wear, tends to be one of grime and dereliction. This is not a true picture despite the fact that the town's prosperity in the 19C came from heavy industries including mining, shipbuilding, engineering and glass making. Most industrial activity was based at or near the river mouth or in the pit villages outside the town.

But with the decline of the major industries even this has changed. It is hard to find a slag heap within 24 kilometres of the town, while on the N side of the town there are the seaside resorts of Seaburn and Roker with their beautiful sandy beaches; many attractive parks throughout the town; over 14 SSSIs within the town boundaries; and much lovely countryside within an hour's drive.

In the 7C Monkwearmouth on the N shore of the river was the centre of European civilisation. It was here that Bede, the first English historian, spent much of his life. Acquiring a different sort of fame in the 19C, Sunderland was then one of the biggest and best-known ports in the world.

1 Barnes Park

Humbledon Hill (NZ 384555).
Sunderland BC.
Approach   Barnes Park is a large pleasant park situated near the junction of Durham Road and Alexandra Road. There are entrances from Durham Road, Barnes View and Ettrick Grove.
History   The park has been in existence since 1909 and an extension was developed after 1952.
Nature interest   The park has many attractive features, including a stream and a pond. There is a great variety of trees, including ash, sycamore, whitebeam and lime. Wild flowers grow on the grassy slopes which attract buff-tailed and red-tailed bumble bees and butterflies. The extension, some three kilometres long, is natural grassland with trees sloping down to a bush-lined stream. Apart from selected grass cutting this area remains as a haven for all kinds of wild life.
Management   Recreation and Libraries Department.
Interpretation   There is a printed nature trail available.
Access   Open at all times.
Contact   Recreation Department.

2 Claxheugh Rock

River Wear (NZ 363576).
Sunderland BC.
Approach   From South Hylton.
Summary   This unique feature of an exposed rock face showing up to 300 million years of geological history, with a tidal swept area of mud flat, is enhanced by a broad grassland area and adjacent planted areas which make it a pleasant area for strolling.
History   During the industrial development of the river this was the site of a lime kiln (the remains of which still exist), cement, pottery and glass works supported by a railway. In recent years there was large-scale extraction of limestone from the rear of the rock which is now filled in with domestic waste and landscaped.

Nature interest   The soil on the top supports pellitory-of-the-wall, orchids and blue moor grass. The defunct railway cut through the rock has pineapple and common mayweed, tansy, sow thistle, knapweed and scabious. On the undisturbed end of the rock the grass area contains a scrub area of hawthorn, elder, rose and bindweed—making it a perfect area for wintering and migrant birds to and from N Europe. Among native species, oystercatchers and redshank are common feeders on the mud flat while cormorants fish regularly in the river.

Management   The area is managed by the local authority as a riverside park with the additional facility of a floating boat staging.

Interpretation   There is a voluntary warden scheme for the river.

Access   Open at all times.

Contact   Recreation Department.

3 The Coast

Seafront (NZ 408593)
Sunderland BC and South Tyneside MBC

Approach   Bus/car coast route.

Summary   The easy access to the beach, rock pools, cliff top, Marsden Rock and onwards makes a full day for coastal exploration with variations.

History   Apart from the construction of a promenade on the lower stretch, the coast cliffs have remained untouched except for the ravages of weather and tide.

Nature interest   The rock pools at the Cat and Dog Stairs contain formations of cannon ball rock found nowhere else in the British Isles. N at Mere Knolls, a wooded area with stream is a wintering haven for migrant birds, while at The Bents bent grass grows in profusion. Here there is an extensive area of rock pools, the home of hermit crabs, starfish and periwinkles, with lugworms, cockles and razor shells on the beach. Orache and thrift are to be found on the cliff face and further on grow scabious, knapweed and birdsfoot trefoil. The grassland along this stretch is home for small mammals and their predators, with wintering migrants such as ring ouzel and redstart.

Approaching Marsden Rock the cliff face supports a large breeding colony of fulmars, kittiwakes and gulls. A common sight on the rocks and beach are oystercatcher, redshank, turnstone, sanderling and ringed plover. Terns and skuas patrol the seashore with the frequent visit of guillemot, puffin, razorbill, eider duck and seal offshore. Scoter, Manx shearwater, whooper swan, geese and gannet can be seen on migration or their flight path between feeding areas.

Management   Local authorities.

Interpretation   The coast is one of the habitats described in the booklet *Sunderland's Wildlife Ways* produced by the Sunderland Urban Wildlife Project.

Access   Open at all times.

Contact   Recreation Department.

4 Cox Green to Ford

(NZ 321539). Sunderland BC.

Approach   Buses along the Chester Road (A183).

Summary   Three kilometres of a stretch of some eight kilometres of disused railway line. Starting near Cox Green Golf Course below the notable local landmark of Penshaw Monument (National Trust), the broad level track is easy walking with parts suitable for wheelchair users. Running roughly parallel with the River Wear, it passes the rolling greens of the golf course, a beechwood, farmlands with glimpses of the N bank of the river as the outskirts of Hylton are approached downstream towards Ford where a more urban scene takes over.

History This is part of the old North Eastern Railway (Penshaw Branch) from Durham to Sunderland, closed some 25 years ago.

Nature interest The route is made up of varying habitats woodland, wetland, hedgerows and steep, dry embankments. Beeches, bluebells, ladies' smock, wild strawberries, roses and hawthorns are part of the variety of wildlife to be seen here, which also includes an equally interesting range of birds: yellowhammers, thrushes, blackbirds, partridge and kestrel.

Management Sunderland BC.

Interpretation See *Sunderland's Wildlife Ways*.

Access Open at all times.

Contact Recreation Department.

5 North Hylton Dene

Hylton Castle, Sunderland SR5 (NZ 357585).
Sunderland BC. 50ha.

Approach Buses along North Hylton Road to Craigavon Road.

Summary Hylton Dene is one of the few surviving examples of semi-natural valley woodland within the urban area, comprising mature woodland, calcareous grassland, flushed marsh and stream-bank habitats forming a 1½ mile corridor through the post-war estates of NW Sunderland.

History Hylton Dene was originally part of the estate of Hylton Caste, built c1400. In 1750 it formed part of the John Bowes estate. The present tree stock is mainly 20C.

Nature interest The banks of the dene are wooded with beech, ash, elm, oak and sycamore. The ground flora includes wild garlic, lords and ladies and wood sorrel. There are blackbirds, thrushes, dunnocks and chaffinches. Kestrels have also been seen.

The grassland around the castle is managed as parkland. Calcareous grassland found on the magnesian limestone in the dene supports flora such as common spotted orchid, field scabious, harebell, bird's foot trefoil and meadow cranesbill. The marsh area is herb rich, supporting marsh valerian, meadowsweet, sneezewort, fleabane, marsh pennywort and angelica.

Management Housing and Estates and Recreation departments. The castle is under the care of English Heritage.

Interpretation Nil on site.

Access Open all times.

Contact Recreation Department.

6 Railway Walk

Between Plains Farm and Silksworth Row (NZ 374538).
Sunderland BC.

Approach Silksworth Road off Durham Road.

Summary A green corridor leads from a reclaimed area to the riverside park.

History   The reclaimed area, once the site of a colliery and pit heap, is now a landscaped recreation area with indoor and outdoor activities including a ski slope. The former mineral line carried coal to the riverside staithes.

Nature interest   The former railway is bordered by ash, hawthorn, elder and rose with willow where there is an adjacent stream. The ground cover is bramble and ivy with umbellifers, rosebay willow-herb, sorrel, bindweed and hogweed, with cranesbill beginning to establish itself.

Management   Sunderland BC.

Interpretation   Nil on site.

Access   Open at all times.

Contact   Recreation Department.

7   Riverside Park

Town centre (NZ 391571).

Sunderland BC.

Approach   From Silksworth Row.

Summary   This riverside park with its combination of industrial history and well-balanced reclamation work makes this site worth visiting at any time of the year.

History   Lime kilns, ship repairs, glass bottle works and extensive coal staithes were the main industries in the history of this site.

Nature interest   The grassed and exposed limestone rock faces, which run along the full length of the park, support spotted orchid and ivy with Oxford ragwort at the base. The planted trees, including rowan and alder along with hawthorn, elder and bramble which combine well with the untouched grass area supporting nettle, thistle, clover, fern, coltsfoot and umbellifers make the area ideal for butterflies and migrant birds. The inaccessible parts of the river bank support herb species such as wall rocket and yellow corydalis, both of which may have been introduced in ballast waste.

Management   An extension to the site is under construction by the local authority as part of its programme to develop a nine mile stretch of the river on educational and recreational lines.

Interpretation   A voluntary warden system exists.

Access   Open at all times.

Contact   Recreation Department.

8   Ryhope Dene

Coastline S of Sunderland (NZ 416520).

Sunderland BC.

Approach   Bus/car coast route to Seaham.

Summary   The gentle sloping footpath follows the line of the stream on to the beach with a wide variety of plants seen from the path. A walk can be extended along the beach.

History   The magnesian limestone coastal denes in Durham are unique in the British Isles and were probably first cut into the limestone during the Ice Age by a torrential stream.

Nature interest   Deciduous trees on the slopes have an understorey of willow and hawthorn. These provide a habitat for a variety of small mammals including bats. It is also home for a variety of resident birds and a stop-over for migratory birds. There is also a large insect population, and the ground flora is particularly rich in spring wood anemones, lesser celandines, bluebells, wild garlic and wild arum. Damp areas by the stream support ferns, mosses and liverworts.

Management   A voluntary warden scheme in existence.

Interpretation   Nil.

Access   Open at all times.

Contact   Recreation Department.

9   Tunstall Hills

(NZ 392545).

Sunderland BC.

Approach   Buses to Leechmere Road from the town centre.

Summary   These hills which reach a height of 110 metres offer a fine view of the town, the North Sea and the countryside. Most of the area is covered with thin glacial drift with rocky outcrops on the surrounding slopes. The S face is formed by a glacial spillway where fossils have been found. A sea cliff fronted by an earlier interglacial seabed forms the steep face to the N. This seabed forms a plateau at 66 metres and is the floor of the valley known as Tunstall Hope.

Nature interest   The underlying rock is magnesian limestone. An interesting flora of lime-loving plants such as blue-moor grass, sea plantain, harebell, rock-rose and salad burnet are just a few of over 300 plants which have been recorded here. Tunstall Hope is an area of natural woodland in which ash, elder and hawthorn are found.

Management   Sunderland BC.

Access   Open at all times—Tunstall Hills only. Tunstall Hope is privately owned.

Further information

Sunderland BC, Department of Recreation and Libraries, Area Office, Broadway, Houghton-le-Spring DH4 4LT (091 5843 222).

Durham University Department of Adult and Continuing Education, Adult Education Centre, 270 Hylton Road, Sunderland SR4 7XJ (091 514 4652).

Acknowledgement   Text written by students of the Durham University Department of Adult and Continuing Education and WEA, organisers of the Sunderland Urban Wildlife Project.